QUEEN VICTORIA
AND
HER PRIME MINISTERS

QUEEN VICTORIA

After the equestrian portrait by Count d'Orsay

QUEEN VICTORIA

AND

HER PRIME MINISTERS

by

ALGERNON CECIL

EYRE & SPOTTISWOODE
LONDON 1953

First published 1953
Reprinted 1953
Reprinted 1953

This book is made and printed in Great Britain
for Eyre & Spottiswoode (Publishers) Limited,
15 Bedford Street, London, W.C.2, by
STAPLES PRINTERS LIMITED
at their Rochester, Kent, establishment

CONTENTS

ILLUSTRATIONS

(The illustrations of Viscount Melbourne, Sir
Robert Peel, Lord John Russell, the Earl of Derby,
the Earl of Aberdeen, Viscount Palmerston, William
Ewart Gladstone, and the Earl of Beaconsfield are by
courtesy of the National Portrait Gallery.)

PREFACE

THE chapters in this book which deal with my father, Queen Victoria and her ten Prime Ministers are not studies in biography, still less have I attempted to treat in any detail the political history of the reign. Had it been my purpose to do either of these things this book must have been at least twice its present length, and probably longer even than that.

My purpose was simpler. It was to study the relations of the Queen with her ten Prime Ministers, their influence upon the Queen and, most important of all, the influence of the Queen and her Prime Ministers in their collaboration on the politics and the social and intellectual climate of their day.

The chapters of this book are essays, then, in the sense which Walter Pater attached to the word in his 'Plato and Platonism'; that is to say, they seek to approach or attain truth tentatively 'as the elusive effect of a particular experience'. They are not in line with much that is assumed in the dogmas of to-day, but they are not, as it seems to me, any the worse for that.

I have debts in various quarters. Some, like that to my father, are touched on in the text. Others must go for the most part unacknowledged, though not, any the more for that, unvalued. Here I must content myself with saying that my obligations, both direct and indirect, to Mr. J. C. Allan are very large; and that I am very grateful to the Editor of *The Quarterly* for raising no difficulty to the republication of the study of the late Lord Rosebery, which originally appeared in that periodical and has, with a few minor alterations, been reproduced here. I think it is John Morley who has observed somewhere that, when one has said anything as well as one can, one should not repeat the attempt—unless, as, doubtless, he would have added, the circumstances compel.

My best thanks are also in especial due to Mr. Douglas Jerrold and Mr. Frank Morley and others at Messrs. Eyre & Spottiswoode's, who have most kindly assisted me with advice in dealing with the proofs.

I am also especially grateful to the present Lord Salisbury for facilitating the reproduction of the portrait of his grandfather in his robes as Chancellor of Oxford University.

June 1952.   A. C.

QUEEN VICTORIA
AND
HER PRIME MINISTERS

PORTRAIT OF A VICTORIAN

CHAPTER I

PORTRAIT OF A VICTORIAN

TO add another book to the world's seemingly inexhaustible supply appears towards the close of one's life a graver responsibility than at the beginning. A sentence from Gibbon's *Decline and Fall* has, for many years, haunted my mind and disturbed my peace like the solemn tolling of a passing-bell mourning over an empire in disintegration. 'A cloud of critics, of compilers, of commentators', so it runs, 'darkened the face of learning'. This book may deserve, for all I can tell, to be dismissed as a mere criticism, compilation or commentary. It has manifestly some elements of all three. Nevertheless, it may perhaps be accounted some small excuse for my temerity if I say that this is not just a book about Victorians—or, as it happens, about ten of the more eminent Victorians—but emphatically a book by a Victorian, one of that rapidly diminishing species. And by a Victorian I mean one who is of that period in date possibly, but in heart and mind certainly. Registers and records would not, I fear, bear me out if I were to assert that I came into being in the year 1834—the year, in fact, of my father's nativity.[1] Nevertheless, intellectually speaking, it is pretty nearly true. Circumstances I need not dwell upon made me my father's constant companion during an impressionable, though adult period of my life: and so I came to see clearly the force of much that he had to say, to perceive the interest of much that he could express in admirably chosen words, to appreciate the penetrating knowledge of the world that broke through reminiscences of his life and era, sometimes like studies for a portrait, sometimes in sharply defined vignettes of social landscape, sometimes just by way of caustic or satirical phrases.

Whatever year it was that I came into the world, it was assuredly in the cold of January—a month I have never loved; a month cold, bleak and grey; a month compelling one to behold all things in their nakedness; a month with the trees stripped—both of their springtime grace and autumn glory. All too truly it invites a comparison with 'bare ruined choirs'. For me it is a season whose music, sighing through leafless boughs, seems to recall the dying orisons of fallen fanes and to reach the attentive ear faintly, as in Matthew Arnold's *Stanzas from the Grande Chartreuse*, like some echo of a world forgotten. But with my father it was altogether otherwise. His sense

[1] The author's father was Lord Eustace Cecil, third son of the second Marquess of Salisbury. His mother was Lady Gertrude Scott, daughter of the second Earl of Eldon. Victoria's last Prime Minister, the third Marquess of Salisbury, was the author's uncle.

of pathos did not run in the direction of what, had he been able to catch its strains, he would probably have termed a doleful music. He had come upon the scene in April; and his temperament, as my mother used to say, resembled that of an April day—its uncertain glory, its sunshine and shower. The romantic and moving charm of the Middle Ages had no place in his philosophy. Victorian though he was to the finger-tips, he discovered, not surprisingly, a strong preference for Elizabethan architecture over other styles, though in fact the Old Palace at Hatfield was built earlier, and the Great House later than the days of the Virgin Queen. In many respects, too, Elizabeth's character, at any rate as he conceived it, took hold of his imagination. He grew up, so to speak, in close proximity to the thought of her seated in the November of 1558 beneath the immemorial oak and learning the news of her accession. The early contemplation of her portrait,[1] resplendent in a robe, all strewn with symbolic eyes and ears and serpents, must, moreover, have fixed an indelible impression on the fancy of a child. He regarded her, maybe, to the end of his life a little uncritically, so subtly did her story blend with his ancestral pieties. Burghley in his view stood ever at her side; and Burghley must have been a prince of diplomatists to have picked his way without disastrous slip or stumble through the pitfalls of a Court dominated by as clever and capricious a being as ever sat on the throne of England.

There was, however, something more than the never quite elucidated reactions of Monarch and Minister to attract my father's mind. He had been brought up upon Paley's Evidences, a defence of Christianity which achieved in England a transcendent success on utilitarian lines, just at the date when the French Revolution passed from the hands of the Terrorists into those of the Thermidorians: and to his mind Paley had never been answered; nor am I prepared to say that he was mistaken. Yet the diplomatist in him encouraged a rather more ambiguous line of theological thought, and one certainly more consistent with the Elizabethan settlement. The quatrain about to be quoted is, indeed, sometimes given to Donne; but I doubt whether it ever crossed my father's mind to doubt its other ascription to the Virgin Queen; and in truth it is highly characteristic of that Sovereign's astute, non-committal approach to such disputations. It has been endlessly quoted, but its arch-simplicity and engaging cleverness never tires the ear:

> He was the Word that spake it,
> He took the bread and brake it;
> And what that Word did make it,
> That I believe and take it.

There lies sacramentalism entirely congenial to the mind of—in the best

[1] The so-called Rainbow portrait by Zucchero.

sense—a man of the world; and this Odysseus of many counsels, of whom I am speaking, was emphatically that.

Somewhere near this point my father's mind met and, if I may so put it, kissed my mother's. I do not think the junction could easily occur to-day, so much more conscious have we most of us become, where any religious conviction at all remains, of a world wider than our country and consequently of the need of a faith and a universal church to give it expression. But to those early Victorians, not greatly given for the most part to the study of ultimate problems and taught in general to accept their surroundings very much as they found them, there seemed little difficulty in supposing that primitive Christianity had lain for centuries buried under a mass of superstitious accretions and had then suddenly come to consciousness again under the politic hand of the Tudors and the less politic pressure of the early Stuarts. Dean Church, perhaps as judicious an apologist as remained in the Church of England after it had passed through the crucible of the Oxford Movement, lays much stress on the view that the English Reformation was still in progress as late as the reign of Charles II; and, if that was so, my mother's ecclesiastical sentiments deserve to be described as Caroline in the same way as my father's merit to be characterized as Elizabethan. A sure sentiment or fine taste had guided her mind towards the poetry of a time when perhaps it may be said the Church of England was most perfectly true to itself, whether we study it in Clarendon's *History* or with the aid of Matthew Arnold's superb essay on Falkland. Without feeling, I fancy, any particular interest in Charles I, although in her early days the day of his execution was, I think, still set apart for special remembrance in the Book of Common Prayer, she found in some churchmen of Charles's time—in George Herbert, above all, and in Henry Vaughan—an ecclesiastical music that deeply stirred her. So much so indeed that, if I were to try to devise a background for her portrait, I should seek to convey the impression of 'a church porch', as it might be, at Bemerton and with, above it, a 'starry sky or world of light merging itself in eternity'. She met my father, however, on another plane. Year by year and week by week, they would follow in John Keble's *Christian Year* the procession of the seasons; and I don't think that Keble ever failed them. As of him, so also of them, it could have been said that the Church of England was exactly the right size for them.

As for the rest, my mother, quite unconsciously, created a home atmosphere as near akin to that of an Austen novel as I have ever come across. Her values were much the same as Jane's; and, except when my father introduced some observations on history or politics, the talk rarely ranged beyond what, under Cowper's or Jane's guidance, we associate with the teatable. There was an effortless charm and a gentle persuasiveness in these colloquies which can hardly be any longer reproduced, though Coventry

Patmore's *Angel in the House* may afford some notion of them. They had their root, doubtless, in the serenity of a happy period and of a happy child-hood; but they owed much, too, to the peace of my mother's quiet mind. I came to know cleverer women than she was, and in due course I grew to marvel at that great 'Marthadom' of women which has seemed to some out-standing members of the sisterhood of their sex so desirable a development, but I cannot pretend that I have ever really understood why these amazons become so excited by their labours or why they regard them as producing some kind of emancipation of their kind. For this I suppose I must hold my mother responsible. The civilization that she and her own sisters exemplified was modelled beyond any question on the recommendation given in the highest quarters to the character of Mary of Bethany; and it was by what she *was*, rather than by anything she *did*, that my mother set her mark upon her children. When it eventually fell to them to choose a text for her tomb-stone, they found themselves agreed without any shadow of hesitation upon the beatitude assigned to the pure in heart. Not that activity was absent from her life! But, when I think of her in relation to the outside world, I see her always, with a few flowers in her hands, making her way, without fail every week when she was in London, to a slum-parish over Westminster Bridge, where, as she used to tell me, the poor children of the place would gather round her. And, so recalling her, I have sometimes wondered whether, in her unostentatious fashion, she had not cast more sweetness and light upon the world than all those busy women who from coveted seats in Parliament or on committees have been setting the world to rights. Or perhaps I have not wondered: I have known.

But to return to my father! A more pronounced character than my mother's might not, I think, have matched his need. He was, besides, exacting in respect of the other sex. A phrase, derived, I believe, from Lord Chester-field's Letters was often to be heard on his lips: 'The Graces! the Graces! the Graces!' He was sensitive to their absence in women in a way to which changes of all sorts have rendered people indifferent now. And that leads me to mention another reign than Elizabeth's which held a great place in his mind, though Queen Anne had as little claim as could well be to satisfy Chesterfield's requirements and was indeed held up by the King of the Belgians[1] for Victoria's consideration as an example of what a Queen ought not to be. Like other boys of his period my father had left school for Sand-hurst with enough Latinity to quote the Odes of Horace and even the Eclogues of Virgil without self-consciousness or apology. *Rusticus exspectat dum defluat amnis* comes back to me over the vale of years with a familiar resonance; there comes also the louder echo of *Odi profanum vulgus, et arceo*. *Latet anguis in herba*—there lay another congenial tag in line with many simi-

[1] See Queen Victoria's Letters (1837–61), November 19th 1834.

lar warnings couched in the vulgar tongue. So then it was not perhaps surprising that this pupil of the Latin Augustans should lend a ready ear to the English ones. At times he would let Pope sing to him in biting epigrams; or Thackeray read to him in mellow tones the tale of Esmond; or Swift hurl savage gibes and jests at the fallen race of man. More than Shakespeare, more than Scott, though he would read these too. The Augustan ironists reflected, I think, his own criticism of life; and my estimate of his political acumen has gained rather than lost by watching the correspondence of events with some of his sombre forecasts. He showed no indication of faith in the fable of automatic, moral progress which bemused so many Victorians; whilst on the other hand he would, I think, have concurred in Lecky's[1] judgment that between 1832 and 1867 England possessed as good a constitution as at any time in her history. It was not very much his way, however, to express his views in philosophic shades of terminology; but he would have claimed that he was neither a Tory in the manner of Eldon nor a Tory-democrat in the manner of Randolph Churchill (the elder); and I suspect he would have found Burke's observation that 'a perfect democracy is . . . the most shameless thing in the world', because men's 'own approbation of their own acts' has to them 'the appearance of a public judgment in their favour', a reflection both congenial and convincing. There, too, the passage of the thirty odd years since he died has rather increased than reduced my opinion of his instinct and his insight.

I have watched the fine flower of Bloomsbury advance, with their hierophant at their head, and smiled to see them return again with loss from the engagement yet not wholly without admiration for the efficacy of the defence. And I have had, too, a good view of the Fabians descending like wolves on the fold they had set out to destroy and then losing their nerve, renouncing the new Soviet civilization of their dreams, turning for succour to trans-Atlantic aid and in fact surrendering to a State, based to no small degree upon the political ideas prevalent in the days of George III and very much in love still with such liberty as Washington might have harmoniously discussed in company with Burke. The old humanities, at least as they were applied to the ends of government in the nineteenth century, have a humaner look than modern science, so busy as it is with the fabrication of inhuman instruments of human destruction; and I am afraid, had Lucretius been with us, we should have had to suggest to him the amendment of a famous line, so that he who runs might henceforth read *Tantum scientia potest suadere malorum*. The prophets of Progress, with a very big P to it, have been sadly derided by the event, and that in the very department of knowledge and in the very quarter of Europe upon which they had set their hopes.

However, I am, as I said, a mere Victorian and must ask that some kindly

[1] *Democracy and Liberty*, c. I.

allowance may be made for my scepticism. I can breathe more freely in the Victorian air. My own trivial recollections, as well as my father's extensive experience and lively memories, give me the sentiment of that time. It is not nothing to be able to recall the little figure, who made so great an empress and whose personality, rendered venerable by age, seemed to need no other grace nor beauty to melt into distant music and to live on, with horns of elfland faintly blowing, after all the loud orchestration of the reign had died away. I can recall distinctly still, being lined up, with other small people, as Victoria passed from the south door into the armoury at Hatfield. I had watched her, too, from the top of a brougham, stationed (where the police would never let it stand to-day) at the point at which Hamilton Place joins Piccadilly, drive by in procession at the date of her first jubilee in 1887, and I had seen her repeat this spectacular progress with added splendour ten years after. It had chanced, also, that I was President of the Oxford Union at the time she died, and so was called upon, in the briefest possible terms, to move the adjournment of that famous debating society on the melancholy occasion of her death. These trivial incidents naturally all served to stimulate the loyalty and reverence that the conversation of my elders had instilled into me. It remains, however, still true that, if this book be worth publishing at all, it is to my father's influence and conversation that it is owing. I have not, indeed, followed his opinions blindly. He would be shocked and grieved at what I have written in praise of Gladstone, for whom, amidst all the intense feeling generated by the Irish Question, he grew to entertain as much dislike as the Queen herself; nor would he have had much sympathy with such casual allusions to the Oxford Movement as I may have been drawn into making. Nevertheless, his sunshine and shadow fell over many a page and, where I see them brightening or darkening a paragraph, I gain a new confidence that I have written what is true, at least as it seemed to the wiser among Victorians themselves.

I may be forgiven if I pause to add a few words more about this much-loved parent, philosopher, and friend. Completely overshadowed though he was by the personality and talents of his elder brother, Queen Victoria's last Prime Minister, my father was in many respects a remarkable man—more remarkable, I think, than some of his family perceived. If Salisbury exemplified a wise man, Eustace Cecil was an instance of a shrewd one. Though not an eminent Victorian, he was a representative one; and his career, packed as it had been with experience of many kinds, illustrated admirably the material upon which the Victorians could draw largely for unpaid public work.

In my grandparents, on my father's side, the businesslike strains of Cecil and Gascoyne blood had met, and in my father they had mingled. My grandfather, like my father, has been overshadowed and is a good deal lost to view behind the figure of his second son, the Prime Minister; but one at least of his contemporaries, and one who had every reason to know what he was talking about, rated his abilities high and complained that people had forgotten what a very capable man he was. The house at Hatfield owed much to his daring treatment of its problems in his time; and politics, too, may, I suppose, be said to owe him something, since he sat in two of Derby's Cabinets, though in the elegant ease of a Lord President of the Council and of a Lord Privy Seal. He could be alarming; but he was sociable. He liked a joke; and he liked a jaunt. One of my father's favourite stories about him recalled the repartee he received from a dairymaid who, chancing to come to him with her troubles at an inconvenient hour, had been met with an admonition to 'go to the devil'. They were excellent friends; upon which she rejoined politely: 'Certainly, my lord, if your lordship will show me the way.'

Bulwer-Lytton, the novelist, attracted his attention, or perhaps displeasure, on one occasion by being late for breakfast, a formal meal in those days. My grandfather forthwith ordered the gong to be taken upstairs and sounded outside Sir Edward's room. After an interval the dining-room door opened and Bulwer-Lytton advanced into the room declaiming in dramatic tones: 'I heard a great sound; and I thought it was the day of judgment.'

From my grandmother,[1] I imagine, descended to her children most of their finer shades of character. She must have been, if the Lawrence portrait truly portrays her, a very pleasing person to look upon; and Wellington evidently found her a delightful friend. But she died when my father was five; and his sisters both married before he was ten. It was in his aunt, the first Lady Cowley and Wellington's sister-in-law—the best friend, so he once told me, that he ever had—that he found the understanding for which his lively, affectionate nature was longing. She had been British Ambassadress in Paris during Louis Philippe's time; and she had known the world of her day and had liked it well enough to mourn over the loss of it. I always see her sitting with my father over the fire, her Embassy days all past and gone, and (I am not imagining the scene; he described it to me) charging a few commonplace words with a weight of emotion sufficient to make all their banality vanish: 'And now it is all over.' Diplomacy, as she had known it in those distant days had seemed delightful; and I suppose her experience inspired him to see its charms.

Another generation of Cowleys, let me say in passing, reigned at the Paris Embassy during the Second Empire; and it was in their time that my father saw the Empress Eugénie stand, white as a sheet, to be married to the ambitious adventurer who, owing everything to his uncle's ten years of

[1] The first wife of the Second Marquess of Salisbury. She was the daughter and heir of Bamber Gascoyne.

monarchy, contrived to hold his own throne for pretty nearly double that time. My father had no uniform with him on this occasion; and he was consequently rigged out at the Embassy with regimentals as various as Joseph's coat. It was assumed that no Frenchman would detect anything amiss; but the English diplomats had not reckoned with the Paris gamins. As my father came out of Notre Dame the boys began to point and to jeer. 'Regarde donc, celui-là. Son uniforme! Qu'est ce qu'il y a?' The police feared an incident, hurried my father in his bogus array into a cab, and packed him off to the British Embassy. The gaiety of nations had been to a minute extent increased; the peace of nations was preserved.

It was, I suppose, at this time, but it may have been later, that my father, in the course of a talk with Grammont, rather naïvely inquired: 'Qu'est-ce-que cela veut dire, Monsieur, ce mot "canaille"?' 'Ah, Monsieur', was the reply he got, much to his amusement, 'maintenant tout le monde est canaille.' So did the *ancien régime* deal with the Revolution, even when, as in Gramont's case, it had come to terms with it.

Seduced by the meretricious glitter of the Second Empire I have been tempted to let my memories run ahead. Had I been a better artist I should perhaps have been able to show the small, motherless boy emerging from the shadows of the great house at Hatfield, early aware that he would have to fight his own battles, early sensible of what later on he became fully conscious, the obligation of self-help and the good sense of Samuel Smiles. Fortunately, his wits were adequate to his occasions. One trivial story comes back to me. There was a certain Lord Sandys, a corpulent personage, who at that time used to visit the House. He delighted, as old gentlemen can, in his own jests; and he proceeded to direct them at my father. The boy was not equal to verbal retorts and resolved, therefore, upon a more practical rejoinder. The next time Lord Sandys cracked a joke at my father's expense, the small boy converted his head into a battering-ram and made straight for the middle of the old gentleman's corporation. These tactics proved highly successful. Lord Sandys ceased his funning and my father was left in peace.

My father had just turned thirteen when my grandfather married again. Lady Mary Sackville-West, renowned for her beautiful eyes, was to have the, I believe, singular destiny of reigning, not only at Hatfield, but at Knowsley[1]. The two great houses possessed in Victoria's later days much of the glamour and distinction that, writing in 1838, Greville attributed, at a still earlier time than his mention of them, to Hatfield and Cassiobury.[2] Froude, busy with his *History of England*, became a frequent visitor to Hatfield in my step-grandmother's time; and I believe, even now, I could find the little cupboard in the wall of the gallery at Hatfield where he was allowed

[1] She married, after the death of her first husband, the fifteenth Earl of Derby.
[2] Cossiobury?

to keep the manuscripts of his much-discussed volumes on the England of
the Armada and before. I have read through, have possessed, and, under
compulsion, destroyed the letters—entirely innocuous, but nevertheless
spiced, as one might expect, with characteristic reflections—that he wrote to
Mary, Lady Derby, in the course of their long friendship. But Froude made,
of course, only one of a circle where the most representative men in politics
and literature were to be met. I allude to him, as I might with equal truth
allude to Lecky, upon whose friendship my father placed high value, because
he serves to show the kind of background that at their best the country-
houses afforded. Without that background the Victorian era could hardly
have been what it was, so well did it serve the intelligence and the intercourse of the country. 'Tark and dardle' (talk and dawdle), said a lady of,
if my memory holds good, foreign extraction to my mother, 'that's what
you do in your country-house visits.' But at any rate they talked to some
purpose and dawdled to some effect.

My father, the home background of whose early life, both as a boy and
a young man I have tried, as the phrase goes, to 'telescope' in the preceding
paragraphs, had gone at the appointed time to Harrow, where he had met
with all the roughness and hardness that was then considered the best introduction to the troublesome world of men. In due course his father asked
him what he meant to do with himself. He replied that he wanted to go
into diplomacy. 'That's no profession,' replied my grandfather, 'you must
find something else.' And he added significantly that there was a good living
in the family. My father, however, felt no vocation for holy orders. If he
could not be a diplomat, he would be a soldier.

So a soldier he became, and, as such, was sent to South Africa, then
presently to India, and ultimately, after transference to the Coldstream
Guards, to the Crimea before the war there ended. It was, I think, on the
way out to South Africa that he narrowly escaped having to fight a duel
with the formidable bully of the regiment, who picked a quarrel whenever
he could. However, he did escape, as he also escaped the, to his constitution, deadly character of the Indian climate, thanks to the doctor's insistence
that, if he were not intending to leave his bones in Asia, he must return
home.

One great piece of good fortune had befallen him at the outset of his
military career. Wellington, as was said, was a friend of his mother's; and
he entered the army just soon enough to receive a small book of military
regulations, autographed by the venerable hands of the victor of Waterloo.
The book, still preserved by his family, perpetuates the memory of an esteem
and admiration for the Duke, no doubt common to the period, but in his
case emphasized by early contacts at Hatfield and Stratfield Saye. I never
heard my father speak of any of the other considerable men he had known at

all in the same way that he spoke of 'the Duke'. Iron from off the Iron Duke might—not, of course, in the ordinary sense—be said to have entered into his soul. A great simplicity of habit and a great absence of personal luxury governed his way of life; and, when I once contemplated at his side the Duke's little bedstead at Walmer, I felt I had tracked these traits to their source. He was, I think, actually present when Wellington, to some inept inquiry what he thought of Napoleon, replied curtly, 'Wasn't a gentleman!' One can, with Seeley, if one pleases, call Napoleon's legacy to the man who had attempted the assassination of Wellington, 'a Corsican touch'; but it was, even more obviously, the touch of a cad. Perhaps then I never saw my father's soul at closer quarters than when we stood in the Duke's room at Walmer or again when we gazed at the gorgeous tomb of the Emperor in the Invalides. So much that he revered was symbolized in the one; so much that he loathed in the other. I became, if possible, even more sensible of the latter sentiment when at a later date I fell under the influence of Herbert Fisher's intellectual admiration of Napoleonic statesmanship. My father would coldly advise me to read Lanfrey, by whose estimate of Napoleon he set much store. All through the time of Victoria the Duke's type of character is at issue with the revolutionary type, incarnate in Napoleon: and the struggle still goes on, even though the combatants on both sides have decided to dub themselves democrats.

Life, which seemed resolved to give this shrewd Victorian the fullest variety of experience possible, presently pitched the soldier into politics. For twenty years—between 1865 and 1885—my father sat in Parliament for different divisions of Essex. He saw 'the Conservative Surrender'[1] in 1867 and used to quote General Peel's epigram upon it, which I give, if not with perfect exactitude, at least in the form with which I grew familiar. 'Three things I have learnt', Peel had declared in reviewing the manœuvres of Disraeli, 'that there is nothing less vital than a vital point, nothing more insecure than security, and nothing so elastic as the conscience of a Cabinet Minister'. Peel had indeed avenged his father.

No man who had lived through 1867 in the House of Commons could fail, if he had his wits about him, to be cynical; and my father was that, not of course, in his personal conduct, but in his judgment of men. 'Rogues!' was a word not infrequently to be heard on his lips as a commonplace flooding with light many of the doings of mankind; and it was not unusual either to hear him quote from the homily of a Scottish minister of religion who had preached on the text 'I said in my haste, all men are liars', and had promptly followed this up by the announcement: 'What the Psalmist said in his haste I say at my leisure.'

[1] The introduction of the Franchise Bill of 1867 by Lord Derby's third administration. This Bill is discussed later in the chapter on Lord Salisbury.

There were other of my father's stories which had approved themselves to his mind by their genial cynicism. There was a story of the first Lord Cottesloe, who as Fremantle, had been a Whip in Dizzy's time in the House of Commons and to whose eightieth birthday party my father, as a connection by marriage, was invited. All the clan Fremantle—sons and grandchildren, and so forth—were gathered together for the celebration and presentation on the auspicious day: and any still living must forgive me, if the conclusion of my tale should seem to carry an innuendo. My father was, anyhow, on the occasion, full of goodwill towards all Fremantles, if not towards all men and, when the octogenarian host beckoned him aside, expected to hear patriarchal benedictions pronounced on the assembled family. It proved otherwise. The old parliamentary hand merely wished to convey the experience of a lifetime and, therewith, a warning: 'My dear Cecil', he said, 'trust no one.'

These be, however, but toys. My father had no need to await the cynic's caution to learn wisdom in the ways of the world. He had long since learnt to take them as he found them; and in 1874 he had followed his elder brother[1] by accepting office in Disraeli's Administration, in which he became Surveyor-General of the Ordnance. I think he would have liked, and had even perhaps some little reason to expect, the Under-Secretaryship for Foreign Affairs; but his lot still fell in the sphere of military and not of diplomatic action. Then, after another period in Opposition, he wearied of politics, and of the way things were going, and were going to go. As he once said to me: 'I had served my country in the Field and in Parliament; I thought I was entitled to try to do something for myself.'

Here his Gascoyne blood came powerfully to his assistance. The Gascoynes had produced at least one Lord Mayor—Sir Crisp Gascoyne—in the eighteenth century; and Crisp's son, Bamber, my father's grandfather, was a clever fellow, who does not make a particularly pleasing appearance in Lamb's *Essays of Elia*, but whose property at Childwall Hall, near Liverpool, has proved a mine of wealth to some of his descendants. My father's inheritance from his mother, however, took the form of a talent for finance and not of a heritage of landed property. Well advanced in middle life, without any special education for business, and, as he used to say, without anyone to teach him its ways, he 'went into the City', became in due course chairman of various trust companies, was given a seat on the Board of the Great Eastern Railway, and ended by converting a modest competence into a considerable fortune. 'We used to think', one of his co-directors told me after his death, 'that your father had some sort of obsession about Russia, for he never would let us invest money there. We see now how shrewd he was.' His long experience as a younger son, perhaps, told to the advantage

[1] Lord Salisbury, afterwards Prime Minister.

of his younger children. 'The great thing in life', he once said to me as exactly as I can recall his words, 'is to be independent; then you are free to do what you wish.' Needless to say, then, he was a profound individualist; and an exchange of opinion that he had with Bishop Gore, whose grasp at any rate of the superficialities of socialism appeared to me no less tenacious than those of his opponent in the opposite direction, caused him a good deal of amusement. 'I've caught it now', he observed to me once, as he handed me a letter from Gore. And so he had; though I am confident that that apostolic man's argument made no more lasting impression upon the other's mind than another argument from the same source seems, if the story is true, to have done in the case of an ecclesiastical superior. 'My dear Gore, don't be a bore.' So Stubbs, the historian, is said (I believe by Gore himself) to have retorted on a postcard in reply to a lengthy dissertation from his subordinate's too enthusiastic pen on the needs of a certain parish near Oxford.

It is a gross mistake to suppose that the more fortunate Victorians did not give a great deal of thought to the lot of the less fortunate ones. Even in the evil days of George IV, unless my memory fails me, you may find Rush, the American Minister, commenting on the striking generosity of the English upper class. And, five years after Victoria came to the throne, on January 16th 1843, there is a revealing entry in Charles Greville's diary which, coming as it does from the pen of that old society hack, is calculated to give pause to much self-congratulation about our supposedly newly developed social conscience. 'The condition of the people, moral and physical', wrote Greville, 'is uppermost in everybody's mind, the state and management of workhouses and prisons, and the great question of education. The newspapers are full of letters and complaints on these subjects, and people think, talk and care about them very much.' And this was at the very time that Newman was setting the academic world ablaze with Tract 90. The early Victorians devoted an astonishing amount of thought to the things that really matter, both ethical and theological, and they for the most part perceived the connection between them.

What, however, it may be asked me, has all this to do with your father? A great deal! He was only nine in 1843, but he grew up in a world to which charity was no stranger and in which philanthropy had not become the almost exclusive preserve of the politician. His eldest brother, Cranborne, who was blind himself, started a society for giving help to the blind—a society which lasted into our time when its administration passed into the hands of a City company. The description of my father as a criminologist in *The Times*'s obituary notice may, however, have been a little extravagant; yet there lies before me as I write a book of essays collected from the St. James's Medley in 1865, where he deals with his personal observation of the underworld of London and of New York and of the convict settlements of France. Asylums, prisons, slums at home and abroad—with these he made himself acquainted; and much that he saw of the poorer districts of the Metropolis noticeably affected him, who was anything but a sentimentalist. He told me that, after one of his explorations in darkest London (I think it was somewhere round Seven Dials) he happened to meet Lord Shaftesbury, the greatest of his name, at dinner, and took the opportunity of talking of what had just disturbed and distressed him. Shaftesbury listened, and at the end observed: 'Well! all I can say is that it is a great deal better than when I began to work.' And this seems to have been quite correct and to have continued true to the end of the reign. Giffen, the great statistician of the period, declared in 1883,[1] the year of Marx's death, that in the preceding fifty years, in every class of work in which it is possible to draw comparisons, the wages of workers had risen at least 20 per cent, in most cases from 50 to 100 per cent, and in one or two instances more than 100 per cent.

With all its faults, then, the much-abused capitalist system could do so much. The whole Victorian economy was broadly based on the belief that character tells in the long run far more than circumstance in the struggle to do away with evil of every kind. All general principles certainly desiderate place for exceptions; but it is not the less misleading to set up exceptions in place of the rule. The Victorians read their Bibles, I should suppose from what I knew of them, a good deal more than we do; and they read in them that the Psalmist, for all his weight of years, had never seen the righteous forsaken or his seed begging their bread. My father had been brought up along those lines; and he was entertainingly mischievous if anyone started to do what he called 'piling up the agony'.

The clash of two centuries, the conflict of two schools is, indeed, to be heard as Gore's letter rustles down into Stubbs's waste-paper basket. It is not given to all pious men to concur in Dr. Johnson's opinion that 'most schemes of political improvement are very laughable things'; but from Melbourne onwards there have been a good many sensible men who knew how little would really come out of the bustling of the busybodies. Clergymen of a socialistic turn of mind have, I fancy, not infrequently had their reservations. Though it was made fifty years ago, I myself can never forget Canon Barnett's remark to me at Toynbee Hall: 'So far as we have gone we have only made prigs of these people.' Neither can I dismiss the impression received at a charitable committee by the discovery that our 'working-class' members were more often than not of the opinion, not shared by some of their more sentimental and materially more fortunate colleagues, that we should do best to leave certain distressing cases, financially speaking, alone.

[1] Robert Giffen, *The Progress of the Working Classes in the Last Half-Century* (quoted in Lecky's *Democracy and Liberty*, cabinet edition), Vol. II, p. 318.

I suspect a larger and wider experience than my own would tend to bring many praiseworthy men nearer to this view than to its opposite, just as, in fact, it kept the shrewd, kindly man of whom I am writing remote from sentimental philanthropy. The last thing, however, I wish to do is to delineate my father as some mere *laudator temporis acti*. He disliked many of the changes he saw, but his standpoint was more adequately rendered by a snatch from an old French song, which was often on his lips: 'Le temps que j'e regrette, c'est le temps qui n'est plus'.

If I have managed to show how deep a sense of duty to his fellow citizens permeated my father's life, then I have done all I need in this direction. He entertained no extravagant expectation that in a wicked world we should not have the poor always with us; less still that latter-day reformers were going to be able to dispose of distress and disappointment and, perhaps least of all, that they would be able to eliminate the *faux bonhomme* who seeks to exploit the sad state of the poor to his personal or party advantage, instead of trying to lift all the problems of poverty beyond the range of politics.

This pronounced individualism of the typical Victorian could make itself felt in matters far removed from philanthropy. 'If ever there is an attempt to introduce conscription into this country', my father said to me once towards the end of his life, 'old as I am, I'll stump the country against it.' Neither the Crimean War, in which he had fought, nor the War Office, in which he had served, had moved him a jot or tittle from the intense, personal, freedom-loving attitude of his contemporaries. He recognized, of course, every able-bodied man's obligation to defend his own country in case of need, and the place, too, of the militia-ballot in such a scheme of defence; and I believe he looked not unfavourably at Roberts's scheme for universal military training. But Victorian, as I said, to the finger-tips as he was, he had been deeply convinced by Mahan of the influence of sea power upon history. His life had closed long before Captain Russell Grenfell's[1] admirable book on sea power appeared, but I think he would have concurred in most, if not all, of that eminent critic's conclusions and not least, in spite of its source, in those words of Napoleon's which furnish the *envoi* of the book: 'England can never be a Continental power, and in the attempt she must be ruined. Let her stick to the sovereignty of the seas, and she may send her ambassadors to the courts of Europe and demand what she pleases.' How much greater has the force of these words become since the defence of England has grown to require mastery in the air as well as at sea! Only a megalomaniac can suppose we can afford to build up and sustain huge European armies as well as great fleets, naval and aerial!

I hope this slight sketch of *un homme d'autrefois*, to whom these pages owe much, may serve to give them such a background as is required. And,

[1] *Sea Power*, by T.124.

LORD EUSTACE CECIL
From a photograph by the St. James's Gallery

though it is irrelevant, I should like to add that the rather unhappy adolescence and the rather difficult early manhood which I have touched on, concluded, like a Victorian novel, in a long and happy old age. 'I always think of your parents', Arthur Balfour once said to me, 'as the most fortunate pair of people I know.' All, as he went on to say, had gone well for them. They had lost no children; they had had no other major misfortunes; they had reached the fullness of their years. The slippers that, in accordance with custom, had, presumably, followed their carriage as they set off on their honeymoon seemed now to be tripping ahead of them on a rose-strewn pathway as they approached their golden wedding day. The September of 1910 was in fact one of the last to be lit by that after-glow of Victorianism which faded out with the coming of August 1914. The world was still wrapped in peace and the distance seemed bathed in the promise of prosperity. The lot had, indeed, fallen to them in a fair ground, with the blue lagoon of Poole Harbour spreading in front of their windows and the soft purple of the Purbeck Hills (in the cup of which my mother's old home at Encombe lay hidden) colouring the far horizon. It was a goodly possession which they sought to pass on in all its tranquil beauty to their children't children; and there seemed nothing in their conservative creed to suggest that the endeavour was other than an expression of the human right to start a family and to found a home. That clear thought should have woven itself into the fabric of this book; for it was as truly part and parcel of the Victorian idea as it now appears distasteful to the later Georgians. To the rash prognostic of the Fabians the memory of my old home, and of those who made it, seems to stand out in sharp contrast; and, not to close on a harsh or angry note, I turn to Landor's 'Petrarch' for a last word: 'Impossible as it is to look far and with pleasure into the future, what a privilege it is, how incomparably greater than any other that genius can confer, to be able to direct the backward flight of fancy and imagination to the recesses they most delighted in; to be able, as the shadows lengthen in our path, to call up before us the youth of our sympathies in all their tenderness and purity!'[1]

[1] *Landor's Works* (ed. T. E. Welby), Vol. IX, p. 184.

VICTORIANA

CHAPTER II

VICTORIANA

LESLIE STEPHEN, in analysing the elements of a society, drew a useful distinction between what he called the social organism and the social tissue. The former is not hard to define; and in the Victorian era in Britain it was admirably sketched in 1867 by Walter Bagehot. The skeleton of the Constitution, as it existed in the 'sixties of last century, is there displayed. Bagehot held up to critical examination the function, as understood in his time, of the Monarchy, of the Cabinet, of the Lords and Commons, of party and party government; and he who would know in detail how these matters looked to a thoughtful Victorian must turn to his pages for guidance, and perhaps, to gain the best advantage, to the edition of 1927, which contains a preface by Arthur Balfour, the Edwardian Prime Minister.

The social tissue of any society is far more subtle to define than the social organism. The majority of men and women in any age are commonplace people and not unlike those who went before them. But the social tissue is determined, at least in large measure, by the uncommon people; and of these in the age of Victoria there were a great number. They lived in a free society, and there were among them striking divergences of mind and temper. The heirs to the romantic tradition had an almost exaggerated belief in the value of forming their own opinions and speaking their minds; and, though their conventions of conduct worked with great force, as we can see in Parnell's case and in Dilke's, there was little that they declined to consider and discuss. As a result their mental process was rich and receptive. But not so the heirs of Priestley and Bentham! The Utilitarians had nothing rare or strange in their philosophy, which carried conviction none the less to minds ready to surrender themselves to an easy formula, 'the greatest happiness of the greatest number', a phrase that served to convert masses of men and women not eager to puzzle their heads with abstruse or occult considerations.

The Mills were high lights in the Victorian picture; and John Morley's statement in his book *On Compromise*[1] that, when he arrived in Oxford, the star of Newman had set and the sun of Mill—i.e. of John Stuart Mill—had risen, gives us a measure of the vast influence of the Utilitarians, and in particular of Mill's essays on liberty and representative government. This great body of thought lay in Victorian days near the heart of nineteenth-century reflection; but, in my view at least, it was an alien body needing only

[1] *On Compromise*, p. 115.

time to expel it. The fate of the Liberal Party, of which it was the inspiration, goes some way to prove that it was not altogether congruous to the genius of the nation. I shall venture, therefore, to glance at it and pass on to ground which seems to me firmer—the ground of a humanity, deeper, stronger, and stranger than Liberalism has ever afforded.

For human nature—idealists, optimists and Utopians notwithstanding—does not change. If it did, the study of, by common consent, the most profoundly humane of human documents—the study of the Bible, of Homer, of Virgil, of Dante, of Shakespeare, of Molière and of the Immortals in general—would be left to children. In fact, all that really appears to happen in the way of alteration is, then, that, for better or worse, certain manners and customs change. Man, however, remains stable, knowing good and evil, and, in his unregenerate condition, choosing still to do the things that his better self repudiates as bad. Examine the history of our own time, if any lurking doubt remains on this matter, and consider whether the ancient horrors, associated with the quarries at Syracuse, the amphitheatre at Rome, or the day of Saint Bartholomew in Paris, were really worse than such events of our own time as are known to have occurred at Buchenwald and Katyn Wood.

This question of man's moral and intellectual improvement, or stagnation, or deterioration, is fundamental in all historical thinking; and there is nothing, perhaps, that has so much to do with the way a man reaches political conviction. In the case of the Victorians it had all the importance given to it in the first chapter of Peacock's *Headlong Hall*. Some thought one way, and some another. Cobden, for example, floating on a tide of economic optimism, believed that the Islands of the Blest lay but a little way ahead. Though he was unquestionably an eminent Victorian and as such was held by Gladstone and others in the highest esteem,[1] the Manchester School, had laspsed into reckless optimism. Amongst his shining qualities Cobden did not number that of prediction. If such things as occurred in France not much more than half a century before Victoria came to the throne and as happened in Germany and Russia fifty years after Victoria had been dead, could be, then the proof of moral progress stands in much need of assistance. Nor does it become clear, if we bring other tests to bear. The faults of the *ancien régime* have been tediously stressed and unscrupulously exaggerated. Of course it was a blunder to teach the leaders of the *noblesse* that their function was to appear as decorative pieces at Court instead of to look after their estates and dependents; but this negligence does not alter the fact that they excelled in what they attempted and gave all Europe a standard in conversation and manners for which one might search in vain to-day. This was what they had tried to do; and they had done it well. But more than that! It is not clear that the pursuits of democracy will not in time lend

[1] Morley's *Gladstone*, Vol. III, p. 182. (Cp. op. cit., Vol. II, p. 49.)

themselves to as much ridicule as those of these much-abused aristocrats whose elegant performances are even yet found to be pleasing, if only in museums and on the stage. It is possible that someday the flogging or kicking of a ball this way or that, may come to seem less deserving of interest than a lucid exposition or a finished repartee, than the *fêtes galantes* depicted by Watteau, or the finesse in furniture achieved in the age of Louis Seize.

There are few more interesting passages, perhaps, in biography than that in which Taine sets out the circumstances that led him to start writing his history of the origins of contemporary France. In the year 1849, when he was no more than twenty-one years of age, he found himself, as he tells us, required to vote in an election charged with possibilities bearing upon the future fate of his country. People pressed upon him the claims of royalism and republicanism, of democracy and conservatism, of socialism or bonapartism. He had no use for any of these. In his own words: 'I was nothing of this kind, nothing at all. . . . My acquaintances, so full of assurance were designing a constitution like a house according to some lovely, new or simple plan . . . and each declared that his model was the proper abode for man, the only one that a sensible man would live in. To my eye this argument was feeble. Personal tastes were not authoritative. It did not seem to me that a house should be built to satisfy the architect but the future inhabitant. To ask advice of the owner, to submit the outline of its future residence to the nation was too clearly a farce or a cheat: in such a case the question itself always gives the answer and, besides, had the answer been free, France was in no better condition than myself to return it: "dix million d'ignorances ne font pas un savoir."[1] A people if consulted, can, to speak strictly, say what form of government it likes, but not what form it needs: it can only find that out by trials: it requires time to know whether its house is convenient, solid, weather-proof, suited to its habits, to its occupations, to its character, its idiosyncrasies, its angularities. Now, to judge by experience, we have never been satisfied by the design we had chosen: thirteen times in eighty years we had pulled a house down to build anew, and, rebuild it as we might, we had not yet found a house to suit us. If other nations had been luckier, if, abroad, several political structures are solid and enduring, it is that they have been built in a particular way, around a core original and massive, have been supported by some old central building, several times repaired but always preserved, have been enlarged by degrees, and fitted by experiment and adaptation to the wants of its residents.'

For such reasons as these, it is worth while to recall Taine's considered judgment on that old society that the Revolution swept so roughly away, leaving France to search for the plan of another, as indeed she searches still.

[1] Taine's *L'Ancien Régime* (Preface).

I give the conclusion in his own words; for it is fragile, like the *ancien régime* that it describes, and does not invite translation: 'De toutes parts au moment où ce monde finit, une complaisance mutuelle, une douceur affectueuse vient comme un souffle tiède et moite d'automne, fondre ce qu'il y avait encore de dureté dans sa sécheresse et envelopper dans un parfum de roses mourantes les élégances de ces derniers instants. On rencontre alors des actions, des mots d'une grâce suprême, uniques en leur genre, comme une mignonne et adorable figurine de vieux Sèvres.'[1]

This finished perfection of courtesy was not, if Taine is the unbiased historian he supposes, inconsistent with political intelligence of a high order. 'La bonne volonté est complète. Jamais l'aristocratie n'a été si digne du pouvoir qu'au moment où elle allait le perdre; les privilégiés, tirés de leur désoeuvrement, redevenaient des hommes publics et, rendus à leur fonction, revenaient à leur devoir.'[2]

In England, as we know, little or nothing of all this was at first perceived by the revolutionary politicians, poets or publicists of the time. Fox, without any depth of reflection, acclaimed the French Revolution as the greatest and best event in history: Wordsworth looked on with an enthusiasm so reckless that, when, later, his mind came to maturity, it left his muse dull with discomfiture and disappointment: and Tom Paine gave utterance to views which did not appear to possess any very solid foundation. Only Burke can be credited with having possessed real vision from the outset and of having perceived whither the sentimental lucubrations of Rousseau must lead. Johnson would doubtless, had he not been five years dead, have brought his massive understanding and his merciless sledge-hammer of a tongue to the aid of Burke's reflections; and Gibbon, whilst characteristically critical of the stress Burke did not fail to lay on the ecclesiastical aspect of the matter, gave Burke's conclusions his support. Thus the three best qualified British minds of the period may be said to have been aligned against the small attorney's outlook of Tom Paine with its palpable contempt for all that is traditional and institutional in a stable civilization. One does not need to look further than Chesterfield's will and letters to see that some of the most forcible cogitations of Paine on human disparity in fortune and circumstance had passed through the mind of the apostle of the Graces; nor does one need to spend long on the pages of Paine to satisfy oneself that it was quite beyond that dabbler in politics, who presently found himself in prison in France with every prospect of expiating his over-indulgence in free speech by a death on the scaffold, to deal with the problems on which he had delivered his soul with so much confidence and so many thrusts at Burke's *Reflections*. Doubtless, before his liberation at 'Thermidor'

[1] Taine, *L'Ancien Régime*, Book II, Chapter iii, Section 2.
[2] ibid., Book IV, Chapter iii, Section 6.

extricated him from his troubles, he may have found time to reflect that
Burke, after all, had understood the French Revolution better than himself.
'Paine's ignorance', said Leslie Stephen, an outstanding but not orthodox
Victorian, 'was vast and his language brutal; but he had the gift of a true
demagogue—the power of wielding a fine, vigorous English.' We can leave
it at that. Paine could never have understood what Burke had in mind
when he asserted the shamelessness of a perfect democracy or when he
declared that the State was no partnership in 'things subservient only to the
gross animal existence of a temporary and perishable nature'—but required
consideration, as 'a partnership in all science . . . in all art . . . in every
virtue and in all perfection'—and, this much admitted, became a partnership of many generations, a partnership between the living and the dead.
All this was quite beyond Paine whose horizon was bounded by the wealth
which he saw in the hands of the Duke of Richmond and the poverty
which, to the credit of his heart, distressed him on so many sides, and which
he fondly supposed could be alleviated or abolished by the simple expedient
of taking from the rich and giving to the poor. The Tom Paines of the world
can learn only from bitter experience, if at all. History is wasted on them.
They cannot be convinced that they have in human nature a constant, and
not a variable that they can mould to their fancy. There is no book, perhaps,
better calculated to dissuade this kind of optimist from his errors than
Lenotre's searching studies of the French revolutionaries. Here are the men
stripped naked, until we can see that they are but men like ourselves or,
maybe a little worse than ourselves, yet, anyhow, not the angels required to
change the heart of man.

Among Lenotre's figures Pache has long seemed to me as much worth
study as any; for no one perhaps had more the look at starting of being the
very kind of man that was wanted to promote gentleness and goodness in
the public service. Yet of him Lenotre declares that he 'personified' the
Terror and was 'the Tartuffe' of the Revolution. When we first catch sight
of him, however, botanizing with his son among the Swiss mountains or,
at close of day, playing the harp with his daughter, no one promises to
make a more exemplary disciple of his compatriot, Rousseau. But some
baleful chance during 1792 took him to Paris, where one of his admirers,
named Gibert, introduced him to Mme Roland, the Mrs. Sidney Webb of
that time and place. Mme Roland, as her memorable exclamation on the
scaffold betrayed, understood human nature very little; and she understood
Pache not at all. She was fool enough to persuade her husband to place him
at the head of the Ministry of War, where Servan had not been doing any
too well. From that moment of accession to great power, the character of
Pache underwent a remarkable change. After the manner of revolutionary
idealists he seemed to slough the glittering skin of the philanthropist and

without more ado to emerge as a nauseous reptile. Then, thanks to the friendships that he had formed with some of the most odious of the revolutionaries, he was made Mayor of Paris and, in that important capacity, became involved in the downfall of the Girondins (his benefactors—the Rolands—among them), in the defence of the September Massacres, and in the unspeakable horror of the charges brought against Marie Antoinette. 'Thermidor' set a term to his activities. The 'sleek' Pache, as Carlyle calls him, escaped, not without difficulty or distress, to the mountains, where he appears to have resumed, as if nothing had happened, his simple way of life, his harmless pleasures and, presumably, his former diet of milk, black bread and periwinkles. From this rural existence he was never again to be tempted away; not even by Monge, his old friend, whom Napoleon sent in 1803 in a fine conveyance with a footman attached, to enquire for him and, from what little we can learn of the interview, presumably to make him some advantageous proposal.

Pache is a salutary example of one type of man whom a revolution brings to the top and whose head is completely turned for a time by the tremendous experience. It had probably never struck the worthy man that politics is a profound science and, to be practised with safety to oneself and mankind, requires the finished dexterity of art. Democracy makes the affairs of men seem so much too simple. One man, after all, is assumed by democratic standards to be as good as another. The revolutionist has seldom reflected that his catchwords carry him but a very little way and want more exact definition, if they are to serve. Justice, for instance, cannot be equated with equity, still less with equality; and Equality will not run comfortably in harness with Liberty. All the confused talk that goes on among radical reformers is carried on without reflecting that, if a man is to be free to make the best of himself and reap the rewards of industry and intelligence, this will not square with the doctrine that all men are born equal or ought to be made so. Eventually the great gulf, lying hid, at any rate in former days, between the Girondin and the Jacobin, is bound to fly open, as in Pache's case, before the astonished eyes of the revolutionary; and, as like as not, he tumbles headlong into it or, maybe, finds himself without any head on his shoulders to guide him in his retreat. Democracy, as was emphasized by Maine, needs something like the Supreme Court in the U.S.A. to make it safe for the world and, not only that, but the individual need of an exceptionally firm and clear mind, if one is going to pick one's way through its perils and adventures. Pache was too small a man to succeed, where far abler men, like Danton, stumbled and fell. Yet his fate illustrates better than many the complexity of the revolutionary creed, when adopted by a man of modest capacity; and his name, though no more now than a smudge on the page of history, is still there to arrest the eye.

French historians from Taine to Gaxotte have long found the French Revolution out and have plucked it of the peacock's plumes, attached to it by ingenuous admirers. It is not, however, so certain that Englishmen have yet to come to see it clear. Fox's nonsense is still sometimes quoted, and apparently with approbation.

'There are few observers', Gibbon has wisely said,[1] 'who possess a clear and comprehensive view of the revolutions of society; and who are capable of discerning the nice and secret springs of action which impel in the same uniform direction the blind and capricious passions of a multitude of individuals.' It was the merit of the early Victorians that they did, more or less, understand the significance of the Revolution and that, though its cleverest child had been routed by an English Tory at Waterloo, they recognized that it had not been thereby disposed of. Some more conclusive answer than Burke's was needed to the argument advanced against so catastrophic an upheaval. Joseph de Maistre, one of its first and most formidable critics, had remarked at the outset that the proper reply to the revolution lay, not in a counter-revolution, but in 'the contrary-of-a-Revolution'. It was something of this sort, something, that is ameliorative, though on traditional lines, that in England sensible men strove to effect, Whig and Tory, oftentimes, if not openly, working together, and never more so perhaps than in 1832, when 'the Duke' stood by his abiding principle that the King's Government must be carried on, whatever party was in power.[2]

The whole matter, as we can see, was still very much in the public mind, when Victoria came to the Throne. A few years before, the young Disraeli had tried to turn this preoccupation of the period to account by producing a 'Revolutionary Epick'. But the poet, as time showed, was anything but a revolutionary himself; and the muse, whom he had invoked on the plains of Troy, withheld the inspiration which she had accorded to Homer. A profound and passionate poem, though conceived after the manner of a prose composition, was, however, on its way. In the January of the very year of Victoria's accession, Carlyle, his genius fortified to some extent with material supplied by Mill, completed his *French Revolution*. 'You have not had', he told his wife, as he gave it her to read, 'for a hundred years any book that comes more direct and flamingly from the heart of a living man.'[3] A 'savage' book, as he said himself, and written by a 'wild' man; but perhaps none the worse for that! He got under the skins of the French revolutionaries, coloured them 'sea-green' or whatever hue they might call for; and the colours held. Belonging to no party and well acquainted with the sordid battle of life, he was in as good a position to deal

[1] *Decline and Fall*, c. xxvii.
[2] Wellington's administration of November, 1832.
[3] Froude, *Carlyle's Life in London*, Vol. I, p. 84.

out justice as a man could hope to be. He struck, indeed, both to the Right and to the Left with the zeal of a Hebrew prophet, contemptuous alike of cabbages and kings, of mobs and monarchs. Satisfied that no man and no body of men escaped the wrath of God, punishment being concealed in the nature of things, he delivered his blows with even hand upon the indolence of Louis, miscalled *le bien aimé*, and upon the insolence of Hébert, editor of the *Père Duchesne*, 'brutalest Newspaper yet published on Earth'. It is worth sampling such examples of Carlyle's quality before we move on. They might have come from a *vox populi* when, holding to the voice of conscience that is in every man, it draws nearest to the *vox Dei*, that is above every man. Consider the *ancien régime*, embodied in the dead King of France in 1774. Listen to the prophet proclaiming the moral on the very eve of the Victorian age, proclaiming those eternal verities which seem no more than truisms to him. 'Thou hast done nothing, poor Louis. Thy fault is properly even this, that thou didst *nothing*. What could poor Louis do? Abdicate, and wash his hands of it—in favour of the first that would accept! Other clear wisdom there was none for him.' A word here for all Kings—for all such at least as say 'Après moi, le déluge', for all that find themselves judges of the earth! And then consider the judgment of God on the *régime moderne*, on the People of France just twenty years later. '. . . The Hébertists lie in Prison only some nine days. On the 24th March (1794), therefore, the Revolution tumbrils carry through that Life-Tumult a new cargo: Hébert, Vincent, Momoro, Ronsin, nineteen of them in all; with whom, curious enough, sits Clootz, Speaker of Mankind. They have been massed swiftly into a lump, this miscellany of Nondescripts; and travel now their last road. No help. They too must "look through the little window"; they too "must sneeze into the sack" . . .; as they have done to others, so is it done to them. . . . Hébert, Père Duchesne . . . sits there low enough, head sunk on breast; Red Nightcaps shouting round him in frightful parody of his Newspaper Articles, "Grand choler of the Père Duchesne!" Thus perish they; the sack receives all their heads. Through some section of History, Nineteen spectre-chimeras shall flit, squeaking and gibbering; till Oblivion swallow them.'

Like it or not, Carlyle had begun to write history as the rude ferment of democracy demanded. The prose or poetry in him had caught the tumult and din of the age of revolution as cleverly as Gibbon had caught the distant sound of the Roman Empire tramping majestically to its doom. Englishmen, reading in those days these volumes so packed with thought, these phrases so loud and lumbering, could remain in no doubt what the French Revolution was and why one sought to save one's country from any repercussions of it. Both parties, dissimilar as were their remedies, were by the time of Victoria's accession agreed upon that.

Observe, meanwhile, what urbane wisdom Macaulay had begun to pour into the ears of the *jeunesse*, mostly *dorée*, of the time. Still, when I was at school at the end of the century, one's tutor put those marvellous Essays of his into one's hands. Still, ever since 1843, those hard, confident coruscating sentences, that all too lucid argumentation, had given to countless minds, preoccupied in after life with politics, their first idea of and introduction to statesmanship. And, if any sentences more than the rest are to be brought forward as an illustration of Macaulay's best quality and dispositions, they should surely be those in his *History of England* in which the historian, forgetting for a moment all the strength of his Whiggery, turns the brilliant light of his portraiture upon Halifax, the Trimmer, and illuminates that distinguished man's peculiar merit in the following terms: 'He always saw passing events, not in the point of view in which they commonly appear to one who bears a part in them, but in the point of view in which, after the lapse of many years, they appear to the philosophic historian. . . . In temper he was what, in our time, is called a Conservative. In theory he was a Republican.'

Such praise could hardly spring from Carlyle's flaming heart, where passion and mystery, common to all mankind, strove together for the mastery and where the conflict between ultimate good and evil was ever kept in mind. What Carlyle was concerned with were the eternal values and verities and, in stressing them, he carried his countrymen with him.

There were cranks, of course, among the Victorians—like Robert Owen, the friend and to some extent the financier of the Duke of Kent, who, in return for monetary assistance, seems to have given a hearing to Owen's views. But Fabians were still only in the making, as the Victorian era drew to a close; and it is a stretch of fancy to argue that Carlyle or Ruskin would have afforded much, if any, countenance to the Socialist of to-day. The popular philosopher of the Victorians was Herbert Spencer; and a more uncompromising individualist it might be hard to find even in that century of individualists. His unbalanced dislike of state-interference may indeed have had something to say to the violent swing of the pendulum noticeable in Mrs. Sidney Webb. She told me once that, as a girl, it used to be one of her pastimes to watch the movements of the philosopher's mind and, when she had discerned for what theory it was making, to drop an imaginary illustration in his path for him to pounce upon. She had her reward in due course. His next work would contain a footnote, fortifying some opinion of his, with a rider to the effect that 'a certain young lady of his acquaintance had informed him of the following fact'; and then followed the invention of Beatrice Potter's fertile fancy. Thus, we may, not unprofitably, reflect can philosophers be fooled by the friends of humanity!

In one respect Spencer's lucubrations were lacking in a postulate that was axiomatic in the teaching of Carlyle. God for him was 'the unknowable'.

To Carlyle's thought God was indispensable. It would be true in Carlyle's case, as in that of the Hebrews, to say that 'clouds and darkness were before Him', but it was no less true that 'righteousness and judgment were the habitation of His seat'. Carlyle might complain that he could only believe in a God who *did* something and then add, with according to Froude[1], an unforgettable cry of pain, 'He does nothing'. But 'his faith', as Froude observes, 'stood firm'. It must be indeed central in any political system exalting duty, instead of pleasure or mere happiness, which some utilitarians have fancied might be effectively substituted in place of the Deity, yet, after the lapse of a generation or two, can be seen to have afforded no such result. Ruskin's nature demanded no such forcible faith as Carlyle's. His religion was 'the religion of beauty'; and he found enough reflections of God in the loveliness of art and nature to make its foundation there seem valid. None of the ultimate values, perhaps—neither truth, nor beauty, nor goodness—will of itself support the weight of a Christianity which postulates the presence of all three.

It is at this point that Tennyson seems to enter the field. He is the Victorian *par excellence*; he goes just so far in the way of belief as the most part of Victorians felt able to go. Religious faith flickers like summer lightning on his horizon, but there are moments when the heavens are black with cloud, and then the poet from the depth of his distress will cry out, and his words will come echoing back from all the hills around: 'There lives more faith in honest doubt, Believe me, than in half the creeds.'[2] He had in fact taken up the tale where Wordsworth, moved by that intense communion of his with Nature to a trust in God, had laid it down; but, he had noticed on examination that Nature was 'red in tooth and claw', was 'careful of the type', but 'careless of the single life'. His was no overpowering intuition or intimation of immortality such as had been inspired in the older poet by the stories of Enoch and Elijah[3]—no 'sense sublime of something'. . . . 'Whose dwelling is the light of setting suns. And the round ocean, and the living air, and the blue sky, and in the mind of man: A motion and a spirit, that impels All thinking things, all objects of all thought, And rolls through all things.'[4] The force of this sensibility to some degree passed from the minds of men with the passing of Wordsworth in 1850.

Very opportunely *In Memoriam* was published on the first of June of that same year within a few weeks of Wordsworth's death; and it settled in a flash the vexed question who was the proper man to take his place as Laureate. Prince Albert performed one of many services to the nation by championing the claims of a candidate who, as it proved, could speak as

---

[1] *Carlyle's Life in London*, Vol. II, p. 260.   [2] *In Memoriam*, XCVI.
[3] See the Preface to the *Ode on Intimations of Immortality*.
[4] Lines composed above Tintern Abbey.

easily for T. H. Huxley[1] in his *Ulysses* as for the Queen herself in his *Idylls*. Tennyson spanned the foaming waters of the time and rendered into mortal music the moaning no less than the dancing of the ocean—the sound of the grey sea no less than of the blue. There was a change of emphasis here, of which the men of that time were much more conscious than we are. I can remember Augustine Birrell talking to me of twentieth-century poets and confessing his inability to appreciate them, and then adding 'But I have to remember that, when I was a young man, I could talk of no one but Tennyson, whereas my father could get no further than Wordsworth.' Walter Pater, in discussing 'the Genius of Plato' as it manifests itself in the search for knowledge with a lover's desire to assimilate wisdom to some sort of contact with a person—to make it full, that is, of delicate and affectionate perception—has dwelt upon the 'great metaphysical force' which Wordsworth and Tennyson in particular brought into the English language,[2] making its abstractions after this manner 'visible, living creatures' and so giving to our grasp of them a 'real' hold.

In Memoriam is shot through and through with this craving for the powerful and prevailing sense of personality in ideas; and it is almost impossible not to associate with the fact Jowett's contemporary observation that neither philosophy nor science could ever solve the riddle of the universe, but that poetry might.[3] Though Tennyson's grandson appears to maintain that no dogma finds its way into the poem until the 84th stanza is reached and though 'He that died in Holy Land'[4] is conceived as reaching out a shining hand to the two bosom friends, united at last as they attain the goal of their endeavour, yet it is obvious to remark that the very first line of the great poem is violently dogmatic ('Strong Son of God, immortal Love',) and that, before four lines are complete, the invocation is justified by an appeal to 'faith and faith alone' and by a confession that credence, divorced from any rational grounds of faith, is relied on to sustain the argument which runs through the ensuing hundred and thirty stanzas. In fact, when directly challenged by Tyndall, the poet came out with a tremendous affirmation of belief: 'Tyndall, there *is* a God.'[5]

Poetry, if we are able to concur in the judgment of Whitehead,[6] 'has great value in affording an objective view of sense-experience'; and Tennyson beyond much doubt registers the conclusions of the most part of Victorians, if given at all to reflection about ultimate things. Indeed it would probably be correct to say that, more than any other man of his time, he gave expression to the intelligent conviction of the most part of the nation,

[1] See his reference to *Ulysses* in his lecture on 'Evolution and Ethics'.
[2] Pater, *Plato and Platonism*, p. 141.
[3] Quoted by Charles Tennyson in his *Alfred Tennyson*, p. 279. [4] ibid., p. 248.
[5] ibid., p. 346. [6] *Science and the Modern World*, p. 111.

although his powers vastly exceeded theirs. Wesley and other evangelists had left faith in God very firmly implanted in the common man—and woman; and Lecky may well be right in maintaining that Wesley had much to do with the bad reception that on the whole the French Revolution met with in Britain. A story is told of Bishop Blomfield, who occupied the See of London between 1828 and 1857, preaching in a village church from the text, 'the fool hath said in his heart: There is no God'. The Rector afterwards told the Bishop that his discourse was far above the heads of the congregation. The Bishop denied this and suggested they should take the opinion of the first parishioner they met, who happened to be an old woman. She was presented to the Bishop and invited to say what she thought of his sermon. ' 'Twere a very fine sermon, my Lard', she said, 'but I don't agree with your Lordship, for I do think as there be a God.' This old lady's assurance fitted in well enough with the contemporary notion of a Divine dispensation ordering all things for the best and entering into individual life in the form of a particular providence:

> The rich man in his castle;
> The poor man at his gate;
> God made them high and lowly,
> And ordered their estate.

That sort of sentiment, which the egalitarian was, in course of time, to discredit as 'opium for the people', expressed itself in the regard of many a post or trade or profession as a trusteeship indicated by God and deserving the exercise of a courtesy and modesty that had no accompaniment of envy and a proper pride that asked no more of a man than faithful stewardship. This far-reaching sense of a particular providence could no doubt at times be comic enough. In one of Miss Yonge's novels a girl is blamed for travelling third-class instead of, as her circumstances dictated, in a first-class carriage.

The forces, making for 'the-contrary-of-a-revolution', however, gained from the presence in the Nation of this conservation of conduct resting, on the religious side, on the injunction in the English Church catechism to do one's duty in that state of life to which it should please God to call one and, on the secular side, on the not as yet wholly unpalatable consideration that it takes all sorts to make a world. Luck lent a spice to life; and, even if good-luck seemed absent, there was always a chance for it in a community where the government had no greedy hand outstretched to seize whatever it could get, and where, indeed, any such impulse was held in general reprobation.

In the days of Gladstone (and I am not forgetting the Midlothian campaign of 1880) the mob oratory of Lloyd George was remote and even that of the earlier Joseph Chamberlain was not much to the general taste of the community. This was no doubt not only due to the hold which Wesley still had on the Nonconformist Conscience but to that which Newman was gradually acquiring over the youth of the nation, both male and female, both rich and poor. The old lady, whose rustic rudiments of knowledge caused her to bring Bishop Blomfield so sharply to book for his sophistications, was far more indicative of how the matter would have gone, if the existence of God had, in true democratic fashion, been submitted for decision to a poll of all the people in Victorian times than if it had been referred to Spencer shall we say, or Darwin, or Huxley? One is apt to forget this, when one studies such critical estimates of the Victorian era as appear in the B.B.C.'s recent broadcasts on 'Ideas and Beliefs of the Victorians'. The mind of the many is rarely reflected in the views of a chosen few controversialists—and perhaps least of all in a religious skirmish.

The outstanding protagonists on either side of the combat, as it was called, between Religion and Science, were representative men, yet not at all representative of the mass of men, who are for the most part at all times led by emotional rather than intellectual considerations. Most people of any education at all were, however, probably intelligent enough to understand that the battle of belief with unbelief had been joined and some saw that the outcome was problematical. Among opinions of that time that have lately been made public are some contained in the letters to her son, of Emily, Lady Tennyson, the poet's wife. She was, in Jowett's judgment, no less remarkable as a woman than the poet was as a man.[1] And among her letters may be found one which runs thus: 'Papa feels that we are on the edge of a mortal strife for the life of man.'[2]

Tennyson was not alone in this anticipation. The river of life was deeply troubled by other currents running contemporaneously with those of the Cambridge 'Apostles', of whom he had been one. The origins, however, of the Oxford Movement have been too often traced to encourage any repetition of the process here. It is enough to say that, as against Tennyson, moving in regions of high emotion, Newman was preoccupied with the rational grounds of faith—with the cogency of the course of history; with the implications of the individual conscience; with the certitude attending the conclusions of a mind feeling its way from foothold to foothold up the ladder mounting from assent to apprehension and so on to final assurance. Contrast Tennyson's tentative, moving, yet unsatisfactory account of the upward climb of belief with the restrained ratiocination of the Oxford Leader:

[1] Charles Tennyson, *Alfred Tennyson*, p. 416.
[2] ibid., p. 419.

C

'A warmth within the breast would melt
The freezing reason's colder part,
And like a man in wrath the heart
Stood up and answered "I have felt".'

    *   *   *   *

Whatever I have said or sung,
Some bitter notes my heart would give
Yea, tho' there often seemed to live
A contradiction on the tongue. . . .[1]

So runs the Tennysonian account of the road of faith. Very different is the Newmanic! Though it is hardly to be supposed that a poet and a playwright, who had occupied himself with Europe's debt to Dante, with the story of Becket, and with the mournful tale of Mary Tudor, did not traverse some part of ground where Newman seemed to have made himself familiar with every hedge and hollow, yet the treatment of besetting problems in Newman's works is conducted with a restraint and simplicity of thought that of itself refutes the charge of playing upon human emotions with its own God-sent music. In the light of the romantic revival, Newman was following through a jungle of conflicting contentions a path which had been found by Gibbon with no more than the aid of eighteenth-century rationalism, but which had yet been plain enough to drive that intelligent young man, whilst hardly more than a boy, to make his way up to London from Magdalen, to hunt out a Catholic priest.

Gibbon, as he tells us in his *Memoirs*, lay under an obligation to Pascal for that studied pungency in his style which had so much to do with rendering the *Decline and Fall* immortal; and Newman has acknowledged that his *Essay on Development* owed something to the ringing cadence of Gibbon's sentences and to their unchallenged claim to be at the time the one available source in English of ecclesiastical history.[2] Pascal has been called a French Plato; and the subtlety both of Newman's pen and penetration might secure for him, with at least as much right, the title of an English one. His way of looking at things and of presenting it to the world was in its way as telling on the banks of the Isis as was Plato's on the banks of the Ilissus. Some readers of this book may recall the passage in the *Phaedo* where Simmias turns sadly to Socrates with the remark that his collocutor can hardly fail to be aware how almost impossible is the attainment of certitude about such matters as immortality and follows this up by the pathetic observation that, though these things are so, a man would be a coward or faint of heart who did not, nevertheless, commit himself to whatever raft he might for the

[1] *In Memoriam*, CXXIV, CXXV.   [2] Ward, *Life of Newman*, Vol. I, p. 34.

voyage of discovery—unless, indeed, as he adds, he should find some word of God which will more safely carry him.[1]

'Some word of God', cried Bishop Gore (standing in the pulpit of St. Mary's, near fifty years after Newman had left it, yet carrying in the profound and moving sincerity of his approach to spiritual things something of Newman's tradition) —'Some word of God': it has come to us: Crowning the legitimate efforts, supplying the inevitable deficiencies, of human reasonings; satisfying all the deepest aspirations of the heart and conscience. It has come to us, and not as a mere spoken message, but as an incarnate person, at first to attract, to alarm, to subdue us; afterwards, when we are His servants, to guide, to discipline, to enlighten, to enrich us, till that which is perfect is come, and that which is in part has been done away.[2] So far, in the space between the accession of Victoria and her first jubilee, had this Oxford influence, charged as it was with oecumenical purpose, moved forward to its appointed end; receiving no countenance from the Queen, commanding little support in high places, yet exercising a vast effect upon the minds of men and operating like the turning of a tide.

The origin of the Oxford Movement is generally traced to Keble's Assize Sermon on National Apostacy, provoked by the suppression of certain Irish Protestant bishoprics in 1833. A more penetrating observation is made by Dean Church: 'It was not till Mr. Newman made up his mind to force on the public mind in a way which could not be evaded the great article of the Creed—"I believe in one Catholic and Apostolic Church"— that the movement began.'[3]

That decision had the effect of posing again the question which Thomas More had put to his judges four centuries before—the question whether it lay within the competence of one nation or one locality to reverse the course of history; to return, so to say, upon the road of Christendom; to proclaim this or that an innovation, to reckon this or that development inorganic when in fact a similar evolution in the secular sphere would be represented as legitimate growth. R. H. Hutton, one of the greatest of Victorian critics, pointed out in some searching pages that Newman's theory of historical development had anticipated Darwin's theory of biological descent and was indeed so far in advance of it as to entitle its formulator to the name of genius. 'Newman's discussion of the true tests of genuine development is marked', said Hutton,[4] 'by the keenest penetration into one of the most characteristic conceptions of modern science.' The claim of the Papacy to stand at the centre of Christendom involved no more divergence, and indeed not so much, from the Primitive Church than the claim

[1] *Phaedo*, p. 85.   [2] Gore, Bampton Lectures, 1891, p. 201.
[3] R. W. Church, *The Oxford Movement*, Chapter II.
[4] R. H. Hutton, *Cardinal Newman*, p. 165.

of the Crown to decree rites and ceremonies and to decide controversies of faith; but one has only to glance at the letters which passed between Victoria and Disraeli as late as 1874 to realize in what obscurity the matter must have seemed to be enfolded in 1845. The Queen complains to the Prime Minister of a public denial by a member of the Administration that she was 'Head of the Church', the style assumed by Henry VIII. 'Now the Sovereign of this Country', she informs Disraeli, 'has always been considered the Head of the Church, and also of the Scotch Church, but still more so of the English.'[1] Disraeli finds himself compelled to explain to Victoria, thirty years or more after she had come to the Throne, that Elizabeth had waived this high and mighty style, assumed by her father, and had contented herself with that of 'Supreme Governor'; whilst, so far as the Kirk was concerned, no such pretensions as the Queen supposed had ever been advanced, the connection between Church and Crown in Scotland being of a merely civil character.

When such matters stood in need of elucidation in such quarters, it is not surprising that Newman should have aroused as much attention, antagonism, and antipathy as Wesley had done with the evangelicism of his time. The English are not a logical people. There will, however, always be a certain number of them with whom the recommendation of logic weighs; and it was to these that the force of Newman's argument made its appeal. It must be doubtful, however, how many of his fellow-countrymen would ever have worried their minds over Newman's problems, had not Kingsley made a violent, personal attack on his honesty. 'I am henceforth in doubt and fear, as much as any honest man can be', Kingsley wrote, concerning every word Dr. Newman may write. 'How can I tell that I shall not be the dupe of some cunning equivocation . . .?' and so on. The result of these charges was Newman's *Apologia*; and after its appearance, if Kingsley still feared to be taken in by him, probably not another man in the country had any similar apprehension. The *Apologia* made plain both the integrity of Newman's mind and of his argument. From that time forward his opponents could hardly avoid the charge that it was they, and not he, who did not reason cogently. But nothing less than a personal attack and its defeat would probably ever have made this clear.

The *Apologia* appeared in 1864. There remained one task still before Newman could fairly be said to have completed the range of his apologetic. This he may be said to have achieved with the publication of his *Grammar of Assent* in 1870. It is no easy book to summarize effectively, but it does carry the religious argument forward from Butler's position that 'probability is the guide of life' to the contention that Catholicism rests upon certitude. All the probabilities have converged and are associated in a

[1] Queen's Letters, July 21st 1874.

conviction that seems to need no further proof. Just as a capable general on the battlefield can, with a *coup d'oeil*, make sure of the propriety of tactics the reasons for which are too numerous and complicated to disentangle or to show in logical sequence, so can the believer feel certain that he has perceived the rational grounds of faith and carried his assent beyond apprehension to assurance. Great stress, indeed, is laid in the book upon the Aristotelic teaching that a special preparation of the mind is required for different departments of inquiry and discussion. 'It is much the same mistake to put up with a mathematician using probabilities and to require demonstration of an orator. Each man judges skilfully in those things about which he is well-informed. . . .'[1] The full force of Newman's argument cannot be conveyed by extracts; but anyone who will take the trouble to study it in its elaborated form will find that Newman has satisfied the demands of the individual conscience in respect of matters which the *Apologia* and the *Essay on Development* had thrown open to view. There is nothing surprising in the fact that, with his piercing sight and with the method of the Humanities in his mastery, he had held the interest of many Victorians who felt little disposition to follow him all the length of the road to Rome.

It was characteristic of the age that there were few Englishmen in its generations who could be persuaded to think that death was the end of all. There were, indeed, very few who dared with Huxley to make their own the lines from Tennyson's *Ulysses* and say:

> It may be that the gulfs will wash us down:
> It may be we shall touch the Happy Isles,
> And see the great Achilles, whom we knew.

Or, like York-Powell, to say with Fitzgerald—'old Fitz.', whom many of them liked so well:

> One Moment in Annihilation's Waste
> One Moment of the Well of Life to taste
> The Stars are setting, and the Caravan
> Starts for the Dawn of Nothing—Oh, make haste!

Three outstanding poets gazed into the dark distance and made a haunting music of the mists. There was Tennyson with *Crossing the Bar*: There was Browning with *Prospice*: and, greater and sweeter even than these, there was Newman with the mystery of his *Dream of Gerontius*, at the sound of which the magic crystal seemed to clear and for a moment to show the world beyond our mortal vision.

As an example of the 'temper', in the best sense, which the Oxford Movement generated, one may do well to look at Dean Church's University

[1] *Grammar of Assent*, p. 414.

Sermons than which none better, it has been said, were ever preached. It is 'the Oriel school' of writing at its best. Courteously phrased and delicately worded, they possess a peculiar charm which makes it no surprise to find that the author's friendship with Newman had been close or that Gladstone had Church in mind, had he been willing, as a likely nominee for the Archbishopric of Canterbury. It is among Church's writings that the historian will find such carefully weighed and persuasive reflections as that 'Christianity, if not true, is the most extraordinary thing in the world; really much more extraordinary than if it is true'; that 'nothing can take the place of Christianity'; that 'reason is wide and manifold and waits its time; and argument partial, one-sided, and often then most effective, when least embarrassed by seeing too much.'

These would be opportune considerations at any time, but were particularly so at a date when the perennial attack upon Christianity was proceeding strongly along all the three lines of physics, biology and the so-called higher criticism. At the distance of three-quarters of a century—for these admirable discourses were given in 1876, 1877, and 1878—it is no waste of time for a student of the era to turn to them and inquire how their character has fared with lapse of time. The Victorians did not lack temperate judgment; and Church was a very good instance of it. But Science, so-called, was very sure of itself at that time, yet so far as finality is concerned, the atom has now dissolved into a cloud of electrons, protons, neutrons, and what not, in respect of which we were told in 1928 (though, for anything I dare say, the scientist, shifting his ground faster than the layman can always follow, may have substituted another doctrine since) that we could not hope to know both the locality and velocity of a particle,[1] or expect to escape the disintegration, the growing 'randomness' inherent in the Second Law of Thermo-Dynamics.[2] So doubtful of herself, indeed, has Physical Science become, that the same eminent scientist just quoted has declared it 'defensible' to hold one set of beliefs in the Laboratory and another in the Church.[3] Biology, as represented by the theory of evolution, has fared but little better than this. Evolution, of which theory, as we have seen, Newman had early seen the application to historical studies, is challenged now rather when it claims to give a full account of the variety of species, than while it confines itself to the theory of some development of the human shape from an animal ancestry. As for the so-called higher criticism of the Gospels it has, under the guidance of Harnack, beaten an indisputable retreat from positions which Baur and Strauss, not to speak of Renan, had seemed very well assured they could hold.

Nothing in regard to all this great recession of opinions will, perhaps,

[1] Eddington, *The Nature of the Physical World*, pp. 220, 221.
[2] ibid., p. 74.   [3] ibid., p. 194.

seem more astonishing to the student than the indifference with which Victorian statesmen appear to have regarded all these various ventures in sceptical criticism at the time. Even those statesmen, who might well be regarded as the best qualified of all to assess the value of evidence, even the leading Lord Chancellors of the era, even Cairns and Selborne, the one a Conservative, the other a Liberal, were, both of them, earnest and practising Christians. At the height of the intellectual scrimmage between Religion and Science, men in great place appear to have remained almost undisturbed by the contentions of the men of science and the men of faith. They had, perhaps, listened too often to the evidence of experts to attach undue weight to it. And the Prime Ministers of Victoria seem to have taken their stand almost to a man on the great affirmative postulate of religion—on, as Carlyle would have said, its 'everlasting yea'. Not, indeed, Melbourne, who very possibly did not know exactly what he believed; nor Palmerston, who cared for none of these things, being otherwise too much engaged with this present world, or at least its ladies. But, apart from these two brothers-in-law of Regency upbringing, all the rest of the Queen's Prime Ministers, not exclusive of Rosebery, seem almost to discover a gathering force of conviction in the claims of Christianity upon human society.

Such considerations as those adduced by Dean Church were calculated to appeal to statesmen versed, as was the case with the political leaders of that day, in the knowledge of history which was declared by Napoleon, despite his revolutionary antecedents, to afford 'the only true philosophy'. In the final round of the engagement between Christianity and its critics the issue has really turned, from the very first, upon the credibility or otherwise, of certain witnesses. With science, as it is presented now, any fact is credible, any law possible. The question then is whether the evidence for certain events recorded, in regard to a Personality so unusual as to invite the closest inquiry, is sufficient. Towards the close of Victoria's reign—in 1884—Edersheim, at one time a minister of the Church of Scotland and subsequently a clergyman of the Church of England, published in two large volumes a *Life of Christ*, so rich in erudition that it deserves to be regarded as the answer of the British school of thought to the critics of Christianity on the Continent. Edersheim gives his affirmative conclusion, on the most vital question of all, in the most uncompromising terms. ' . . . The theories of deception, delusion and vision', he wrote in estimating the force of the evidence for the Resurrection of Christ, being . . . impossible, and the *a priori* objection to the fact, as involving a miracle, being a *petitio principii*', the evidence compels an acceptance of the fact itself 'which', he adds, and repeats, 'may unhesitatingly be pronounced that best established in history.'[1] There, then, set forth with a racial

[1] 'That grand fact of history, than which none is better attested—the Resurrection of Christ . . . '(Edersheim, *Life and Times of Jesus the Messiah*, Vol. II, pp. 397 and 629).

insight that might have captivated Disraeli, a Teutonic learning that would
have approved itself to Gladstone, and with the prestige that must attach to
a select preacher at Oxford and a Warburtonian lecturer at Lincoln's Inn, is a
late Victorian vindication of the attitude taken up by the leading Victorian
Prime Ministers, and more and more resolutely as time continued; and it
would be no easy matter to shake it now, whether or not Britain, as alleged
by Mr. Sherwood Taylor in commenting on the 'Ideas and Beliefs of the
Victorians', has changed from a Christian to a pagan nation.

The opinions of the Victorian Prime Ministers affecting 'the social
tissue' of society, must be seen against some such background of belief as
has been above depicted; and their quality must be carefully distinguished
from that of the politicians of to-day whose thought hardly appears to
range beyond material things, and whose energies appear to be fully
engaged in the manipulation or mystification of the proletariat. Bagehot,
in his contemporary sketch of the English Constitution in Victorian times,
has claimed that 'the leading statesmen under the system of Cabinet
Government are not only household words, but household ideas.'[1] This
was, in fact, a favourite thought with him and appears elsewhere in his
writings. 'In political matters', he says in his Physics and Politics,[2] 'how
quickly a leading statesman can change the tone of the community! We
are, most of us, in earnest with Mr. Gladstone. We were, most of us, not so
earnest in the time of Lord Palmerston.'

The ten Victorian Prime Ministers, whose portraits I have tried in this
book to throw on the political screen, had, all of them, more or less, the
enigmatic gift of strong personality—of something which is seldom now
apparent in our public men and is scarcely to be expected of those who make
it their pride or their merit to reflect in mentality and manners 'the common man'.

The peculiar ethos of the Victorian era must be sought in its marked antithesis to much that passes current to-day. Justice, as the Victorians, like the
Platonic Socrates, perceived, is a minding of one's own business; Liberty at
its best, is, as the New Testament proclaimed, a perfect law—a law that is,
commending itself, not by compulsion, but by high good sense; and Reason,
when flowing along transcendental rather than empirical lines, furnishes a
pretty nearly uncontaminated spring of moral obligation from which man,
in his humane and civic capacity alike, can draw the water of life. 'The moral
progress of mankind', wrote a Balliol philosopher,[3] whose life began just
before Victoria came to the throne and concluded nearly two decades before
the close of the reign, but whose influence upon his contemporaries was
outstanding, and whose portrait may be found in the Mr. Gray of Robert
Elsmere—'The Moral progress of mankind has no reality except as resulting

[1] English Constitution, Chapter I.   [2] p. 90.   [3] T. H. Green.

in the formation of more perfect characters.' So from one generation to another, and with growing conviction, the wisest of the Victorians believed: and their confidence lay at a great remove from the faith of the Fabians, who put their trust in the pressure of circumstances, exhibited so as to substitute for the individual conscience—for that 'aboriginal vicar of Christ, a prophet in its informations, a monarch in its peremptoriness, a priest in its blessings and anathemas', as Newman called it[1]—a moral consciousness of the community, an organ of which the existence appears to be certified only by the anatomy of dialectical materialism and which all too plainly tempts a critic to observe that, to judge by the chaotic volume of nonsense and noise it produces, it is evidently voice and nothing, or at least little besides.

There is, however, no occasion to dwell on the quaint creed of the Fabians, provided it is clearly understood that to arrive at any comprehension of the English nineteenth century along this avenue is even more hopeless than to seek to do so from the side of Thackeray's *Four Georges*. The world of the Fabians is, if possible, further removed from the genius of the Victorians than is the society of the early Hanoverians, with its crude imitation of the *ancien régime* as observed in the *salles*, or the *bosquets* of Versailles. These societies furnish at either end a measure of the Victorian achievement, but the state-struck philanthropy of the one no more affords a criticism of it than does the studied elegance of the other. There was that in the Victorians which distinguished them essentially from all who had gone before and perhaps from all who will come after; and it is not wholly absurd, with human nature and Christian civilization very much in our thoughts, to see in them the heirs of all the ages. Despite their not inconsiderable negligences and ignorances, none perhaps, has ever come so near to the designing of a true type of society. None, anyhow, has succeeded better in bringing the best men to the top, if that be any test, nor have any mingled more happily the qualities of the heart and the head. Their times have come to look like easy times; but we have to ask ourselves how much that seeming ease was owing to the good sense of those, both men and women, who guided and tempered their movement. As Gladstone wrote to General Grey in 1869: '*We* know at what a cost of internal danger to all the institutions of the country, she (England) fought her way to the perilous eminence on which she undoubtedly stood in 1815.'[2] They knew, because they had had to bring the ship of state out of the danger-zones, past reef and rock and quicksand, until she floated fair and free in relatively tranquil waters. In the first thirty years of Victoria they had seen the nation recover its strength;

---

[1] Reprinted in *Difficulties of Anglicans Considered*, but which appeared first as a pamphlet addressed to the Duke of Norfolk in 1875 on the occasion of Mr. Gladstone's 'Expostulation' regarding the duality of Catholic allegiance.

[2] Morley, *Life of Gladstone*, Vol. II, p. 317.

Sovereign, Parliament and people co-operating, amidst all their petty strife, to reach a larger end. Then, at what has been called 'the great divide' of the reign (economically, that is, if we are thinking in such terms, after the Limited Liability Act of 1860), Gladstone and his contemporaries saw England attain such a plenitude of power as it is unlikely she will see again. Of the capacity of the Ministers who brought about this pre-eminence there can be no serious question. There was in them a native, delicate regard both for the values of authority and liberty and, as has been said, of head and heart, for which one might look long and far to find the match. Call it, if you will, a *je ne sais quoi*; call it the finesse spirit of the time. But, whatever name is given it, its essence is more. It is, perhaps, best apprehended by turning the pages of such non-political but contemporary volumes as Newman's *Idea of a University*, or Matthew Arnold's *Notebooks*, for its essence is to be found there, if below the surface. But, to see it in detachment and merely as a sentiment, one might do worse than look for an example at the letter to Gladstone from G. F. Watts, in which the painter refuses a baronetcy. The letter gave pause even to a Prime Minister, accustomed as he must have been to many solicitations for pretty ribbons to wear on one's coat; and, as he observed in his reply, it 'made the nineteenth century stare or blink, as those blink who stand in a great brightness and have not eyes for it'. Yet, not only elect persons, but many who had fallen under the spell of Watts's or of some other masterpieces of that age, would, if I mistake not, have felt him to be in this way their spokesman. Anyhow, here are his words: 'I feel that it would be something like a real disgrace to accept for work merely attempted, reward and payment only due to work achieved. I should have the ghost of the Lycian chief[1] reproaching me in my dreams. . . . Living mainly in a world of my own, my views are narrowed (I hope I may say also simplified) till a sense of the four great conditions which to my mind comprise all that can be demonstrated of our existence, Life and Death, Light and Darkness, so dominate my mental vision that they almost become material entities and take material forms, dwarfing and casting into shadow ordinary considerations. . . . Labouring beside the poet and the statesman, the artist may deal with those great ideas. . . .'[2]

Almost might it have been Michelangelo standing in the sacristy of San Lorenzo and tracing in meditation the lines and features of those enigmatic figures, destined to keep vigil century after century beside the tombs of the Medici and named by tradition, 'Day and Night; Twilight and Dawn'? So near could the great Victorians come in heart and mind to the great Florentines, so instinctively would they turn to art to express the things that cannot otherwise be adequately uttered!

---

[1] viz. Sarpedon.
[2] Quoted from Morley's *Life of Gladstone*, Vol. II, p. 542.

It would be a pity to miss this Italian touch in the men of that period; for it worked very strongly in some of them. The old sense of Italy as the seat of Christian civilization and of Rome as the capital of Humanist culture had been to some extent kept alive by the 'grand tour' which young men still took to complete their education, and by such poets as Byron and Rogers as well as by memories of Keats and Shelley. The Oxford Movement had taken up the tale; and the two convert Cardinals—Newman and Manning—restored on the religious plane an interest to which Tennyson, in his tribute to Dante, and Browning, in countless lovely lines, such as those towards the beginning of Sordello,[1] ministered to on a more secular one. Englishmen like Ruskin 'found' themselves in Italy; and there were enough who felt they could live nowhere else if they were to *live* anywhere at all. And those of us, who can look back to better days than these, can never forget 'mornings in Florence', when we were young, hours in Rome when the year was still at the spring, and days on Como when Primavera began to scatter her flowers and favours of every kind over lakeside and mountain. It was a Savoyard who made the first effective reply to Rousseau's political doctrine. It was the Victorians who first gave his penetrating dictum force and meaning. Revolution, as preached by Rousseau, is always with us, for its temper will never die as long as human nature can be soured by inequality of conditions. Only when the eye extends the vision with the aid of those beauties which the Italian painters saw so clearly, do earth and heaven seem to meet and kiss in an all-embracing tranquillity; only then can change become, in the words of a late Victorian, 'the revolutionism of one who has slept a hundred years'.[2]

[1] 'Sordello, foremost in the regal class
Nature has broadly severed from her mass
Of men, and framed for pleasure, as she frames
Some happy lands that have luxurious names
For loose fertility . . .'
[2] Pater, *Diaphaneitè*.

VICTORIA

CHAPTER III

VICTORIA

IT was still dark when they took the road from Windsor on that June day of 1837 which was to inaugurate the longest, and in some respects the greatest, reign in English history; but the sunlight, breaking from behind the clouds just as they drew towards Kensington, cast an auspicious glory on palace walls, raised long since to regal splendour by the coming there of 'the Whig Deliverer'. The ageing Archbishop, it is on record, observed the omen; whilst his lay companion, the Lord Chamberlain, reflected on the fact that the proclamation on the morrow of a new Sovereign would coincide with the pride and pomp of midsummer. These two Court Mercuries—one of them, it appears, so soundly Erastian as to maintain, even contemporaneously with the existence of the Fourth George, 'that the King could do no wrong either morally or physically'[1]; the other, the son of that Lady Conyngham, whose influence, as the mistress of the monarch mentioned, had to be reckoned with even in ecclesiastical appointments—these two Court Mercuries were not ill-chosen to ring out the passing of 'the Four Georges', with the Fourth William now coffined in their wake—and in the same hour the passing, too, of the Hanoverian Electorate to the Duke of Cumberland—and to ring in the reign of a woman who probably possessed a dominant share of Coburg genes and, therewith, no little susceptibility to Coburg influences. Fortune gave Victoria sages, if not about her cradle, at least about her Court; and Leopold, the relict of Princess Charlotte and later King of the Belgians, comes early upon the stage as an uncle greatly beloved. Behind Leopold lay his nephew, Albert, and, of course, beside Albert, Stockmar. We can descry, not too fancifully, their spirits poised above the adolescent reign, and moving the young Queen towards 'the noble life'—that particular object of romance and chivalry which, at its best, elicits honour and devotion from others in a manner no presidency, conditioned of necessity by popular election, nor imperium, drawn, like Caesar's or Napoleon's, out of the needs or opportunities of the time, can ever inspire. Loyalty to persons, as Newman presently was to observe, springs eternal in the human breast; and in its high humanity lay, as he saw, the purest source of political and religious life, just as in treachery lay man's most infernal foe.

The three German sages just mentioned, soon to travel in heart or mind

[1] D.N.B. on Archbishop Howley.

47

from Coburg, were exceptionally equipped for the work they had to do. Leopold had had every reason to expect that, as Princess Charlotte's somewhile husband, he would have occupied the place which Albert was to fill, and had thus become early acquainted with what the others, in course of time, were to make a close study of—the English Constitution, its genius and development. They came, as it chanced, upon the scene at an hour of rare flexibility even in the case of an always-flexible Constitution; and they perceived, perhaps better than any Englishman could have done at the time, the part the Sovereign might play in this era of constitutional evolution. They are seen, then, first in the background of the stage, but gradually Albert advances—kinglike as Arthur, though never, like Philip of Spain or William of Orange, invited to wear the English crown.

Before these figures, looming on the horizon as the first sunlight strikes the reign, Victoria's parents tend to seem as shadows departing. Yet they had had their obvious share in the making—and her mother also in the moulding—of their daughter's destiny. Edward, Duke of Kent, her father, a martinet, a spendthrift, a man living long in sin and leaving Madame St. Laurent at last, not for conscience' sake, but for the sake of a dynasty in mortal fear of dying out, had no great good in him to pass on, and, anyhow, little time in which to pass it. Still, if to Victoria rather the shadow of a name than the impression of an influence, this Fourth-Georgian personage was indisputably the transmitter to his daughter of Norman blood, of Plantagenet ancestry, of the roses of York and Lancaster, white and red, of the Tudor-born supremacy over the English Church Establishment and of the Orange-bred presidency by virtue of a lay commissioner in respect of the Scotch one, both of them brought somehow into line by that comfortable latitudinarianism of the Hanoverians which enabled the Sovereign to readjust his religious convictions as he crossed the Border. All this mixture of blood, all this confusion of faith, materializing into a monarchy, still of three kingdoms united in one Parliament and under one Sovereign, the Duke of Kent, who never wore the Crown and, indeed, remained so remote from it to the end as to lead a penurious existence and leave a load of debt for his daughter to discharge, passed on to the child whose lot not merely constituted a goodly heritage, but fell to her in the fair ground of youth.

To her mother the young Queen owed more, if moral and intellectual tendencies can be traced after the manner of looks. The elder Victoria was no 'ugly duchess' either in morals or manners. 'The Duchess of Kent', wrote Mrs. Arbuthnot, 'is a very sensible person and educates Princess Victoria (who is the most charming child I ever saw) remarkably well.'[1] 'I was', wrote Walter Scott in the same year (1828), 'presented to the little Princess Victoria . . . This little lady is educating with much care and watched so

[1] *Journal*, Vol. II, p. 186.

closely that no busy maid has a moment to whisper "You are heir of England" . . . She is fair like the Royal family, the Duchess herself very pleasing
and affable in her manners.'[1] In any appraisement of the Duchess of Kent,
that kindly estimate on the part of one who had had so many historical
reputations passing through his hands and had dealt with them in general
not unfaithfully, deserves to be recalled. And so also does Victoria's own
tribute on her sixteenth birthday,[2] which, though the Queen in later years
seems to have supposed her childhood to have been sad, bears no trace of
subdued melancholy or subtle reproach: 'From my *Dear* Mama I received
a lovely enamel bracelet with her hair, a pair of fine china vases, a lovely
shawl and some English and French books . . .' With all that, but above
and beyond it, stood out in Victoria's mind the musical entertainment given
in her honour, with Lablache, Tamburini, Rubini, Madame Malibran, but,
best of all, Grisi, participating. 'My dear Mama's great present was that
delicious concert, which I shall never forget.' There was not much, then, to
complain about; except, perhaps, afterwards, looking back, in the light of
the felicity that was to come to her with the advent of Albert. Even after her
accession, however, she toyed with the idea of being another Virgin Queen,
while the Duchess of Kent lived on at the Court. And when, in 1861, the
Duchess died, the outburst of grief, which can be followed in Victoria's
letters to the King of the Belgians, leaves no room for doubt that such differences with her mother as critics have dwelt on, a little too eagerly, have been
given more importance than they can justly bear. Such sentences as follow
leave no room for the idea that the relations between mother and daughter
had been seriously strained!—'She is gone. That *precious, dearly beloved, tender*
Mother—whom I never was parted from, but for a few months—without
whom I can't imagine life.' 'The constant intercourse of *forty-one* years cannot
cease without the *total want* of *power* of *real enjoyment* of *anything*.' 'I think *so*
much of dearest mamma and miss her love and interest and solicitude
dreadfully: I feel as if we were no longer cared for, and miss writing to her
and telling her everything, dreadfully.'[3]

These and other passages that could be quoted from the Queen's letters
render the familiar view of the Duchess as a meddlesome, inconvenient old
mother impossible; but doubtless, like most of us, she made mistakes in
handling a very difficult situation dominated by a half-crazy old 'salt' and
later by a daughter, only just of age. Perhaps she showed herself a little too
eager in King William's last years to pave her own path to a regency, or
her daughter's to the throne, with red carpets, and to advertise the impending
accession with premature royal salutes; but we may feel certain that she
would equally have been blamed, had the heiress presumptive to the Crown

---

[1] *Lockhart's Life*, May 19th 1828.   [2] Diary, May 1835.
[3] Queen's Letters, 1861, *passim*.

been forbidden to see anything of a world, all agog to know what she was
like. Even as it was, Greville comments on the world's ignorance of, and
curiosity about, Victoria. But, however all that may be, the ostentatious
operations of his sister-in-law attracted the old King's ranging eye and
rattling tongue to a lamentable degree; and there was one large dinner party
at Windsor, towards the end of his time, when the monarch's garrulous
and all too ready eloquence outran all bounds of hospitality or discretion
and compelled Victoria to distressful tears and her mother to rapid retreat.
The Sovereign wanted, so he said, to see more of his successor and less of
the Duchess; and the young Princess, whilst she wrote, after William was
dead, that he was 'odd, very odd', as in truth his Ministers found him, does
not seem wholly to have resented his desire. Still, the Duchess can hardly
be blamed for having wished to keep the girl out of the old man's way—
he being, as Greville remarked, 'something of a blackguard, and something
more of a buffoon'.[1] If the monarchy was to continue, its abuses would
evidently have to be swept away. An end would have to be made to the
indelicacy we can discern, not only in the prominence of those *maîtresses-
en-titre* like Lady Hertford and Lady Conyngham who had cumbered the
Court under George IV, but also to the elevation of a *batardise*, as they
called it, such as had issued from William's unlawful association and was at
his accession invested with a precedence only inferior to that approved by
Charles II for his illegal offspring. The Court was no circle for Victoria to
mix in; and any mother, seeking to form her daughter after the likeness of
the virtuous woman in the Book of Proverbs, would have avoided sending
her child to the Palace.

Doubtless it had been unfortunate for the Duchess's reputation that she
looked to her Chamberlain so largely for advice, though it is likely that her
relations with Conroy were as innocent as those, which contemporary
society also glanced at critically, of Queen Adelaide with Lord Howe.
Possibly, as Mrs. Belloc-Lowndes records in her *Merry Wives of Westminster*,
Victoria was maliciously induced to believe that some enlargement of Conroy's style of living came of his Palace connection, and not, as in reality,
from an accession of fortune received by his wife, to whom he was in fact
much attached.[2] Possibly, as Greville seems to have gathered from Wellington,[3] Conroy was surprised by Victoria in some unspecified familiarities
with her mother that can hardly have been of a very grave character, since
Baroness Späth, her lady-in-waiting, ventured to remonstrate with her about
them. The Baroness was subsequently dismissed—to the indignation of her
friend, Baroness Lehzen, Victoria's governess, who, at the time and for some

---

[1] *Memoirs*, June 21st 1837.
[2] This view is adopted in Dormer Creston's *The Youthful Queen Victoria*.
[3] See Strachey's *Queen Victoria*, p. 44, footnote.

time after, remained very influential in Victoria's life, though in the end she, too, fell out of favour. Twenty years later, when the Duchess fell gravely ill in 1859, the Queen wrote to King Leopold: 'I hardly myself knew how I loved her or how my whole existence seems bound up with her—until I saw looming in the distance the fearful possibility of what I will not mention.'[1] But the last word on the whole matter seems to lie in Victoria's letter to King Leopold at the time of her mother's death in 1861: 'Oh! I am so wretched to think how for a time two people' (presumably Lehzen and possibly Conroy) 'most wickedly estranged us.'[2]

One or two things, anyhow, are quite clear. Victoria disliked Conroy, was resolved he should be no *maire du palais* of hers, and paid him off for his services to her mother handsomely but immediately with a baronetcy in addition to a pension of £3,000 a year. It is also plain that the Duchess suffered no material loss apart from that of her Chamberlain. She lived on with Victoria; she had her whist parties nightly arranged for her at the Palace; she accompanied her daughter on social, though not political occasions; she was treated by the Queen, according to Greville's observation, with cordiality and affection; and, if she casually said to Princess Lieven,[3] whose sharp tongue would not have let the words lose in the telling, that, after her daughter's accession, she counted for nothing any longer, it is obvious to reply that, so far as sovereign-power went, she had counted for nothing before. Her own disposition to favour the Whigs, and particularly Lord Durham, was, however, reflected in the early political preferences of the Queen; and here, since it aided the four years' administration of Melbourne, the country had little cause for regret. Not to dwell unduly on an incident that has attracted in general more interest than it merits, one might say that Victoria managed the awkward business of putting her mother in her right place and thwarting any aspiration Sir John Conroy may have entertained of dominating the Royal Household with a dexterity that older heads might have envied. Unable to criticize the Queen for ineptitude or inexperience, Society, when it grew tired of singing her praises, fell back on the comment that her prudery and caution were unnatural to the point of unseemliness in a girl so young.[4] But, in the world we live in, one cannot hope to be well spoken of for long, if only because people grow tired of saying and hearing the same thing. To escape one charge is only therefore to incur its opposite. It was a great part of Victoria's strength that, without being a strikingly clever woman, her mind was straight and clear, her judgment in general sound, and her adaptability very considerable. She had of course, her likes and dislikes, and she could swing over from sharp hostility

---

[1] May 25th 1859.
[2] Queen's Letters, April 9th. Also March 16th, 26th, 30th 1861.
[3] *Memoirs*, July 30th 1837.
[4] ibid., August 10th 1837.

to warm regard. In sixty years, too, there was time for the occurrence of some negligences, ignorances, and follies—the muddle, for instance, over Lady Flora Hastings,[1] for which Sir James Clark's faulty diagnosis and chattering tongue must take the principal blame; the culpable neglect of Ireland, which the favour shown to Scotland did something to accentuate; the Queen's failure 'to instruct her sorrows to be proud'[2]—and her consequent inability for a decade and more after the death of the Prince Consort to put herself at the head of her people as they went from strength to strength. We may smile at the royal caprice which exalted John Brown to an altitude in the Queen's household, as well as at the exaggerated promotion of a less notorious figure—the Munshi from whom Victoria learnt Hindustani and to whom she imparted some unnecessary confidences.[3] We may be critical of such indiscretions, but spread over sixty years they don't come to much. So then let such trifles be. They added something to the gaiety of men, and even of nations, but do not detract from a high estimate of Victoria. No man nor woman, after all, can hope to walk through such a world as ours without affording countless targets for the barbs of ridicule; and still less can King or Queen under the glare, proverbially fierce, that beats upon all thrones. The only danger is that such an artist as Lytton Strachey, dexterously elaborating a pastiche, should lead us to miss the portrait of a lady, so subtly traced by the finesse of her education that she could sit beside an Empress (and that Empress, one of the loveliest women in Europe), and make Eugénie, as was said, seem a parvenue, whilst she herself remained in the well-worn phrase every inch a Queen. I remember a well-qualified eye-witness telling me how much it had amused him to watch Strachey's face falling as, at the request of some hostess, a critic no less fine than himself and far more competent—Arthur Balfour—sketched an impression of Victoria as her Ministers saw her. The fancied figure of fun dissolved like some effigy cast in snow beneath the sunshine of this intimate valuation. Victoria had a grandeur, wrought of time and experience, that no statesman could deny. As Salisbury observed after her death, 'No Minister in her long reign ever disregarded her advice or pressed her to disregard it without afterwards feeling that he had incurred a dangerous responsibility.[4]

Balfour, it is true, was born only in 1848; and his contact with Victoria can only have been close in the 'nineties. But she could from the first impress the eyes of statesmen, the least susceptible and the most experienced, with her peculiar dignity. Not in vain had Lehzen laboured! Not in vain had that once-beloved preceptress worked upon a character singularly straight, duti-

---

[1] See *infra* p. 95. See also Domer Creston's *The Youthful Queen Victoria*.
[2] *King John*, III, i.
[3] There is an account of this incident in Ponsonby's *Recollections of Three Reigns*.
[4] Speech in the House of Lords, January 25th 1901.

ıl and resolute, to give it knowledge of the things a Queen of England
ught to know. Doubtless Esher is right in suggesting that Victoria's Latinity
vould have left Roger Ascham dissatisfied: still Melbourne could talk to her
bout Lalage *dulce ridentem, dulce loquentem*,[1] and she could note it in her
liary; which, perhaps, Elizabeth, for all her scholarship, might not have
een at the pains to do. Victoria's penmanship, though devoid of literary
legance, was not wanting in point or power. She felt the charm of Mme
e Sévigné's letters—femininity at its fairest—and King Leopold declared
hat her own fulfilled their precept in so far that the reader might suppose
he was speaking.[2]

For the rest Britain had no cause to regret in the coming age that the
Queen was neither pedant nor prig, neither dubious virgin nor potential
virago, as might perhaps have been charged against Elizabeth, but a woman
nost womanly, who as a child had loved her dolls, and as a wife was able
o worship her husband. There ran in Elizabeth's body the blood of the
oughest of tyrants and of the fastest of flirts; and this was doubtless protec-
ion enough against any too scholarly sweetness and light. But Victoria, had
he been, like her own eldest daughter,[3] a more intellectual woman, might
ave made a far less successful Sovereign. She had capability; and that was
nough. As Melbourne warned Peel, she knew there were many things she
ould not understand, but she could appreciate a case simply and shortly
xplained to her.[4] And, as she told herself, at the outset she was 'very young,
nd perhaps in many things, not in all things, inexperienced, but . . . sure
hat very few had more goodwill and more real desire to do what is fit
nd right than she had'.[5] What Elizabeth would have been without the
allast of Burghley in her counsels, we can never even guess; for even in
hose last five years, when he was gone, his son, seised of all his wisdom
nd perhaps subtler than himself, took his place, though not his office, and
teered the State through the crisis of a succession which the Queen herself
vould never fairly face. Victoria's lot was very different. Whereas the Tudor
Queen in forty years had but one chief Minister, whom she chose herself
vith, perhaps, an instinct that his solid qualities would make good her
apricious defects, Victoria in her sixty years and more had ten Prime
Ministers thrust upon her by her people. It is no small tribute to her character
nd capacity that she contrived to work well enough with all but two or
hree of them; and that from one of these latter she drew the following
ribute: 'Often as I have been struck by the Queen's extraordinary integrity
f mind—I know of no better expression—I never felt it more than on

[1] Esher, *Girlhood of Queen Victoria*, Vol. I, p. 268.
[2] Queen's Letters, February 15th 1856.   [3] The Empress Frederick of Germany.
[4] Greville, *Memoirs*—Victoria, Chapter XII.
[5] Esher, *Girlhood of Queen Victoria*—Queen's Diary, June 20th 1837.

hearing and reading a letter of hers . . . about the Danish question. He
determination, in this case as in others, not inwardly to "sell the truth" . .
overbears all prepossessions and longings, strong as they are, on the Germa
side, and enables her spontaneously to hold the balance, it seems to me
tolerably even.'[1]

Palmerston, who made light of her wishes; Gladstone, who bombarde
her ears with his eloquence, were neither courtiers born nor made; an
Russell, who with his pernickety precision, could provoke her to clas
him with Palmerston as 'a dreadful old man',[2] all these tried her to th
uttermost. But, for all that, the association of the Sovereign with Ministe
who, according to our make-believe Constitution, were accounted servan
of the Monarch but in fact were in process of becoming tribunes of th
People, worked better under her than ever it had done under her grand
father or her uncles. 'She showed a wonderful power on the one hand',
Salisbury remarked, 'of observing with the most absolute strictness th
limits of her action which the Constitution draws, and, on the other han
of maintaining a steady and persistent influence on the action of her Ministe
in the course of legislation and government.'[3] Doubtless the stars with whic
custom bejewelled her as a woman fought now and again in their cours
for her as a monarch. And, doubtless too, her sex surrounded her with
glamour, which made Disraeli, half in jest and half in earnest, call her
Faery Queen, and prescribed a courtesy of loyal devotion which no princ
however fair, could probably have commanded in equal measure.

It is Richardson's Lovelace who, asserting in the same breath that 'wisdo
never entered into the character of woman', observes that 'women mak
better sovereigns than men', because, as he says, 'the women-sovereigns ar
governed by men, the men-sovereigns by women'.[4] The rake had hit upo
an aphorism at least as true as such scintillations of wit need to be; and ther
is no better place than English history to look for its vindication. How super
is the spectacle where the Armada sinks into the sea and the star of Shake
speare begins to rise on the horizon; how arresting the picture, presented i
Esmond, of pen and sword combining in Addison's prose and Marlborough'
campaigns to render the reign of Anne Augustan! Time has mellowed t
a majestic splendour the reigns of the last Tudor and of the last Stuart Queen
But the Age of Victoria still waits to assume its full historic proportions—
to be recollected, like some pageant that has passed, in tranquillity; to b
seen as the apex to which Britain, in the long pursuit of her destiny, onc
climbed, and from which, like other empires and other states, sometime ric

[1] Morley, *Life of Gladstone*, Vol. II, p. 192. (Gladstone to the Duchess of Sutherland
anuary 4th 1864.)
[2] Queen's Letters, February 25th 1864.
[3] Speech, House of Lords, January 25th 1901.
[4] *Clarissa Harlowe*, Vol. III, Letter I.

n repute and ready for epic celebration, she gradually lapsed. Decline may be infinitely slow; but neither classic Greece with all its intellectual beauty, nor pagan Rome with all its solemn grandeur, nor Florence aflame with art, nor Paris lusting after glory, nor Prussia drunk with love of power, have ever been able to escape the day of doom. The ineluctable follows the immortal hour, and sometimes is not far behind it.

No man, of course, could see what that long midsummer day of 1837 was going to bring forth, any more than any man could tell on the short November day, when Elizabeth received the news of her accession at Hatfield, that a great epoch was beginning. Only the historic Muse—spectator as she is of all time and existence—could rightly be supposed to possess the genius to perceive that, given a statesmanship equal to its occasion, there were powers at work in the world and in men's minds which would carry the reign far in grace and high in glory. The first of those powers was the romance that hung about the young Queen—a romance fortified by the sense of a prodigious escape from the kingship of Cumberland, which grave men thought would have made an end of the monarchy.[1] Scott, however, as he sat beside Princess Victoria at the Duchess of Kent's table, had probably little idea that he had anything to do with preparing her path; though, in fact, it most certainly was so. For he had contrived to say in language which all could understand—in song, in story, and through that great love of the past which spoke out in the perfection of his Border minstrelsy—things that the Revolution in France, and all that came of it, had striven to suppress.

Victoria heard that music, charged, like the sound of church bells, with a mystery beyond our penetration and reminiscent of an age less earthbound than our own. She heard it through his every sentence and in his every line; heard it, as her girlhood's diary tells us, so that she could set down that Scott was her *beau idéal* of a poet; that one who could write such beautiful poems never could in *her* opinion write an *ugly* line; that she did 'so admire' him both in poetry and prose; even that there were two lines in *Rokeby,* itself all 'full of loveliness, sweetness, grace, elegance and feeling', which struck the Dean[2] ('who is, s'il est permis de le dire, poetry-mad') as 'most splendid' and made her feel that she wanted to copy out the whole. Alas! she does not say—or at any rate the published extract from her diary does not tell—what lines they were that stirred her thus deeply. But her response is enough to show how ready was her girl's heart to receive the music, in the widest sense of the word, of the coming age. She was, after all, in good company in setting Scott so high. Byron, rebel as he liked to think himself, puts Scott above all the British poets of his time, and far above Wordsworth

[1] Esher, *Girlhood of Queen Victoria,* Vol. I, p. 175.
[2] Davys of Chester.

and Coleridge; calls him the undoubted 'monarch of Parnassus and the mos
English of bards' (Letter of November 24th 1813); and declares in a letter to
Stendhal of May 29th 1823 that Scott was 'of all men the most open, the mos
honourable, the most amiable' and 'as nearly a thorough good man as man
can be'. Call the movement mock-romantic if you must, and provided that
at the same time, you style the pagan taste of the Revolution pseudo-classic
Human nature has to repeat itself, so rare is real novelty in the soul of man, so
seldom can we safely say, 'This has never been before'. But Scott, though a
man of instinctive modesty, was well aware, as a notable passage in Lockhart's
Life discovers, that he had absorbed, and not imitated the genius of the
romantic past. 'They have', as he observed of his own imitators, 'to read old
books and consult antiquarian collections to get their knowledge; I write
because I have long since read such works and possess, thanks to a strong
memory, the information which they have to seek for.'[1] Chivalry and all the
code of conduct for gentle and simple that centres round the symbolic
words *noblesse oblige* had its being, and not just its reflection, in his soul; nor
can we ever hope to reach any true understanding of the Victorian Era unless
we understand that. It met and matched, and for a long time it also scotched,
the slogans of the Revolution by a deeper thought and a finer fence. It confronted the new paganism with its cruelty and its greed by courtesy and
compassion. It combated error by setting forth truth. And in this work
Scott's influence was supreme. 'His services, direct and indirect', as Lockhart
claims, 'towards repressing the revolutionary propensities of his age, were
vast—far beyond the comprehension of vulgar politicians.'[2]

It was Scott, after all, who most impressed upon the early Victorians the
power of the past, the fashions of chivalry, the traditions of loyalty, the
grace of order and degree, the debt of mankind to the dead. He was not
insensible to the force of the reasoning which had led to the expulsion of
the Stuarts and had given him the Fourth George for a Sovereign; and his
reminiscence of that depraved and dishonourable personage, to which
Thackeray took such exception in the Book of Snobs, is probably the most
generous we have. Yet, for all that, he saw clearly what sermons lie in
stones, what worship lingers in old ruined abbeys, what high devotion could
come, to lord and vassal alike, from the loyalties and courtesies of manor
and castle, how much wisdom lay in ancient ways, and how much bleaker
society might grow, if these were to vanish and civilization to disintegrate
under the pull-devil, pull-baker conflict of equality with liberty and of that
highly militant type of fraternity which found expression in the Terror and
in the Revolutionary and Napoleonic Wars. 'Had Sir Walter never taken
a direct part in politics as a writer', asserts Lockhart,[3] 'the visible bias of his

[1] Lockhart, *Life of Scott*, Chapter LXII.   [2] ibid., last chapter.
[3] ibid., last chapter.

mind on such subjects must have had a great influence; nay the mere fact that such a man belonged to a particular side would have been a very important weight in the balance.' With Newman, the deepest religious and anti-revolutionary intellect of the coming age, we have his own word that Scott's literary influence operated as a powerful auxiliary in his labours, stimulating mental thirst, feeding hopes, conjuring up visions, indoctrinating noble ideas, and thus meeting the demand of the time for a deeper philosophy and a more radiant outlook.[1]

Scott, of course, was only reflecting in a Caledonian mirror the image of the Europe which had risen, as one might say, phoenix-like from the ashes of Troy, had served its wander-years with Odysseus and Æneas, and had winged its way at length from Hell to Heaven in Dante's Vision. But for the intervention of the Reformation, this comprehensive, developing design of a Christian Commonwealth might conceivably have travelled on along the path of the Renaissance into more serene dominions than even Shelley's music dreamed of. Outstanding Humanists—Erasmus, Thomas More, Montaigne—had seen the blunder Europe was making in the sixteenth century, but had been powerless to avert it. But now spring was once more in the intellectual air; and Scott caught the magic rhythm of the enchanted adventure in which knight and clerk had roamed alike in the forest of the imagination, spies of God, praying, working, singing, succouring with sword or pen a world from whence, as physical and metaphysical scientists have themselves warned us, we exclude the sense of mystery at our peril. His imagination regained for Europe the balance which the Reformation culminating in the Revolution had shaken. The pomp and circumstance, the chivalry and courtesy, of the Middle Age, recovered much of their charm and discarded much of their coarseness. Shrewd as a Lowlander, Scott did not overstate his case, yet we who look back can see that the minstrel had left the banks of the Tweed and climbed to Arthur's Seat and had beheld from thence the richness of a land into which he himself would never fully enter, but whither his disciples would one day press—all that Brotherhood of the Pre-Raphaelites, with Rossetti leading; Newman with a great multitude of followers listening in the old University City to the sound of church bells—'that peculiar creation', as Froude called it in an immortal passage, 'of the medieval age which falls upon the ear like the echo of a vanished world': Barry, with Pugin at his side, raising Gothic spires; Tennyson solitary, splendid, drawing exquisite melody from a harp tuned to his theme, as the Round Table passed before his vision and the dead knights rose, and the arm, clothed in white samite, mystic, wonderful, caught Excalibur and waved it again above mysterious waters. These all painted, spoke, built, sang to Scott's inspiration; whilst out in Italy Browning felt the tense pressure of

[1] Newman, *Apologia*, p. 96.

the laden air and returned Italian eclogues, Florentine legends, and one long, forgotten tale of Rome, in which the Pope's concluding summary stands for the last word of wisdom. Then, at long last, like soft notes dying after the climax of the piece is past, came 'John Inglesant'—'a Romance' indeed, meeting with an unexpected welcome and read in all directions.

Facing Scott's monument, at the entry of that long avenue of the Victorians, straight in design as a Roman road, yet cut in its course by a thousand beckoning glades and alluring vistas, there rises before the imaginative mind another figure mounted on horseback, wrought in iron and towering, as Scott would have been the first to say, high above his own. As he told Ballantyne with an emphasis intended to exclude all doubt or objection, one only of the many notabilities he had met had struck him with a sense of awe —Wellington.[1] Here was at once a great soldier and a great statesman—the greatest, so he declared, in either kind.

One can hardly hope to understand the particular quality of Victorian statesmanship and the particular response it could count upon without stressing the character of the Iron Duke and seeing how large a part he played in forming the standards of his time. A very trifling illustration may help to show the depth of the impression he made. A quarter of a century ago I was asked to look through and advise upon a box of mementoes preserved by a great lady of the period who had reigned in more than one of those 'stately homes of England', celebrated just before Victoria's time by Felicia Hemans, and whom I can recall in her old age, when pomp and circumstance had given place to the dignity and distinction of time. Among the relics of her past life that I came across was a packet which, on examination, revealed Wellington-worship carried to its utmost limit. The parcel contained just a pair of gloves. An accompanying inscription, however, registered the fact that the owner had been wearing them when, on first entering Society, she had shaken hands with the Great Duke.

As happened to Mary, Lady Derby, when, with those famous *beaux yeux* of hers, she contemplated the hero of Waterloo, so it befell likewise many choice spirits of the other sex. They set eyes on the hero, only to fall in love with the gentleman. I never, as I have said, heard my father refer to anyone as he did to the Duke; he was not much given to veneration. Still here, plainly, was a man above common stature; here was he—whom every man at arms would wish to be. A very famous, if not a very happy warrior! For after Waterloo, they say, he wept; and always his commonsense and his humanity told him that peace was the supreme need of his country. His despatches after that decisive battle, like his conversations with Stanhope, are full of a political sagacity, for lack of which a later age has chosen its occasions for joining issue badly, has fumbled in its war-making, and has

[1] Lockhart, Chapter XXXV.

failed in its ultimate purpose of making peace. He was too great a gentleman to court the smiles of Jack Cade, as he was too astute a statesman to expect that even the wisest policy could bring Europe, with its stricken soul in it, more than 'a little peace'—in this case the not unbroken, yet, broadly speaking, enduring peace of the century between 1815 and 1914. Not for a nature like his was that worship in the house of the under-dog, which we have seen carried to such surprising heights of superstition.

But he did not, for all that, fall himself into the folly of attempting to hold positions that had become by political erosion totally untenable. He was wise enough to surrender, when he could do no other; but he saw, as indeed he said, that education without religion made clever devils. Thersites stoned his windows at Apsley House; as Thersites also stoned Walter Scott in person at Jedburgh. But the humour of Wellington was more than a match for the malice of the mob. 'Well, gentlemen', he had cried, when a crowd refused to let him pass home unless he would first cry 'God save Queen Caroline', 'have it your own way. God save Queen Caroline; and may all your wives be like her !' In the end they respected one whose essential aristocracy (in the true meaning of that much-abused word) they could not discern at the beginning. His popularity grew to a great height, though he seemed scarcely aware of its demonstrations. In his last years the whole audience rose when he entered the Opera House; and, when he died, men took his body for burial, not to the immemorial Abbey, but through 'streaming London's central roar' to St. Paul's, so that, as Tennyson declared, 'the sound of those he wrought for, and the feet of those he fought for' might 'echo round his bones for evermore'. He had always tried to see things as they really were, both in war and peace; and, in the end at least, his fellow countrymen, almost to a man, saw him as he really was.

It needed, perhaps, such a passing to show how much a single figure by its detachment, its devotion to duty, its almost Johnsonian common sense had done to keep Englishmen free from Continental illusions in the conduct of their country's affairs. If a distinguished historian of our own time is right in teaching us to think of the Black Prince and of Charles II as exercising far beyond their own time an outstanding, formative influence over the changing English conception of a gentleman, it is as certainly true that the shadow of Wellington stretched across the whole reign of Victoria, pointing to whatsoever things in human character were honest and just, lovely and of good report. The hand of the historian is, however, constrained to pause before completing the familiar association of words by adding 'whatsoever things were pure'. I can indeed recollect an eminent Oxford Professor of History casually dismissing such a tribute as not worth consideration in the case of any great soldier. Yet, despite that rash generalization, which would not go for much in the witness-box, it might be hard to prove that Wellington, who, as he himself said in his correspondence,[1] was no libertine, and who, as the poet said for him, 'Let the turbid streams of rumour flow Thro' either babbling world of high and low', was ever more than a flirt. Let us see how some of this idle talk looks under close examination.

Lady Shelley, who knew well both persons concerned and often saw them together, declares in her diary that she was satisfied, after much opportunity of observation, that the Duke's association with Mrs. Arbuthnot, which Greville insinuates was a liaison,[2] was no immoral connection but just a great man's friendship; and, since this book started on its way, Mrs. Arbuthnot's Diaries have come out to confirm her. Arbuthnot's affectionate intimacy with the Duke renders her view probable. Wellington, as is well known, had married Lady Kitty Pakenham, long after his rejection in early life by her parents as too poor a match, merely because he heard, on his return from India, that she still cared for him. This characteristic chivalry, however, did not suffice to make a happy home; and he sought companionship elsewhere. In the days when Charles Greville came to know him (and to hear more of him perhaps through his own brother, Algernon, who was the Duke's Secretary) he had reached an age when assiduous attentions could well be dismissed as no more than the innocent flirtations of an eminent old man with his lost youth. Greville describes them in fact as the 'senile engouements' of 'a privileged person'; and I remember my father, who, as I have said, knew the Duke himself and must have heard the gossip both of the Brigade of Guards and of the Hatfield circle, commenting on them more respectfully, but somewhat to the same effect. As regards earlier days, where Greville presumably had to rely, if not directly on his brother, but upon remoter hearsay, the Duke is credited with having been 'extremely addicted to gallantry'; with a *grande passion*, nearly involving him in serious difficulties, for a lady in Spain; with excessive attentions to Lady Frances Webster at the time of Waterloo, and with other connections 'most of them . . . certainly' (so he says) 'very innocent'. Human nature in this and many other respects is so far fallen that no one can be greatly blamed for putting a bad construction upon much that yet lies very far from being 'proven' by any standard a conscientious juryman could accept. The only direct first-hand testimony available is, however, I believe, Harriet Wilson's—and who in the world is going to accept one such as a credible witness, when she was engaged in a piece of bookmaking and, as we now know,[3] offered to leave Wellington's name out of her book if he would pay her for doing so.

---

[1] Despatches, September 17th 1823 and January 6th 1832.

[2] *Memoirs*, August 5th 1834.

[3] See *The Journal of Mrs. Arbuthnot*, Vol. I, p. 378; cp. Greville's Diary, September 18th 1852.

These considerations are curiously reinforced by others arising from passages in some letters lately published.[1] These are of the date of the Peninsular War, and are addressed by Wellington to William Wellesley-Pole (subsequently the third Lord Mornington) and deal, among other things, with the depraved private life of their eldest brother, Richard, Lord Wellesley. The Duke's candour in discussing Wellesley's licentious habits verges on coarseness. A Hebrew prophet, denouncing the sexual shortcomings of his race, could hardly have used more uncompromising language. But what is still more to the point in the present connection is to recognize that very few men—and perhaps, least of all men, Wellington—would have cared to use such disdainful words in respect of anyone to whose shortcomings they were themselves addicted. As the editor of the letters observes without, it would seem, quite appreciating the full force of his remark, 'He (Wellington) always applied to others the same standard which he set for himself'.

Let the Duke's reputation, then, go undimmed by tales unproven until the secrets of all hearts are revealed. And for a portrait of the man, high-souled and in Victoria's time graced with all the dignity and distinction that age can bestow, take some words from Greville's concluding estimate and to them add Carlyle's description of him as he appeared at Bath House two years before his death. These together give as good an impression of the effect of his personality in its final phase upon the Society of that time as we can well hope for. First, then, Greville: 'He had more pride in obeying than in commanding, and he never for a moment considered that his great position and elevation above all other subjects released him from the same obligation which the humblest of them acknowledged . . . There never was a man whose greatness was so *thrust* upon him.'[2]

And now for Carlyle: 'Journal, June 25th 1850. Last night at a grand ball at Bath House—the only ball of any description I ever saw . . . By far the most interesting figure present was the old Duke of Wellington, who appeared between twelve and one, and slowly glided through the rooms —truly a beautiful old man; I had never seen till now how beautiful, and what an expression of graceful simplicity, veracity, and nobleness there is about the old hero when you see him close at hand. His very size had hitherto deceived me. He is a shortish, slightish figure, about five feet eight, of good breadth however, and all muscle or bone. His legs, I think, must be the short part of him, for certainly on horseback I have always taken him to be tall. Eyes beautiful light blue, full of mild valour, with infinitely more faculty and geniality than I had fancied before; the face wholly gentle, wise, valiant, and venerable. The voice too, as I again heard, is "aquiline" clear, perfectly equable—uncracked, that is—and perhaps almost musical, but (an)

---

[1] *Camden Miscellany* (3rd series, volume 79).
[2] *Memoirs*, September 18th 1852.

essentially tenor or almost treble voice—eighty-two, I understand. He glided slowly along, slightly saluting this and that other, clear, clean, fresh as this June evening itself, till the silver buckle of his stock vanished into the door of the next room, and I saw him no more. Except Dr. Chalmers, I have not for many years seen so beautiful an old man.'[1]

'The tottering throne', Scott had written in the very line that precedes the most famous quatrain in all his verse—his tribute to the Younger Pitt. Let forty years go by, however, and Scott's anxious fears assume the look of a region cloud, hanging only over the first four Georges. More than any other men of the time, though they had no mean collaborators, the Border Minstrel and the Iron Duke had wrought this change in sentiment. Neither Spenser nor Shakespeare had sung the romance of royalty before the Virgin Queen more fervidly than Scott in his prophet's mantle did for Princess Victoria; and the debt was fittingly repaid when, as Queen, she made her best-loved home in Scotland. And if Raleigh spread his cloak before Elizabeth's feet with more immediate dramatic effect, Wellington's hand pointed unswervingly to the path Honour and Devotion must tread. Victoria did well, in her letters to Leopold,[2] to single him out when he died as the greatest man this country ever produced, the most devoted and loyal of her subjects; for she had never, in all her length of days, another who excelled him in the personal loyalty that invests patriotism with a grace and glamour it cannot otherwise command. In the magic attraction of the monarchy, however unworthy the monarch, lay the compelling magnet of the British tradition; and the conqueror of the French Revolution at Waterloo taught his countrymen to seek it there.

So then Victoria, stepping out from Kensington Palace on that June morning of 1837, into the long avenue of her reign has, so to say, these colossal figures like statues in the background behind. All eyes are upon her; and soon all tongues are singing her praise, so simply, yet with such dignity, does she discharge the office for which God, as she deems, had designed her. Wellington watching her, when she read her speech, was, equally with Peel, astonished, and told Greville he could not have wished to see a part better played, had his own daughter been called on to take it. Lehzen and the Duchess had done their work well. Victoria had emerged from their hands a passionate lover of music; and, though no Venus, she was yet to many as a piece of music passing through the quivering air of her accession.

Just after that opportune event a very clever man—'known, liked and honoured' as the epitome of the *Dictionary of National Biography* goes out of its way to tell us, 'for his manliness, honesty and exuberant drollery and wit' —in a sermon, preached presumably at St. Paul's, for that was where Sidney

[1] Froude, *Carlyle's Life in London*, Vol. II, p. 46.
[2] Queen's Letters, September 17th 1852.

Smith was a canon, ventured to set out what idea, as he considered, the young Queen ought to conceive of her duties and on what points she should endeavour to rest the hoped-for glories of her reign. First and foremost, he said, the new Queen should bend her mind to the very serious consideration of educating the people. Of the importance of this, no reasonable doubt, he said, could exist; and it was the more urgent that many countries in Europe were ahead of England in this kind of effort. Objections to the general education of the people were, in his view, utterly untenable; and he added that 'the great use and the great importance of education properly conducted is, that it creates a great bias in favour of virtue and religion, at a period of life when the mind is open to all the impressions which superior wisdom may choose to affix upon it'. But, in the second place, the great thing which it was needful to impress upon the mind of the Sovereign was 'a rooted horror of war—an earnest and passionate desire to keep her people in a state of profound peace'.

'The greatest curse', Sidney Smith continued, 'which can be entailed upon mankind is a state of war. All the atrocious crimes committed in years of peace—all that is spent in peace by the secret corruptions, or by the thoughtless extravagance of nations, are mere trifles compared with the gigantic evils which stalk over the world in a state of war. God is forgotten in war—every principle of Christian charity trampled upon—human labour destroyed—human industry extinguished—you see the son, and the husband, and the brother, dying miserably in distant lands—you see the waste of human affections—you see the breaking of human hearts—you hear the shrieks of widows and children after battle—and you walk over the mangled bodies of the wounded calling for death!' Then, in a new burst of eloquence, such as few preachers to-day would have the power to emulate or the courage to release, and which is the more characteristic of the moral foundation of the Victorian age, he apostrophizes the Queen in words that the historian may find it well worth while to record: 'I would say to that royal child, Worship God, by loving peace—it is not *your* humanity to pity a beggar by giving him food or raiment—*I* can do that; that is the charity of the humble and the unknown—widen you your heart for the more expanded miseries of mankind—pity the mothers of the peasantry who see their sons torn away from their families—pity your poor subjects crowded into hospitals, and calling in their last breath upon their distant country and their young Queen—pity the stupid, frantic folly of human beings, who are always ready to tear each other to pieces, and to deluge the earth with each other's blood; this is your extended humanity—and this the great field of your compassion. Extinguish in your heart the fiendish love of military glory; from which your sex does not necessarily exempt you, and to which the wickedness of flatterers may urge you. Say upon your deathbed, "I have made few orphans in my reign—I have made few widows—my object has been peace. I have used all the weight of my character, and all the power of my situation, to check the irascible passions of mankind, and to turn them to the arts of honest industry: this has been the Christianity of my throne, and this the gospel of my sceptre" . . .'

The brilliant *habitué* of the Holland House circle had borne a more courageous witness to the wickedness of war than many who have subsequently had the same mission of preparing the paths of peace. Still the preacher cannot satisfy himself that he has said enough, and his tongue takes up the theme again: 'It is all misery, and folly, and impiety, and cruelty. The atrocities, and horrors, and disgusts of war, have never been half enough insisted upon by the teachers of the people; but the worst of evils and the greatest of follies, have been varnished over with specious names, and the gigantic robbers and murderers of the world have been holden up, for their imitation, to the weak eyes of youth. May honest counsellors keep this poison from the mind of the young Queen. May she love what God bids, and do what makes men happy.' There follow a few paragraphs in which the preacher deplores the bad effects of fanaticism in religion, and then he completes his portrait of what he calls 'the Patriot Queen' with a prophet's vision of the glory that such a woman as he had depicted, 'rich in the rudiments of wisdom and mercy', may bring to her people. 'I, of course', he adds, 'can only expect to see the beginning of such a splendid period; but, when I do see it, I shall exclaim with the Psalmist—Lord, now lettest Thou Thy servant depart with in peace, for mine eyes have seen Thy salvation.'

*   *   *   *   *

'Clio, a Muse', must, I fancy, have felt, in that auspicious hour when the girl, born to be Queen, and resolved to be Patriot Queen, mounted the steps of the throne, while all the listening world around stood tiptoe to get at least some little glimpse of her whose likeness Time had stretched upon the waters, that the stream of history was carrying a reflection of rare charm and interest. There was nothing at all to compare with it in the story of any other English queen's accession; nothing in Matilda's ineffectual struggle to claim her father's heritage; nothing in Mary Tudor's rally of the legitimists against the ill-starred, usurping Jane; nothing in Elizabeth's bold assumption of a crown that half Europe might have assigned as of right to Mary Stuart; nothing in the Second Mary's compliance in the dispossession and deposition of her father; nothing in Anne's continued occupation of a throne which she herself, in her own dull way, half felt to belong to her brother, already proclaimed King of England, if only at St. Germains. All the circumstances of Victoria's accession befitted the high majesty of June; and all the midsummer pomps seemed to advance to greet her like a Sovereign long awaited. After three old Kings—here at last was gaiety and goodness, an English Queen—even, one might say as Disraeli, half in love and half in irony, called her, late in time, a Faery Queen. From 'a palace in a garden' she stepped out; and all the land watched as she took hold of her inheritance. A girl still; yes, but prudent; yes, but capable of being mistress of her house, her throne, her kingdom! A girl on occasions merry; even, as Mr. G. M. Young has it, a 'gay, self-willed little Whig'. She could dance —oh! sometimes with such infinite pleasure—longing for a waltz ('the only dance', according to Byron, 'which teaches girls to think[1])—yet limiting herself for regal propriety's sake to the stately or staid quadrille. She could sing, but, better still, could listen with passionate enthusiasm to Grisi singing; she could play under Lablache's discreet instruction, but none the less could know her own mind, even with all conventional views against her, about operatic and theatrical performances. She would read mostly good books, yet, in rebellious moods, a novel or two; which performance her mother regarded as a trifle 'fast'. She knew, as we saw, a little Latin, but, like the greatest Englishman of all, less Greek. She could acclaim a remark of adored Mme de Sévigné as of a quality worthy of Tacitus or Machiavel. She could insert with ease French and Italian and German quotations in her journal. She could be very depreciatory of her small stature and slight presence, when she found a crowd assembled to have a look at her. She could at the same time be very generously alive to the charm of her Coburg cousins—of their interesting talk about interesting things, and, above all, of Albert's light touch in conversation and his never-failing gaiety.

Matters of more import than these took their place in Victoria's thoughts, at first through the medium of Dr. Davys, Dean of Chester and subsequently Bishop of Peterborough. I should guess that under his tuition she came to know, after the manner of Stevenson's young woman, about as much theology as her Albert liked. As much, anyhow, as her rôle as Sovereign required—Christian ethic, if not Christian dogma! To turn over the pages of her correspondence is to derive the impression that neither high church-men nor low churchmen were congenial to her. She disliked the aims of the former, the devotions of the latter. She found in the Established Church of Scotland 'the real and true stronghold of Protestantism'.[2] In the exercise of her office as supreme Governor of the Church of England she found 'the two dear Deans, Stanley and Wellesley' most congenial and, when they were no longer there towards the close of the reign, she turned for counsel to Randall Davidson,[3] whom she was reluctant, from a personal point of view, to see withdrawn from the Deanery of Windsor and elevated to the Episco-pal Bench. She hardly seemed aware, when she crossed the Border, that she

[1] *Don Juan*, canto xi, stanza 68.
[2] Queen's Letters, September 21st 1879.   [3] ibid., December 20th 1882.

D

had crossed the dividing line of two Churches as well as of two kingdoms; and this was in a way the more striking that she was sensible of the fascination of her Stuart ancestress, the Queen of Scots, and took Mary's part against her Tudor rival, the champion of the English Church and the occupant of the English throne.[1] But let this inconsistency pass, for it is common enough.

So, then, once again Victoria stepped out from the Palace at Kensington, a Queen into her kingdom—into her island kingdom, containing, perhaps at that time, some twenty-seven million souls, but with the population of an empire looming large in the distance; a kingdom, where still great cities were scarce and, as we should think, small; where London in 1831 had a million and a half inhabitants and Bristol only twenty thousand; a little world, where yet the countryside was but little spoilt by the presence of mechanical transport and where the internal-combustion engine was not yet for some sixty years to threaten the tranquillity of the scene; a little world, where still, as we may gather from an article on Mrs. Norton in the *Quarterly Review* in 1840, women moved intellectually among men with a freedom and sense of purpose hitherto unknown on this side of the Channel; a little society which the middle class, more especially, were urgent to make rich, not only with coal mines and manufactures, but with the fashion of old art returning and expressing itself anew in stone and canvas, in song and worship reminiscent of the Middle Age; a fine, fair heritage—for all its sordid streets and most distressful cases of infant mortality, giving, they say, a return, about 1840, of one death to four births among the children of the least fortunate part of the population, as against only one in ten for the most prosperous; a goodly, great dominion which was in the coming time to raise England to such vast power and influence as to give its Queen a certain strange pre-eminence even in that world, still blazing with emperors and kings.[2] Nor were the nations entirely at fault in seeing the English Queen as a phenomenon. Listen, if you doubt it, to the voice of Bernard Shaw, who begins to be heard towards the close of the reign, and see how even he falls under the magic spell, as he flits about, jeering, like Beaumarchais before him, as he destroys a social edifice:

Lubin: I did not discover any new truth revealed in these books, Mr. Barnabas.

Franklyn: What! Not the truth that England was governed all that time by a little woman who knew her own mind . . .

Lubin: . . . Which woman do you mean?

Franklyn: Queen Victoria, to whom your Prime Ministers stood in the

[1] See the letter to Lord Rosebery of July 7th 1887.
[2] See G. M. Young, *Early Victorian England*, Vol. I, pp. 167-9.

relation of naughty children, whose heads she knocked together, when their tempers and quarrels became intolerable. Within thirteen years of her death Europe became a hell.

Burge: Quite true. That was because she was piously brought up and regarded herself as an instrument. If a statesman remembers that he is only an instrument and feels quite sure that he is rightly interpreting the Divine Purpose, he will come out all right . . .[1]

*　　*　　*　　*　　*

There, then, even with the background of the Shavian mirror, does Victoria appear, an enduring reproach to the character and quality of the statesmanship that came after her. And the estimate is not perhaps so very wide of the mark. At all events, with this as a compass to carry, we have something to steer us through the various administrations by which the Queen's Government was carried on by 'the Ten', whose persons and personalities form the studies in this book.

Victoria is not, however, the only design—to change the metaphor—in the architecture of the reign. Less obvious to the eye, but hardly less notable in the structure, is the year 1861, when Albert died. As Strachey has well expressed its significance, what happened then was this: 'In addition to his intellectual and moral qualities, the Prince enjoyed by virtue of his position, one supreme advantage which every other holder of high office in the country was without; he was permanent. Politicians came and went, but the Prince was perpetually installed at the centre of affairs.' The Queen strove, indeed, always to carry on on Albert's lines. We might, perhaps, borrow from one of the less-known Victorian poets and say

> Love an eternal temper took,
> Dipp'd, glowing, in Death's icy brook![2]

Still, though that was the case, there was something plainly wanting. By common consent the prestige and the popularity of the Sovereign never sank so low as in the decade which followed the fatal year when Victoria lost her mother and her husband and the vital energy of her youth. It alarmed even Gladstone; and he did what he could to stem the flowing tide, which was actually at its most threatening some ten years after the Prince's death. The Queen recalled her obligation to him many years later: 'I shall ever gratefully remember his devotion and zeal in all that concerned my personal welfare and that of my family.'[3] She had not found Gladstone's sympathy uncongenial at the time of her great grief. 'Of all her Ministers',

---

[1] *Back to Methuselah*, Part II: 'The Gospel of the Brothers Barnabas'.
[2] Patmore, *The Victories of Love*, Book II, viii.
[3] Morley, *Life of Gladstone*, Vol. II, p. 426.

Dean Wellesley had written to him, 'she seemed to me to think that you had most entered into her sorrows . . .'[1] But, as Morley points out, there was something in their natures which tended to keep them apart. The Queen, he says, dreaded 'enthusiasm'; whereas Gladstone had a full measure of enthusiasm for causes, and the Irish cause in particular.[2] Disraeli was far cleverer. He saw that the Albert legend offered the true point of entry into Victoria's counsels; and he was so fortunate as to have appreciated at their proper valuation the Prince's gifts and influence. Strachey quotes him as saying: 'With Prince Albert we have buried our Sovereign. This German Prince has governed England for twenty-one years with a wisdom and energy such as none of our Kings have ever shown.'[3] By 1874, when Disraeli came to power, the time was ripe for what might, perhaps, be described as 'the sublimation of the Queen', if not yet of the Prince Consort. And there was no one better qualified to set that movement in motion than the strange man, whose political advice she grew to value almost like Albert's. Once before an adventurer had known how to make his way with her— the Third Napoleon. He had moved in the Blessington Circle: he is 'the Prince Florestan' of *Endymion*. And now again another figure out of that Byronic côterie captured her fancy and talked to her in a language she liked.

The second part of the reign was thus started; the two jubilees were visible on the far horizon. A change came over the Queen, inaugurated by her Oriental vizier, but not a little accentuated by reaction from his scholastic rival. The converging influence of Disraeli and Gladstone, by way of attraction and opposition, cannot well be exaggerated. 'What your loss to me as a Minister would be', she wrote of the one, 'it is impossible to estimate.'[4] 'What the Queen is especially anxious to have impressed on Lord Hartington and Granville', she wrote to Ponsonby of the other, 'is firstly that Mr. Gladstone *she* could have nothing to do with, for she considers his whole conduct since '76 to have been one series of violent, passionate invective against and abuse of Lord Beaconsfield . . . and that he . . . made the task of the Government of this Country most difficult in times of the greatest difficulty and anxiety, and did all to try and prevent England from holding the position which, thanks to Lord Beaconsfield's firmness, has been restored to her.'[5]

It was the turn of the tide for Victoria; and before long there followed a turn of the tide for her people also. She did not feel that she had changed; it was the ever-restless ocean, now threatening the Island-Empire, with which in heart and soul she had become associated, that seemed to be forcing her towards a new orientation of thought. When she received Beaconsfield's

[1] Morley's *Life of Gladstone*, p. 425.   [2] ibid., p. 425.
[3] Strachey, p. 220 (quoting Vitzthum).   [4] Queen's Letters, April 7th 1880.
[5] ibid., April 8th 1880.

telegram (of a few days before the letters just quoted) announcing his certain defeat at the polls, she wired to Ponsonby: 'The Queen cannot deny she (Liberal as she has ever been, but never Radical or Democratic) thinks it a great calamity for the Country and the peace of Europe !'[1]

It was not till the beginning of the following year that Victoria completely regained her balance. I know of no passage in her Letters so human, so appealing as the following entry on New Year's Day 1881—none which, after forty years and more on a throne, shows a finer sense of human frailty and a deeper modesty and faith. 'God spare all I most love', it runs, 'for many a year, and help me on ! I feel how sadly deficient I am, and how over-sensitive and irritable, and how uncontrollable my temper is, when annoyed and hurt. But I am so overdone, so vexed, and in such distress about my country that that must be my excuse. I will daily pray for God's help to improve.'

There stands the woman without any of the trappings of majesty; and there can be read an endorsement from the most intimate source of the rough old Archbishop's[2] claim that, because this woman had occupied the throne, countless people were leading better lives. None of 'the Ten', great as their influence was, can lay claim to so much.

[1] Queen's Letters, April 2nd 1880. (Cp. Victoria to Gladstone, July 25th 1884: 'The Queen will yield to no one in TRUE LIBERAL FEELING, but not to destructive, and she calls upon Mr. Gladstone to *restrain, as he can*, some of his wild colleagues and followers.')
[2] The elder Temple.

LORD MELBOURNE

WILLIAM LAMB, 2nd VISCOUNT MELBOURNE
born 1779 died 1848

Entered Parliament (Member for Leominster) 1804
Chief Secretary for Ireland (Canning's administration)
1827 to 1828
Home Secretary (Grey's administration) 1830 to 1834
Prime Minister July 1834 to November 1834
April 1835 to August 1841

CHAPTER IV

LORD MELBOURNE

THERE are two subjects, I can recollect hearing the late Lord Oxford remark, that would suit Lytton Strachey—Shelburne and Melbourne. The so-called 'Jesuit of Berkeley Square', political sponsor though he was of the Younger Pitt, patron of Bentham and Priestley, and (perhaps his most memorable claim to remembrance, in cypress, if not in rosemary), concessor of American Independence, is, however, the weaker partner in this jingling association of names. Melbourne, dawdling out from Holland House, cutting a dandified figure in the days of Beau Brummel; contracting a mad marriage with Caroline Ponsonby; moving, debonair if not dissolute, through the world of the Regency and the reign of the monarch self-styled, with unconscious irony, the first Gentleman in Europe; figuring in the Courts, though not found guilty, on a charge of seduction; described in Disraeli's *Letters of Runnymede* in 1836 as 'sauntering over the destinies of a nation and lounging away the glories of an Empire'; and then by a marvellous metamorphosis, which it seemed to need the brain of a Prospero to plan and the hand of an Ariel to execute, appearing in 1837 as the mentor of Victoria and the first begetter of the Victorian Age. Melbourne, when his accomplishment is assessed, leaves Shelburne behind; Brocket may boast a master such as Bowood never knew.

There is indeed a transient mood in which the first of 'the Queen's Prime Ministers' suggests the last. Different as they were in so much, Melbourne and Salisbury shared a disbelief in the multitude, a distrust of enthusiasm, a disdain of agitation, a wise cynicism of judgment, that tempt one to say that the political philosophy of the reign·was as a wheel coming round full circle and resting, after repeated revolution, on impressions of life and aphorisms of experience not so unlike those of Solomon. Such men as Melbourne and Salisbury have little use for the froth and bubble upon which politicians mostly thrive; for they perceive that to the most part of mankind stability is of more value than change and that the more complex human society grows, the more pregnant with peril does change become. In their eyes the process and method of political development should be modelled, as Bacon long since declared, on the process of Nature; on alterations, that is to say, coming about so quietly and unobtrusively that one notices the completed fact without marking the precise moment of the occurrence. There is no sound of tumbrils, no dancing of carmagnoles, no singing of sanguinary songs, no waving of red flags, no shouting in the streets, no assault of citadels. Fashions change, but without ferocity; institutions develop, but without violence; life is made easier, but through the applications of physical science, not the strife of tongues; morality moves, but in the manner of charity. How small, indeed, of all that human hearts endure, the part which laws or kings—Punches in Parliament, or Judys at the polling-booth—can cause or cure! No wonder that Johnson, with his wealth of humanity and commonsense, styled himself a Tory and was tempted to make mock of reformers, caressing the underdog, as he howled for the moon. When it is heart's ease that men really seek, it is precious little good dosing them with mind's unrest, glorifying discontent as divine, or soothing sores with quack remedies from the demagogue's dispensary.

Some few remarkable men do give a real, and not merely a notional, assent to the fact that what stands like stone amidst all this surge of froth and bubble is made from finer marble than Parliament can quarry; and these deserve the name of statesmen, for they are conscious of the nature of their limitations. Melbourne, for all his indolent pose, was such a one. Not for nothing had he mingled from adolescence in that brilliant circle which Lady Holland[1]—*maîtresse-femme*, if by no means *femme charmante*—had the talent to assemble and, thanks to the vulpine accumulations of the old dig-fox, her husband's grandfather, the means to regale at Holland House.[2] Not for nothing had Melbourne breathed the air of the New Whigs, aristocrats, or at least oligarchs, alive with ideas novel, or at any rate come alive again. Not for nothing had he known Charles James Fox, magnificent in debate, captivating in conversation, disreputable in morals, and dishonoured for all time by his explicit denial on 'direct authority' in the House of Commons of the Prince of Wales's marriage to Mrs. Fitzherbert. Not for nothing! The spell, however, that Fox could cast—the spell of which Pitt acknowledged the power; the spell from which Burke in the end recoiled as from an evil thing—left young William Lamb neither bewitched nor contentious. He saw, if others did not, that the dreams which dazzled the Whigs had found their way up into our sorry world through no gate of horn. He lived with the Reformers, but disliked the Reform Bill; and, when he died, Greville, bending over his bier and composing his epitaph, could declare him to have been 'a thorough conservative at heart'. His whiggery was only circumstance; his conservatism was character. And that is why his shrewdness with its pungent 'why can't you let it alone?' has about it a foretaste of Salisbury's more con-

[1] Lady Holland was born Elizabeth Vassall and inherited a large fortune from her father, Richard Vassall of Jamaica. She first married Sir Godfrey Webster, who divorced her because of her connection with Henry Richard, the third Lord Holland, whom she afterwards married.

[2] Henry Fox, first Baron Holland, whose manoeuvres as Paymaster-General were said to have brought a quarter of a million pounds into his estate.

sidered, but not so dissimilar sagacity at the close and consummation of the reign.

Holland House, where could be heard the third Lord Holland's wide-ranging, tolerant talk; Macaulay's opulent speech, confounding all resistance, like the hard cash of a multi-millionaire dumped down on the counter of knowledge—Sydney Smith's powerful wit operating like a prelate's mace in the thick of battle; Allen's acid invectives against Christianity; and Greville's chill criticism of himself and his times—the Holland House of that date and distinction was, more truly than Eton or Cambridge, Glasgow University or Lincoln's Inn, though to all these Melbourne went, the academy in which he graduated. He marked the talk and no doubt assisted from time to time in the tournament; but when in 1839 the Queen told him she got bored with perpetual talk of politics, he replied, 'Nothing so disagreeable, very tiresome; and that's the worst of Holland House'.[1] Its genius had changed, as he added, after the time of Fox, who had much preferred conversation about poetry and literature. Anyhow the Holland House circle of his early recollection left him politically very much of a sceptic. He was too wise to attempt much in the way of songs before sunrise. Had he not seen, when no more than a boy of ten, the 'evening sun of July' 1789, sinking behind the ruins of the Bastille; had he not beheld, at the age of twenty-six, 'the sun of Austerlitz' casting its beams upon a Europe already red with battle, and could he really suppose that the old world of the Humanists, pagan and Christian, was going to be satisfactorily supplanted by the sinuous ideology of Rousseau, the lethal knife of Robespierre or the sanguinary sword of Napoleon? He sat on chatting with the Whigs, but he took office as Irish Secretary first in 1827 with the Tories, or perhaps more strictly, under Canning and with a Conservative Party waiting in embryo to be born. When Canning, after his Hundred Days Premiership, died, Melbourne lingered on under the phantasmal Goderich, and later under Wellington with whom his relations, to the great advantage of the country, continued cordial even after he had ranged himself with the Reforming Whigs and served as Home Secretary under Lord Grey. The times were troubled; and Melbourne surprised his contemporaries by his energy in keeping order, and burdened his biographers with his defence for severity in suppressing sedition. The 'Tolpuddle Martyrs' were transported under Whig rule, though beatified later on under Trades Union influence. An Act limiting child-labour in factories stands, however, to Melbourne's credit; and that meant a good deal in a world greatly perplexed by the apparently conflicting claims of freedom and compassion. Somehow Melbourne slipped past and supplanted Grey—Lord Grey of the Reform Bill—and, King William IV notwithstanding, settled into the Premiership which neither Grey, jockeyed out of office by an intrigue of

[1] Queen's Diary, September 26th 1839.

Brougham's and Littleton's, nor Peel had proved long able to retain. And there the new reign found him, the very man for the place, as Wellington quickly recognized—a grand seigneur cut out to be 'Regius Professor' (as the wits were presently to name him), not indeed at either University, but at Windsor Castle and St. James's Palace.

Melbourne's still, at the time, imperfectly formed thought on the merit of inaction and the function of the police had appeared clearly in his treatment of public disorder as Home Secretary. On the whole he did well. He set his face against prosecutions of the Press and the encouragement of informers, but, though he worked smoothly, he failed, perhaps through latent Whig prejudices, to give full credit to the police force which under the direction of those remarkable men, Rowan and Maine, was displacing the descendants of Dogberry and Verges as guardians of the law. He used, it is true, these new-model men to stop trouble in 1833, but a recent writer accuses him of 'a disgraceful attempt . . . to deny that he had given orders to Rowan to prevent the meeting at Coldbath Field and to insinuate that Rowan's statement of the fact in his evidence was untrue'.[1]

The charge accords so ill with all else that we know of Melbourne that one is inclined to suspect something remained undisclosed, or that there was some official in the background, whom he wished to shelter, even, conceivably, his ill-bred but efficient private secretary, Thomas Young, 'a remarkable character . . . rough-hewn, vulgar, presuming, but also shrewd and capable, and devoted to those whose pay he took'.[2] There are some later words of Melbourne's, which the Queen relates, worth recalling in this connection. Her record of the conversation reads thus: 'Talked of Richelieu, his character, and Lord M. said that, if the people were alive and here, they could often tell us in a moment why they did things, whereas we write volumes to prove the reasons why people did so-and-so; he said people always accused Lord Burleigh of being so unkind to his nephew, Bacon, and Lord M. said he was certain, if Lord Burleigh were alive, he would give his good reasons for it, and we knew "what an infernal scamp" Bacon was.'[3]

Anyhow, by hook or by crook, Melbourne steered his way as Home Secretary through the era of the Reform Bill—a Bill, as we have seen, that he disliked but did not oppose. In his eyes the really valuable feature of the old system lay precisely in those pocket-boroughs which were so easy to attack, yet served to bring many valuable men into Parliament who might not, otherwise, have found their way there. From his angle of vision, consequently, the Reform Act of 1832 represented change rather than improvement—a distinction soon to be obliterated for many minds by ubiquitous

---

[1] Reith, C., *A Short History of the British Police*, p. 66.
[2] Dunckley, *Lord Melbourne*, p. 125.
[3] Queen's Diary, March 13th 1839 (in Esher's *Girlhood of Queen Victoria*).

but credulous believers in automatic progress, who excusably mistook the many inventions and achievements of the Victorian era for the manifestation of some universal law. Though Lecky maintained that England never had a better constitution than the one she enjoyed between 1832 and 1867, there were long to be found critics of the change, and some in places where one might least expect to encounter them. Gladstone himself, who entered the House of Commons at this time, left it on record[1] that in his opinion the composition of the new Chamber was in the main inferior to that of the old; but progressively-minded persons may take comfort in the reflection that the provision of lavatories at any rate had been improved out of all recognition, since in the former House Gladstone declared he could not recall any accommodation for washing his hands.[2]

Melbourne's weakness as a political preceptor lay in the fact that he had no liking for the middle classes, though they were to play a great part in creating both the commercial prosperity and the artistic distinction of the new reign and though Victoria herself showed to especial advantage both in her understanding of them at home and in her relations with the bourgeois monarchy of Louis Philippe and the parvenu empire of Louis Napoleon. All said and done, we are a nation of shopkeepers. Melbourne was none too ready to acknowledge it, 'I don't like the Middle Classes', he told the Queen. 'They say that the Upper and Lower Classes are very much like each other in this country; the Middle Classes are bad; the higher and lower classes there's some good in, but the Middle Classes are all affectation and conceit and pretence and concealment.'[3]

A sentiment not well suited to the sound middle-class stock of capable land-agents, lawyers and bishops, from which Melbourne was legally supposed to descend, but appropriate to the son of the last Lord Egremont, whom the social world of his time gave him for a father! For Egremont was a man who made Petworth popular by his lavish hospitality and aesthetic taste and England populous after the manner of Charles II, but who left no regular progeny to succeed him. A portrait of this grandee hung at Brocket; and Landseer, the artist, when he first caught sight of it, is said to have turned round, so strikingly did the man depicted resemble his host, to look at Melbourne, who was showing him round the house. Melbourne met the covert attack on his mother's honour with characteristic insouciance. 'Ay, you have heard that story, have you?' he said, 'But it's all a lie for all that.'[4] Perhaps it was—who can now be sure? But all the rest of the evidence bearing on the matter tells against Melbourne's denial—the marked distinction shown by the first Lord Melbourne between his treatment of his elder son, who died

[1] See Hunt and Poole, *Political History of England*, Vol. XI, p. 318.
[2] Morley's *Life of Gladstone*, Vol. I, p. 101.   [3] Queen's Diary, January 23rd 1840.
[4] See, for the story, Dunckley's *Lord Melbourne*, p. 237.

young, and this second son who succeeded him; the notorious reputation of
Lady Melbourne herself; the political ability of the Prime Minister, so much
more in keeping with a Wyndham than a Lamb ancestry; the facial likeness
to Egremont just noticed; and, of course, the common gossip of the time
recorded by Greville. Still Melbourne's elaborate account, given to the
Queen, of his Lamb descent[1] stands beside his remark to Landseer as a
challenge to the popular suspicion. Victoria, meanwhile set down his strictures on the Middle Class in her diary, but wisely enough made no attempt
to make her reign other than the magnificent tribute that it is, both artistically
and industrially, to that section of her subjects.

Whatever his paternity, William Lamb's mentality, both in its religious
and political aspect, had all the seemingly effortless charm of the *ancien
régime*. He thought, and he read, profoundly; but a certain nonchalance,
very characteristic of a grand seigneur, hid his conclusions, or rather his
tendencies, in theological and political science. There was certainly a door to
which he found no key; there was a veil past which he could not see: and he
was content that it should be so. Esher may be justified in asserting that
Melbourne, though 'not religious,[2] was a firm believer in the doctrines of
Christianity'. Nothing, however, lends strong support to this not in itself too
clear estimate of his views. To call oneself 'a quietist' in the style of Mme
Guyon; to profess oneself an episcopalian but 'in such a funny way' as to
make Victoria laugh;[3] to read much theology; to take trouble about the
appointment of bishops; even to kneel beside the Queen at the altar on one
very special occasion[4]—these things can be otherwise explained, or explained
away. Probably his shrewdness told him that, in Harcourt's phrase, there was
'a sort of a something' behind the veil, but he was not the man to commit
himself like his contemporary, Rivarol: 'Tout Etat, si j'ose le dire, est un
vaisseau qui a ses ancres dans le ciel.' That was far too bold an addition for
an old habitué of Holland House to make to the time-honoured metaphor
of the ship of State.

The Queen's Diaries show, indeed, that all Melbourne's charms and graces
did not suffice to blind her to his shortcomings in the matter of church-going;
and one entry there betrays an anxiety in this respect almost as striking as
another recording her pleasure at his taking communion with her on the
Christmas Day before her marriage. 'It was a fine and solemn scene', she
wrote on that occasion, 'in this fine old Chapel. I felt for one, my dearest
Albert,—and wished he could be by my side,—also dear Lehzen,—but was
very glad Lord Melbourne was there, the one whom I look up to as a father,
and I was glad he took it (i.e. communion) with me.'[5]

---

[1] Queen's Diary, November 16th 1838.
[2] *Girlhood of Queen Victoria*, Vol. II, p. 1.   [3] Queen's Diary, March 10th 1839.
[4] ibid., Christmas Day, 1839.   [5] ibid., Christmas Day, 1839.

'Fatherly' and 'filial' were in fact the operative words defining the relationship between the two; and neither party we may feel sure, despite the critics, ever dreamed of, or desired any other. For two idyllic years, until Albert appeared, they were both able to gratify a sentiment which neither had previously experienced—a sentiment devoid of passion, but rich in all that age can ever offer to youth or youth give back to age. For once youth was very much disposed to learn, and age in a very good position to teach. The vision of the high-spirited girl, devout in her self-dedication, on that summer morning of 1837 in the Old Palace at Kensington seems to sway gently, like some image reflected on the surface of time's river, and to bend before the breeze of a mind mature, shrewd, kindly and humorous. The experience was such as Victoria had never had before, and Melbourne could never hope to see again; a thing beautiful in its brief season. He who had been captivated by the wayward grace of Caroline Ponsonby, only to find out the fickleness of her fascination; he who had sported a little incautiously, yet innocently enough, with Amaryllis in the shade or, as the novelist has it, with Diana at the Crossways, only to find himself cited, perhaps with a view to casting on him political obloquy on the very eve of the new reign, as the third party in a domestic difference; he it was who found now in the end that Fortune had not played him false, but had set him, just before the day closed in, the noblest of all his labours. At length a good woman, and a wise, had come into a life that had hitherto known only an affectionate indeed, but wanton mother, a little witch of a wife, and a son defective, if not deranged.

Melbourne rose to his romantic occasion, whilst the Queen had, as she later confided to him,[1] felt convinced that he deserved her confidence because he had sided with William IV in the dispute over her allowance as Princess, though he knew that William's reign was closing and that he had consequently every selfish reason for supporting the claim of the heir presumptive. Even the most friendly judges, however, were a little overpowered by the rapid growth and wide extent of the confidence she reposed in him. Her own words in her diary give its measure within two years of her accession. 'God knows', she wrote, '*no* Minister, no friend ever possessed the confidence of the Crown so entirely as this truly excellent Lord Melbourne possesses mine.'[2] Both Sovereign and subject found what they had long been severally and subconsciously seeking; and the two came to love one another dearly. One can see it in the mass of little confidences that the Queen made to the Minister and in a mass of little reassurances, and admonitions too, that the Minister gave to the Queen. She told him early how conscious she felt of saying 'stupid things in conversation',[3] how impossible she found it to conceal her feelings or deceive a man (it was Peel she had in mind at the

[1] Greville's *Memoirs*, March 25th 1838.
[2] Queen's Diary, March 22nd 1839.   [3] ibid., February 7th 1839.

moment,[1] but it remained as true fifty years later with Gladstone); how much she minded being so short in stature;[2] how keenly ashamed she felt of her ignorance about so many things.[3] And Melbourne encouraged her as fond parent would, telling her how well she did her work; how the greatest men—even Pitt himself, when he was going to make a speech—felt nervous, and that she might probably never get over her feeling of apprehension on public occasions, since shyness was the common accompaniment of high and right feelings, and tension the result of a peculiar temperament, 'sensitive and susceptible'.[4] 'He was so kind and paternal to me', she commented when setting down the incident in her journal. And when, some months later, on the occasion of his sixtieth birthday, they had a little talk and she said she hoped he would always tell her what he heard said of her, since she felt sure she made 'a great many mistakes', he replied that he didn't know that at all, but that she was said to be 'lofty, high, stern, and decided', yet that this was much better than her being thought familiar—far better than her being thought weak. He added with satisfaction that Lord Stanley had with emphasis denied to him that weakness was attributed to her, though this and indecision were the natural accompaniments of girlhood. She answered modestly that he must see for himself that she was often 'very childish'; which, however, he gallantly, and perhaps rightly declared he did not do in any respect.[5]

So the education went on and, of course, Melbourne, devoting himself to the achievement of the one thing needful—to the thing which would really matter long after any time he could hope to see—to the making of the Queen, came in for a share of criticism, for being so much at Windsor and so little at Whitehall, for making a courtier of himself, and so on and so forth. Brougham was especially offensive on the point, but then Brougham enjoyed being offensive, and had his own reasons for being out of love with Melbourne, who did not keep him in office and whose omission has been called 'the boldest and most perilous' act of Melbourne's life. One letter from the old rascal came under the young Queen's eye, and caused her especial annoyance. It was, as Melbourne observed, an attack on hereditary monarchy; and it led to Melbourne's quoting 'with tears in his eyes', Eldon's dictum, 'The King of England is always king; king in the helplessness of infancy, king in the decrepitude of age.'[6] The little scene, as Victoria records it, speaks out of the fullness of the heart—in that age when loyalty still had magic in it. Not one of her Prime Ministers, though not all of them with the same emotion, would have failed to echo Eldon's sentiment. Brougham was just a vulgarian, insensible to those finer feelings of which we can trace the effect in Wellington's

[1] Queen's Diary, June 12th 1839.   [2] ibid., February 23rd 1838.
[3] ibid., August 20th 1838.   [4] ibid., August 16th 1838.
[5] ibid., March 15th 1839.   [6] ibid., December 15th 1838.

abiding maxim that at all costs the King's Government must be carried on, no less than in Gladstone's pathetic distress at his failure to secure his Sovereign's regard. There is a world of difference between this and the worship of amorphous abstractions such as appeal to revolutionary minds, but seldom, if ever, submit to precise or lucid definition. Melbourne's loyalty came as naturally to him as the patriotism ringing in Scott's incredulous recoil from a dead soul which never to itself has said, 'This is my own, my native land!' It was for him a great sentiment that made good sense. Greville's description of him under its influence can in fact hardly be improved upon by the historian: 'He acted in all things an affectionate, conscientious and patriotic part, endeavouring to make Victoria happy as a woman and popular as a queen.'[1]

Wellington, though, as was said, recognizing Melbourne's exceptional talent for his work, thought the Prime Minister jested rather too much with the Queen; and Melbourne himself, when he heard of this opinion, turned it over in his mind reflectively and then characteristically reported it to Victoria. 'It's a very odd thing, Lord Melbourne said' (so the Queen sets down in 1840),[2] 'the Duke of Wellington said to Clarendon, "I like Lord Melbourne. I've a very good opinion of him, and I think he's the best Minister the Queen can have, and he has given her very good advice, I've no doubt; but I'm afraid he jokes too much with her and makes her treat things too lightly which are very serious." "Now there may be some truth in that," Lord Melbourne added. I said, Oh! no, but that perhaps, as [sic] I often scolded him, he jested a little about religion, which he denied. "It shows the shrewdness of the man"—forsooth, Wellington—Lord M. said.'

The passage deserves a moment's pause, for it illustrates incidentally one or two not uninteresting features in this strange conjunction of youth and age for the carrying-on of the Queen's Government. Victoria scolded her well-beloved Minister a lot; and he her a little. She scolded him, not only for non-attendance at church, but for snoring out of due season: 'I said to him', she records, 'he mustn't go to sleep before so many people, for that he generally snored! "That proclaims ... too much", he said, in which I quite agreed.'[3] 'Talked of my being so silent, which I thought wrong and uncivil, as I hated it in others, and that it annoyed me when he was silent. "I'm afraid I'm so sometimes", he said, "won't say a word." Yes, I said, that nothing could be got out of him sometimes. "And that you dislike?" he said. Yes, I said, it made me unhappy, which made him laugh.'[4]

Thus, daughter-like, she would go for him, and queen-like, come off best in these sofa-cushion battles. Yet he was no way dismayed by these defeats. 'He never scrupled,' remarked Greville[5] 'to tell the Queen what none other

[1] *Memoirs*, November 25th 1848.
[2] Queen's Diary, February 2nd 1840.
[3] ibid., August 25th 1839.
[4] ibid., July 11th 1839.
[5] *Memoirs*, November 29th 1848.

would have dared to say; and in the midst of that atmosphere of flattery and deceit which kings and queens are destined to breathe, and by which their minds are so often perverted, he never scrupled to declare boldly and frankly his real opinions, strange as they sometimes sounded and unpalatable as they often were, and to wage war with her prejudices and false impressions with regard to people or things, whenever he saw that she was led astray by them.' He told her, casually but yet not without purpose, that the Tories were not so bad as she thought them; and some day she was to find out he was right. ' "I don't dislike the Tories", said Lord M. (as she records), "I think they are very much like the others." We agreed J. Russell disliked being supported by them. "I don't care", said Lord M., "by whom I am supported; I consider them all as one; I don't care by whom I'm helped, as long as I *am* helped", he said laughingly.'[1] It was good advice, and for a long stretch of months— from May 1839 to August 1841—Melbourne went on instilling other such telling observations into her ear. He told her, as we know from her Diary, things which it would have been well for Britain if publicists and politicians long after his time had understood and remembered. He made her notice that Austria was 'the *only* country sincerely friendly to England'.[2] He told her that she should visit Scotland and Ireland, but that 'it would be an immense thing' if she visited the latter.[3] Victoria unfortunately found the native land of Scott so much more to her liking that she had little disposition left to listen to the moving and melancholy music of the Hibernian harp. The moors and glens about Balmoral were, though after Melbourne's time, to thrill her with their rugged beauty, the Highlanders, as exemplified in John Brown, were to fascinate her with their rough forthrightness of speech in a way that the lakes and mountains, the bogs and the blarney of the Emerald Isle had no power to do. And so this wise admonition of Melbourne went little observed; and three-fourths of a nation, still very capable in its wild way of devotion to the Throne as well as to the Altar, was finally lost to the United Kingdom.

It is to Melbourne's credit that he marked so clearly on the chart of the coming reign the course the Queen should take and the rock on which the imperial idea might founder. He had made some little impression in Dublin as Irish Secretary by his good sense and good temper. But the inability of Pitt to follow up the Union, as he had intended, by the enfranchisement of the Catholics had queered the Irish pitch for all his successors. The plan which the Crown had disrupted by its ill-judged opposition, only the Crown could re-adjust by judicious gestures; and it lay with Victoria to atone for the folly and prejudice of her grandfather. The opportunity, however, slipped by; and a British Parliament, left to wrangle as to what ought to be done, ended by

[1] Queen's Diary, September 23rd 1839.
[2] ibid., January 1st 1840.   [3] ibid., June 16th 1839.

leaving the great problem of the reign unsolved. It is proverbially easy to be wise after the event; but Melbourne *was* wise before it; and it is a fair conjecture that, if Victoria had brought herself to cross the Irish Sea year by year, or even rather less often, she would have won the hearts of her Irish subjects. As it was, Salisbury was still struggling with the Irish question at the close of the reign; and, as he saw, more than Eire hung upon the result. 'If Ireland goes', he once told his daughter, from whom I had the story, 'India will go fifty years later.' Ireland went; and India, to all intents and purposes, not so much as fifty years after.

So precise is the Queen's record of her conversations with her first Prime Minister, that we can watch the exchange of amenities and pleasantries with an assurance, probably unrivalled in history, of knowing exactly what passed. Again and again she takes photographic snapshots of her beloved foster-father in characteristic attitudes, and leaves impressions that might tempt a painter's hand. Take such an example as this:

'We were seated as usual, Lord Melbourne sitting near me. He said he was quite well, but never *felt* quite well . . . and that he never felt quite free from some little ailing, nor did anybody. When he was young, he said, he never felt unwell, and used "only to live for his amusement", and that, if he were to begin life again, he would do only that and not enter Politics at all. I said I thought people who only lived for their amusement bad, and that I was sure we should all be punished hereafter for living as we did without thinking at all of our future life. "That's not my case", Lord M. said; and we talked of living our life and beginning it again and, if it were possible, we agreed, we should try and correct ourselves.'[1]

Or glance at the following entry:

'Sept. 25. 1838 . . . Spoke of the impious and dreadful things the French now introduced upon the stage, whereas formerly, Lord M. said, they never killed anybody on the stage and accused us of doing so; and Lord M. said he believed that in none of Racine's or Corneille's Tragedies, anybody was ever killed on the stage. Spoke of these French Tragedies which Lord Melbourne admires very much; and, though he says that Corneille had the most power, I'm glad he agrees with me in admiring Racine the most, and he said "that for beauty of feeling and taste" he thought there was nothing like Racine; he mentioned *Phèdre* and *Athalie* as his finest; spoke of Voltaire's *Zaïre* and *Semiramis*; he said that Voltaire copied a good deal from the English: "like a great Master he infused the same spirit" without taking the same words. *Zaïre* was very like *Othello*

---

[1] Queen's Diary, January 30th 1840. I have ventured very slightly to vary the Queen's English in respect of grammar and punctuation.

and *Semiramis* very like *Hamlet,* he said; he admired the acting of these Tragedies, and Madame Duchenois's acting as very fine, though herself *so* ugly.'

Of Byron Melbourne seems to have said little more to Victoria than that he was 'treacherous beyond conception'.[1]

All such talk discovers in the Queen some intellectual interest not always outstanding in royalty! In her choice of books she might even in her day have been styled 'dashing', for she was criticized by her mother for reading a realistic novel. Lehzen had taught her something of values in literature and art; and Melbourne, like not a few of the Prime Ministers of those times, was well-equipped to lead conversation down the glades of the Graces to the temples of the Muses. Indeed, he carried his large learning lightly and knew how to toss into the talk items worth remembering and promptly recorded by the Queen in her Diary. To know him was, indeed, in its way a political and social education. Take from the Queen's Journal of the time such casual observations as these, and derive from them a general idea of the 'Regius Professor' at work, or, if we prefer, at play.

June 5th 1838:

'Lord Egremont used to say that Society was not near so amusing as it used to be; people were all so well educated that there were no more any originals to be seen.'

Again on June 10th 1838 we read:

'Lord Melbourne told us that Talleyrand said, "La *meilleure* éducation, c'est l'éducation publique Anglais; et c'est détestable!" . . . "*My opinion* is", said Lord Melbourne, "that it does not much signify *what* is taught, if what's taught is *well* taught." Then he added, "People too often confound learning and knowledge with talent and abilities; for that the two former could not make the two latter." '

On March 31st 1839 appears an old chestnut of a story that has seen many fights since:

'Lord M. said that Carlini, a famous Clown at Paris, went to a Physician and complained of being so ill, upon which the Physician said, "Go and see Carlini". 'This is the original story, which, the Queen adds, 'I have heard told of Garrick and Liston'.

Or take a more memorable piece of conversation upon which a prudent commentator will make no comment:

'Feb. 10th 1839. Lord Melbourne made us laugh very much with his opinions about Schools and Public Education; the latter he don't like, and,

[1] Esher, *Girlhood of Queen Victoria,* Vol. I, p. 304.

when I asked him if he did, he said, "I daren't say in these times that I'm against it—but I *am* against it" . . . He thinks it much better . . . left to Voluntary Education and that people of any great genius were educated by circumstances, and that the education of circumstances was the best; what *is* taught in Schools might be improved, he thinks. "All this was beginning when I was a boy", he said, "when I was with a clergyman at Hatfield, all those Sunday Schools were beginning . . ." Then he talked of those Normal Schools, where they are going to educate Schoolmasters, and he said, "You'll see they'll breed the most conceited set of blockheads ever known, and that'll be of no use whatever; now mind me if they don't", he added, turning to me.'

How much in Melbourne's table-talk is provocative paradox and how much genial scepticism, is of course disputable. An age like our own, obsessed by wishful thinking, which has largely lost any subtle sense of the ridiculous and almost all hard grasp of reality; which has attempted to swing over in the wake of an exhausting war from a system of individual freedom to one of state-controls, cannot be expected to sense the bouquet in Melbourne's well-matured, shrewdly sparkling wine of life. He scented from afar the ambiguity of 'progress', and suspected the shallow lamentation of the fortunate. When the Queen asked him if he liked rail-roads in general, he replied, she tells us, 'I don't care about them', in a way which made her laugh; and that might well be, for he had been caught in a railway speculation. Every Socialist, however, who prefers that such misadventures should be left to the tax-payer must at least approve his sharp retort to Lady Portman, who complained that the county of Dorset was so poor: 'That's because you don't give enough wages.'[1]

This humane commonsense needs always to be kept in mind when Melbourne's more familiar comment on Dickens's *Oliver Twist* is instanced. England was then within two or three years of another of those periodical accesses of violent philanthropy that overtake from time to time a nation on the whole kind and generous, but confused in respect of any lucid definition of justice and consequently apt to raise by sentiment as many problems as it settles by reason. Melbourne's comments on *Oliver Twist* must be read with a lively recollection that the England of his youth had seen the so-called 'Speenhamland Act of Parliament' 'passed' by the Berkshire justices in 1795, and the abolition in the same year of the workhouse test. Indeed, Greville was in 1839 to write: 'We are just now overrun with philanthropy, and God knows where it will stop or whither it will lead us.'[2]

'It's all among workhouses and coffin makers, and pickpockets,' Melbourne

[1] Esher, *Girlhood of Queen Victoria*, Vol. II, p. 302.
[2] Greville's *Memoirs*, March 31st 1844.

told the Queen in discussing Dickens's memorable novel which it is right to remember that at the moment he had only half read, 'I don't like that low debasing style; it's all slang; it's just like *The Beggar's Opera*; I shouldn't think it would tend to raise morals; I don't like that low debasing view of mankind.'

'We defended Oliver', the Queen remarks, 'very much, but in vain.'

'I don't like those things'; Melbourne repeated. 'I wish to avoid them; I don't like them in *reality*, and therefore I don't wish to see them represented.' Everything one reads, he told the Queen, 'should be pure and elevating. Schiller and Goethe would have been shocked at such things'. Lehzen challenged this opinion, only to elicit from him the observation, 'She don't know her own literature; Goethe said one ought never to see anything disagreeable . . . It's a bad taste which will pass away like any other, but depend upon it, while it lasts, it's a bad, depraved, vicious taste. Now just read *Jonathan Wild*', he said to Lord Torrington, 'and *Amelia*, and see if it isn't just the same thing.'[1] Neo-pagan sentiments, perhaps, but anyhow matter for a diverting debate between the new film-addicts and the old Regency buck. We miss, however, the flavour of Melbourne's dissertation, if we fail to notice that Victoria adds, 'Lord Melbourne kept us in fits of laughter by all this'. To the not, perhaps, wholly disinterested champions of the underdog, with their peculiar ululations at the indifference of the 'wicked rich' to the always, though only by hypothesis, virtuous poor, Melbourne's attitude towards Dickens's sob-stuff must seem intolerably callous. Yet Victoria's account of the scene shows clearly enough, at any rate to those who understand the Victorians, that the audience set the value Melbourne intended on what he was saying. The story of his life indicates that he was neither lacking in pity nor in courtesy, if not quite in the manner of those 'friends of humanity' who, as soon as their fine sentiments come into contact with brute facts, find themselves confronted with the alternative of confessing themselves dupes or carrying on as liars. Dickens did well, no doubt, to remind us that in this 'loud, stunning tide of human care and crime' there are to be found little Olivers, little Nells, little Emilys, and little Dorrits; but he who peoples his picture of the world with them will suffer disillusionments as sharp as he who looks into Dickens's private life for any exemplification of his professional morals. Melbourne was a better man than Dickens. Though his talk outside the royal circle could not be relied upon to satisfy the demands of exact propriety, at least as the Victorian Age was to understand it, he was by general consent a great gentleman and was so regarded by the greatest gentleman of them all, his foremost opponent in the House of Lords and his firmest supporter at Court.[2]

[1] Queen's Diary, April 7 1839.
[2] Wellington, who supported Melbourne in the Norton affair. See footnote, p. 96.

'Lord Melbourne kept us in fits of laughter by all this.' So, as we have seen, Victoria set down. And the lively lesson was not lost. The Queen was never betrayed into becoming a bustling, moral prig, nor into chattering the ill-considered nonsense of Mr. Brooke in *Middlemarch*, a type much in request among reformers at this date. She never made herself cheap; if anything she let the incurable ache from the loss of her husband become too ready an excuse for almost complete retirement; and it needed all the long-stored strength of her people's loyalty to sweep her back into view on the tide of her jubilees and bring her a publicity and a renown such as no dealer in those commodities could ever have obtained for her. Yet still her quiet life had all the while been inspiring thoughts, themselves inspired, from Tennyson's moving dedication to the Idylls to Kipling's rough, not too acceptable reference to 'the widder at Windsor'. Little by little and line by line she set her impress upon her people's imagination, focused their thought, framed their standards, satisfied their sentiment, until for those who can recall her, she became imaginatively and symbolically the everlasting occupant of her imperial throne. Child, and grandchild, and great-grandchild have sat there, and by sovereign right of inheritance; yet still always it is She, who seems to give it an ampler majesty than her successors with the utmost industry have contrived to confer upon it. Character, not circumstance, constituted the supreme element in her manifestation of sovereignty, so that what she was mattered much more than what she did. And Melbourne, in his quaint debonair way, had early argued her out of a diffidence that for all her remarkable assurance at exigent moments was undoubtedly there, and had put her in the way of making her life into a sort of music not unbecoming one to whom music, in its narrower meaning, meant so much.

A trivial incident belonging to a much later date, now very possibly unknown to any person living but myself, may make the subtle operation of this particular virtue in Victoria clearer. She had been due to attend an afternoon service in Salisbury Cathedral, but by some accident was late. The canon-in-residence, a son of Lord Aberdeen, with whom the decision rested, decided not to wait for her and ordered evensong to begin. She arrived in due course and took her place. But later she sent for Canon Gordon and thanked him for his conduct. That was Victoria; and therein her quality appeared. The first Elizabeth, perhaps, without actually threatening to unfrock the ecclesiastical authority responsible (as she is supposed to have done with the prelate in the familiar story) would have reproved the presumptuous canon; and Anne, perhaps, would have pouted and been piqued. But to Victoria it seemed entirely as it should be that the common service of God should go forward regardless of royal personages and worldly considerations.

For the rest, the Queen showed little taste for controversies of faith; and she might be set down in her own way as something of a throned 'quietist'. And, if this description be admitted, some slight influence upon her mind of Melbourne's religious detachment may be suspected. For he, who took so much care in the appointment of bishops, and devoted so much time to the study of the Primitive Fathers of the Church, described himself, under the Queen's anxious interrogation, as a disciple of Fénelon and Mme Guyon.[1] Of course, as the contest shows, he was hard put to it at the moment to find a reason for not attending church three times of a Sunday, as Victoria and her attendants mischievously insinuated that he should do; and it was convenient enough to counter their attack by claiming that he had grown so perfect as to be exempt from the obligation of external observances. All the same, Victoria's recording of the conversation shows that it made a little mark upon her mind and was not altogether out of keeping with the religious elasticity required in a Protestant, to whom the faith professed at Rome alone represented the unpardonable sin.

In matters of religious thought the coming period was to possess something of the quality of spring-time. A north-westerly wind, sweeping before it storm-clouds of honest doubt, races across the reign; but even the storm-clouds are lit with lambent beauty by an undimmed belief in what revealed religion had argued to be admirable. George Eliot's novels hold their high place there, because, though confidence in the Christian dogma is wanting, the values are everywhere those of Christian ethic. It says something for Melbourne's fine intelligence that, sceptical though he was about so many things, both high and low, it amused him to profess himself a pupil of the *cygne de Cambrai*, the first eminent Frenchman, as Acton maintained, to see the urgency of the social problem. For Fénelon went about his work with a quiet mind, rather than a bustling mentality such as has since come so much into vogue as the test of benevolence and has thrown the unostentatious activity of the Good Samaritan—finding occasion only 'as he journeyed', only as the opportunity came to him—so much into the shade.

Melbourne's own view of the much vexed question of the proper attitude of the state to the individual is tersely summarized in some words which he used to the Queen and of which her record runs, 'All government has to do is to prevent and punish crime'.[2] 'Why do you bother the poor? Leave them alone', was a remark of Scott's that he quoted for Victoria's consideration.[3] And it was worth quoting. Out of the fullness of a heart less wise and generous than its author's, such a sentiment might have been distrusted as a piece of selfish evasion inconsistent with charity. But in Scott it was the honest outcome of a hatred of the sounding brass and the tinkling cymbals which differ-

[1] Queen's Diary, September 14th 1839.
   See the Queen's Diary, p. 148, in Esher's *Girlhood of Queen Victoria*, Vol. II.
[3] Queen's Diary, February 20th 1839.

entiated the new revolutionary method of dealing wholesale with bodily
suffering from the old comprehensive treatment of the whole man, body, soul
and spirit—a much more difficult matter. Few people perhaps have any longer
the fine perception to distinguish the over-confident and not always politically
pure activities of the reformer from the delicate grace of compassion; yet it is
here, in the sense and spirit of that time and formed the definite division for
those capable of detecting it between a pagan society and a Christian civilization.

The zeal of the crusader was as little congenial to Melbourne as to Salisbury;
for both were penetrating enough to perceive that the fervour with which
philanthropic causes are recommended to the multitude is of the most
transient value unless productive of such a change of heart as to bring mankind to contemplate the things of others, not enviously or angrily, but as
objects of a stewardship resting on a divine institution and working into a
divine design. This change of heart, with its implicit mysticism, has the
effect of bringing patience into the place in political philosophy that Pitt had
given to it as the most valuable quality a statesman could possess, and so of
illuminating with larger meaning the promise addressed to the patient that
they should inherit the earth. The forceful, ever since the Christian heritage
came into sight, have seen its desirability and sought to take it by force, but
the open sesame of the Kingdom of God does not yield entry to violence,
and reveals it as essentially the reward of the gentle, the long-suffering, the
slow to take offence. Such persons do not for the most part make either
crusaders or revolutionists, yet they have found out the secret of human
regeneration, which old men in a hurry to achieve, like young men in a
fever to reform, so commonly miss.

Enough, however, of a problem which like the subject of it will be always
with us to a greater or less degree, whether we turn ourselves inwards or
outwards. The Liberals thought they could solve it with liberty; the
Socialists think they can solve it with equality. But in truth it is only soluble
by such a regeneration in men as only Christianity has the power to effect,
but to which Christians to-day appear able less than ever to render persuasive.

It remains to consider Melbourne in his penultimate phase—after Albert
came on the scene and before he himself resigned office.

'I observed', the Queen records of a conversation of hers with Melbourne
on April 18th 1839, 'that marrying a subject was making yourself so much
their equal, and brought you so in contact with the whole family. Lord M.
quite agreed in this and said, "I don't think it would be liked; there would be
such jealousy". I said, Why need I marry at all for three or four years? did
he see the necessity? I said I dreaded the thought of marrying; that I was so
accustomed to have my own way, that I thought it was 10 to 1 that I shouldn't
agree with anybody . . .' So that was how marriage looked to Victoria

nearly two years after she came to the throne. Then there came a change. On October 13th 1839, however, she gave Melbourne the hint of a change by telling him her views about marriage had a good deal changed, and why. She set down in her diary three days before that Albert was 'beautiful' and that she had beheld him with emotion. 'Certainly a very fine young man, very good-looking!' was Melbourne's comment on her information; but he added that she would need another week to consider.[1] Yet by the very next day her mind was quite made up; and, the day after, she sent for Albert and made her sentiments known to him and said that it would make her 'too happy' if he would consent.[2] They then embraced. He was, she set down in her diary, 'so kind, so affectionate' and, when she said she was quite unworthy of him, his manifest happiness 'das Leben mit dir zu zubringen' (as he put it) made her feel the moment the happiest and brightest in her life.[3] Two hours later she was telling Melbourne she had 'got well through' her business with Albert. 'Oh, you have!' said Lord M. with a detachment worthy of Wellington when Uxbridge announced at Waterloo that he had lost a leg. Other conversations followed, Melbourne as usual, and even more than usual, boldly dispassionate.

'Talked of Albert's indifference about Ladies', records the royal diary,[4] 'and Lord M. said "A little dangerous, all that is—it's very well, if that holds, but it doesn't always," Lord M. said. I said this was very wrong of him and scolded him for it. "It's what I said at Windsor; I think I know human nature pretty well." I said, "not the best of human nature." "I've known the best of my time," he said, "and I've read of the best." '

Still, as it turned out, Albert's exceptional rectitude was to be proof against these prudent counsels; so that Victoria had in the event the best of the argument. She had looked for a Galahad and had been lucky enough to find one to fit into her idyll of a Queen. The choice did her judgment credit, though it was only long after Albert's death that her people fully grasped how wise King Leopold had been in promoting it and how well Victoria had done for herself as a woman and for her country as a queen. Some five weeks later she announced her engagement formally to the Council. When she told the Duchess of Gloucester this was impending, the Duchess inquired if it were not 'a nervous thing' to have to do, and received the answer, 'Yes; but I did a much more nervous thing a little while ago—I proposed to Prince Albert'.[5]

It was a good thing for Melbourne's administration that the excitement of the marriage came when it did, so as to efface the apathy succeeding the accession. 'The great characteristic of the present time', Greville had been

---

[1] Queen's Diary, October 13th 1840.   [2] ibid., October 14th 1840.
[3] ibid., October 15th 1840.   [4] January 19th 1840.
[5] Greville's *Memoirs*, November 15th 1839.

writing in March of 1839, 'is indifference: nobody appears to care for any-thing; nobody cares for the Queen; her popularity has sunk to zero, and loyalty is a dead letter; nobody cares for the Government, or for any man or set of men.'[1] It was the expression of a mood, partly national and partly personal; but then mankind, considered as a whole, is, after all, for the most part little better than a succession of moods and a bundle of nerves. Melbourne to some extent was the victim of the common boredom and desire for change which lies in wait even for the best of administrations; and Greville, whose concluding estimate of the Prime Minister is so flattering, betrays again and again by casual, uncomplimentary observations his own susceptibility to the comments of the clubs and the country-houses. For instance: 'Melbourne seems to hold office for no other purpose but that of dining at Buckingham Palace, and he is content to rub on from day to day, letting all things take their chance.'[2] When in May, 1839, the Prime Minister at length resigned over the affairs of Jamaica, the Whigs developed as perhaps never before or after in their history, a strong sense of the romance of royalty. They stood by the Queen in the much-debated 'Bedchamber business' and supported her assertion of the royal prerogative to have the choosing of the women about her. In her old age Victoria admitted she had not, perhaps, been very wise about the Bedchamber question; but Melbourne had not her excuse of political immaturity. It did not really matter so very much what ladies the Queen had about her—and all the less that, as indeed she told Peel at the time, she never talked politics to them,[3] being herself totally blind to the existence of what are now called 'women's rights', her own of course excepted. The girl's attitude, according to her own account, had been that she wished to retain about her all her women and such men as had no seat in Parliament. Peel had consented in respect of the men and was ready to consent in respect of most of the women; but Lady Normanby, the wife of an ex-Minister described by Peel as his 'most formidable enemy', appeared in his eyes to constitute an insuperable obstacle to any such general rule, and so, as a matter of general principle, he had urged that the choice of the Mistress of the Robes and of the Ladies of the Bedchamber should rest with the administration. To Victoria's argument that this had never been insisted upon before, he replied that she was a queen-regnant, not queen-consort, and that this fact made the whole difference. Wellington was called in to compose the breeze between Sovereign and Minister, but without success. The Queen wrote Melbourne a memorandum explaining her predicament; and he, after consulting his Cabinet, which his resignation had, however, plainly dissolved, advised her to inform Peel that she could not consent to adopt a course contrary to usage and repugnant to her feelings.

[1] Greville's *Memoirs*, March 12th 1839.   [2] ibid., March 25th 1839.
[3] Queen's Diary, May 9th 1839.

Advice thus tendered by the Opposition could not possibly be reconciled with correct constitutional procedure; but so, however, it was that the Whigs shaped their loyalty at the time.

The incident was no more than a storm in a tea-cup; and, had Melbourne turned for advice to his classical studies, he might have quelled it as successfully as did Neptune the winds which Æolus at Juno's behest let loose upon the fleet of Æneas. The *Sortes Virgilianae*, however, do not seem at the moment to have tempted his curiosity or tempered his paternal impulse to rush to the rescue of the Queen in a distress, occasioned perhaps quite as much by the thought of losing him as of losing her ladies. His colleagues, with, be it noted, men as trusted as Grey and Spencer backing them, stood, as was said, behind him; and Peel relinquished the rudder that he had stretched out his hand to take.

The caprice of the Queen, the loyalty of the Whigs, the suppleness of an unwritten constitution, thus, fortunately for the nation, prolonged for nearly two years more the power of the man best qualified for the principal work in hand. Victoria still needed Melbourne as a sympathetic counsellor; and so much the more that her marriage was not yet decided upon. And Britain needed a monarch a little more advanced in wisdom and stature than even Victoria's surprising intelligence and strength of purpose had yet shown her to be. The time for change was, however, coming; and with it there came the man. Victoria was astonishingly lucky in that, or perhaps rather astonishingly sensible in seizing her luck at the moment of opportunity. Albert's *amour-propre* would not have suffered him to wait for ever.

It has been supposed that Melbourne raised no opposition to this marriage of first-cousins, because he knew that in fact they were not so. Mr. Bolitho appears, however, to have dispelled the doubt about Albert's legitimacy so far as this is humanly possible.[1] Duchess Louise of Saxe-Coburg-Gotha, 'clever and fascinating'—to borrow Victoria's adjectives—did not despair of her worthless husband or begin to go wrong herself until at least a year after Albert was born; and, if Albert's tremendous conscience and all-dominating sense of duty seem not particularly easy to account for on hereditary lines, education, as personified in Stockmar, must be given the greater credit. Stockmar moralized mercilessly, and Albert was able to absorb political moralities quite as methodically as a Wesleyan absorbs evangelical truth and as thoroughly as a boa-constrictor its sustenance. All the same we have to recollect that Stockmar was extremely intelligent in the German style. 'I think he is about the cleverest man I ever knew in my life',[2] Melbourne told the Queen. For all that, Albert had to await a change of Ministry before he could obtain any such place in the Queen's counsels as

---

[1] Bolitho, *The Reign of Queen Victoria*, p. 25.
[2] Queen's Diary, January 14th 1840.

he already possessed in her affections. Besides, as Mr. Roger Fulford in his biography of the Prince Consort[1] very justly remarks, the Queen 'would have acted with great recklessness if she had immediately given the Prince a dominating influence in politics and in the Household. The English Constitution was changing course; and Albert was to play a great part in the change; but the direction was not yet clear nor was the pilot ready. For Melbourne, as for Wellington, it was the Sovereign's Government that, first and foremost, had to be carried on. William IV had virtually turned Melbourne out of office; and Victoria had virtually kept him in. Epigrammatically it would be true to say that people still reckoned in terms of 'the King's Government' quite as much as in those of 'the Prime Minister's administration'. The Sovereign had not as yet been reduced, so far as political activities were concerned, to the condition of a cipher whose assent on all ordinary occasions might be assumed, nor to that of a *deus ex machina* to be invoked, for whatever his or her intervention might be worth, at extraordinary parliamentary or ministerial crises. Sovereignty, that is, had not yet passed altogether to the People. The social influence of the Monarch was still very great; and his constitutional power still very obscurely and imperfectly defined. Development, however, was in process; and the Queen's Consort was to affect that development considerably. Not, however, at once! Both the Queen and Melbourne were prudently jealous; and, when, in this connection, any urgent issue arose, recourse was had for precedents to the life of Prince George of Denmark, whom Victoria described as 'Queen Anne's very stupid and insignificant husband', whom Melbourne damned as 'infernal', and whom Macaulay wrote off as 'impenetrably stupid'. For all that, the Prime Minister was forming a very favourable opinion of Albert's capacities; so much so indeed that, when in 1841 he finally took leave of the Queen, he told her that, since the Prince with all his accomplishments remained at her side, to leave her was easier than it would have been two years earlier.

The four fateful years of Melbourne's administration, as we look back at them, seem to show very little of great moment, even though beneath the soil so much lay waiting to spring up. Chartism, indeed, showed its head simultaneously with the Queen's accession—Chartism alive with new ideas, some of them (the ballot, payment of Members of Parliament, manhood suffrage) presently to be slowly adopted; others (annual parliaments, equal electoral districts), too symmetrical even for revolutionary reformers, 'date' through neglect. Melbourne, who had established an acquaintance with Francis Place, much as Balfour long afterwards was to form one with the Sidney Webbs, may be presumed to have viewed the movement of the Chartists with something of the same quizzical scepticism as his remote

[1] p. 56.

successor in the premiership that of the Fabians. Another movement destined to be of much deeper interest to thoughtful men throughout Victoria's reign hardly seems to have stirred his interest. It was in 1833 that Keble set Oxford thinking by that famous assize sermon on 'National Apostasy' which was to have consequences the preacher never contemplated. As Herbert Paul cleverly observes in the *History of Modern England*,[1] 'There are men for whom the Church of England is too large, and others for whom it is too small. It was exactly the right size for Mr. Keble.' Before Melbourne's administration ended, the movement that Keble was credited with starting was making itself felt in the stronger articulation of 'Tracts for the Times'; and in the year in which Melbourne fell appeared Tract 90, that famous failure, as very many of both parties judged and in the end its author himself, to bring the Thirty-Nine Articles of the Church of England into line with Catholic belief and practice. This body of thought would go forward, impelled by the theory of historic evolution, which physical science was to do so much to recommend; and ultimately raised by the power and pathos of Newman's *Apologia* to an ethereal beauty which long held the imagination of the Victorians, and has but very slowly grown pale with reminiscence. Almost simultaneously the Anti-Corn-Law League, in a sphere as material as that of the Oxford Movement was spiritual, leaped in 1838 into prominence under the auspices of Cobden and Bright at Manchester; whilst the Irish Question was electrified by the Chief Secretary's winged observation in the same year that property has duties as well as rights. Melbourne had done well by Ireland, at least in the matter of good intentions—better, as some have thought, than he did by England.[2] Further west, Durham's famous report, drawn up by Charles Buller, began to weld the French and English Canadas into a workable unity, which, with the subsequent unification of India under the Crown, was to constitute one of the great imperial advances of the coming time. 'The measures of the Melbourne Government', wrote Disraeli,[3] 'were generally moderate, well-matured and statesmanlike schemes.'

The political promise of the period was thus rich beyond the ordinary. But for Melbourne the end was come. When an uninteresting adverse vote in August 1841 on the duties to be paid respectively on foreign and colonial sugar finally terminated his administration, there remained for him little probability of any return to power. He had done the work he was peculiarly qualified to do. He had brought the young Queen safe through the critical years of girlhood and delivered her into the able hands of Albert and of Stockmar. Of the two outstanding mistakes of his administration which Greville signalizes; one—his attitude on the Bedchamber question—served

---

[1] Vol. III, p. 178.
[2] Hammond, *Gladstone and the Irish Nation*, p. 29.
[3] *Life of Lord George Bentinck*, p. 16.

his country well, for it lengthened by two years or more the life of his administration. The other mistake that is pilloried by the diarist—the episode associated with the name of Lady Flora Hastings—deserves perhaps graver strictures and less attention than it receives.[1] For once Melbourne had been too easy-going. He ought to have kept the affair quiet; and he could the more easily have done so, since there was nothing whatever in it. As it was, the young Queen's Court was besmirched with an ugly scandal and Lady Flora was made notorious. In the record of that exemplary reign the incident lives on, is repeated by chronicler after chronicler, and has to be reckoned with still by the historian who wishes to escape a charge of shutting his eyes to a smudge that disfigures a court morally almost impeccable.

Still, when this has been dealt with, Melbourne can be said to have imparted to the youthful personality and early circle of Victoria a charm that no man then living had it in his power to confer upon them. Not Wellington, for all his greatness! Not Peel, for all his political dexterity! Not Palmerston, though he had Emily Lamb, Melbourne's sister, one of the most brilliant of hostesses, to wife; not Russell, though he was as clever as his family could make him. No, nor anyone else! And when Melbourne's service came to be assessed, memory could speak of him rather quaintly and happily as 'The Regius Professor', for, as has been said, 'no such lot as his had ever fallen to any statesman in the whole course of our history'.[2] His genial philosophy of politics afforded what dry-as-dust professors must have striven in vain to convey, and was neither out of place in the making of a queen nor ill-timed in the case of a woman who before she came to the throne could enter in her diary: 'Everything that is pleasant, alas! passes so quickly in this wide world of troubles . . .'[3]

The old Minister, years ahead of his young Sovereign, and moving fast, even at the date of the Queen's accession, towards sixty, knew as no child of eighteen could know that this melancholy meditation could become a plaguy platitude. Even in 1837 he was senescent; and the Queen had soon become alive to it. She noticed, as she records,[4] how he talked to himself loud enough to make her turn round, though not loud enough to be understood. She noticed, as we have seen, how he dropped off to sleep in company; tired, perhaps, as some of us become, of carrying on familiar conversations of

---

[1] Lady Flora Hastings, an unmarried lady-in-waiting to the Duchess of Kent, was dismissed because she was suspected of being pregnant. The suspicion was afterwards found to be incorrect, the unfortunate lady's appearance being caused by a malignant disease, but the case engendered a lot of public indignation, loudly ventilated in the Tory Press, and the Queen came in for a good deal of censure. A very full account of the affair can be found in Miss Dormer Creston's *The Youthful Queen Victoria*.

[2] Dunckley, *Lord Melbourne*, p. 205.

[3] Queen's Diary, August 8th 1836.

[4] ibid., December 27th 1837.

which the purport grows less and less apparent as the shadows of life grow longer and longer. She marked his pronunciation of 'Rōōm' and 'Gōōld', the quaint habit of a day that was gone, and no doubt as comic as 'gurl' and 'cheerio' appear to antiquated persons who recall the one as a social solecism, and view the other as an invitation to a waltz of wishful thinking. There had, of course, been a young Melbourne, whose portrait has been traced in our time by defter and more delicate hands than my own;[1] the young Melbourne of whom we caught a glimpse in the rococo framework of the Regency and who gambled on the charm of Caroline Ponsonby and lost his bet, but who was nevertheless worked, together with his wife, into a bowdlerized romance at the close of the last century by Mrs. Humphry Ward in *The Marriage of William Ashe*. Fiction, too, has provided a middle-aged Melbourne— Disraeli's Monteagle in *Venetia*, where, upon his wife's remarking that it was odd that both he and Herbert (a personification of Shelley as he might have appeared in later age) should have had bishops for their tutors, is made to say, 'It is very strange, and it only shows that it is quite useless in this world to lay plans or reckon on anything . . .' As for the old Melbourne of these pages, he is familiar to us all as Lord Dannisborough in *Diana of the Crossways*. But this drawing has no more life in it than Diana's laboured epigrams have sparkle; and Diana herself observes that she has a fatal attraction for antiques.

In face, however, of these portraits by eminent hands, Melbourne, if he paces the Elysian fields, may rightly reflect that he is held as much in memory by the elect of our terrestrial sphere as any Prime Minister can reasonably expect to be. He had proved himself beyond question to be an interesting man, and in the early education of Victoria he had proved to be an effective one where a more definitely purposeful man might well have failed. So obviously indicated was he for the Queen's counsellor even before her accession that Wellington is reported to have said that, if he were driven out of office by the Norton affair, he himself—Wellington—would join no other administration.[2] Greville not altogether aptly compares him to Sallustius Crispus, of whom Tacitus observed that 'in choosing to emulate Maecenas, without holding senatorial rank, he outstripped in influence many who had won a triumph or the Consulate; and while by his elegance and refinement he was separated from the past, he more nearly approached the present by the lavish scale of his appointments. For all that, beneath a

---

[1] Lord Melbourne, when Home Secretary, gave a police magistracy to the Hon. George Norton, who had married Caroline, one of the three beautiful daughters of Tom Sheridan, the son of the dramatist. The appointment caused some scandal, and Norton, who was both impecunious and violent, accused Melbourne of a guilty association with his wife. He brought an action against Melbourne, at the instigation of some of the less reputable members of the Opposition, but the suit was dismissed.

[2] Torrens's *Memoirs*, Vol. II, p. 191.

VISCOUNT MELBOURNE
From the portrait by J. Partridge

semblance of apathy and indifference he possessed a vigour of soul equal to the greatest enterprises.' Sydney Smith, who must have met him time and again at Holland House, had earlier drawn an engaging portrait in the course of his second letter to Archdeacon Singleton: 'Viscount Melbourne declared himself quite satisfied with the Church as it is; but if the public had any desire to alter it, they might do as they pleased. He might have said the same thing of the Monarchy, or of any other of our institutions; and there is in the declaration a permissiveness and good humour which in public men has seldom been exceeded . . . If the truth must be told, our Viscount is somewhat of an impostor. Everything about him seems to betoken careless desolation: anyone would suppose from his manner that he was playing at chuck-farthing with human happiness; that he was always on the heel of pastime; that he would giggle away the Great Charter, and decide by the method of teetotum whether my Lords, the Bishops, should or should not retain their seats in the House of Lords. All this is the mere vanity of surprising, and making us believe he can play with kingdoms as other men can with ninepins. Instead of this lofty nebulo, this miracle of moral and intellectual felicities, he is nothing more than a sensible, honest man who means to do his duty to his Sovereign and to the country: instead of being the ignorant man he pretends to be. Before he meets the deputation of tallow-chandlers in the morning, he sits up half the night with Thomas Young talking about melting and skimming, and then, though he has acquired knowledge enough to work off a whole vat of prime Leicester tallow, he pretends next morning not to know the difference between a dip and a mould . . . Neither can I allow to this Minister (however he may be irritated by the denial) the extreme merit of indifference to the consequences of his measures. I believe him to be conscientiously alive to the good or evil that he is doing, and that his caution has more than once arrested the gigantic projects of the Lycurgus of the Lower House. I am sorry to hurt any man's feelings, and to brush away the magnificent fabric of levity and gaiety he has reared; but I accuse our Minister of honesty and diligence; I deny that he is careless or rash: he is nothing more than a man of good understanding, and good principle, disguised in the eternal and somewhat wearisome affectation of a political roué.'

There, then, is Melbourne, as he lives in fiction and as he looked to the eyes of contemporary observers. He had both good fortune, and bad; but he was certainly fortunate in the hour of his death, which occurred in 1848, the famous year of revolution, when all the thrones of Europe quaked except those of Russia, securely despotic, and of England, securely free. He has left us two proverbial pieces of political wisdom—the Conservative's advice to all sensible men: 'Why can't you let it alone?' and the cynic's advice to all doubting Cabinets: 'It doesn't much matter what we say, provided we all say the same thing.'

E

Such statecraft, however, though often sagacious, lays itself open to satire; and Praed's lines are worth recalling as a counterpoise in criticism:

> To promise, pause, prepare, postpone,
> And end by letting things alone;
> In short, to earn the people's pay
> By doing nothing every day.[1]

[1] Quoted from F. W. Hirst's *Gladstone as Financier and Economist*, p. 37.

SIR ROBERT PEEL

Second Baronet
born 1788 died 1850

Entered Parliament (Cashel, Tipperary) 1809

Under-Secretary for War (Duke of Portland's administration) 1810

Chief Secretary for Ireland (Lord Liverpool's administration) 1812 Resigned 1818

Home Secretary (Lord Liverpool's administration) 1822. Resigned 1827

Home Secretary and Leader of the House of Commons (Duke of Wellington's administration) 1828-30

Prime Minister and Chancellor of the Exchequer December 1834 to April 1835

Prime Minister September 1841 to July 1846

CHAPTER V

SIR ROBERT PEEL

MELBOURNE fades from view—witty, mellow, insouciant, *débonnaire*—leaving upon the political tapestry of the time some faint suggestion of that elegant enchantment which meets us in its full fascination in the paintings of Watteau, or rises to haunt us in the gardens of Versailles or the Trianons. All that requires to be recalled before we try to mark the exact place that Peel occupies in the succession of Victorian Prime Ministers. He is *par excellence* the founder of conservatism, the conservator of certain values in the national tradition that come from a more solid appreciation of what the so-called *ancien régime* had to give than is afforded by the contemplation of the trimmings of pageantry and the graces and elegancies which had so long been associated with them. The calico-printers who laid the fortune of the Peels had no more inheritance of finesse than the corn-dealers who built up the prosperity of the Gladstones. Yet these two middle-class stocks were to produce scions who saw, and sought to preserve, certain features in the old society which a man despises at his peril and for which the weight of numbers offers no substitute.

'C'est toujours le beau monde qui gouverne le monde', says the adage. The Tories, and still more the Whigs, might have done justice to what of truth may be discerned in that tribute to modes and manners. But the collapse of the *ancien régime* in France had laid open to sight the half-forgotten hills of Christendom; and, as the Paris of Louis Quatorze fell, figuratively speaking, into fragments, the splendid ruin of Latin civilization burst the clearer into view, solemn and awe-inspiring in the distance. Melbourne's eyes, curious student though he was of the past and casual sceptic of change, were too dim to make much of a scene that signified a great deal to a man like Chateaubriand. It was a panorama, however, that did not need the imagination of a poet and a Breton to be arresting. Peel and Gladstone were men of business whose vision had been clarified by the Humanities; and they saw that the old order had comprised in its compass things that Democracy in America would not easily foster and that Democracy in France would not easily sustain—things that had been deep-set in the structure of the past, but that were neither frivolous nor vain. 'The truth I take to be', wrote Gladstone in a letter concerned with the value of the Humanities, 'that the modern European civilization from the middle age downwards is the compound of two great factors, the Christian religion for the Spirit of Man, and the Greek, and in a secondary degree the Roman, discipline for his mind and intellect. St. Paul is the apostle of the Gentiles and is in his own person a symbol of this great wedding—the place, for example, of Aristotle and Plato in Christian education is not arbitrary, nor in principle mutable'.[1]

It might have been better expressed—this vision of the distant hills of Sion across the Isles of Greece—but Gladstone, though he spent many hours with Homer and Dante, was no sweet singer of Israel nor any deft epitomizer of epic or other thought. He saw, like the intelligent man of business that he was, that the goods he was inspecting were of first-rate value; and he did not want to let them escape him. But we shall come back to this. We have to do here with Peel, Gladstone's first master in politics and like himself, an Oxonian, a double-first, and a financier. And it is worth notice, in passing, that the coming party leaders of the latter part of the reign both in some sense derive from Peel—Gladstone from congruity with his temperament; Disraeli from hostility to it.

Melbourne's Ministry had, in a manner, represented the sequel of that governance of England by an hereditary aristocracy which had prevailed since the days of Queen Anne. But, in any finely constituted polity, the best men intellectually must find an equal and honoured place beside those political animals whose inherited tendencies and traditions give them the same sort of pedigree value in politics which on the racecourse we attach to a thoroughbred; and we can see clearly in the fortunes of Burke that this element was wanting in the political philosophy of the Whigs. Indeed, the Tories were, perhaps, better disposed to open their doors wide to those who, in the Middle Age, would have risen through the medium of the Church to the highest positions in the State. At all events it is rather through the ranks of the Tories that talent without adventitious advantages regained its proper place in the counsels of the nation. It might have fallen to Canning or to Huskisson, had they lived, to establish this most necessary restoration; circumstances caused it to become effective in Peel.

Peel came of a north country family who had done well in cotton and calico; and he was heir to a new-made baronetcy whose founder—the first Sir Robert—though a trifle uncouth, had all the intelligence of the successful manufacturer, and, as such, had been consulted by Pitt. Sir Robert the Elder, let it be said in passing, was one of the rare men at that time to perceive that a measure of State interference, where women and children were involved, was necessary to the working of the new factory system. His wealth led him to send his son to Harrow, where the younger Robert had Byron for a contemporary and also a competitor in classical studies and polite declamation, and then on to Christchurch, Oxford, where he distinguished himself

---

[1] Letter of 1861 to Lord Lyttelton (printed in Morley's *Life of Gladstone*, Vol. II, p. 647).

by being the first man to get a double-first in the newly separated schools of Classics and Mathematics. He left the University with the Tory label of his father, but neither by temperament nor opinion did he show any leaning towards the Stuart pretensions, just dying out then in the person of 'Henry IX',[1] nor even towards the Bolingbroke version of 'the Patriot King'. Let us put Peel, then, at once in his place, and do so in the words of Disraeli, his most savage opponent: 'What he really was, and what posterity will acknowledge him to have been, is the greatest Member of Parliament that ever lived.'[2] That bold—some may think overbold—estimate is the more impressive if we recollect that Parliament was in his time at its greatest.

The essence of Peel's Conservatism lay in his possession of a calm and open mind, the necessary condition of all true development in art, in science, in law, and even in that which has been called the queen of the sciences—theology itself. Whilst the Chartists, and a few Tories with them, were liberating their souls on the long hours of work and the employment of small children in factories; whilst the manufacturers were denouncing the exploitation of miners by landlords; whilst 'the wicked rich' in town and country were being denounced by the not wholly virtuous poor; whilst Cobden was describing the Corn Laws as 'baptized in blood, begotten in violence and injustice, perpetuated at the expense of the tears and groans of the people'; and whilst O'Connell was asserting that the venison of landlords was 'sweetened with widows' tears', and 'their claret dyed with orphans' blood'; whilst, in fact, demagogy was running riot, Peel had the sense and the education to appreciate that a sound economy and a stable finance was a surer remedy for all the distress and discontent than indiscriminate abuse and impatient indignation. 'If', observes Elie Halévy,[3] the recent French historian of the age of Peel and Cobden, 'there was a statesman in whose mind problems of political economy took precedence of purely political questions, who cared little for his reputation and whose chief preoccupation was the material conditions in which the people lived, he was Sir Robert Peel, and everyone knew it.'

Into Parliament Peel had come in 1809, as Member for Cashel, an Irish seat and, since Catholics were not enfranchised until twenty years later, as rotten a borough as could easily be found—at least in the accepted modern use of the term, though not so rotten, perhaps, for all that, in the eyes of Peel and his Protestant associates, to whom Catholicism represented pretty well the last word in bigotry and ignorance, and the first in political corruption. As we have already seen, he entered the House as a Tory; but his father is said to have intimated that he might not remain so if his abilities went

[1] Cardinal York, the younger son of James the Old Pretender.
[2] Life of Lord George Bentinck, Chapter XXVII.
[3] Halévy, Age of Peel and Cobden (translation), p. 10.

long unrecognized. However that may be, three years later Liverpool gave him the Irish Secretariat; a poor appointment at that time, though by the end of the century destined to become as great a prize and peril as man could desire or dread. Even so, he contrived to make some name for himself in Ireland; though, of course, the temptation to call him 'Orange Peel' was not resisted, and, with the then Duke of Richmond, a Protestant stalwart, at the Viceregal Lodge, was, perhaps, irresistible. There was nothing to be done in regard to the essentials of the Irish problem until Catholic Emancipation could find its way past the Sovereign's Coronation oath, as Pitt in 1800 had intended that it should do. The mental condition and moral obstruction of the Third George had rendered this impossible; and the Fourth George, though he had so far emancipated himself from the religious restriction imposed upon the heir to the throne as surreptitiously to marry a Catholic widow, despite the provisions of the Bill of Rights, the Act of Settlement and the Royal Marriage Act of 1772, remained fiercely opposed to the emancipation of his Catholic subjects from their incapacity at the polling booth. In the last year of his reign, however, the delicacy of his conscience was constrained to yield to the exigencies of circumstance. Wellington and Peel, both of them opposed in theory to Catholic Emancipation, perceived, when O'Connell was returned for County Clare, that concession had become inevitable. The King's Government must be carried on. Wellington was too great for anyone to suspect him of playing for his own hand. Peel's shift of policy required a subtler defence; and a later Prime Minister has made some severe, if at the same time not wholly unsympathetic, strictures upon his conduct in this connection. Rosebery points out, in a judgment all the weightier that it comes from a successor well acquainted with the difficulties of a leader's position, that the reasons given by Peel do not really satisfy the ethical standards of a political moralist. In May 1828, as he says, Peel had been the champion in Parliament of the opposition to Catholic claims. Before August he had become convinced that those claims would have to be allowed; yet in August he was equally satisfied that he himself ought not to be the Minister to effect a settlement. Then, in January 1829, as difficulties gathered about the devoted head of Wellington, he offered to remain in office if the Duke wished for and required his assistance. Wellington can hardly be blamed for closing with the offer, since it was made; but the responsibility of making it lies heavy on Peel's reputation.

His treatment of two other matters—police and the poor law—had, however, raised Peel's reputation high before Victoria came to the throne. Liverpool, who was an abler man than Liberal critics have been inclined to allow, had early perceived what William Pitt had perceived even before the ideas of the French Revolution were well on their way, that in the disturbed state of the country it was essential to have some means of keeping order which would not oblige the Government to make use of the soldiery. The so-called 'Peterloo Massacre' had proved a clinching argument in respect of this trend of thought; and Wellington had sent a memorandum to the Cabinet calling upon it to lose no time in forming a police force in London. Peel was appointed to the Home Office in 1822 in order to inaugurate the new system; and this he had so effectively done that the modern policeman has long retained variations of Peel's christian and surnames as pet soubriquets. It cannot be denied that the gaiety of the nations of Great Britain was somewhat eclipsed by the disappearance of Dogberry and Verges, and the substitution for them of Peel's highly uniformed force, costing in 1830 the sum of £6 a man to fit out with blue coat, brown cloth overcoat, hat, boots and the rest of his equipment. Still, there are few Conservative measures which illustrate better what the State can really do to assist the espousals of liberty and order. Some of the Whigs, nevertheless, did not like the measure, and supposed it might violate personal freedom by the encouragement of spies and informers, a race of beings whose presence in large numbers is more damaging to the character of a government than almost any other auxiliary that can be named.

Peel's dealings with the Poor Law cannot be said to have secured general assent to the same degree as his dealings with the police; but then the new Poor Law of 1834, the crowning achievement, as it has been called, of the first Reformed Parliament, was a sharply controversial measure in its own day and has become more so since. It attracted the support of the progressives of that time who had been trained in the school of Bentham, but it excited the opposition of Disraeli and other more conservative friends of the poor, and in these latter days it attracts the indignation of all 'friends of humanity' whose unsleeping endeavour is to find grievances, old and new, for the under-dog. The maintenance, or perhaps rather the discovery, of an exact right balance between a relief that is soppily sentimental and a relief that is repulsively prudent is, in truth, distressingly difficult; and British Administrations in this, as in other matters, have wavered between excessive kindness and extreme severity. The Elizabethan Poor Law was hard; the system of the Berkshire magistrates in 1795, which was so generally adopted as to be known as the Speenhamland Act of Parliament, was soft; and successive changes, including the Act of 1834, register passing emotions in the interminable struggle between sense and sensibility. At a period like our own, which has been largely influenced by the Webbs and the Hammonds, there is no need to stress the merits of sentiments of humanity or the advantages of State intervention. It is wholesome, however, to recall in the interests of mental equilibrium the observations upon this Poor Law of 1834 of Brodrick and Fotheringham, the one the most famous of all Wardens of Merton, and the other a lecturer in Classical Literature at King's College, London. These historians, writing at the end of the nineteenth century, draw attention to the fact that the summary of information collected by the Royal Commission of 1832 astounded the public of that time by its revelation of ruinous, official infatuation, pursued on the largest possible scale, and setting a premium upon improvidence, if not on vice, by the wholesale practice of giving outdoor relief in aid of wages. 'Had some theorists of a later generation', they remark, 'witnessed the social order then prevailing in country districts, they would have found several of their favourite objects practically attained. There was no competition between the working people; old and young, skilled and unskilled hands, the industrious and the idle, were held worthy of equal reward, the actual allowance to each being measured by his need and not by the value of his work; while the parochial authorities, figuring as an earthly providence, exercised a benevolent superintendence over the welfare and liberty of every day labourer in the village community. The fruits of that superintendence were the decline of a race of freemen into a race of slaves, unconscious of their slavery, and the gradual ruin of the landlords and farmers upon whom the maintenance of these slaves depended . . . It was clearly found that, where outdoor relief was abolished or rigorously limited, where no allowances were made in aid of wages, and where a manly self-reliance was encouraged instead of a servile mendacity, wages rose, honest industry revived, and the whole character of the village population was improved. Fortified by these successful experiments, the Commissioners took a firm stand on the vital distinction, previously ignored, between poverty and pauperism.'[1] Cobbett and *The Times*, though evidently from opposite standpoints, raised loud lamentations over what Cobbett called the 'Poor Robbery Bill'. It was at this point that Peel came in; and his intervention in favour of the more austere school of economics was effective in defeating the coalition of extremists on both sides who else might have triumphed. His 'admirable public spirit' has received the praise of the authors above quoted, and it is significant that on this issue he went into the same lobby with such a Radical as Grote. High principle had a greater hold upon both these men than a careless generosity.

Whatever we may think of Peel's conduct in respect of Catholic Emancipation, or of his wisdom in dealing with the Poor Law, it is certain that his reputation both at home and abroad stood extraordinarily high for the few years that preceded Victoria's accession. Rosebery has gone so far as to declare, what is in effect a great compliment to his character, that no one who examines his career can doubt that he attained the highest point of his reputation twice, and on both occasions when he was not in office. The second occasion fell in the four years between his final resignation and his premature death; of that, what little needs to be said can be said later. But

[1] *Political History of England*, 1801–1937, p. 342.

the first time occurred in 1834-5 when, in Rosebery's words, 'England waited breathlessly for his return from Rome to form an administration'— the Whigs having fallen, and Wellington no longer considering himself the right person to lead the Tory Party and therefore taking up the position of a caretaker in all the great administrative departments until Peel could be brought back to form the King's Government. This long delay, with the old Tory Prime Minister magnanimously holding the reins of power until his former subordinate could arrive to take them over, has no parallel in British history: nor, I believe, can any other British Minister claim that his speeches made such a stir in Russia under the Tsars, as to have been translated into Russian and sent to all the Russian universities because of the admiration entertained for them by the head of the government. Yet this is what actually happened after Peel went to Glasgow in 1836 to address the students there. Londonderry, the British Ambassador accredited to the Russian Emperor at the time, recounts the repercussions in Russia of Peel's Glasgow speech in the following terms: 'I could not resist informing you of the very extraordinary effects your two most wonderful speeches have produced in this capital. In society nothing else is talked of, and the Emperor expressed himself yesterday to me in a manner that convinced me of the admiration he experienced in reading them. Would to God our soi-disant patriots could feel for their country as these Russians seem to feel for us . . . The translation of your dinner speech . . . is given in all the Russian papers . . . I have just heard the speech of the Lord Rector is to be translated and sent to all the Russian universities.'[1]

This astonishing tribute to Peel's understanding of what was common to European civilization at the time came in the early months of 1837, and gives as good evidence as could be wished for of the place he held in Europe at the date of Victoria's accession. At home he had made his position clear two or three years before in the famous Tamworth manifesto. He had made no pretence of approving the Reform Bill of 1832; and the thought of abandoning a political career had even crossed his mind, though only to be rejected. If he remained in politics, he recognized, however, that the Reform Act would have to be accepted as an irrevocable settlement, and that patriotism would require of him and his followers to do their utmost to make it workable. Though, as he said, declarations of general principle were necessarily vague, he made it plain that he stood for a perfect equality of all the King's subjects in respect to civil privileges, and that he was prepared to review such questions as the treatment of municipal corporations, of Church rates and Church property, of the admission of dissenters to the university, and of public finance and economy in the light of this general conception of justice. The wisdom of the Victorians had found its first clear utterance;

[1] Parker, *Sir Robert Peel*, Vol. II, p. 331.

and all the promise of a true polity, as opposed to an unbridled democracy, seemed latent in the manifesto. Its very claim to address that class of citizens who are less interested in the contentions of party than in the cause of good government, said much in its favour. This was enforced by the author's explicit declaration that he had never been, either before or after the Reform Bill, a defender of abuses or an enemy of judicious reforms. He takes occasion to remind his hearers of the part he had taken in currency questions—a matter upon which something more will be said later on—and, as a further proof of his sympathy with enlightenment, of the system of trial by jury. His conclusion is especially characteristic, and discovers the political economist in almost every phrase, for he summarizes his purposes as the maintenance of peace, the honourable and scrupulous fulfilment of all engagements with foreign powers, the maintenance of public credit, the enforcement of strict economy, and the impartial treatment of all agricultural, manufacturing and commercial interests.

Such, then, very briefly was the Tamworth manifesto, in which, on his assumption of the leadership of the Conservative Party, Peel had put forward his aims. It was the work of a wealthy, highly educated and certainly benevolent man of business, and, though it has, of course and inevitably, marks of its middle-class origin, it can be truthfully styled a highly patriotic document. It would hardly be too much to say that the political principles of all those little Victorian Liberals and Conservatives, of whom Gilbert, later on at the end of the reign, was to make kindly sport, had their root in the thought and method of Peel. Disraeli, as we shall see, had his own visions and philosophy, but Peel's influence is to be perceived in Salisbury and Balfour, as much as in his direct disciple, Gladstone. The last-named writes of Peel in 1853 as 'my great master and teacher in public affairs',[1] and towards the close of his own life, as Morley notices, Gladstone repeats, what in effect he had said in 1868, that he himself had 'never swerved from those truly conservative objects and desires with which he entered life'; that is from the principles of Peel's conservatism. One other tribute to their author may be appropriately added. In a memorandum by Prince Albert, dated Christmas 1845, there is included, together with a sketch of Peel's ultimate aims, the observation: 'His character is not easy to read, because his mastery of Parliamentary methods masked an intense dislike of the Party system, while his frigid efficiency covered an almost passionate concern for the welfare of the people.'[2]

The temperamental sympathy between the Prince Consort and Peel made the much-needed bridge by which Peel passed into the counsels and confidence of the Queen. But for Albert she might never have understood him.

---

[1] *Life of Gladstone*, Vol. I, pp. 177–9.
[2] Quoted from G. M. Young's *Early Victorian England*, Vol. II, p. 450.

Thanks to Albert she came to recognize him as one of the greatest of her Prime Ministers.

This conjunction of Peel and the Prince Consort was not the least piece of good fortune that befell Victoria. Peel, as the affair of the Bedchamber showed, had no power of ingratiating himself with the Sovereign. He had, as Wellington, who criticized himself at the same time for lack of small talk, pointedly put it, 'no manners'. He was serious; he was high minded; he had an infinite capacity for taking pains, though without any sparkle of genius; in fact, he was *bourgeois*, if by that term is signified a freedom alike from the affected indolence of the aristocrat and the carping ignorance of the proletarian. Mr. Fulford notices another peculiar point of resemblance between the Prince and the Prime Minister—that they were 'only completely natural and at ease' in the company of their wives. Victoria, as was said, came in time to think of Peel as one of the ablest of her Prime Ministers; yet he had needed to be explained to her, and Albert had supplied the explanation.

Peel's Ministry of 1834 had not lasted long, nor come to much. Some minor matters, ecclesiastical and civil, such as tithes and civil marriage, were regulated in accordance with the opportunism of the Tamworth manifesto; but it is enough to say that Peel proved himself—in the words of Guizot— to be 'the most conservative of liberals and the most liberal of conservatives, and the most capable man of all in both Parties'. Peel's Ministry of 1841, however, if we follow the verdict of Gladstone,[1] who was a member of it and intimately acquainted with its working and personnel, was one that surpassed in many important characteristics any of its successors, Liberal or Conservative. Its outstanding traits, according to Peel's pupil, were its financial strictness, its loyal adherence to the principle of public economy, its purity in the exercise of patronage, its jealous care for the rights of Parliament, its strong aversion to any extension of territorial responsibility, its fair and equal regard for the rights of foreign countries and its single eye to the nation's interests. If this high testimony be accepted as historic truth, then it is safe to conjecture that Peel's administration owed much to the fact that the Prime Minister, who in 1834 had himself held the Chancellorship of the Exchequer, thoroughly understood finance, and to the circumstance that the Foreign Secretary, who was Aberdeen, managed foreign affairs with rare integrity. These two departments rank in importance far above the rest; indeed, the Foreign Office was considered in those days to stand in a special relationship to all members of the Cabinet, and its papers were, theoretically at least, supposed to be available for general inspection. And it is worth notice that foreign affairs and finance do, in fact, fill a more than usually large space in the history of those years. The good

[1] Morley, *Life of Gladstone*, Vol. I, p. 643.

relations between England and France were not a happy harmony natural to the English and French peoples, but the very particular work of Aberdeen and Guizot; and, almost as soon as the silver cord of Aberdeen's faultless rectitude was loosed, the golden bowl of the Anglo-French understanding lay broken by the notorious affair of 'the Spanish marriages',[1] and the two nations resumed their traditional suspicion of one another's designs.

The financial and economic business of the Administration requires more to be said of it; for, though Peel was no longer his own Chancellor of the Exchequer—an office that fell to Goulburn—his mind was preoccupied with his budgets and matters akin to them.

Since Pitt's time one of those minds which transcend fashions of thought had dominated this department of political science. Adam Smith is the Aristotle of public finance; and his approach to economics has the qualities required of a perennial philosophy. To extricate oneself from the network of speculative notions that prevail in one's own time is no small part of the work of the historian who wishes to deal faithfully with the past; and this is not least important in treating of the economic acts of Peel. The matter is perhaps best introduced by recalling a few of those maxims or aphorisms which figure so prominently in the shrewd Scotsman's enquiry into the nature and causes of the wealth of nations; and it is well to recollect at the outset that Adam Smith was not merely one of the Commissioners of His Majesty's Customs in Scotland, but had also been, before he published his famous book in 1776, Professor of Logic and subsequently of Moral Philosophy at Glasgow. The master of Pitt in economic thought, he need not astonish us when he observes that 'great nations are never impoverished by private, though they sometimes are by public, prodigality',[2] or when he casually observes that 'Versailles is an ornament and an honour to France, Stowe and Wilton to England'. But Adam Smith strikes a deeper, an almost mystical, note when he lets fall the remark that the individual, whilst directing industry to his own gain, is in many cases 'led by an invisible hand to promote an end which was no part of his intention', and that 'by pursuing his own interest, he frequently promotes that of the society more effectually than when he really intends to promote it'.[3] One of his phrases that 'defence . . . is of much more importance than opulence' has been dragged from its original context and made into a household word by the tariff reformers of

---

[1] Palmerston, who succeeded Aberdeen as Foreign Secretary when Lord John Russell succeeded Peel as Prime Minister in July 1846, supported the suit of Don Enrique de Bourbon (a radical intriguer detested by the Queen Mother) for the hand of the Spanish Queen Isabella II and tried to arrange the secret betrothal of the Infanta to Prince Leopold of Saxe Coburg. Louis Philippe and Guizot intrigued more successfully. Isabella was married in October 1846 to the negligible Duke of Cadiz and the Infanta to the Duc de Montpensier. Palmerston took his defeat badly and told the French Foreign Minister that it was clear that no friendly understanding was desired.

[2] Book II, Chapter III.   [3] Book IV, Chapter II.

the first decade of this century; but they might as usefully have popularized another 'the natural progress of opulence',[1] for that has done more than Free Trade or Protection could ever accomplish to raise the standard of living. Still, this maybe is too much to expect of such as Adam Smith, in an unusually violent and cutting aside, denominates as 'insidious and crafty animals vulgarly called statesmen or politicians'.[2] More important, however, for the welfare of a country than the nature of its rulers is their regard for the true principles of taxation. Adam Smith's four classical maxims will, if dealt with honestly, long survive the interested attempts of second-class economists to dispose of them. 'The expense of government to the individuals of a great nation', he says, 'is like the expense of management to the joint-tenants of a great estate, who are all obliged to contribute in proportion to their respective interests in the estate. In the observation or neglect of this maxim consists, what is called the equality or inequality of taxation.'[3] That is the first maxim; and the other three ride in behind it. Taxes, that is to say, need to be certain, and not arbitrary. Taxes should be levied at a time and in a manner most likely to be convenient to the persons taxed. And taxes should be contrived so as both to take out and to keep out of pockets of the people as little as possible beyond what is brought into the public treasury. In other words, industry should not be obstructed more than can be helped: taxes should be conceived so as not to tempt men to evasion, or worse; and what Adam Smith styles 'the odious examination of the tax-gatherers' should be controlled so as to create the minimum of vexation.

These principles clearly cannot commend themselves to a community or any section of a community which gratifies its personal malice or political purposes by the punitive taxation of wealth, honourably acquired. It is, therefore, the more necessary to notice that Adam Smith, in concluding his treatment of the subject observes that 'the evident justice and utility of the foregoing maxims have recommended them more or less to the attention of all nations', and even dares to claim in the following sentence that 'All nations have endeavoured, to the best of their judgment, to render their taxes as equal as they could contrive; as certain, as convenient to the contributor, both in the time and in the mode of payment, and, in proportion to the revenue which they brought to the Prince, as little burdensome to the people.'[4] Such, then, were the principles and practice of sound taxation as they had appeared to a British economist of unsurpassed reputation, who had talked with Turgot before the advent of the European catastrophe in France, which their application might have averted. It follows that we should regard Adam Smith as the pioneer of that 'contrary-of-a-revolution' policy

[1] Book IV, Chapter II.   [2] ibid.
[3] Book V, Chapter II.
[4] ibid.

which it was the aim of Peel and the great Victorians after him to bring to fruition, if not to perfection.

From these prolegomena, then, we are in a position to pass on and glance at Peel's solid achievements in finance and economics. For, although his great Administration of 1841 terminated in the disastrous party split of 1846, his work forms, none the less, an integrated economic whole, and within its sphere foreshadows the considered policy of the era.

Memoranda (for more cannot be attempted here) of this policy in commerce and finance may perhaps be grouped around three Acts of Parliament —what goes by the name of Peel's Act of 1819; the Bank Charter Act of 1844; and the famous Act which committed the country to the abolition of the Corn Laws. The Act of 1819, to take that measure first, indicated a recovery in the country from wartime conditions of currency. Payments in coin, or of banknotes payable on demand in coin, had been suspended in 1797; and the suspension had continued throughout the Revolutionary and Napoleonic Wars. The Bank Restriction Act, by which this was effected, represented, therefore, the substitution of an inconvertible for a convertible paper currency, or, if we prefer American phraseology, the substitution of 'soft' money for 'hard'. As time went on, the paper coinage thus introduced lost value, and in 1810 Francis Horner published in the *Edinburgh Review* an article which became famous, and originated the still more famous report of the Bullion Committee, advising the resumption of cash payments within two years. It was in vain that the egregious Vansittart induced Parliament to affirm that a banknote was as good as coin. Parliament, which is said to be able to do anything except to turn a man into a woman and a woman into a man, was unable to make people believe, so long as they were powerless to exchange one for the other, that a scrap of paper was as good as a golden sovereign. Peel's Act of 1819—so called because he presided over the committee whose recommendation to restore cash payments by stages was put into effect—was long thought to have established a principle in regard to currency from which the country would not again depart; but circumstances familiar to all of us have once more proved politicians to be unstable as water, and paper money of dubious quality has again replaced gold and fallen in value as the years have passed. A modern Parliament is hardly less susceptible than a medieval king to the temptation and advantages of debasing the currency.

The Bank Charter Act of 1844 completed the policy of 1819, which had left the banks with the right to issue paper money. Peel's great speech on this occasion has been described by a competent authority as 'the parliamentary foundation of all sound thinking on the subject and . . . the most authoritative exposition of the true position of the national currency'. The measure he advocated had the effect of separating the issue and the banking

SIR ROBERT PEEL
From the portrait by J. Linnell

departments of the Bank of England, and of bringing the issue department under the control of the Government, whilst leaving it nominally under the management of the Bank directors, who retained, however, a real control of the deposit side of the Bank's activities. As things stood after Peel's measure was passed, the issue of notes, which as a rule did not exceed fourteen millions, was fixed at that amount; and this sum was covered by a holding of Government securities. Beyond that amount no paper money might be issued which was not covered by gold stored at the Bank, and with this gold the bankers might not tamper; so that public creditors enjoyed the certitude that the value of any paper currency could be met on demand. Before the end of the century the Act had come under criticism, because, on three different occasions during a financial crisis, authority has been given to the Bank to issue paper money in excess of what the Act permits. But the criticism seems ill-founded. At any time the State can place, and at these times mentioned did place, its own unrivalled credit at the service of the Bank; and the suspension of the rule could have caused no anxiety to anyone who had confidence still in the honesty of the nation itself. What Peel had effected was, therefore, to establish the equivalent of a guarantee to all public creditors of a currency as stable as currency can be rendered. Beyond such security no man, humanly speaking, was in a position to go. Ingenious arguments have been produced by modern economists to persuade an ingenuous public that what amounts to a debasement of the coinage need not operate disadvantageously, and may, indeed, promote the full employment of the nation. The task of the charlatan in a democracy is never difficult. Sound finance, however, though content to allow exceptions in extraordinary circumstances, must always strive after such a currency as Peel established. Whether the Bank Charter Act did anything to avert or reduce the duration of a commercial crisis is another question, to which John Stuart Mill devoted much attention in his *Political Economy*, concluding on the whole in a negative sense; but the argument both for and against is too lengthy to be examined here.

The third fence which Peel had to take, and in the taking of which he fell, was the abolition of the Corn Laws. Adam Smith had expounded the theory of Free Trade so convincingly that in a world where all nations lived in peace and amity little doubt could remain that its adoption was statesmanlike, and that it made both for the wealth and welfare of nations. The difficulty, which the Victorians for the most part did not sufficiently face, is that men are excessively quarrelsome, and that Cobden's optimistic idea that unilateral Free Trade would engender universal peace does not find any sufficient justification in the pages of the past or the prospects of the future. Adam Smith had allowed that defence is greater than opulence, and, as a result, that home-grown grain, although more costly, may yet afford the nation more security than cheap grain imported at a risk. Cobden and his followers were able to persuade an urban electorate, only too ready to believe it, that swords were on the point of being converted into plough-shares, and that cheap food was a boon that could not be overvalued. Peel, though he easily saw the full force of the argument for Free Trade, moved, of necessity, with greater hesitancy. Neither Whig nor Tory in 1841 would have confessed a creed which appeared to strike, whatever Cobden might circuitously argue, at the welfare of the rural population no less than at the rents of the great landed proprietors: and the difference between the two Parties lay in the preference of the Whigs for a fixed protective duty on the import of corn, and the preference of the Tories for the sliding scale already in operation but susceptible to change.

'Probably', declares Northcote, 'no budget was ever awaited with more interest, anxiety or curiosity than that of 1842. Serious financial difficulties had been accumulating for several years. Five times in succession the revenue had fallen short of the expenditure by amounts averaging about a million and a half per annum.'[1] Something had clearly got to be done, for, by general admission, public finance was in a deplorable condition. Peel, in the great Budget of 1842, which, rather to the disparagement of his Chancellor of the Exchequer, the inconsiderable Goulburn, he handled himself, remitted a great weight of taxes, affecting both raw materials and articles partly manufactured. This remission of duty, which covered no less than seven hundred and fifty articles, involved the young Gladstone, who was Vice-President of the Board of Trade, in labour which would probably have worn out any man of less than his stupendous strength. Yet all this tre-mendous effort left still a tax upon corn and sugar, commodities of prime necessity; so that Peel could be taunted at public meetings with having taken the tax off dried fruits, cosmetics, satins, and caviare, but having left it still upon bread. Nevertheless, the Budget was recognized as epoch making; though, as Northcote points out, Peel's predictions were far from proving correct in the first year of putting into force the new taxation and only gave the desired stability in the Budget of 1844-5, and though the income tax, alleged to be only imposed for a time and at the rate of sevenpence in the pound to make up for what was being surrendered in indirect taxation, was never, in fact, again completely remitted.

This conversion of a war tax into a permanent burden, though it was not envisaged as an enduring impost at the time, was perhaps the most epoch-making feature of Peel's finance. Bold, however, as the Prime Minister was, he was not bold enough for Cobden, impatient of the delay in carrying a measure which appeared to him more urgent and more incontestably bene-ficial than any other—the repeal of the Corn Laws. His enthusiasm led him

[1] Northcote, *Twenty Years of Financial Policy*, p. 5.

to declare, a good many years afterwards, that Peel had been always a Free Trader in theory, and abstractly as sound as Adam Smith or Bentham in political economy; but, if we follow John Morley's opinion, we shall admit this to have been only partially true in the year 1842. Another close student of the period has passed a very adverse verdict on Peel's conduct at this time: 'For anyone who retains his freedom of mind moral dogma will seem to have a higher validity than economic; and whether he thinks the repeal of the Corn Laws a good thing or a bad, he will find it hard to discern any such pressing necessity for their repeal at the particular moment chosen as to justify a statesman in violating his pledges and breaking up his Party.'[1] This is but an amplified endorsement of Rosebery's judgment. Russell was doubtless the proper man to have carried Free Trade; and the Irish distress arose more from lack of oats than of potatoes. On the other hand, delay was the proper policy for Peel to have followed, and not, as Wellington said in some well-known words, to have given way to a 'damned fright', caused by 'rotten potatoes'. But the clouds in their courses were fighting for the Manchester School. The years 1843 and 1844 were not, indeed, such bad seasons; and for a time it looked as if Peel's measure had been sufficient to restore equanimity, if not prosperity.

But in the autumn of 1845 there came 'the rain that rained away the Corn Laws'. No man living, it is said, could recall so persistent a downpour. And what was happening in Great Britain was nothing to that which happened in Ireland. The potato crop there was ruined; and the Irish thought themselves on the very verge of starvation. The Whig leader seized his opportunity and addressed from Edinburgh to his constituents in London the memorable letter accusing the Government of failing in their duty to Queen and country. The effect was immense; and the total repeal of the Corn Laws became inevitable. Peel seems to have realized in how bitterly compromising a situation he had been placed. 'I never in my life', Wellington told Croker in describing Peel's state of mind in October 1845, 'witnessed such agony.'[2] But Russell, who had called so loudly for action, proved himself unable to take it, when Peel, on the 5th December, resigned. For the magnitude of the crisis was not sufficient to induce Grey[3] to withdraw a very natural objection to joining an administration if it meant, as it did, the return of Palmerston to the Foreign Office; and without Grey in the Government Lord John felt himself unable to get on. Peel, therefore, on his own initiative and to the great satisfaction of the Queen, withdrew his resignation and returned to office, but only to find himself face to face with a furious party and, what was perhaps of more consequence, with a party led from behind

---

[1] Monypenny, *Life of Disraeli*, Vol. II, p. 346.   [2] *Croker Papers*, Vol. III, p. 67.
[3] Charles, second Earl Grey, the son of the former Prime Minister. He was Secretary at War from 1835-39 and Secretary for Colonies from 1846-52.

by a young Israelite, master of every wile in political strategy and tactics, and merciless in his use of them. What *Père* Joseph is supposed to have been to Richelieu, and more, Disraeli was to Lord George Bentinck; and we have the narrative of the struggle written in this 'grey cardinal's' script, or, if the metaphor runs better, the record of the race, won by Bentinck over Peel, broadcast in the trainer's words. 'It should not be forgotten', observes Disraeli in this famous monograph, 'that the most authentic and interesting histories are those which have been composed by actors in the transactions which they record. The contemporary writer who is personally familiar with his theme has unquestionably a great advantage; but it is assumed that his pen can scarcely escape the bias of private friendship or political connection. Yet truth after all is the sovereign passion of mankind; nor is the writer of these pages prepared to relinquish his conviction that it is possible to combine the accuracy of the present with the impartiality of the future.'

If Disraeli did not exactly succeed in depicting with naked truth the last days of that fateful Parliament during which Britain swung over from an agricultural to an industrial basis and, forsaking Protection, poised her weight anew upon the adoption of national and upon the expectation of international Free Trade, he certainly contrived to dramatize with telling political effect this episode in our economic history. *The Life of Lord George Bentinck* is the work of one who in his time had fancied himself an epic poet and then, when Calliope failed him, had taken to politics. The stress of his song falls first on the Man and then upon the Arms required to compass the fall of 'the greatest member of Parliament that ever lived'; the sombre landscape of circumstance is touched in with an artist's skill; and the figures in the foreground seem to move to a dramatist's desire. The eye falls first on Lord George, with Newmarket and the racecourse at his back. Then Westminster with its fields seems to spring to view beneath his feet and to rouse his mind to an energy hitherto undreamed of. Two countries simultaneously become visible on the horizon—Ireland, where no future promise of cheap corn could supply subsistence to a starving peasantry in place of the present crop of rotting potatoes; England, where the Country Party was slow to sacrifice its vision of golden harvests, raised by English hands in a protected prosperity, to the townsman's dream of cereals, imported from overseas in shiploads and exemplifying through the blessing of cheap food the benefit of an expanding commerce where all men and nations would be producing exactly what they were most fitted for.

The drama, developed by the cunning of a great impresario who, in fact, though he avoids mention of himself, had taken a major part in it, draws with well-timed pause and judicious digression to its climax. The last scene discovers Peel sitting aloof, attentive and approving, whilst Chandos[1]—

---

[1] Duke of Buckingham and Chandos.

destined in due course to be the last to wear the ducal coronet, for which the Temple-Grenvilles had struggled so hard and to such little lasting purpose —seeks to sustain the falling Minister by throwing his great family influence into the scales at the critical hour. 'Very pale' the young man looked, and not unlike 'the early portraits of Lord Grenville', his ancestor two or more generations back, impassive, cold, earnest, unrhetorical, arguing that tariff considerations could supply no test of Conservative principles. It was, however, all in vain. He won cheers from the Treasury Bench; but, soon after he resumed his seat, the eighty odd, rebellious Protectionists, not pausing to salute him who was about to fall, defiled into the hostile Lobby before the eyes of the doomed Minister. Amongst them was the literary artist who had contributed so greatly to bring about the impending catastrophe. To Disraeli, as he looked back upon that midnight scene, it appeared impossible that Peel could have marked this deviation of his sometime followers without the deepest feeling. 'They were men to gain whose hearts and the hearts of their fathers had been the aim and exultation of his life. They had extended to him an unlimited confidence and an admiration without stint. They had stood by him in the darkest hour and had borne him from the depths of political despair to the proudest of living positions. Right or wrong, they were men of honour, breeding, refinement, high and generous character, great weight and station in the country, which they had ever placed at his disposal. They had been, not only his followers, but his friends; had joined in the same pastimes, drunk from the same cup, and in the pleasantness of private life had often forgotten together the cares and strife of politics.'[1] So, then, they passed on, as if they were symbols of the coming change that it would need a full century to complete, these gentlemen of England, these 'country gentlemen'—the Mannerses, the Somersets, the Bentincks, the Lowthers, the Lennoxes; 'Bankes, with a parliamentary name of two centuries', 'Christopher, from the broad Lincolnshire which Protection had created'; Mileses and Henleys, Duncombes and Yorkes, Liddells and Longs. It was the dumb-show preluding the play that was to come. And Peel sat there, watching the great fissure in the ranks of his followers as it widened; another Marius seated upon the ruins of Carthage or, as it seemed to Disraeli at the time, another Napoleon at Dresden—'an emperor', in Metternich's phrase, 'without an army'. St. Helena itself, with its Prometheus bound, hardly tendered to the imagination a more striking spectacle than Westminster that fateful evening when its greatest Parliamentarian lay prone.

Not Disraeli only was fired by a fierce, if partly factitious, indignation at Peel's conduct. The speeches with which he had planted envenomed arrows in Peel's all too vulnerable breast, found a strange echo in the words

[1] Disraeli, *Life of Lord George Bentinck*, p. 299.

of one who, though his own hour had struck, was yet to be seen, like some ghost of other days, a guest at Windsor. The old Melbourne was sitting there next the Queen, when in allusion to Peel's apostasy, he suddenly burst out with: 'Ma'am, it is a damned dishonest act!' Victoria sought to soothe him, but found that this was merely to add fuel to the flames. 'I say again', Melbourne declared, 'it is a very dishonest act': and he proceeded to denounce the abolition of the Corn Laws. The Queen laughed; but presently, as he would go on, she said: 'Lord Melbourne, I must beg you not to say anything more on this subject now; I shall be very glad to discuss it with you at any other time.'[1] The anecdote was trivial enough, but possessed, nevertheless, a certain importance. Prince Albert was a Free Trader; and the Queen, by 1846, doubtless shared his opinions. But there had, of course, been a time when whatever Melbourne said, as we should say, 'went'. For a little while, indeed, after his resignation he had, much to the alarm of Stockmar, maintained a correspondence with the Sovereign, but, after that, even this relic of his old influence had been dropped, and so much so, indeed, that Victoria could write 'the dream is past'.

Peel's race also was now run, though few guessed it. As soon as the Corn Laws were abolished, the great Minister, defeated in the House of Commons, made known his resignation. In the words in which he took leave of his office there is much that is moving, for he sketched his epitaph: 'I shall leave', he declared, 'a name severely censured by many who on public grounds deeply regret the severance of party ties . . . I shall surrender power, severely censured by others who, from no interested motive, adhere to the principle of protection . . . I shall leave a name execrated by every monopolist who, from less honourable motives, clamours for protection . . . but it may be I shall leave a name sometimes remembered with expressions of goodwill in the abodes of those whose lot it is to labour and to earn their daily bread with the sweat of their brow.'

Four years, as it proved, remained to the fallen Minister: and those four years were enough to let passions subside and to give him again that great outstanding position in public affairs which he had known once before, and, in like manner, when out of office. Then, in 1850, there occurred the fall from his horse which brought the end. He was a bad horseman, but it appears that he had also a bad horse, against which he might have been warned, if he had been less shy and stiff, by an acquaintance who recognized the animal and perceived the danger Peel would be put in if he rode it. Death was not instantaneous and for three days he suffered intense pain, which he was ill-constituted by nature to endure. But at length he passed on his way; and his mourning countrymen, seeing now the man and not the causes with which his name was associated, made no secret of their

[1] Greville's *Memoirs*, January 13th 1846 and January 22nd 1848.

sorrow. Gladstone, in those lovely lines, composed by Scott in memory of
a greater than Peel, voiced all the profundity of their regret.

> Now is the stately column broke,
> The beacon light is quenched in smoke;
> The trumpet's silver sound is still,
> The warder silent on the hill.

LORD JOHN RUSSELL

Afterwards 1st EARL RUSSELL
born 1798 died 1878

Entered Parliament 1813 (Tavistock)

Paymaster-General of the Forces, without Cabinet rank (Grey's administration). Admitted into Cabinet 1831

Home Secretary and Leader of the House of Commons (Melbourne's administration) 1835

Colonial Secretary (Second Melbourne administration) 1839-1841

Prime Minister, July 1846 to February 1852

Foreign Secretary (Aberdeen's administration) December 1852. Resigned February 1853

Colonial Secretary (First Palmerston administration) February 1855. Resigned July 1855

Foreign Secretary (Second Palmerston administration) June 1859 to October 1865

Prime Minister October 1865 to June 1866

CHAPTER VI

LORD JOHN RUSSELL

IN the annals of English families who have advanced from small beginnings to great estate, there are few more curious chances to record than that which led to the rise of the house of Russell. In the winter of the year 1506 the Archduke Philip, the husband of the mad Joanna, and the brother-in-law of Katharine of Aragon, fell so abominably seasick as he cruised in a gale down the English Channel, that he put into Weymouth harbour to seek relief from his sufferings. The local potentate, Sir Thomas Trenchard, thereupon invited the storm-tossed prince to stay with him at Wolverton Hall; and around that trifling circumstance the Fates started to weave the long tapestry of the Bedford inheritance. Lacking the gift of tongues, Trenchard sent for his neighbour and kinsman, John Russell, who could talk the language of the Archduke; and this young man made himself so extremely agreeable to the convalescent prince that he received an invitation to join him at Windsor where he was due. There Henry VII took a fancy to him and provided him with a place in the royal household; and thence the family started what in the retrospect appears a facile ascent to the seats of the mighty. With one exception—that of Lord Russell, commonly and incorrectly called Lord William Russell, who became involved in the Rye House Plot and lost his head in consequence—the Russells cultivated the virtue of prudence. Estates and titles—large estates and lofty titles—piled up through the perilous period of the Reformation. Cheneys, Tavistock, Woburn and, most valuable of all, the Protector Somerset's forfeited property of Covent Garden, laid the foundation of enormous wealth; and meanwhile, a barony blossomed into an earldom, which again with the coming of the Whig Deliverer, was exalted into a dukedom. An astute flexibility must have had something to do with this prodigality of success; and, indeed, it is hardly probable that without it one head of the family should have been the friend of Thomas Cromwell and also have given away Mary Tudor at her marriage to Philip of Spain, while another should have commanded the Parliamentary Horse at Edgehill in 1642 and have fought for the King at Newbury in 1643. Yet for all the spacious splendours and august advantages that fell to their share, no Russell before the reign of Victoria had held the position of First Minister of the Crown. That was left to the subject of this essay to achieve; and that he did achieve it is all the more to his credit, inasmuch as he was a delicate boy, and grew up without strong health or any grandeur of presence such as serves, at times, to win for a public man an esteem and an influence beyond his deserts.

With the earlier part of Russell's biography this book is not much concerned. It is interesting to recollect that he had fallen under the magic of Charles James Fox, and that he had written a life of him that can hardly be said to have survived. It is interesting, too, to recollect that the young Russell had visited Wellington during the war in the Peninsular and that the Duke became a frequent visitor at Woburn, where his Tory principles were more tolerable than the unstable views of Canning.[1] It is more interesting, perhaps, to add that some few years after the Peninsular War Russell visited Napoleon at Elba, and described him in a notebook as looking 'not unlike the whole length figure of Gibbon', with fat cheeks and a rather turn-up nose, a dusky eye, and a mouth both contemptuous and decided; very different, in fact, from the Roman with classic features which his coinage and portraits had sought to portray. Russell describes him as good-natured and easy in his talk, as possessing an agreeable laugh and smile, and as repeating garrulously a number of pointless questions.

Russell had been as closely associated in the public mind with the Reform Bill of 1832 as any man, except Grey; so indeed that Sydney Smith, exemplifying the mild jests in which one has to deal in order to sustain a reputation for jocularity, styled him 'Lord John Reformer'. Russell had not the social address of a popular leader, but he was most frequently on the popular and, in the view of the period, progressive side: yet the name of 'Finality John' which he acquired in Melbourne's time, on account of his avowed intention in Melbourne's time of associating himself with no further extensions of the suffrage, betrays some qualms of aristocratic doubt and justifies the name of 'the last Whig Government' by which his great administration goes. It was the way and the weakness of the later Whig philosophy to assume the airs and graces of the grand manner whilst countenancing and encouraging ideas subversive of that order of things which had done much to secure its intellectual ascendancy. If we look close at the Whig technique it appears not unlike what I have known an artist describe as the foundation of a Gainsborough landscape—an assortment of small hills and hillocks upon which the Whigs had sat themselves down and from which they by no means intended to be dislodged. In the nature of things, however, there is clearly a limit to such complacent condescension and easy generosity as theirs. The time must inevitably come when the benefactions, both political and economic, which the Whig magnates could confer without serious loss to their position or prestige become exhausted. Still, when John Russell formed his administration in July 1846 the Whigs made no small show with historic names, though there was no denying that they were kept in

[1] See G. W. E. Russell, *Collections and Recollections*, p. 17.

power not so much by the favour of the nation as by the mutual hatred of the Peelites and the Protectionists. Russell wanted, indeed, to include some Peelites, with Peel at their head, in his Cabinet, if he had been able; but their leader would not consent, nor would his followers serve without him. This independence of Peel's rather tended to emphasize the ascendancy over all the other politicians of the time which, notwithstanding his changes of opinion, he had now for the second time in his career manifestly established in the eyes of the nation. Russell could never hope to surpass him in this sort of esteem. Honourable, courageous and clever, Russell was still a slight man intellectually as well as influentially; and, for all his indisputable ability and industry, overshadowed within the Cabinet by Palmerston—abounding in vitality, dashing in action, rich in experience, and a very Podsnap in assurance that the ways of his fellow countrymen were as a light unto the world—and without the Cabinet by Peel, to whom Cobden could write in 1846: 'You represent the IDEA of the age, and it has no other representative among statesmen.'[1]

Cobden, indeed, went so far as to fancy that Peel, had he wished, could have drawn to his standard as leader of a new party both the wayward enthusiasm of the masses, living always in hope of better things, and likewise the commercial intelligence of the middle class in a manner and to a degree not contemplated by Grey or Russell at the date of the Reform Bill. But, however that may be, 'the last Whig Government' went unchallenged by Peel, its old opponent, and fell presently before a deft blow from Palmerston, its own familiar friend and for some time associate. 'Pam' as the world called him, was no doubt temperamentally unfit to fight as brother-in-arms beside the House of Grey, which, appropriately enough, manned the last bastions of Whiggery and merited the name of its 'old Guard'. At the Exchequer Russell had placed Charles Wood, distinguished, like Peel, by a double-first, and married to a daughter of the Lord Grey of the Reform Bill; whilst over the Colonial Office presided the then-reigning Lord Grey, whose opposition a year earlier to the formation of a Whig administration had prevented Russell from going down in history as the repealer of the Corn Laws.[2] Then, at the Home Office, sat Sir George Grey with all the grace of a gentleman, though without any equipment in other ways remarkable. Under his department came at that date the duty of policing Ireland; and Ireland was fast becoming a problem of the first magnitude. O'Connell's race was nearly run; and Catholic Ireland which, had rather more leading Protestants been as wise as Pitt or rather fewer influential Protestants not been as unwise as George III, might have become integrated with England, was starting to cut away and driving the dour colony of Scots in Ulster to cling the more tenaciously to the United Kingdom.

[1] Morley, *Life of Cobden*, Vol. I, p. 392.   [2] See Morley's *Gladstone*, Vol. II, p. 244.

Neither in 1846 during the closing months of the old Parliament, nor after an appeal to the country in 1847, which made little change in the relative position of parties, had the Whigs that clear majority over the rest which would have enabled them to take a clear line of their own. The country, so far as can be ascertained, liked the thought of Peel at the head of affairs better than that of Russell; and in Parliament it was the dislike of the Protectionists for Peelites and of the Irish for the English which gave the last Whig Cabinet such power as it possessed. Lord John, though his frame was frail, had as firm and tenacious a will as the most part of his family; so much, indeed, that Sydney Smith assured him that Euclid would have had a poor chance with him, had he happened to form the opinion that the interior angles of a triangle were not equal to two right angles. Yet the policy of the administration in respect of Ireland, which was by far the greatest matter they had to deal with, is described by a Liberal historian 'feeble and futile',[1] and, though the words are strong and sweeping and require at any rate some qualification, they must be accepted as on the whole appropriate. Russell had diagnosed the Irish problem by the epigram: 'Your oppressions have taught the Irish to hate you, your concessions to brave you.' And he had written to Tom Moore the poet: 'I wish I knew what to do to help your country. But, as I do not, it is of no use giving her smooth words.'[2] There seems no particular reason to suppose that Russell's grasp of the Irish problem had grown stronger with time. He seemed to most people, and certainly not least to the Irish themselves, whose jurymen at inquests on victims of the famine would sometimes bring in verdicts of wilful murder against him personally, to fumble and fail. Certainly matters did eventually improve, but at the cost of a gigantic emigration which reduced the population of Ireland from something like eight million to five or less. It had risen between 1800 and 1840 by just about the amount that it fell after the famine; but the conditions of life (or existence) enjoyed (or suffered) by this increase of inhabitants as it is depicted in the Report of the Devon Commission, which came out in 1844, are so appalling that the decline, though it be made a subject of reproach to the English Government, can hardly be made a subject of regret for the historian.

Russell acted as any strong individualist and staunch Protestant might have been expected to do in the desperate circumstances in which he suddenly found himself placed. Other men of other opinions to his might conceivably have shown a deeper understanding or taken a more inspired initiative. Disraeli, for instance, analysed the Irish situation with the keener imagination of a race which also had greatly suffered for its faith. And Peel in 1844, when he trebled and made permanent the Government grant to the Irish Catholic

[1] Paul, *History of Modern England*, Vol. I, p. 117.
[2] Walpole, *Life of Russell*, Vol. I, p. 182.

Seminary at Maynooth, had made a gesture of sympathy which in John
Morley's opinion deserved to rank as 'one of the boldest things he ever did'.[1]
Peel's memorandum, too, of April 1849, which was drawn up after a
solicited interview for the information of Clarendon, the Viceroy, shows
slightly more imagination than can be claimed for Russell. The policy that
commended itself to the Conservative leader included the appointment or
a Commission to superintend public relief given in the Irish Unions; a
return to the Irish Poor Laws of 1838 which required the able-bodied pauper
to enter the workhouse, if room was available, in order to obtain relief; the
transfer of properties hopelessly encumbered; the establishment, perhaps in
Connemara, of a model estate under the direction of Commissioners; and
the adoption of a policy of road-making, similar to that which Marshal
Wade had instituted more than a century before for the pacification of the
Highlands of Scotland. So by degrees, Peel thought, might the Irish be
weaned from dependence on their priests, as the Scotch had been weaned
from dependence on their chieftains. This was to come nearer to the heart
of the matter than the Whigs, and yet not quite to get home. A grudging
and suspicious toleration of a nation's proudest convictions was not enough.
If the soul of Ireland was to be won, a courtesy hitherto unknown in the
treatment of its religion must displace a contempt which all too plainly
declared that modern Protestantism, for all its boasted tolerance, did not
truly recognize a freedom of faith in others analogous to its own demand
for religious liberty. There was nothing unreasonable in believing that, if
God had revealed Himself at all, He had also provided a seat of authority,
a Chair of Faith, where His revelation might be preserved in totality and
defined with certainty. The Irishman was satisfied that it was so; and the
notion of hierarchy was as congenial to his thought as to that of the Hebrews.
But to the most part of Englishmen all this had for some while past seemed
fabulous; and the fable doubtless repelled him the more that at this very
hour, in the oldest and most romantic of English universities, John Henry
Newman, the leading, kindly light of that place and time, had found it to
be no fable at all. John Russell swore by the English Reformation in religion
and by the French Revolution in politics; and he put his faith in Luther
and Charles James Fox, between whom a later Prime Minister[2] was to discover a singular resemblance of character. The full force of his feeling was,
a year or two later, to appear in his famous letter to the Bishop of Durham,
breathing fire and fury against the Pope for restoring in England a Catholic
hierarchy obedient to the Holy See. A pure rationalist would have seen that
it was as sensible to rail against St. Augustine, whom Pope Gregory indisputably despatched on the unpromising mission of making the Angles into
angels and had as certainly constituted first Archbishop of Canterbury. But

[1] Morley, *Life of Gladstone*, Book II, Chapter IX.   [2] Rosebery, in his *Pitt*, p. 3.

Russell's indignation did not give him time for reflection; and his 'very imprudent, undignified and, in his station, unbecoming' letter, as Greville calls it,[1] produced in Ireland an unspeakable mischievous effect, as Greville learnt in a letter from the Viceroy. The unwisdom of Russell's violence was, however, at the time very acceptable to many of his countrymen; and it was only some while after it had been stamped on the statute book by the abortive Act of 1851 against the use of territorial titles not authorized by Parliament, that public opinion came round to the view, held by all sensible men, such as Aberdeen, from the first, that the Prime Minister had excited himself both unduly and undesirably. Later, there appeared in *Punch* Leech's memorable cartoon, depicting little Johnny Russell chalking 'No Popery' on a wall and then taking to his heels. The cartoon was supposed to have proved damaging at the polls; but the naughty little boy, being at heart rather a nice old man, sent for the artist and inquired if he could do anything for him. Leech asked for a nomination for his son at the Charterhouse; and Russell gave it.[2] Thus was humour served and thus did *noblesse oblige*.

Russell, to give him his due, had long been statesman enough to see that, feel as he might about Papal interference in England, the endowment of the Catholic clergy in Ireland, and the maintenance of their churches there, would have gone a great way towards the solution of the Irish problem. In 1848, that year of Revolution, he may be found consulting with Clarendon,[3] a Catholic and a landlord, about this idea which he had long entertained. The scheme, however, smashed on the stumbling-block of finance. No Whig could readily consent to despoil the Established Church of the Protestant minority in order to endow the Rome-oriented Church of the Catholic majority. It might be just; it might be reasonable; it might be right. But Mr. Podsnap, convinced that it was 'not English', would never have stood it. It was safer to stick to a secular policy. That meant the encouragement of emigration, the enforced sale of encumbered estates; the making of roads, even if unwanted, for the sake of the workless; the distribution of relief, even if the British taxpayer groaned and grumbled, to the starving. There were those who thought waste land should have been reclaimed; but, besides the evident unfairness involved in giving such State aid to one property and not to another, there was the further difficulty that the plan would bring an unearned increment to the fortunate landlord, who would often enough have done little enough to deserve it. There were those again, like Lord George Bentinck, who wanted railways put in hand as relief works; and here Russell laid himself open to a charge of inconsistency by first rejecting the plan on the ground that the proportion of such expenditure which would go to unskilled

[1] *Memoirs*, November 10th 1850.
[2] Stuart Reid, *Lord John Russell*, p. 192.
[3] The fourth Earl, afterwards Foreign Secretary 1853-8, 1865-6 and 1868-70.

LORD JOHN RUSSELL
From the portrait by G. F. Watts

labour under the schemes was too small to be effective, and then subsequently yielding and making some use of the suggestion.

Russell's policy, in fact, bore all the look of casual opportunism; yet, for all that, it served the Viceroy well enough to make the visit of Victoria and Albert to the distressful isle in the August of 1849 a distinct success, in itself a tribute to the policy pursued. Victoria and Albert—they acted more and more in association during the last Whig administration—received a warm welcome, which in the Queen's speech of the following January was warmly recognized. Had this gesture but created a precedent, had the Queen returned again and again, the rift between Hibernia and her English and Caledonian sisters might quite possibly never have widened into the present, to all appearance final, breach. One of John Russell's oldest friends, as already noticed, was Tom Moore, whose *Memoirs* and correspondence after the poet's death he set himself to edit. It was a thousand pities that neither Minister nor poet knew in that age of romance how to wake the harp hanging mute in Tara's halls and to strike the strings into a harmony that might have filled the isles of Britain with a new music, but the chance was missed. Neither 'home rule' nor 'twenty years of resolute government', the two rational alternatives, was calculated to provide the basis for a congenial understanding such as would gradually destroy centuries of maltreatment and restore a mutual courtesy of thought symbolized by a common monarch invested with a triple crown. The test of statesmanship is its power of integration. A crisis falling, in John Russell's phrase, like 'a famine of the thirteenth century upon a population of the nineteenth' was an hour when benevolence and understanding had their fullest opportunity. 'That was a period', observed Disraeli of Ireland at this time, 'when all classes of the community were pervaded by an admirable sympathy; religious rancour and political discord alike vanished; the clergyman and the priest laboured in the same vineyard; the contributions of private charity, especially those collected and managed by a committee of London Merchants, were princely in amount and distributed with skilful zeal . . .'[1] Peel thought along much the same lines.[2] But, if the hour for statesmanlike action had come, the man had not. The last Whig fumbled with the Irish problem until he fell, doing a little good but never able to bring himself to deal with the matter on larger lines such as Peel was presumably feeling after when he appointed the Devon Commission in 1844, or such as Disraeli adumbrated. Russell was a little too dry, a little too cautious, a little too lacking in vitality to find exactly the right approach to the question; and Palmerston, the other leading figure in the Cabinet and an Irishman to boot, was content to be jaunty and to attribute the troubles of Ireland to its climate. As for the great

[1] See Villiers's *A Vanished Victorian*, p. 169.
[2] *Life of Lord George Bentinck*, pp. 357-8.

F

clan of Greys in the administration, their inertia seemed to grow with time: and so the psychological moment died away, never really to return.

John Russell, for so delicate a man, was a hard worker and a good speaker. The last Whig administration bears the mark of this, not only in these efforts of uncertain aim in Ireland which fill so large a space in its history, not only in the passing of the Ecclesiastical Titles Act which took up so much of its time, but in that Bill of 1850 for giving self-government to the colonies of Victoria, Tasmania and South Australia, which the Prime Minister himself, an Imperialist before the most part of his fellow statesmen, steered to the statute book, and in those other Bills which, though of private origin, obtained Government support—the Free Libraries Act of 1850, and the Factory Act of 1847, limiting the hours of labour to a still-excessive ten hours for women and young persons. In connection with education also an administrative decision of first-class importance was brought into force. Teachers were, as the word was, to be 'apprenticed' in certain selected schools, to be paid during training and in due course to be employed in State-inspected schools, where their salaries could be raised by half as much again from State grants, and were finally, after fifteen years, to become eligible for pensions.

In this matter, and perhaps, too, in some others, Russell did not display any marked clarity of thought. As a Liberal he was committed to freedom of opinion for parents and to equality of opportunity for religious denominations. As a Protestant, however, he was not attracted by the idea of the State endowment of any religion that did not represent, as he and the most part of his fellow countrymen understood it, the pure word of God: and as a Prime Minister, just about, in the year 1847, to face a General Election he was alive to the inexpediency of imperilling the evangelical vote. Consequently he temporized and finally extricated himself from his difficulties by expressing a pious or, perhaps more justly, a platonic hope that, later on, he might be able to make a grant to Catholic schools whose claim, in principle, he did not deny.

John Russell cuts at times, though not invariably, rather a brave little figure in his long struggle with self and circumstance, but the political magnitude of Peel was still there in 1847 to make him look small, and the popular address of Palmerston was pushing him more and more out of view. England, as we all know, dearly loved a lord in the middle of the nineteenth century; and 'Pam' had the peculiar qualification of being, not, as John Russell was, a mere lord by courtesy, but the real thing—a peer in his own right, yet only an Irish peer, and thus qualified to sit in the House of Commons, whilst still enjoying the still considerable prestige of a peerage of sorts. A breezy, genial, jaunty way with him; a John Bullishness on occasion sufficient to set all the Podsnaps shouting for joy; a blarney of thought and speech both very much in character with John Bull's other island; a fine house in Mayfair in which to assemble his followers and his friends; and a wife as accomplished as any hostess of the period to grace the head of his stair—of all these things this gay Mephistophelian personage of whom they said abroad that, if the Devil had a son, he was surely Palmerston, was possessed.

What had Russell to put into the balance in comparison with all this? It seemed as far a cry from the Palace in Piccadilly, where Palmerston and Lady Palmerston held their court, to Pembroke Lodge in Richmond Park, where Russell, domestic, retiring, conscientious and scholarly, made his quiet home, as the disposition of the Foreign Secretary was politically remote from that of the Prime Minister. The ill-assorted couple managed, however, to collaborate somehow, though the constitutional machine groaned and creaked noisily under the effort. The source of trouble was twofold. Palmerston cared not a hang what his colleagues thought or whether he carried out their intentions. But, even so, the current of resentment in ministerial circles might have been contained, if it had not been that Palmerston was as indifferent to the views of the Court as he was to the views of the Cabinet. Victoria herself had a remarkably strong will; and Albert possessed a good acquaintance with the Continent and a fine judgment to make use of it. To have the Foreign Secretary, who was by nature an incurable meddler in the affairs of other countries, provided he could, or thought he could, keep clear of war, despatching instructions which the Court had not approved, or of which it was completely unaware, was more than an intelligent Sovereign or her husband could be expected to put up with. There was constant friction; and had it not been that Palmerston achieved an outstanding parliamentary victory, which is still very much remembered, in the famous case of Don Pacifico,[1] by means of a magniloquent, if on closer inspection, rather ludicrous peroration, it might have been impossible for him to retain office as long as he did. It was in vain for Gladstone to point that, under the law of Nature and of God, no one Christian nation had any title to free itself from the obligation to respect the rights of the rest implicit in the idea of Christendom; or that a Roman citizen had been

---

[1] The King of Greece had expropriated the property of various British subjects without redress, whereupon Palmerston took summary action. His most spectacular performance was in defence of a dubious financier, Don Pacifico, whose house had been sacked by the Athenian mob. The British Foreign Secretary ordered Admiral Parker to blockade the coast and seize merchantmen, the French tried to arbitrate, but their emissary was treated so inconsiderately by Palmerston that he was recalled. Lord Stanley moved a resolution against the government in the Upper House, which was carried by twenty-seven. The Cabinet, however, stood by Palmerston, and the Radical free trader J. A. Roebuck was selected to bring forward a vote of confidence. Palmerston was triumphant in the ensuing debate and the vote of confidence was carried by forty-six.

privileged, as the member of a conquering race, to ride roughshod over the claims of justice in a manner that England could neither desire nor aspire to imitate. Over such fine ethic arguments the phrase *Civis Romanus sum* easily carried the day; and Palmerston, whom Russell had incautiously hailed as 'the Minister of England', went from strength to strength, or perhaps more justly from folly to folly. Masterfulness, however, is pretty sure in the end to meet its match; and in that very summer of 1850, when Palmerston achieved his supreme parliamentary success, the Queen's patience expired. On the twelfth of August, in an historic memorandum addressed to the Prime Minister, the Queen laid down that she required the Foreign Secretary to state distinctly what he proposed to do in any given case, to await her sanction which, when conveyed to him, must be neither altered nor modified on pain of dismissal; and furthermore, to apprise her of anything important that had passed between himself and other Foreign Ministers, and to let her have foreign despatches requiring her consideration and assent, in good time. Russell kept the contents of this memorandum very much to himself and, though it was communicated to Palmerston, it remained unknown to the Cabinet and escaped the searching eye of Greville. Two days after it was written Palmerston, who continued in public to show no sign of discomfiture, solicited an interview with the Prince Consort, and seems to have excused himself in agitation and tears. Character, however, is not easily changed by crisis; and Palmerston rapidly resumed his accustomed habits in diplomacy.

The attention of Europe was at that time preoccupied with events in France, where the Prince-President was busy transforming himself into Napoleon III. On December 2nd 1851, disregarding his oath to maintain the Constitution, he arrested his more dangerous opponents, dissolved the National Assembly, and appealed to the people to elect him President for ten years with full control of the administration. Resistance to these designs was forcibly suppressed; and matters moved forward towards a plebiscite which ensured to the unscrupulous but popular adventurer the position and power that he desired. Palmerston, liking the President better than the Assembly, or perhaps trusting him more, approved his proceedings and, without consulting the Prime Minister or his colleagues, informed the French Ambassador that he was in sympathy with what had been done. Three days later he advised the British Ambassador in Paris that the Queen's Government desired to abstain from all interference with the internal affairs of France; but when Lord Normanby, the Ambassador in question, communicated these instructions to the French Foreign Minister, the latter replied that Palmerston had already signified approval of the *coup d'état* through the French Ambassador in London. The Queen was furious: Lord John summarily dismissed the Foreign Secretary, though with the offer (which was not accepted) of the Lord Lieutenancy of Ireland; and the Cabinet approved what Lord John had done. Except upon paper Palmerston was seldom indiscreet, and his words concealed his thought. He was all smiles and soap with his successor, Lord Granville; and he made little attempt to answer Russell's crushing exposure of his conduct—an exposure rendered the more devastating by the production of the pertinent part of the Queen's memorandum. 'There *was* a Palmerston', observed Disraeli, as he looked on; and for just on two months it was permissible to think so. But in February of 1852 that devil's son of an ex-Foreign Secretary caused the last Whig Government to be defeated on a Militia Bill, and thus gave his historic 'tit-for-tat' to Johnny Russell so effectively that it was not until after Palmerston's death in 1865 that his rival regained the Premiership.

To trace John Russell's career during that interval of thirteen years is not the purpose of this essay. It is enough to say that, after the brief Derby administration, he resumed office under Aberdeen in 1852, when for a short time he held the Foreign Office. Herbert Paul the historian, who had no love for John Russell, has described him as 'the evil genius of the Coalition' of Peelites and Whigs that under the leadership of Aberdeen had been formed into something very like a Ministry of all the Talents. The judgment is harsh, but it is not altogether without justification. Russell had been persuaded by Macaulay that it was his patriotic duty to join the new administration, but he had not been persuaded that it was his private duty to forget himself. He remembered perpetually that he had been Prime Minister; and he was difficult to the last degree. He wished at first to have the Foreign Office as well as the leadership of the House of Commons, but presently added the condition that he should be able to throw up the former as soon as he wanted, and pass it over to Clarendon. Aberdeen, who did not think he could manage without Russell's assistance in Parliament, consented to this unusual arrangement. During his brief tenure of the Ministry of Foreign Affairs, Russell made, however, several vital decisions which bore heavily upon the situation in the Near East, where a dispute had arisen between Turkey and Russia over the guardianship of the Holy Places at Jerusalem. More will be said about this when we come to consider Aberdeen's administration. What needs to be said here is that Russell took the tremendous decision of sending Stratford de Redcliffe back to Constantinople—Stratford de Redcliffe, whom the Russian Emperor had refused to receive, who detested Nicholas in consequence, and whose influence over the Turks it is impossible to overestimate. That, alone, was an action on Russell's part of which the consequence can hardly be exaggerated; and with it must be coupled the fact that Russell rejected the overtures of the Russian Emperor through Sir Hamilton Seymour for a secret understanding between Russia and Britain for the settlement of the Eastern Question.

Nicholas had long believed that this was the true way of approaching the problem, and had explicitly said to the British Ambassador at St. Petersburg that, if Britain and Russia were agreed, he was entirely without anxiety as to what the rest of Europe might do. To have rejected these overtures was thus a mistake whose importance cannot be measured.

Russell, though generally condemned as an ineffective Prime Minister, is as generally praised as a competent Leader of the House of Commons. His reputation in this capacity, however, was gravely damaged by his conduct in 1855, when owing to the mismanagement of supplies and services for the Crimean War the Aberdeen administration came under heavy fire in Parliament. There can be no dispute that, confronted by Roebuck's motion for an inquiry, John Russell ran away instead of standing his ground; and that in the retrospect he recognized his fault, though he qualified the admission by charging himself with a worse mistake in having taken office at all. At the time, however, he pleaded that he could not see how Roebuck's motion could be resisted; and proceeded to resign. Other men did not see how a politician—and one, in particular, who had been so largely instrumental in promoting hostilities—could honourably withdraw at the moment when the conduct of the war, for which he was as much responsible as any man in the Government (Sidney Herbert the Secretary-at-War, and Newcastle the Secretary-for-War, alone, perhaps, excepted) came under discussion.

The Aberdeen administration, deserted in its hour of crisis by its commander in the Commons, suffered a staggering defeat; and the Sovereign turned to Derby to carry on her Government. But the Rupert of debate was no Rupert in counsel; and discretion in a political crisis appeared to him, not on this occasion only, to be the better part of valour. To the consternation of his party at the time, and to his lasting condemnation in the pages of history, Derby refused to form an administration. The Queen then turned to Russell, who was by no means averse from resuming the high office to which he probably felt he had as good a right as any man with some title to be considered. His recent pusillanimous defection was not, however, forgotten; and though, as the saying went, Johnny was always in the end forgiven, the time for pardon had not yet come. He very soon found that no one of any importance would serve under him; and Palmerston thus became inevitable. That game old fighting-cock consequently attained the supreme office in the State for the first time when he was over seventy and, with a short interlude, held it for a decade until he died.

Russell with his frail health was no match for that bold and buoyant spirit who, mastering a situation which Russell had not stayed to defend, might be said to have given his old associate 'tit-for-tat' more effectively even than before. The weaker vessel was compelled to content himself for the time with the Colonial Office.

In the event, as all the world knows, the Russian generals, Janvier and Février, 'turned traitor' to the Emperor Nicholas, and did him to death in the month of March;[1] and this circumstance enabled Russell to find more congenial employment at Vienna, where, on the Emperor's death, peace negotiations were resumed. Anyone who has read what Russell has written in his *Life* of Fox in condemnation of Pitt's entry into the Revolutionary War in 1793, may well fancy that no more earnest peacemaker could have been chosen. The fascination of Palmerston, however, was for Russell greater than the fascination of Fox; and, as it had been before the Crimean War broke out, so it was still, now that the war was on. Palmerston's high spirits retained their ascendancy over Russell's cooler judgment. There was no really good reason why Count Buol's proposal to settle, on the basis of Russia's retaining the same naval force on the Black Sea as before hostilities broke out, should not have been accepted; and Russell was demonstrably ready to come to an agreement on these lines. But neither Palmerston nor the Prince Consort, nor perhaps Stratford de Redcliffe, favoured such terms, though their main objection could not be confessed. By allying ourselves with France we had allied ourselves to a Government dependent, for all the pretence put forward in the famous phrase 'L'Empire—c'est la paix', upon recurring military successes. The maintenance of the dynasty demanded the capture of Sebastopol; and Palmerston favoured an Anglo-French *entente* based on the Bonapartes. Consequently the conclusion of peace needed to be deferred until after the fall of the fortress. Russell was too honest to be a skilled prevaricator in debate, but not so honest as to refuse to go back on his conversations with Buol. The Austrian Minister was quite justifiably indignant at what he regarded as British duplicity. He made public the truth; and Russell dared not deny it in the House of Commons. This ignominious exposure excited the fury of the Press and the public; and they fell upon Russell again and drove him into resignation. His apologists claim that he had saved the situation and sacrificed himself for his colleagues. It is not so easy to say that he had preserved the reputation of Britain for standing by her word.

However that may be, John Russell passed out of office and did four years' penance between the July of 1855 and the June of 1859, when he again accepted office as Foreign Secretary, and in that position he remained until 1865, when Palmerston died. The stronger personality had conquered, yet of these 'two dreadful old men',[2] as Victoria styled them, the feebler frame achieved the longer life. During the years of Russell's management of

[1] The Tsar had said that these two famous generals, signifying the bitterest months of the Russian winter, would always fight for him. But the Turkish victory of Empatoria in February 1855 was one of the decisive battles of the Crimean War, and the Tsar died a month later.

[2] *Queen's Letters*, February 25th 1864.

external affairs more than one highly critical issue came up for decision, but the importance of his own contribution to the outcome may be questioned. The Prince Consort revised on his deathbed the despatch relating to the seizure of the Confederate commissioners, Slidell and Mason, on a British steamer, and this revision is generally credited with having prevented hostilities with the U.S.A.[1] When the famous *Alabama*[2] case occurred in the following year there was no longer a Prince Consort to temper Russell's mismanagement. In respect of the unification of Italy under Cavour, who was backed by Napoleon III, which involved the spoliation of Austria, our old ally, the sympathies of the Court ran counter to those aggressive doctrines of nationality which attracted the minds both of Palmerston and Russell, and did so much to destroy the old intellectual solidarity of Europe. Fortunately, nothing more was asked of the Prime Minister and the Foreign Secretary than fair, fine words and benevolent approval in respect of a movement which frightened the French Emperor into unconscionable intrigues and acts of violence inconsistent with the Treaty of Vienna. The case of Schleswig-Holstein, however, which came up for consideration in 1863, touched Britain more nearly. The heir-apparent to the throne had been married in the spring of that year to the King of Denmark's daughter, and the King of Denmark was Prince Christian of Schleswig-Holstein. More of this matter will be heard when we come to the premiership of Palmerston. But Russell's ineptitude in the conduct of the business was all too evident to his contemporaries and to the Queen. In one of the essays which a future Foreign Secretary, some day to be reckoned very sagacious, was at that time contributing to the *Quarterly Review*, Russell's diplomacy was trounced in trenchant terms. 'It would be, perhaps, too much', the critic observes, 'to say that any of the despatches in the papers that have been published formally and absolutely pledge England to go to war, but they exhaust the resources of the English language to contrive threats that just fall short of this. They hint that she will; they declare that she may; they refuse to say that she will not; they intimate that she will treat the seizure of Schleswig for a material guarantee as she treated the seizure of the Principalities on the same plea in 1854; they regret that England and the German Powers are on the point of becoming enemies . . . In fact, Lord Russell seems to have thought that, so

[1] Slidell and Mason were two commissioners dispatched by the Confederacy to obtain sympathy and possibly arms from the governments of England and France. They sailed on a British steamer, which was boarded by a Federal ship, whose captain removed the commissioners. This international incident, which might have had serious consequences, is discussed in Chapter IX, p. 181.

[2] The *Alabama* affair (1862) dragged on for several years. The Federal government claimed compensation because the vessel, which was built at Birkenhead, and carried a partly British crew, acted as a Confederate privateer and raided Federal shipping. Lord John Russell peremptorily refused the Federal demand and the affair remained unsettled when Gladstone took office.

long as he qualified it with a "might" or a "may" or a "probably", there was no form of menace that it was improper for him or his ambassadors to utter.'[1] The Danish Foreign Minister, indeed, as the essay goes on to observe, told a British diplomatist that he knew it to be as hard to find the form of words that would bind Lord Russell as it used to be in medieval legends to find the oath which would bind the Tempter.[2]

Russell, in a word, pursued Palmerston's policy of meddling, without Palmerston's drive or decision. He lacked, too, all the other's skill in presenting a bad as if it were the better cause to Parliament. It was well for him, and indeed for his country, when upon Palmerston's death in October 1865 the Queen called upon him to form the new administration, and that in this way the Foreign Office passed back into the abler hands of Clarendon. For some few months until June 1866 Russell carried on what was hardly more than the titular direction of the new administration from the seat in the House of Lords which he had accepted in 1861. The Whig Party, however, was evidently split in the Commons where Gladstone, the protagonist of an extended suffrage, and Sir Robert Lowe, the champion of a Lower House manned by the best men in the nation, however they might be best obtained, fought Homeric battles over the last Reform Bill of which 'Finality John', falsely so called, had long been an advocate. It was not a very startling Bill, for it did little more than propose to reduce the qualification for the county franchise from a rental of fifty pounds to one of fourteen, and of the borough franchise from a rental of ten pounds to seven; but wild and whirling words were used, and the greater of the two chief combatants (Gladstone) declared in later life that he had known no more formidable antagonist than the lesser (Lowe). The struggle terminated rather tamely in the defeat of the Government by eleven votes on a motion of Lord Dunkellin's to substitute a rateable for a rental value as the basic principle of the borough franchise. Russell, as Gladstone thought, 'secretly conscious that he had arrived at the last stage of his political existence',[3] was inclined to stake the life of his Ministry on a general vote of confidence; but Granville, and Gladstone himself, were so much against this that they advocated resignation, and the Prime Minister yielded in spite of the Queen's disapproval. His last premiership had fallen in a tricky time, what with the nation divided over the case of Governor Eyre,[4] the frightful calamity of a cattle plague, and a tremendous

---

[1] *Essays of Robert, Third Marquis of Salisbury, on Foreign Politics*, pp. 218, 219.
[2] ibid., p. 227.   [3] Morley's, *Gladstone*, Vol. II, p. 207.
[4] Eyre was Governor of Jamaica and in 1865 he quelled a native insurrection by a number of summary executions and harsh punitive measures. After much public outcry Eyre was recalled and a commission of enquiry condemned his methods, but the influential Jamaica Committee, under John Stuart Mill, agitated for a public prosecution of the ex-governor, though other sections of opinion supported him. In 1869 a prosecution was initiated, but the Grand Jury threw out the Bill.

commercial panic in the city; and the old man was probably wise to make way for younger Ministers.

'My dear Lord Russell', Gladstone had written to him a few months before, 'I have received to-night by telegraph the appalling news of Lord Palmerston's decease . . . Your former place, your powers, experience, services and renown do not leave room for doubt that you will be sent for. Your hands will be entirely free. You are pledged probably to no one, certainly not to me. But any government now to be formed cannot be wholly a continuation; it must be in some degree a new commencement.'[1] The letter was kindly meant, but it was also highly significant of the approaching absorption of the old Whig Party into the coming Liberal Dispensation of which Gladstone had become the prophet. The Reform Bill over which Russell's last administration stumbled and fell, formed a suitable conclusion to his political career. He had first become known through his association with the Reform Bill of 1832; and it was not inappropriate that he should finish his course on the eve of the Reform Bill of 1867 which was carried by Disraeli, and furnished the basis for the advancing faith in democracy. Russell's Bill, which failed, would, it is calculated, have added four hundred thousand voters to the electorate. Disraeli's Bill, which was passed, added nearly a million. Lecky recalls the fact that the old Prime Minister spoke with very considerable apprehension of the possible effects of the 1867 Reform Act, observing that he feared there was too much truth in the saying that the concessions of the Whigs had once been concessions to intelligence, but had become concessions to ignorance. Up to the very end of his public life Russell had been able to play the rôle of the benevolent aristocrat in sympathy with Radical catchwords, yet secure from their operation; and he remained as late as 1863 in Disraeli's idea of him 'the incarnate creation of High Whiggism'.[2] It was agreeable to talk about equality, and yet to feel as comfortably raised above the common herd of men as 'the Venetian oligarchy' of Disraeli's novels. But it was not a satisfaction that could be prolonged for ever; and it must be doubtful whether the new Whigs of Fox's breed saw like the old Whigs of Burke's tradition whither they were bound. It may well be true, as Froude asserts in his 'Short Study' of Cheneys and the House of Russell, that 'there is no instance, ancient or modern, of any long protracted national existence where an order or aristocracy and gentry is not to be found preserving their identity, their influence, and their privileges of birth through century after century'. Yet the doctrines of the French Revolution, unscientific and contradictory as they are, were already in Russell's time so far advanced in the minds of Englishmen as to threaten the Whig oligarchy in the most formidable degree. There is no maintaining

[1] Stuart Reid, Lord John Russell, pp. 335-40.
[2] Buckle, Life of Disraeli, Vol. IV, p. 390.

at one and the same time that all men are equal and that certain elect families are from generation to generation the best qualified to be the repositories of power. Whig sentiment said one thing; Whig doctrine another. The English Revolution of 1688 had been the making of the Whigs; the French Revolution of 1789 was their undoing. When Russell gave, as he said, his first advice as Prime Minister to the Queen in the words 'There is nothing so conservative as progress', he coined a good epigram but killed a great party. The Whigs went down before the Liberals, as the Liberals in our own time have gone down before the Socialists. They had not thought out their creed.

Russell was well liked by those who knew him well, though he was not at all times easy, even to those who knew him best. In the large world outside his immediate circle, where one well-chosen word or genial gesture counts for so much in making or maintaining a leader, he did not excel. But, taking him for all in all, recognizing his long service to the State, and not forgetting that simple faith which made him a protagonist of the Evangelical Party in the Church, he may well be reckoned an eminent Victorian. His home was happy, his tastes were modest, and his children were a constant joy to him. Yet when all that has been acknowledged and praised, it must be allowed that colleague and critic alike discerned in him a narrow attachment to great place and a keen eye for the main chance, neither of them quite worthy of a man of so much private virtue. Of this, however, he seems himself to have been unaware. 'Johnny', as Clarendon remarked, 'had always such high motives for doing himself a good turn.'

That, however, is not perhaps the note one would wish to sound in playing the old man out; and those who seek a kindlier memory should turn to the chapter in *Collections and Recollections* which George Russell— that burly, amusing raconteur of good stories about well-known men, whom some few of us may still recall as a diner-out giving good value for his dinner —devoted to the memory of his uncle. In a single lengthy sentence he has embalmed his memory of the table talk at Pembroke Lodge; and it would be a pity to curtail it. 'It was a curious and interesting privilege', he wrote, 'for a young man to sit in the trellised dining-room at Pembroke Lodge, or to pace its terraced walk looking upon the Thames, in intimate converse with a statesman who had enjoyed the genial society of Charles Fox, and had been the travelling companion of Lord Holland; had corresponded with Tom Moore, debated with Francis Jeffrey, and dined with Dr. Parr; had visited Melrose Abbey in the company of Sir Walter Scott, and criticized the acting of Mrs. Siddons; conversed with Napoleon in his seclusion at Elba, and ridden with the Duke of Wellington along the lines of Torres Vedras.' 'Never was so robust a spirit', continues this kindly kinsman, 'enshrined in so fragile a frame', and he goes on to solicit our compassion for one whose feeble digestion and (physically) faint heart rendered him incapable of discharging his duties otherwise than by resurgent determination. According to Sydney Smith, if that wag can be credited, the electors of Tavistock when they first saw the little man, were so appalled at the modest dimensions of the candidate soliciting their suffrages, that they had to be told that he had once been of larger size but had withered away, owing to his excessive exertions in the cause of Reform. Socially indeed, from shyness or awkwardness, he could be strangely wanting. His nephew illustrates this trait by the story of his behaviour at a concert at Buckingham Palace, when he deserted a seat beside the Duchess of Sutherland for one, at some distance off, beside the Duchess of Inverness. The incivility was so patent that someone asked him later why he had made the move. He replied that the fire beside Her Grace of Sutherland had been hot to the point of making him faint. The inquiring friend thereupon remarked that he hoped he had explained to the lady the cause of his move. To which he replied: 'Well!—no. I don't think I did that. But I told the Duchess of Inverness why I came and sat by her.'[1]

The manners of the *ancien régime* had evidently not altogether descended to the head of the last Whig administration; but, after all, the New Whigs affected to admire the political, if not the social, accomplishment of the *sansculottes*. Manners for them no longer made man; though to be quite fair to him, poor 'Johnny' on his deathbed reproached himself for the lapses from geniality which had marked his career: 'I have seemed cold to my friends, but it was not in my heart.'

Enough, however, has been said of the man; and it is time to seek for the verdict on the statesman. It is clear at a glance that Russell never had the stature of Peel or Palmerston among his contemporaries, or of Disraeli or Gladstone among his successors. In comparison with them he was a light weight. Yet the mention of almost any other among the Prime Ministers of Victoria leaves one with the sense that he fell below the mark. Neither Melbourne nor Aberdeen would have committed the absurdity of publishing the Durham Letter; the former because he would have thought the use of ecclesiastical titles by the Pope, or anybody else, a matter of small importance; the latter because his mind was instinctively tolerant and recoiled from any kind of religious discrimination. John Russell, however, was in religion a Whig of 1688, and in politics a Foxite of 1789; and that is pretty nearly as much as to say that on neither issue had he fully cleared his thought. 'Finality' was a word with which he coquetted, but at which he also boggled. What was really final to him was the reign of the Whigs. Whiggery was dying; and Russell's best claim to remembrance perhaps was that he kept

[1] G. W. E. Russell, *Collections and Recollections*, p. 13.

it alive so long by those qualities of his to which Greville[1] does justice in no very amiable spirit—great ingenuity, rare cleverness, but also smallness of mind, all helpful in their way to one seeking to stretch his opinions so as to last his time. He never really faced the problem which Mill, in the year 1847, just after Russell had come for the first time into power as Premier, diagnoses in a letter to Comte. Halévy does well to throw it into prominence, for it was greatly to engage English thought for the next hundred years and at the end, without much reflection, to be settled by sentiment. Mill wrote in these terms: 'We have embarked on a system of charitable government . . . To-day all the cry is to provide the poor, not only with money but, it is only fair to say, with whatever is thought beneficial, shorter hours of work for example, better sanitation, even education, primarily Christian and Protestant, but not excluding a modicum of secular information. That is to say they are to be governed paternally, a course to which the Court, the nobility and the wealthy are quite agreeable . . . They (i.e. the three above-mentioned classes) entirely forget, or rather have never known that well-being cannot be secured by passive qualities alone and that, generally speaking, what is done for people benefits them only when it assists them in what they do for themselves.'[2] From this passage, now just over a century old, it may well be inferred that we do more in the way of revolving round our deepest problems than we ever do in the way of solving them. There is some excuse, for all systems have their merits and all systems have their defects; and it is only natural to notice more particularly the defects of the system that is actually in operation. But whilst Disraeli looked to a Tory democracy to unite 'the two nations' of rich and poor, and Gladstone believed that Liberalism would do its boasted work and that money would fructify in the pockets of the people, the Whigs in their last representative man continued to arouse the spirit of a Reform of the Suffrage and then trembled as they saw it rise. There was neither light nor leadership nor the force of strong personality in John Russell; but something admirable may yet be found in his attempt to do his duty in that state of life to which it had pleased Providence to call him. He makes less appeal perhaps than any other Victorian Prime Minister to the spectator; and yet no member of his able and distinguished family has ever risen higher than he.

[1] Diary, January 30th 1846.
[2] Quoted from Halévy's *History of the English People*, 1841-52—'The Age of Peel and Cobden'—(English translation), p. 144.

LORD DERBY

EDWARD GEORGE GEOFFREY SMITH STANLEY
14th EARL OF DERBY
born 1799 died 1869

Entered Parliament (Member for Stockbridge) 1820

Under-Secretary for the Colonies (Canning's administration) 1827, resigned 1828

Chief Secretary for Ireland (Grey's administration) 1831 to 1833

Secretary for the Colonies (Goderich's administration) 1833. Resigned 1834

Secretary at War and for the Colonies (second Peel administration) 1841. Resigned 1845

Prime Minister February to December 1852
February 1858 to June 1859
June 1866 to December 1868

THE EARL OF DERBY
From the portrait by F. R. Say

CHAPTER VII

LORD DERBY

IT was in the year 1834 that Disraeli, a young man of thirty at the time, found himself dining in Storey's Gate with Mrs. Norton, one of the three famous Sheridan sisters.[1] Lord Melbourne—Home Secretary in Grey's administration at that time, and Mrs. Norton's particular friend—was also dining there; and to him Disraeli was introduced after dinner. The young politician made the most of his opportunity; and showed to such advantage that the elder man was moved to inquire whether he could be of any service to him. 'Tell me', he said, 'what you want to be?' The reply was given, it is said, with quiet gravity: 'I want to be Prime Minister.' Melbourne observed, no less seriously and with a sigh, that there was no chance of that in their time, that everything in that respect had the look of being ordered and settled, and that Grey would certainly be succeeded by one who had every requisite for the position of Prime Minister, a man in the prime of life and reputation, with old blood, high rank, great fortune, and greater ability to his credit. 'Nobody can compete with Stanley', he said, 'I heard him the other night in the Commons, when the party were all divided and breaking away from their ranks, recall them by the mere force of superior will and eloquence: he rose like a young eagle above them all, and kept hovering over their heads, until they were reduced to abject submission. There is nothing like him ... You must put all these foolish notions out of your head; they won't do at all. Stanley will be the next Prime Minister, you will see.'[2]

Curiously enough, in the very year when Melbourne uttered his vaticinations, Derby and Disraeli were alike, intellectually speaking, on the wing and moving from Left to Right; and it was within the ranks of Toryism, not of Whiggery, that their minds were to find contact, and also antipathy. Born and bred a Whig, Derby had early shown a leaning towards the creed of Canning, under whom he had served as Under-Secretary for the Colonies during Canning's 'hundred days' of power in 1827; and, after those days were done, he had remained in office under Goderich. As for Disraeli, he had found himself compelled by the failure of his poem[3] to seek new pastures

---

[1] Mrs. Norton's sisters were Helena, who became first Lady Dufferin and afterwards Lady Giffard, and Jane Georgina, who married Lord Edward Seymour, afterwards the twelfth Duke of Somerset. They were the daughters of Tom Sheridan, son of the dramatist.

[2] Monypenny, *Life of Disraeli*, Vol. I, p. 255.   [3] The Revolutionary Epick.

in politics and was wavering, about the time of his encounter with Melbourne, between some sort of association with 'Radical Jack'—the first Lord Durham —or a more prosaic and promising allegiance to Sir Robert Peel.

The strange relationship which presently arose, some ten years later after the fall of Peel, between these two converts to the 'Right' can perhaps only be understood if we bring ourselves to recognize in how great a flux almost all men's minds were left by the passage of the Reform Bill of 1832 and the anticipation of some further change that would again unmoor the ship of state and carry it towards coasts unknown and unexplored. We can see manifestations of this sense of apprehension in the new projects of Reform which, until Disraeli inconsiderately made off with the clothes of the shivering Whigs, obsessed the mind of Lord John Russell. We can see it more clearly still, perhaps, in the long dissertation on the change in the Constitution in which Greville apprehensively indulges on August 14th 1854. Ever since the disruption of the Conservative Party in 1840, he asserts, the House of Commons has been in a state of disorganization and confusion, and the great Party ties have been severed. Derby's first administration had fallen a year or two before; and Greville analyses the causes of its collapse in sentiments without restraint. 'The wretched composition of it', he says, 'its false position, and the mixture of inconsistency and insincerity which characterized it, deprived it of all respect, authority and influence, and it was more weak because divided and dissatisfied within, and because all the more honest and truthful of the party were disgusted and ashamed of the part they were playing.' But he continues with the significant admission, 'It was easier to turn them out than to find a good and strong government to replace them'.[1] If now we turn to a passage of some four years later in the same Diary, we come upon another significant entry. The Queen had just visited Radically-minded Birmingham, but had been well received there— 'with an enthusiasm', so Greville notes, ' . . . said to have exceeded all that was ever displayed in her former receptions at Manchester or elsewhere'. 'This great fact', he proceeds, 'lends some force to the notion entertained by many political thinkers that there is more danger in conferring political power on the middle classes than in extending it far beneath them, and in point of fact that there is so little to be apprehended from the extension of the suffrage, that universal suffrage itself would be innocuous.'[2]

The proper qualifications to sustain the demand for a vote, or for more votes than one, troubled most often men of that time almost to the point of obsession.

Neither Derby nor Disraeli, however (though for different reasons), found this particular difficulty troublesome. Disraeli, as we shall find when we come to examine the political philosophy of Sidonia in *Coningsby*, put little

[1] *Memoirs*, August 14th 1854.   [2] Greville's *Memoirs*, June 16th 1858.

confidence in reason as the quality required for the management of man, and much in those of passion and imagination. Derby, on the other hand, was not given to philosophizing. His three fundamental convictions, as Saintsbury in rather different language has observed, resolved themselves into a loyalty to the Church of his fathers, which never wavered; an almost exclusive concern for the landed interest which might be compared to that of the French Physiocrats for the Land itself; and a comfortable confidence that his own Order of Society would prove equal to any and every occasion. The breeder of racehorses or of prize livestock has no obvious cause to think that the laws of descent and pedigree are suspended in respect of political as distinct from other kinds of animals; and Derby, whose personal qualities left him little reason to quarrel with his mental and moral inheritance, went on his way without troubling overmuch about the egalitarian argument, which afforded an unstable foundation for the democratic mode of thought. He had, indeed, too robust and too witty a mind to be attracted to political systems. He saw that certain things had worked pretty well in the society and nation of which he was a member; and he was content to leave the matter there. To suspect or accuse him on this account of any narrowness of political vision is surely to misconceive his kind of mind. A man who can feel equally at home, as he could, mingling with a racing crowd or, alone by himself, rendering Homer into English—and this with admittedly good success—has spanned the earth, if not the heavens. But in fact Derby, for all the fun he extracted from the Turf or from those sharp and sudden frays in Parliament which got him the name of the Rupert of debate, never forgot the stars above. From the day in 1834 when he abandoned his Party and his prospects, because 'Johnny' (that is, John Russell) had, as he phrased it, 'upset the coach' by advocating some secularization of ecclesiastical property, to the day in 1868 when, with failing strength, but an eloquence all the more moving, he made his protest against the Disestablishment of the Irish Protestant Church, Derby fought, as it seemed to him at any rate, on the side of the angels.

Disraeli—we have, of course, his own word for it—supposed himself to be battling on that side, also. But no two champions of a cause were ever more subject to disagreements both of character and temperament. Derby had taken very much to heart Wolsey's famous charge to fling away ambition; but there was nothing in the world that Disraeli was less inclined to do. Eton and Oxford, abundant vitality and uncommon fortune had confirmed Derby's disposition to play politics like a game; to rush, shouting, into action like a Homeric warrior; and to let the Siege of the Whig citadel hang on for ten years or twenty. Disraeli, on the other hand, played like one sitting with coin and counter at the gaming-table, the eye never less than alert, the mind ever waiting on opportunity, with a bank to be broken or a fortune won by the luck of a stake or the expectation of a system.

How uneasy was this most singular partnership between, as contemporary observers called them, 'the Jockey and the Jew' can be read, not between the lines alone, but here and there in words that betray the tension on one side or the other. Turn for instance to a letter from Disraeli to Frances Anne, Lady Londonderry, a woman of some note in her time and a correspondent to whom the Tory leader in the Commons imparted matters of no small interest. Here in August 1854 (nearly six months before Derby's 'great refusal' to take office in February 1855, which Disraeli could never forgive) Derby is thus depicted by his lieutenant: 'As for our chief, we never see him. His house is always closed; he subscribes to nothing, though his fortune is very large, and expects everything to be done. I have never yet been backed in life. All the great personages I have known, even when what is called ambitious by courtesy, have been quite unequal to a grand game ... If ever there were a time when a political chief should concentrate his mind and resources on the situation, 'tis the present. There cannot be too much vigilance, too much thought and too much daring. All seem wanting.'[1] As for Derby's reaction to Disraeli let an entry of some six years later in Greville's *Memoirs* give the opposite side of the picture. 'March 18th 1860 ... Lyndhurst told me the other day that Derby had told Lady Lyndhurst he was so disgusted with the state of affairs at home and abroad, that he had serious thought of withdrawing from public life, and Clarendon told me that an eminent Conservative, who had begged not to be quoted, had said that he knew Derby was violently discontented with Disraeli, and prepared to dissolve their political connection.'

Froude, in that brilliant monograph which he executed in honour of the shade of Disraeli, has compared his subject's career to that of a racehorse straining for the goal. It would have been easier for Derby if he could have seen his colleague so. But, for the points of this particular Arabian, Derby, great lover of the Turf though he was, had no eye. Nor was Lord George Bentinck, whom Disraeli invested with the mantle of a hero and set in the midst of his classic account of the fall of Peel, much more to Derby's taste as a politician. In reply to a question from the Queen how Bentinck, had he been alive in 1852, would have behaved, Derby replied that 'Bentinck would have made confusion worse confounded'.[2] It is not surprising in these circumstances, though critics have often wondered at the omission, that there is so little mention made of Derby in Disraeli's *Life of Bentinck*. The two men were as alien temperamentally as men could be; and it is to their mutual credit that only one serious clash, of which we have only the account from Derby's side, appears to have occurred in the whole course of their corre-

[1] Monypenny & Buckle, *Life of Benjamin Disraeli*, Vol. III, p. 547.
[2] See Queen's Letters for Albert Mem. of November 29th 1852.

spondence; and this was in 1858, over the reconstitution of the Government of India after the mutiny, when Disraeli ignored in the House of Commons the agreed resolutions of the Cabinet on a 'very material point'. Both men clearly carried on their business with one another with much discretion, though discretion was precisely the quality in which Disraeli told Greville he found Derby lacking.[1]

There was, however, more than difference of temperament to take into account. The two men were able to work together, not because they were agreed upon fundamentals, but because, as Saintsbury puts it,[2] 'Derby's own lack of a settled theory of general politics . . . coincided with Disraeli's indifference to political particulars'. It made an uneasy combination, but was still for practical purposes a convenient one. Even so, this analysis must be regarded with some reserve. If we look at the main issue of the moment—the question of Protection and Free Trade—there is a sensible difference in the approach of the two men to it. In Derby's great speech of May 25th 1846 in the House of Lords, which was estimated by Palmerston as the finest of all his speeches, the sincerity and conviction of the orator are as apparent as his eloquence. In his mind's eye he saw the nation as a whole, and not those 'two nations' of rich and poor which chiefly occupied Disraeli's attention; and he saw the constituent parts of the nation, like living members of a body that must none of them be lost, and least of all those to whom the country looked to provide dynamic energy and focal fire for the cultivation of the soil. A balance, he argued, had to be maintained between 'the ancient monarchy', 'the proud aristocracy' and 'the reformed House of Commons', if the nation was to continue in its organic tradition. And there followed the famous apologia for the English squirearchy, of which, as leader of the Tory Party, he had become the accredited champion: 'Do not mistake me', he told his hearers, 'when I speak of the aristocracy. I do not speak exclusively or mainly of that body I have the honour to address. I speak, my Lords, of the great body of landed proprietors of this country. I speak of men unennobled by rank, and many of them undistinguished by great wealth, but who, and their ancestors before them, for generation after generation have been the centre each of his respective locality—who have the prestige of old associations attached to their names; who conduct the business of their respective counties; who influence the opinions and feelings of their respective neighbours; who exercise a modest and decent hospitality, and preside over a tenantry who have hereditary claims upon their consideration and affections. My Lords, these are the aristocracy of this country to whom I allude. Reduce these men, and you inflict an irretrievable, an irreparable injury upon the country.' For the protection of this order of society, more

[1] Greville, *Memoirs*, January 26th 1856.
[2] Saintsbury, *The Earl of Derby*, p. 81.

educative at its best than many masters in the manners that make man, more
concerned with development of the Colonies in which his far-ranging mind
had discerned, before the day when it became popular to do so, a true
expansion of England, Derby pleaded with a force and an eloquence which
nobody could deny. Disraeli, too, had indeed urged the claims of the Country
Party, but Disraeli had his eye upon the townsman's vote, upon the potentialities of urban wealth, and, to be just to him, upon the miseries that were
springing up among the vast aggregations of men, women and children
depending upon factory work for their subsistence. Not that it should be
supposed that Derby was indifferent to the lot of his less fortunate compatriots! The works of relief which he inspired during the Lancashire cotton-
famine of the 'sixties, the personal exertions which he made at that time and
in that cause, though his health was none too good and the other calls upon
his time were very considerable, place his deep interest in the relief of distress
entirely beyond question, and discover, more than any other part of his
political work as leader of the Conservative Party, that old talent of his for
getting things done, which had been noticeable in his early days at the Irish
and Colonial Offices. As chairman of the Central Executive Committee of the
Relief Fund he took steps to ensure that no case went unexamined, or, if
deserving, unhelped; that no money subscribed should be idly wasted; and
that no lead in generosity should be wanting. His voice was raised at a vast
Lancashire gathering in December 1862 in an eloquent appeal for funds; and
his hand was open simultaneously to make good his words with a gift of five
thousand pounds. No doubt, as he would himself have been the first to say, a
widow's mite counted for far more in the books of the Recording Angel; yet
still the sum was great, and, perhaps in its time, without parallel on any single
similar occasion. This large and energetic benevolence established the local
esteem felt for the House of Stanley for years to come, and, if it be true, as
Saintsbury observes, that a politician has seldom had such an opportunity
given to him, it is also true that no such opportunity was ever better taken.[1]

Derby on this occasion had shown his capacity to work in the spirit of
Shaftesbury, the greatest philanthropist of the time; and in his presence,
personality and power of speech there was such an assemblage of distinctions
as any believer in aristocracy must be well content to see. Yet it was part of
the man's genius that he could put off the grand seigneur and put on the
good-companion as easily as Prince Hal in the tavern at Eastcheap. Everyone
knows Greville's account of Derby as he appeared at Newmarket in the
April of 1851, evidently in the best of spirits, and consorting with a crowd of
blacklegs, betting men and loose characters of every description with whom
he was chaffing, joking, laughing and shouting. Here was a statesman without
inhibitions; a sportsman without exclusion; a countryman with as firm a

[1] Saintsbury, *The Earl of Derby*, p. 148.

tread on the Turf as any burgess could boast in the market-place or banker
in the counting-house; and, to conclude, a churchman, as completely at
his ease in contemplating the racecourse as in championing the cause of the
Altar and the Throne. Versatility could hardly farther go.

Not everybody, however, liked the man or his manners! His tongue was
too rollicking at times and his repartees were too mordant. Saintsbury goes,
perhaps, rather far when he declares that he can think of no statesman of the
first rank in England of whom so many sayings of 'absolutely the first order
in point of wit'[1] are recorded: and certainly the story he tells to illustrate this
opinion, though good enough in its way, fails to reach the required level.
Charles Greville had deliberately failed to appear in his place as Clerk of the
Council immediately after Derby's acceptance of the Premiership; and
Derby's notice was drawn by some busybody to the circumstance. With
admirable quickness he replied, 'No, really? You know I'm the most inatten-
tive fellow in the world about these things. I never notice, when I ring the
bell, whether John or Thomas answers it.' Saintsbury reckons this retort to be
the equal of anything that sprang from the lips of Retz, or Rochefoucauld or
Talleyrand; but Talleyrand's reply to some fool of a revolutionary who
sought his advice how best to start a new religion is immeasurably better: 'Go
and get yourself crucified, and rise again the third day.' So is Louis Philippe's
terse exclamation when they brought him news that the dying Talleyrand
was suffering all the pains of hell: 'Quoi? Déjà!' Doubtless, however, Derby's
caustic rejoinders could burn deep; and, if the particular instance given above
reached Greville's ears, it may have had something to do with the Diarist's
remark that of all men Derby was the one to whom he felt the greatest
political repugnance.[2] But the remark was no unfair retort to an intended
slight.

During his twenty years' leadership of the Conservative Party there can
be no doubt Derby found Disraeli a thorn in the flesh. He had, however, a
high standard of honour in his political dealings; and, as he told Prince
Albert in 1852 in so many words 'he could not in honour sacrifice Mr.
Disraeli, who had acted very straightforwardly to him.'[3] Interest, and even
convenience, might doubtless have encouraged him to behave less consider-
ately. He wanted nothing more than to reunite the two sections of the
Conservative Party; and it seems pretty clear that nothing stood more in the
way of this than the presence of Disraeli in high places among the Derbyites.

With these general observations in our minds, we must now follow the
succession of Derby's refusals and acceptances of the Premiership. The first
invitation to him to form an administration seems to have been made

[1] Saintsbury, *The Earl of Derby*, p. 203.
[2] *Memoirs*, March 20th 1858.
[3] Queen's Letters, 2nd Memo. of Prince Albert, November 28th 1852.

during the crisis of 1845–6,[1] after Peel had resigned on the issue of Repeal and John Russell had failed to implement his Edinburgh Letter advocating an unconditional abolition of the Corn Laws. It was not, however, till March 1846 that Derby was formally elected Leader of the Protectionist Rump; and it would have been near madness, with such men as he had at his disposal, to take office. During 1850 Russell came out with a Protestant manifesto, known as the Durham Letter, and in February 1851 he resigned on a franchise question. As a result Derby (or Stanley, as he remained until his father's death in the June of 1851), was approached again, not once, but twice. Feeling his party too weak in talent, however, he still held off. But when in 1852 February came round again—and February was frequently a fateful month for him—Derby yielded, and formed what goes by the style of the 'Who? Who?' Government. This singular appellation may be regarded as Wellington's last legacy to the Party which he had once led. It is said that, as Derby attempted to acquaint him with the names of the new Cabinet, the Duke, whose hearing had become very poor, kept audibly inquiring, 'Who? Who?' 'We have a most talented, capable, and courageous Prime Minister,' wrote Victoria to Leopold, 'but all his people have no experience.'[2] They were certainly not a very distinguished lot. Apart from the Prime Minister, Disraeli alone managed to make much mark; and that was mainly by throwing over in his first Budget the Protectionist traditions of the Party, and declaring himself a Free Trader at least in all but name. He praised the cheapness and abundance and general prosperity which had followed upon the adoption of a Free Trade policy by Peel; and he gave facts and figures to prove his point. Derby, in a conversation with Prince Albert[3] in the February of 1851, had told him, in reply to an enquiry, that he wished to see the word Protection 'merged'. If this meant that Protective principles were to disappear by a sort of absorption into taxes for revenue, there is, I suppose, some sense to be made of it; but the long and short of the matter is that in the twelve months during which he held power, Derby, without committing himself to any clear policy, allowed his principal lieutenant to beat a retreat. He even told the Prince, in reply to an indiscreet inquiry,[4] that in his opinion Disraeli had never had a strong feeling one way or the other about Protection or Free Trade, and that he would make a very good Free Trade Minister. At the General Election in the preceding July the Conservative Party had in truth spoken with two voices; the County candidates being for the most part Protectionists in their language, and the Borough candidates Free-Traders.

---

[1] So Saintsbury (*Life of Derby*, pp. 53, 57); but I find no evidence of this in the Queen's Letters; only Prince Albert's observation on December 25th 1845 that 'if Peel had resigned in November, Lord Stanley and the Protectionists would have been prepared to form a Government'.

[2] Queen's Letters, February 22nd 1851.   [3] ibid., March 9th 1852.

[4] ibid., November 28th 1852.

The Election had left the Parties pretty equally divided, with the Irishmen holding the balance. One historian has described the resulting situation as the equivalent of what mathematicians call 'unstable equilibrium'. There was a consequent, uncomely struggle to find words which might conceal thought; and Palmerston, whose sympathies were with Protection, if they were anywhere, found a formula which enabled the Government to swallow Charles Villiers's motion approving the repeal of the Corn Laws, without the stinging addition originally attached to it, to the effect that Repeal had been a just, wise and beneficial measure. Greater things, however, were in the air than these echoes of a battle lost.

In the middle of September the Queen was writing to the King of the Belgians to say that England had suffered an irreparable loss in the death of Wellington, who, she added, 'was the pride and the *bon génie*, as it were, of this country . . . the GREATEST man it ever produced, and the most devoted and loyal subject the Crown had ever had'. The Duke had been, she added, 'a true kind friend and most valuable adviser'. To think that all this was gone; that this great and immortal man belonged now to History, and no longer to the present, was a truth which she could not realize. 'We', she concluded, 'shall soon stand sadly alone; Aberdeen is almost the only personal friend of that kind we have left. Melbourne, Peel, Liverpool—and now the Duke—*all* gone.'[1]

The hero had just lived long enough to pay a tribute at the Academy banquet to the heroic dead who had gone down in the troopship *Birkenhead*; but his death occurred, appropriately, a month or two before, in Paris, Louis Napoleon revived the Imperial title, and before the throne of France was again occupied by a Bonaparte. Malmesbury, who was Derby's Foreign Secretary, with indecorous haste saluted in glowing terms the elevation of one whose acquisition of supreme power laid him open to the charge of breaking his oath and of violating the liberties of his fellow-countrymen; but these things were soon to be forgotten in an attempt common to both British Parties to establish with the Second Empire that cordial understanding which had once existed with the Orleans Monarchy. The days of the 'Who? Who?' Ministry were, however, numbered; and the autumn Budget of 1852 brought its downfall. Disraeli introduced his financial measures with his customary cleverness; and his ingenuity secured a certain amount of immediate praise from, amongst others, the Prime Minister. Derby, in a letter, congratulated the Chancellor on 'a masterly performance', added that he had had the satisfaction of listening to the five hours' exposition, the first half-hour only excepted, and could truly say that he had heard it with entire satisfaction, had admired the clearness and breadth of the statement and the skill with which the speaker had traversed some very difficult ground. This

[1] Queen's Letters, September 17th 1852.

first favourable impression did not, however, endure. Northcote, a future Chancellor of the Exchequer, was one day to observe that Disraeli's Budget presented too many assailable points to have much chance of success; and Derby at the time, in a communication some ten days later than his letter just quoted, observed that the administration had staked its existence upon the passage of the Budget as a whole, but that he no longer believed that they could carry the reduction of the Malt Tax, and that, as this was the only relief granted to the Agricultural Interest, the Budget did not provide that compensation for the acceptance of Free Trade which the Country Party had been led to expect. Skilful manoeuvring might delay defeat; but he added that in his view it was better to be defeated honestly in a fair encounter than to escape under a cloud from the reproaches of disappointed friends and from the sneers of malevolent opponents. Disraeli was thus left to fight a rearguard action, in which style of fighting he was a master. So far as his share in it went, this last phase of the lost battle was brilliantly conducted; and, in concluding, Disraeli coined a phrase destined to be immortal: 'This', he said, 'I know; that England does not love coalitions'; and he appealed from the victors of the hour to the mild and irresistible influence of public opinion, stronger than Parliament and sustaining those august and ancient institutions which without it would become the baseless fabric of a vision. His language roused a great enthusiasm among his sympathizers but then, contrary to custom, and much to the indignation of Ministerialists, Gladstone rose, like some shadow of Peel ingeminating wrath upon a foe caught in Time's revenges. Disraeli sat impressive, as the diatribe proceeded; whilst Derby sitting in the Gallery is said to have dropped his head upon his arms and muttered, 'Dull!' Not many thought the speech that; for, besides its invective, it had ranged in a masterly fashion over the whole subject of the Budget and had rested more especially upon the novel and, as it seemed to the men of that time, improvident policy of taxing precarious, or, as we say today, earned incomes, less heavily than invested ones. Macaulay sat musing over and marking the course of a debate which occasioned the first duel between the two coming protagonists in the approaching age. He has left it on record that in his opinion all Disraeli had to say could have been better said in two hours than in five; that the substance of the Budget might be epitomized as a diversion of the money of townsfolk into the pockets of malt-growers; and that the cheering which followed the adverse vote of nineteen and heralded the fall of the first Derby administration was terrific. But Macaulay's sense of values was different from Derby's; though, even if they had been the same, no honest historian could call the transformation of the Protectionists into Free-Traders precisely elegant.

Disraeli, however, took his leave of office, if we borrow Morley's words, 'with infinite polish and grace', thanking the House for the generosity with which they had treated him, and apologizing for any words, that might have slipped from his lips, in maintaining an unequal struggle, and given pain to his opponents. All said and admitted to their disparagement, the Derby administration in its ten months of office had carried a National Militia Act, given a constitution to New Zealand, adumbrated a good understanding with France, and of course carried on the Queen's Government, when the Whigs failed her. A fine example of Derby's oratory, when Wellington died, did something to redeem the lapse into supposedly unconscious plagiarism which disfigured Disraeli's too ambitious tribute to the Hero: and on the whole the personnel of the Derby administration had done themselves more credit than might have been expected of so raw a team of Ministers. But they had not done well enough to give Derby confidence.

The victorious elements of opposition coalesced into an administration under Aberdeen. That administration, which fared well at starting, fell into disorder under the impact of the Crimean War, and by 1855—in the accustomed fateful month of February—Derby found himself wrestling with the question of taking office again as the head of a purely Conservative administration. In the last days of January he had sounded Palmerston as to his willingness to join him, and Palmerston might have done so, but for Clarendon who, on his own admission to Greville,[1] dissuaded him. Gladstone when approached at the same time,[2] though not, as it would appear, as part of the same overture, might also have joined, had Palmerston been willing and had Aberdeen approved his doing so: but some little obscurity envelops this transaction. What is clear is the unanimous, or almost unanimous, verdict, both of historians and politicians, that Derby should have gone forward, whether or not Palmerston or the Peelites were willing to cooperate. Gladstone thought so; and still more did Disraeli think so. Nevertheless it is no light thing to take over the conduct of a war in which, had Derby been in charge, so Disraeli maintained, we should never have become involved, but which, so far as it had gone, had been sadly mismanaged. If it was Derby's patriotic duty, after the collapse of Aberdeen and the discomfiture of John Russell, to take over the Premiership, then it would also appear to have been the patriotic duty of anyone whose assistance he sought in the national emergency to give him what aid they might. Derby may fairly have said to himself that Palmerston was a necessity, and that Gladstone was a desirability, if he was to succeed; and every man has a right to exact conditions which seem to him requisite for the successful execution of a task he is pressed to undertake. It may be, as his critics maintain, that the nation would have rallied to him in any case, and that his daring would have brought

[1] Greville's *Memoirs*, November 10th 1856.
[2] Morley, *Life of Gladstone*, Vol. I, p. 527, footnote.

recruits flocking to his standard. Disraeli thought so, and could never really forgive his Leader for missing this singular opportunity of giving his party occasion to render the country high service. But in fact no one can be sure; and the importance of Palmerston, from a national point of view, is shown not only by his subsequent success in Derby's place as Premier, but also by the confidence which the country afterwards placed in him, excepting only during the fifteen months between February 1858 and June 1859 when, owing to his mismanagement of the Orsini Plot[1] affair, Derby's second administration displaced him.

That was the great administration which carried the Government of India Act, transferring supreme power from the India Company and the President of the Board of Control to a Secretary of State for India, with a Council of fifteen, chosen, eight of them by the Indian Secretary, and seven of them by the Directors of the Company. Later on, the number of councillors was reduced to twelve, and all the nominations were transferred to the Secretary of State, whose decision, except in regard to matters of revenue, was to be final, and could, in effect, determine almost every question of political importance without consultation with his Council. The Act was, of course, a sequel to the Mutiny, and the Mutiny had incidentally produced friction between Lord Canning, the Governor-General and Ellenborough, the President of the Board of Control. It would be tedious to examine the rights and wrongs of their quarrel; and it is enough to say that the Government supported Ellenborough, but that Ellenborough was nevertheless wise enough to resign. In his place, as last President of the Board of Control, had been installed Derby's son, Stanley, who became in due course the first Secretary of State for India. Though a man of outstanding ability, Stanley was not as eloquent as his father, and, when it came to drafting the Royal Proclamation that the Indian Government would thenceforward be carried on in the name of the Queen alone, Stanley did not prove equal to the occasion. The Queen turned to the Prime Minister to find those sentiments appropriate to the event; and Derby discharged this duty to perfection. On the one hand he caused the Queen to affirm her belief in Christianity, and on the other, to affirm her resolve that no subject of hers should suffer disadvantage for the profession of a different faith. All in authority in India were warned that any interference with the belief or worship of her Indian subjects would be visited with her utmost displeasure; and that neither class

---

[1] Orsini attempted to assassinate Napoleon III in January 1858 and it transpired that the conspiracy had been planned among anarchists in London and that the bombs thrown, which killed and injured a number of people, were manufactured in Birmingham. The French protested violently and injudiciously; British public opinion reacted against their demands, and Palmerston's Conspiracy Bill, introduced to please the French, provoked a vote of censure against him which was carried by a majority of nineteen.

nor creed should exclude from office those who were competent to discharge its duties. The Proclamation has been described as Derby's best monument; and it seems correct to add that it laid a foundation for the subsequent adoption by the Sovereign of the title Empress of India under Disraeli's Ministry.

The India Act became law in August 1858, and by the end of the year the Mutiny was declared to have been extinguished. In the autumn Gladstone accepted the Government's invitation to go as High Commissioner to the Ionian Islands to investigate the desire of the inhabitants to be ceded to Greece; and the responsibility for the subsequent regrettable loss of the islands to England in 1863 was eventually blamed on this mission; but at the time, the fact that so strong a Peelite had consented to serve in the inquiry excited more interest as an indication that he might join the Derby Ministry. Nothing, however, came of the idea. The last months of the Derby administration were occupied with the question of Parliamentary Reform; and on the last day of February 1859, Disraeli introduced a Reform Bill, which, had it been carried, would have identified the rural and urban franchises, and deprived the forty-shilling freeholder of his County vote. There is not, however, much point in following this moribund affair in its details. It is enough to say that it had no success, and that after a defeat on the first of April the Conservatives gained some twenty-five seats in the Election, but not enough. When Parliament reassembled in May an amendment, condemning the Government, on the Reform issue at home, and upon its failure abroad to avert the war between France and Austria, was carried by a small majority, and resulted in the downfall of Derby. Palmerston took his place, and from 1859 to the June of 1866 he and, after his death, Lord John Russell, had charge of British affairs. Then Derby returned to power for two years and a half, with by far the strongest body of colleagues he had yet been able to assemble. He could not, indeed, secure the assistance of Robert Lowe and the so-called 'Cave of Adullam'; but younger Conservatives of marked ability had begun to make their appearance and, with Lord Stanley as Foreign Secretary and Lord Cranborne as Secretary of State for India, Derby had no longer to rely upon the capacity of Disraeli alone. This administration, however, is remembered, and almost solely remembered, for its struggles with the question of Reform. Palmerston had never smiled upon any alteration of the suffrage, and Derby had not been ill-content to come to some sort of understanding with him that so long as he pursued a Conservative policy at home, Conservatives would not interfere with his tenure of power. But 'Lord John Reformer' was not the man to leave Reform alone. How far the country really desired Reform is open to discussion; but it is certain that the Queen herself pressed upon Derby the necessity of dealing with it, and that Derby did not dissent from this view. Disraeli, who would have been content to let sleeping dogs lie for a little longer, was therefore compelled to deal with the matter, and as Leader of the House of Commons, was obliged to take most of the odium attaching to the so-called 'Conservative surrender'. The broad result of the new Act was to give household suffrage in the towns; whilst certain compensating securities, such as dual voting, and educational and property franchises, were gradually dropped. Cranborne protested, in trenchant terms both with tongue and pen; and General Peel and Lord Carnarvon followed him into opposition. Of the phrasemaking of the time, one phrase in particular has survived—'a leap in the dark'. Some say that Cranborne was the first to use it; but it is certain that Derby himself adopted it at the Bill's third reading in the House of Lords. So, then, the Reform Act went through; and, when February of the succeeding year came round, Derby resigned office. Had he retained it a few months longer, his administration would have had the credit of abolishing public executions and of reconstituting the governing bodies of the great public schools, which improvements in fact were accomplished by his successor, Disraeli. His health, though it forced him to resign, left him still capable of a great speech, which appropriately enough he delivered against the impending disestablishment of the Irish Church, now urged by Gladstone, intent on reuniting the Opposition in a common effort to overthrow Disraeli. There was death to be read in his face and detected in the cadences of his voice, as he rose to plead against the abandonment by the English Government of Christianity in the form that seemed truest to him, and which, over long years, Protestantism has rashly supposed that the Irish would ultimately accept. The pathos of his eloquence moved many who could not subscribe to his tenets; and when at last it came to his famous adaptation of Meg Merrilies's classic apostrophe in Guy Mannering the topmost heights of his oratory were attained. 'They may say', he urged, ' "Go your ways, Ministers of England, ye have this day, as far as in you lay, quenched the light of spiritual truth in fifteen hundred parishes. See if your own Church stand the faster [sic] for that." ' And there was more in the same vein. The resonance of the once powerful voice may have lacked its former force; but the impassioned quality of the appeal left upon the listening senate an impression which no charm of youth nor energy of manhood could have commanded. Derby, and the churchmanship he championed, alike, were doomed; but the great scene in the House of Lords, when Chatham, exhausted by illness, rose, protesting in a final effort against the severance with America, was greater only by a little than Derby's final plea for the institution that seemed to him worthiest to be preserved. But, as with Chatham, his day was done; and as we look back at him now, his Premiership seems rather the monument of a grace and dignity to which we no longer seem able to produce a parallel. He was a Conservative in the best sense: he knew that change must come; and he made no resistance to the passage of time, but rather, cultivated the national garden so that it might yield fruit in due season as it ever had done. He figured among the Prime Ministers of Victoria as among the translators of Homer

> The brilliant chief, irregularly Great,
> Frank, haughty, rash, the Rupert of Debate.

THE EARL OF ABERDEEN
From the portrait by J. Partridge

LORD ABERDEEN

GEORGE HAMILTON GORDON, 4th EARL OF ABERDEEN
born 1784 died 1860

Entered Parliament as Scottish representative peer 1806

Chancellor of the Duchy of Lancaster, with Cabinet rank (Wellington's administration), January 1828

Foreign Secretary June 1828

Secretary at War and for the Colonies (first Peel administration) December to April 1834

Foreign Secretary (second Peel administration) 1841 to 1846

Prime Minister December 1852 to January 1855

CHAPTER VIII

LORD ABERDEEN

ABERDEEN is, perhaps, the least remembered of Victorian Prime Ministers. Yet, as the reader will have noticed, Victoria spoke of him when Wellington died, as almost the only man left to her upon whom she could lean for advice; and the Queen had not been alone in regarding him as a counsellor of the highest distinction. In the letter which Lady Peel, after her husband's death, wrote to Aberdeen, there occur the words, 'My beloved one always talked of you as "*the* friend" whom he most valued, for whom he had the sincerest affection, whom he esteemed higher than any'. But there is another testimony to the rare quality of Aberdeen's character, which some may place higher yet than these. In an appendix which Morley has added to his *Life of Gladstone*, there is preserved a tribute to this rare and noble human being, more searching and analytical than those already quoted. It cannot be cited in full here, though no one who is interested in Aberdeen can afford to neglect it. A few sentences may, however, be extracted from this estimate of him from the hand of the greatest of the Peelites. 'I will name . . . the following characteristics', says Gladstone in a letter to Aberdeen's younger son, the first Lord Stanmore, 'one and all of which were more prominent in him than in any public man I ever knew: mental calmness; the absence . . . of all egoism; the love of exact justice; a thorough tolerance of spirit; and last, and most of all, an entire absence of suspicion . . . His mind seemed to move in an atmosphere of chartered tranquillity which allowed him the view of every object, however blinding to others, in its true position and proportion. It has always appeared to me that the love of justice is one of the rarest of all good qualities, I mean the love of it with full and commanding strength. I should almost dare to say there are five generous men to one just man. The beauty of justice is the beauty of simple form; the beauty of generosity is heightened with colour and every accessory. The passions will often ally themselves with generosity, but they always tend to avert from justice. The man who strongly loves justice must love it for its own sake, and such a love makes for itself a character of a simpler grandeur to which it is hard to find an equal. Next to Lord Aberdeen, I think Sir Robert Peel was the most just of the just men I have had the happiness to know.'

It is not unusual in this evil world for the just man to meet with adversity; and Aberdeen forms no exception to the familiar rule, at least during the days of his premiership. He had been a noticeably able Foreign Secretary in a period when Prime Ministers were quite as likely to be looked for in the ranks of those who had been engaged in the conduct of foreign affairs as among those who had had charge of finance; the Foreign Office and the Exchequer being tacitly recognized as the two departments of the most vital consequence to the welfare of the nation.

George Gordon (he added 'Hamilton' later as a tribute to his father-in-law, Abercorn, by his first marriage), fourth Earl of Aberdeen, was an elderly man of sixty-eight when circumstances, far more than any wishes of his own, compelled him, in the year 1852, to become the head of a Ministry of—shall we say, since Derby and Disraeli were lacking to it?—most of the talents. Born five years before the French Revolution began, Aberdeen had taken, when still a very young man, the opportunity, afforded by the Peace of Amiens, to visit the Continent, and had been presented to Napoleon, whose winning smile, brilliant conversation and piercing eye made a great impression upon him. From France he had passed on into the Balkans—fascinated, like Byron, who gave him in *English Bards and Scotch Reviewers* the style of 'the travelled thane, Athenian Aberdeen', by the fame and fate of Greece. With Pitt and Dundas for his guardians he soon attracted the attention of Castlereagh, who in 1813 sent him as a special envoy to the Court of Austria where, in due course, he became English Ambassador. The last Coalition against Napoleon was in process of formation; and this fact threw him into the closest association with Metternich, whom he described to Castlereagh as 'not a very clever man, but tolerably well-informed'. The critical, adverse judgment of a man under thirty upon one over a decade older and of vastly more experience may give rise to a suspicion of priggishness in the junior, but Aberdeen was probably concerned to prove his independence in the eyes of Castlereagh, especially as he and Metternich got on well together and saw a good deal of one another. Of the war he had glimpses enough to conceive a great hatred of the misery which wars entail; and the most ardent pacifist will find an anticipation of his sentiments in Aberdeen's horror and disgust at the scenes through which he passed in the wake of the Allied Armies. He was not, however, blind to the splendour or insensible to the excitement of military operations, yet, as he observes, 'the scenes of distress and misery have sunk deeper in my mind'. 'The continual sight of the poor, wounded wretches of all nations', he goes on, 'haunts me night and day.' Readers may well be glad to be spared Aberdeen's description of his entry into Leipzig after the battle; and there seems no reason to inflict this upon them, provided the early impression of war upon the young man's mind is recognized and remembered, when, within two years of the opening of his premiership, the old statesman found himself confronted in the Near East by a situation which, if the utmost care were not exercised might easily end in hostilities.

For the rest it is enough to say that, as Foreign Secretary under Peel between 1841 and 1846, Aberdeen stands out as the first begetter of that understanding with France which a hundred years later was to play so great a part in the development of European and English history. He had of course invaluable auxiliaries in Louis Philippe and Talleyrand, the latter of whom arrived as French Ambassador to the Court of St. James in the late September of 1830; but he was wise enough to let this new development of Franco-British relations remain a work of tact and not of treaty. It is improbable that, had he remained in power, the misunderstanding with Guizot over the Spanish marriage[1] would have occurred. When Palmerston maintained that in his policy he was defending the Treaty of Utrecht, Wellington called his argument 'damned stuff', and stuff and nonsense it had very much the look of being. Anyhow the *entente*, such as it was, collapsed, and the House of Orleans not long after it; though how closely the two events were connected remains a matter for conjecture. With the recovery by the Bonapartes of the throne of France, the Franco-British understanding was, rather surprisingly, renewed. The unscrupulousness of the Third Napoleon was something of which Palmerston was uncritical. He was quick to condone the questionable methods of the President's accession and, when the new ruler pretended that, in his own words, 'L'Empire c'est la paix', the falsity of the man was not such as to anger the soul of the Foreign Secretary. The nephew, like the uncle, acted, if with greater reluctance, upon the principle that a showy war affords the best support to a shaky throne. And Palmerston's procedure was calculated to afford him every assistance in his policy.

Few, if any, persons now defend the Crimean War. Charles Greville had the good sense to perceive its folly at the time, though, with social, if not patriotic discretion, he appears to have kept his views to himself. The Prime Minister and the most part of the Cabinet, were not far from thinking as he did. Aberdeen had been at the Foreign Office in 1844, when the Emperor of Russia visited England; and, though Malmesbury's subsequent allegation that a secret memorandum, recognizing the Russian Protectorate of the Greek Christians in Turkey, was then drawn up by Nicholas and signed by Wellington, Peel and the Foreign Secretary himself, is unsubstantiated, there can be little doubt that there was some talk, initiated by the Emperor, about the inevitable dissolution at no distant date of the Turkish Empire and that there was also some sort of agreement that, if this occurred, England and Russia should act together. Partition Treaties concluded across sick men's beds are not very pretty things nor always particularly successful. Charles II of Spain struggled hard to keep together the crumbling Spanish Empire which Louis XIV and William of Orange had prudently agreed to dismember; and he manoeuvred so successfully that, when his death occurred,

[1] See footnote on p. 110 above.

the conspirators fell to fighting with each other. So likewise it happened with the Russian project of setting up little Kingdoms under Russian protection in the Balkans and leaving England to take Egypt if she liked. The Sultan of Turkey, or whatever 'Mayor of the Palace' managed him, had no more mind than the Spanish King to suffer the sharing out of his possessions; and, whether by design or accident, he managed to get the Catholic Emperor of the French and the Orthodox Tsar of all the Russias into acute controversy over the protection of their respective co-religionists under his rule. This squabble was no concern of Britain's; but within a little while it began to lose its religious motive, which was in fact sufficiently settled by Lord Stratford de Redcliffe's able diplomacy of giving the Latins the key of the Church of Bethlehem and putting an Orthodox priest in charge of the door without the right to shut it against the adherents of other forms of faith.

Stratford de Redcliffe, though a skilled negotiator, was not, however, precisely a man of peace, at least where the Russians, whom he hated, were concerned. And Menschikoff, who represented Russia, was no diplomatist at all and had been instructed, in accordance with the rising temper of his master, to obtain a guarantee confirming all the rights of the Orthodox Church in Turkey. Still, if Aberdeen had been Foreign Secretary with a Cabinet composed only of such solid persons of sense as all Cabinets should consist of, it is unlikely that this agitation of the Near Eastern Question in 1853 would have eventuated in hostilities between England, France and Russia. Unfortunately the French Emperor appears to have been eager to humiliate his fellow-sovereign at Petersburg, who had humiliated him by refusing him the customary style of brother; and very unfortunately, too, there were to be found in the existing and the previous English administrations persons well disposed towards the new Sovereign of France. Malmesbury, Derby's Foreign Secretary, had been intimate with Louis Napoleon as a young man and had mistaken his dislike of bloodshed for a hatred of war. Palmerston had hailed him as at least preferable to the Second Republic, which was full of dreams and disorder. And Clarendon, who had certainly known Mme de Montijo[1] very well in the 'thirties, was perhaps a little kind to one married to a beautiful woman of whom scandal whispered that he was himself the father. This tale can hardly be dismissed as mere idle gossip, since Lady Clarendon's diary records the account of a conversation which her husband had had, some twenty years later, with the lady implicated, when she discussed the question in the most dispassionate manner possible and declared that she had told the Emperor that there was nothing in it: 'Les dates ne correspondent pas.'[2]

The main point deserving consideration is how Napoleon contrived to

[1] The mother of the Empress Eugénie.
[2] George Villiers, A Vanished Victorian, pp. 80 and 262.

inveigle such intelligent Victorians as had been assembled under the leadership of Aberdeen into the one great war of Victoria's reign. Aberdeen could never forgive himself for what occurred, and appears to have believed that, if he had met with proper support, especially from John Russell, then in charge of the Foreign Office, all the machinations of Stratford de Redcliffe and Palmerston would have failed. And Russell ought to have afforded him this support. Herbert Paul, the historian, has collected one or two damaging sentences from Russell's despatches in January 1853 to Cowley, at that time representing England in Paris. The ambassador of France, Russell said, had been the first to disturb the *status quo* in which the matter rested—that is, the matter of the respective rights of the disputatious ecclesiastics—by speaking of the use of force and threatening the intervention of the French Fleet. The Cabinet, Russell went on to say, would deeply regret any dispute leading to conflict between two of the great Powers of Europe, and then added, that, when we reflected that the quarrel was over exclusive privileges in a spot near which the Heavenly Host proclaimed peace on earth and goodwill towards men, the thought of such a spectacle was melancholy indeed.[1] If these were the considerations which moved Russell before he transferred the Foreign Office to Clarendon some three weeks later in February 1853, there should have been no doubt that he would support Aberdeen on the main issue of peace and war, in company with those 'silent members of the Cabinet' all of whom—so Granville assured Aberdeen during the summer of 1853—were with him. It is no wonder, then, that we find Aberdeen himself writing retrospectively to Russell in March 1854: ' . . . I believe that there were, in the course of the negotiations on two or three occasions when, if I had been supported, peace might have been honourably and advantageously secured. I will especially refer to the opportunity afforded by the transactions which took place at the meeting of the two Emperors at Olmütz. But I repeat that the want of support, although it may palliate, cannot altogether justify to my own conscience the course which I pursued.'[2]

Aberdeen, indeed, never really forgave himself; and the familiar story tells how towards the close of his life he failed for no apparent reason to repair a church on his estate which was falling into disrepair, and how, after his death, the mystery attaching to the delay was solved by the discovery that he had marked in his Bible the passage describing David as a man of blood and unworthy in consequence to build the Temple of the Lord. Very different was the mind of Palmerston, who ridiculed 'peace at any price men', as he called them, strengthened his ties with Walewski, the French Ambassador, and very soon made a convert of little Lord John, just at this time to be

---

[1] Paul, *History of Modern England*, Vol. I, pp. 301, 302.
[2] Spencer Walpole, *Life of Lord John Russell*, Vol. II, p. 213.

seen politically at his poorest. Palmerston was not, indeed, Foreign Secretary, but none the less busy with foreign affairs; and Clarendon's attempt to find some diplomatic middle way was useless in face of two such Russophobes as Palmerston and Stratford de Redcliffe. The world, looking back on the complicated negotiation with the impartiality of Time, has in general judged that the crux of the affair was reached at the date of the Vienna Note, which, badly drafted by the French, but accepted by the Russians, was rejected by the Turks in August 1853. The Note was so worded as to preserve the independence of the Porte, whilst recognizing the traditional claim of the Tsar to protect Turkish Christians. A strong Government in England would have insisted that Stratford de Redcliffe should compel the Turks to accept this solution, on pain of losing the support of the Western Powers; and that was what Aberdeen definitely wanted done. Had Russell supported him, or, as Prince Albert thought,[1] had Aberdeen known what the Queen's opinion was, Palmerston should have been rendered comparatively innocuous. As things went, however, the Turkish Commander on the Danube required the Russians to evacuate the invaded Principalities of Moldavia and Wallachia within a fortnight on pain of war, which, as the Russian General declared he had no authority to treat, followed in due course. Since the Turks had now made war upon land, where they got rather the best of it, there was no reason why the Russian Black Sea Squadron should not destroy eleven Turkish warships at Sinope; and destroy them they did on November 3rd 1853. But the British public had, meanwhile, passed beyond the range of reason and declared the action at Sinope to be a massacre. In this state of affairs there was no longer much chance that the judicial mind of Aberdeen, who had always been disposed to trust the assurances the Tsar had given of his honest intention to deal with the Turkish problem in conjunction with Britain, and who was indisposed to believe in any possibility of ameliorating the Turkish Government, would be able to avert war. His sobriety and distinction of mind became, indeed, provocative to the temper of a nation by now abandoned to strong words and bitter feelings. The Prime Minister and Prince Albert, who was likewise gifted with political prudence, became the targets of all the excitable and ignorant people who grow hot with ill-considered indignation whenever war is on the horizon and assume that anyone who does not agree with them must be a tool of the enemy and a traitor to his country.

For a time, Aberdeen held on his way coolly enough. A Treaty-of-Vienna man and more Conservative in his foreign than in his domestic policy, he supported, in the early spring of 1854, John Russell's ill-timed project of Reform against Palmerston's vigorous opposition and subsequent resignation. It was certainly not a moment when a British Government could afford to be

[1] Queen's Letters, October 16th 1853. Memo. by Prince Albert.

divided; and Aberdeen's firmness, assisted by the arguments of Newcastle and Gladstone, brought Palmerston back into the fold just before the last faint hope of peace was blotted out by the entry of the British and French fleets into the Black Sea. Aberdeen indeed would not even then allow himself to despair; but in the opening months of 1854, whilst John Russell played with his Reform Bill, Palmerston fanned the flames of war. Still the Prime Minister stayed at his post refusing to believe that all hope was gone, and, even after the declaration of war on March 28th 1854, he struggled to hold the Cabinet together until, as has been told, Russell betrayed him almost without warning, and brought Aberdeen's administration down with a stab in the back. So good a man has seldom fought against greater political adversity. 'We abolished the Aberdeen Cabinet, the ablest we have had, perhaps, since the Reform Act', wrote Bagehot, '—a Cabinet not only adapted, but eminently adapted for every sort of difficulty, save the one it had to meet . . . As was said at the time "We turned out the Quaker and put in the pugilist".'[1]

Aberdeen would have assented. As the Prince states in another Memorandum of December 1854[2]—'Lord Aberdeen states his great difficulty to be, not only the long antecedent and mutual opposition between him and Lord Palmerston, but also the fact that Lord Palmerston loved war for war's sake, and he peace for peace's sake.'

Twenty years after the Crimean War began—in 1874—the Emperor Alexander II of Russia was staying at Windsor. Sitting by the Queen he recalled old memories, and how his father enjoyed himself as Victoria's guest. Then he added 'Tout a malheureusement changé.' 'Vous avez été mal servi', he went on, 'mais celui n'est plus qui l'a fait.' The Queen took the reference to be to Palmerston, and, in recording the conversation in her journal, adds the comment that the charge was doubtless true and that she had replied that there had certainly been misunderstandings which she much regretted.[3] Her verdict is the verdict of history, which attests the rectitude of her regard for Aberdeen and of her disapproval of Palmerston.

[1] *The English Constitution*—the chapter on 'The Cabinet'.
[2] Queen's Letters, December 9th 1854.
[3] ibid., May 13th 1874.

LORD PALMERSTON

HENRY JOHN TEMPLE, 3rd VISCOUNT PALMERSTON
born 1784 died 1865

Entered Parliament (Member for Newtown, Isle of Wight) 1807

Junior Lord of the Admiralty (Duke of Portland's administration) 1807

Secretary at War 1809

Foreign Secretary (Grey's administration) 1830 to 1834; 1835 to 1841

Foreign Secretary (Lord John Russell's first administration) 1846. Resigned 1851

Home Secretary (Aberdeen's administration) 1852 to 1855

Prime Minister February 1855 to February 1858
June 1859 to October 1865

CHAPTER IX

LORD PALMERSTON

O N February 15th 1855, at the age of 70, Lord Palmerston became Prime Minister, at the head of a Whig-Peelite Coalition, called to office by the discontents arising from the reverses inseparable, as it would seem, from the beginnings of any continental campaign fought by Great Britain. As so often in such cases the man called to power by popular acclaim appeared less heroic to those close to the political scene. Disraeli, twenty-four years later, drew a portrait of Palmerston as Lord Rochampton in his novel *Endymion* which was not unflattering—he was credited there with force and flexibility of character, with courage and adroitness, with a capacity to capture the imagination and confidence of the nation. At the time, in a letter to Frances Anne, Lady Londonderry, dated —— 1855, he spoke differently: 'Though he is really an impostor, utterly exhausted, and at the best only ginger-beer, and not champagne, and now an old painted pantaloon, very deaf, very blind, and with false teeth which would fall out of his mouth when speaking, if he did not hesitate and halt so in his talk, here is a man whom the country resolves to associate with energy, wisdom, and eloquence, and will until he has tried and failed.'[1]

Yet, whether from luck, which is sometimes so very active in the affairs of politicians, or through imposture, which is also of great assistance to them and of which, as we have seen, Disraeli credits Palmerston with a share, 'the old painted pantaloon' held the premiership for the best part of a decade after this estimate was written and contrived, except for one brief lapse from power, to content the British people.

The 'inevitability' of Palmerston, for so it was described and so it was, was due perhaps to two causes. The first was his age, his experience and his public reputation. He had been offered, and refused, the Chancellorship of the Exchequer (by Spencer Perceval) in 1809; he had been Secretary for War in the successive Perceval, Liverpool, Goderich and Wellington administrations, serving them in that office for twenty years. He had been a member of Canning's, Goderich's and Wellington's Cabinets, until he resigned with the Canningites in 1828 to re-enter the Cabinet in 1830 as a Whig. From 1830 to 1831 and again from 1835 to 1841 he had been Foreign Secretary to the Grey and Melbourne Whig administrations. He had returned to the Foreign Office with the Whigs under Lord John Russell in 1846. Forced out of the

[1] Monypenny & Buckle, *Life of Disraeli*, Vol. III, p. 567.

Foreign Secretaryship in 1851, he had, as we have seen, brought Lord John Russell's Government down nine days later, and after the brief interlude of the first Derby-Disraeli administration, had joined the Aberdeen Peelite-Whig Coalition as Home Secretary.

Despite his long tenure of the office of Secretary-at-War, Palmerston had never claimed to be a student of war, and his conduct of foreign affairs over a long period had aroused the suspicions of his colleagues on account of its vigour and received, at one time or another, even if it had not merited, the condemnation of men as different as Wellington, Grey, Aberdeen, Gladstone and John Bright, to say nothing of the Queen and the Prince Consort who seems, in this connection, to have bestowed on him the name of 'the immoral one'.[1]

In 1845, during one of the few periods when he was out of office (during Sir Robert Peel's second administration) Palmerston wrote a memorandum, to rebut what was evidently already a widespread accusation that he was a reckless and trouble-making diplomatist. In this he claimed not only to have attached the greatest importance to the preservation of peace but to have preserved it for the ten years when, under the Grey and Melbourne administrations, he held office (between 1830 and 1834, that is, and between 1835 and 1841). During this period, in his view, England was only in danger of war on three occasions—at the accession of Louis Philippe; again, when England joined with France to take Antwerp from the Dutch and give it to the Belgians; and, finally, when Mehmet Ali occupied Syria, declared his independence of the Sultan and spoke of marching on Constantinople. In every case, his activities, so he said, had preserved peace; and anyhow peace was preserved. The charge against him consequently resolved itself into the alleged tendency of his policy to produce hostilities.

Thus modified, the criticism could hardly be held, whatever Palmerston himself would have urged, to have been without substance by those who had to do with him at home or abroad. With a pen in his hand, he was apt to become a dangerous man, in spite of his happy knack of presenting the matter to the House of Commons in such a way as to secure approbation and of his hardly less invaluable gift of making himself popular with its members in the intercourse of the lobby. In his department, however, his sharp minutes; in his despatches, his instructions, drafted or revised with small regard to the wishes of Court or Cabinet; and, in his conduct generally, his disposition to dissociate his private conversations as Lord Palmerston from his public commitments as Foreign Secretary, were all the source of annoyance and indignation both to his subordinates and his superiors. He was the least diplomatic of diplomatists. I can remember being told, some fifty years after his death, by one in a position to know what he was talking about, that the

[1] Bell's *Palmerston*. Vol. II, p. 23, for the story in detail.

suspicion of English foreign policy still entertained on the Continent was due to the methods and manners of the Palmerston period. Those in England best acquainted with the affairs of Europe at that period—Wellington, Prince Albert, Aberdeen—all deplored Palmerston's inconsiderate methods; and even Russell, whose forebearance was hardly to be distinguished from weakness, was, as we have seen, moved at last to join issue with the Foreign Secretary and in 1851 to get rid of him. Not, however, before he had insulted the Government of Austria by condoning an assault upon General Haynau in London; and not before, in contravention of the views of the British Court and Cabinet, he had abandoned the intended policy of neutrality in respect of French affairs by intimating to the French Ambassador in London his approval of the Prince-President's *coup d'état*! Russell, roused at last, had taken the drastic course of reading out to the House of Commons (in February 1852) some part of the Queen's memorandum of August 1850 in which she had insisted that her Foreign Secretary must distinctly state what action he was proposing to take in any given case and that, after receiving her authority to act, he must not alter or modify what she had agreed to; a disclosure which Palmerston seems to have said at the time he could never forgive.[1] By general consent the Foreign Secretary's defence was of the feeblest; and the utter collapse of the too insolent Minister was epitomized by Disraeli when discussing it with Bulwer, in the dramatic words 'There *was* a Palmerston'. Yet the Queen, who had written in July 1850 that 'there is no chance of Lord Palmerston reforming himself in his sixty-seventh year',[2] found herself in 1855 with no choice but to accept him as Prime Minister in his seventy-first.

The fact is that in the crisis of war, the majority of men look for a leader with great experience, but who has nevertheless precisely those qualities of independence, unconventionality, initiative, and above all boldness of speech and swiftness of action which they most distrust in peace.

There was, moreover, another factor in the politics of those days which told in Palmerston's favour. English public opinion was becoming increasingly middle class, increasingly insular, increasingly self-satisfied. John Bull at this time fancied himself very much in the guise of Mr. Podsnap, a gentleman who in fact made his first appearance on our national stage towards the close of the Palmerstonian era and has given almost as much pleasure to all healthy-minded Britons ever since as Falstaff or Pickwick. It is a fairly safe guess that among Palmerston's many adherents in the decade of his power there were numbered many Podsnaps. 'Podsnappery' covered a wide range of thought; as wide a range, perhaps, as can be comfortably compressed into the discovery that some institution, or course of conduct, was 'not English'. Whether Lord

[1] Queen's Letters, Vol. II, p. 446.
[2] ibid., Vol. II, p. 306.

Palmerston was among the guests at that famous dinner given in the house, situated 'in a shady angle adjoining Portman Square', in honour of Georgiana Podsnap's eighteenth birthday, history does not say; but a later Victorian may perhaps presume to guess that, had he been there, he would have found the company, if not very much to his liking, at least very well adapted to the sort of instruction Mr. Podsnap administered to his friends and followers, 'the foreign gentleman' alone excepted.

'Other countries'—countries, that is, not blessed with the British Constitution—the foreign gentleman naturally inquired of Mr. Podsnap after the lecture was well on its way,[1] 'They do how?' 'They do, Sir,' said Mr. Podsnap, with an alacrity and, if we may borrow a little foreign assistance to exalt the quality of his reply, with an aplomb, 'They do—I am sorry to be obliged to say it—as they do.'

'It was a little particular of Providence', said the foreign gentleman, laughing, 'for the frontier is not large.'

'Undoubtedly,' assented Mr. Podsnap; 'But so it is. It was the Charter of the Land. This Land was Blessed, Sir, to the Direct Exclusion of such other Countries as there may happen to be. And, if we were all Englishmen present, I would say', added Mr. Podsnap, looking round upon his compatriots and sounding solemnly with his theme, 'that there is in the Englishman a combination of qualities, a modesty, an independence, a responsibility, a repose, combined with an absence of everything calculated to call a blush into the cheek of a young person, which one would seek in vain among the Nations of the Earth.'

To the Podsnaps, growing as rapidly in influence as in numbers, Palmerston was on the whole a congenial figure, a man with a good spice of the Regency buck in his blood, an enviable thickness in his skin and a pilgrim staff, near allied to a sword-stick, in his hand. Yet it must be admitted that his rise to a rare height of power provides a very strange finale to the early Victorian era. If Mr. Fulford gives, as I am not doubting that he does give, a correct account of the state of things at Windsor before Albert came there with what Melbourne decried as his 'damned morality', there was a shocking incident during the Paget regime in the early days of the reign, when Palmerston, at the time Secretary of State for Foreign Affairs, was caught red-handed attempting to invade the bedroom of one of the Queen's ladies,[2] who was no willing recipient of his attentions and called for assistance. The matter was concealed from Victoria at the time, but it came to her knowledge later and appears very naturally to have affected her attitude towards the old sinner whose affairs-of-the-heart were so ill-concealed as even to penetrate into the

[1] I have adapted the original a little in both these passages.
[2] Fulford, *The Prince Consort*, p. 61. There is also a reference in Bell's *Lord Palmerston*, Vol. II, p. 21.

VISCOUNT PALMERSTON
From the portrait by J. Partridge

correspondence of the Foreign Office.[1] By 1855, however, this rollicking relic of Georgian England, married in 1839 to Lady Cowper, one of the most brilliant hostesses in London, if not from her first husband's standpoint one of the best of wives, may be presumed to have reached years of discretion. Victoria herself speaks with astonishment of the sympathy and understanding she found in him when, just after Albert's death in 1861, she consulted him about the treatment of the Prince of Wales, at that time just reaching manhood and in no small need of dexterous handling.

Nevertheless, the gay old consultant, whom the irony of circumstance had provided as the proper person to give Victoria advice on the finishing governance of the heir to the throne, was perhaps of all her Prime Ministers the one least qualified by personal conduct to give it. 'Pilgerstein', she called him in corresponding with Leopold, but no palmer or pilgrim in pursuit of any Holy Land was he; and his domestic policy, in most respects marked by conservatism, had as perhaps its outstanding feature an extension of facilities for divorce, so as to bring the rupture of the marriage-tie within the reach of those who could not afford the expense of a private Act of Parliament. The change was in all equity fair enough, and not one of which any supporter of a Church established or reformed by Henry VIII could with any show of reason complain. Still it is worth notice in what terms an able contemporary historian, attaining just in that Palmerstonian decade the apogee of his ecclesiastical fortunes as Dean of Ely, dealt with the issue involved from the standpoint of civilization. Merivale is writing of the history of Ancient Rome in the interval between the First and Second Punic War—somewhere about 230 B.C.—when, as he sees it, the constitution of the State had become strongly popular whilst yet the spirit of aristocracy had survived in the appointments to and administration of the public service, so that for a fleeting hour a happy balance of forces was attained and some sentiment for the few lingered on in the minds of the many. It was precisely in this hour of flux that the Roman Republic first abandoned its ancient reverence for an inviolate rule of marriage. 'The law of divorce', argues the historian, 'became more widely extended and more frequently resorted to, and nothing tended more to sap the morals of the Romans than the laxity which was thus introduced into the holiest and most delicate of all human relations.'[2] The moral change consequent on this new outlook on marriage was in some respects analogous to that which occurred about 1850 in England. The movement of opinion, however, had, of course, to wait for a new generation of men to become familiar with it; and the threatened edifice of Christian civilization was

---

[1] As I may be challenged about this statement, I had better say at once that my authority was Sir Thomas (afterwards Lord) Sanderson, whose memories of the old Foreign Office I heard from his own lips, when writing a chapter on it for the *Cambridge History of British Foreign Policy*.

[2] Merivale, *General History of Rome*, Chapter XIX.

further buttressed by the influence of the Court and the religious convictions of Palmerston's successors in the premiership.

Palmerston had, for the rest, reached an age when few men find alterations to their taste; and in domestic affairs he had at no time been eager for them. It was consequently easy for Derby and Disraeli to come to a working arrangement with him to do nothing, or nothing very much, in respect of that extension of the suffrage which had always possessed a rather amorphous attraction for Russell and was now beginning to catch the eyes of Gladstone, but which Disraeli at any rate was resolved to make the prize of the Tory Party before the Liberals turned it to their advantage.

Fortunately for this inertia of Palmerston in domestic affairs, which diverged but little from his brother-in-law, Melbourne's, broad-based preference for letting things alone, imperial and foreign policy largely pre-occupied public attention in the decade of his premiership; and this was ground where the Prime Minister was possessed of all the advantages of experience, if not all the graces of tact. There was a European Peace to be negotiated in Paris; and Clarendon, who, as Foreign Secretary, took charge there, contrived to effect a settlement sufficiently showy to bring credit to the British Government. The sick man at Constantinople rose again from his bed. The Russians resigned their protectorate over the Turkish Christians, withdrew their warships from the Black Sea, dismantled the fortifications of Sebastopol, and restored to Turkey the city of Kars. And this settlement lasted all the time of Palmerston and looked well enough to the eye of the observer. But in diplomacy there is nothing final, nor can be. After Palmerston was dead and Napoleon III dethroned, the Russians, at Bismarck's instigation, repudiated the Black Sea clauses of the Treaty, and a few years later, in 1878, resumed their pressure upon Turkey with the result that Kars was regained and with it the strip of Bessarabia, lost to Russia in 1856. The sick man, indeed, again stood on his legs at the Berlin Congress of 1878, and for another forty years was endowed with the attributes of sovereignty; but Clarendon's particular labours on his behalf went for the most part the way of mortal things.

Greville, indeed, as we have noted, held from the start that the war was a foolish adventure; and so it looks to most people to-day. Can this be said of the suppression of the Indian Mutiny in 1857? To the men of Palmerston's time the loss of India would have appeared such a consummation of disaster, as should have caused the statue of Chatham at Westminster to veil its eyes and the monument to Clive in Whitehall to totter on its pedestal. The integration of India, to which so many Britons gave their lives and labours, and its assimilation to the composite structure so strangely and, as it seemed to some, mystically brought to a unity under Victoria's sway, owed not a little to those anxious months of 1857, when George Canning's son, calm, judicious, fearless, and imperturbable, to a degree that his own father might have envied, seemed to set the star of India's destiny in the heavens, until the Oriental came who plucked it and placed it on his Sovereign's brow. The British people have little vision left of that idea of Empire which once inflamed their imagination. But the Victorians saw clearly that an India, integrated as never before, could be merged without loss of identity or dignity in a larger conception; and that British statesmanship was equal to this occasion. Not, however, Palmerston! He regarded the Mutiny with a jaunty assurance that refused to recognize its danger. Victoria and Disraeli, however, had a better understanding of the gravity of the situation; and it was upon her initiative that large reinforcements were sent out and the situation saved.

The old incompatibility of temper between the Sovereign and the Prime Minister had thus quickly begun to reappear; and the great personal popularity of the latter in the country, which in the spring of 1857 had returned him to power by an overwhelming vote, rendered the difference of outlook so much the tenser. The British people, though much attracted towards a master, who exemplified as perhaps never before all the supposed characteristics of John Bull, was not, however, completely bewitched. The appointment in 1858 of Clanricarde as Lord Privy Seal shocked all men capable of understanding that, *mutatis mutandis*, the Ministers of the Sovereign have the need of the same qualification for their public, as Caesar's wife for her private office;[1] and when a little later Palmerston, after Orsini's attempt on the French Emperor's life in Paris so far forgot, as it seemed to his countrymen, the nation's pride as to listen to the acrid complaints of the French Ambassador and the clanking sabres of the French Colonels and to frame a Bill making conspiracy to murder felonious, public indignation, accentuated by the opportune disclosure that the Third Napoleon was still paying the legacy, conferred by the First upon Cantillon for attempting to assassinate Wellington, drove the Prime Minister to resign. The majority of nearly 150, which he commanded on February 14th, was converted over night into a minority of 19; and for a few months the Conservatives under Derby returned to office, if hardly to power.

Beaten on Reform in the spring of 1859, the Tories dissolved in April, but failed to get a majority. The Opposition sunk its differences. Radicals, Liberals and Whigs united to defeat the Government in the House of Commons, and in June 1859 the last survivor in public life of George III's Ministers formed the first Liberal administration with Mr. Gladstone as Chancellor of the Exchequer.

---

[1] Clanricarde's reputation had fallen so low that the Queen had already in 1852 refused to sanction his appointment as Ambassador in Paris.

Napoleon III was now at the height of his influence and also as it happened, at the apex of his alarms. The Orsini Plot had shown him the long hand of those secret societies with which in times past he had incautiously consorted. The cause of nationality was indeed one which he could gracefully champion as an *idée Napoléonienne*, but the unification of Italy was not in line with the Treaty of Vienna. Palmerston countenanced this so-called liberation movement abroad, though he had not the clarity and consistency of mind to favour a like principle in Ireland or India. Victoria, however, stood by the Vienna settlement and regarded as aggression the attempt of the House of Savoy, itself in its origins a non-Italian power, to dislodge the Habsburgs, to whom they had owed a good deal of their own greatness, from the Italian Peninsula. People have grown a shade more shy of applauding the unification of Italy and of Germany, since these Powers united to destroy any lingering unity that Europe still retained in the year 1939. But, in 1859 and long after, the cause of Italian unity made a charming sentiment, if not, in the light of Italian history, a very profound one. The Italy of the Middle Age, like the Greece of antiquity, which pleased the imagination and ministered to the arts, was a country of small States, both republican and monarchical, and could never have developed the diversity of its genius, had it not been so. Even Henry Adams, that thoughtful and dispassionate American, could say in the late nineteenth century that 'Rome before 1870'—that is Rome when still under the Papacy—'was seductive beyond resistance'.[1] One could not expect Palmerston 'the incarnation', as Herbert Paul has styled him, 'of a Philistine', to sympathize with such a sentiment any more than Garibaldi, the re-incarnation of a *condottiere*; but it is to Victoria's credit that she, like Aberdeen, upon whose gift of judgment Gladstone (even though in this particular instance he was at variance with it) set so much store, perceived nothing especially admirable in the dispossession by methods, not lacking in force and fraud, of the reigning houses of Italy. The merit of change is as a rule far too problematical to deserve advancement by any but the most honourable and straightforward means; and the politicians who think otherwise lay themselves open to the charge of believing that the end—in the popular, though not the original sense of the phrase—justifies the means. Integration is without doubt a statesmanlike policy; but the moral and spiritual integration of the world was not very obviously promoted by the political integration of Italy or Germany, attended, as they were, by all those concomitants of racial domination and territorial ambition which have since come clearly to view. Acton was soon to point to Britain and Austria[2] as examples of those superior unities of association which, in fact, hold more promise of some possible future brotherhood of man than any exclusive

[1] *Education of Henry Adams*, p. 89.
[2] 'The History of Freedom and Other Essays', p. 298 (*Home and Foreign Review*, 1862).

assertion of the rights of nationality. Much as he disliked the Austrians, Palmerston had the sense to accept Palacky's contemporary phrase and to admit that, if there were no Austria, one would have to be invented. Time has abundantly shown the wisdom of that word, even though circumstance has not allowed Time's shadow to move back so much as one degree on the dial of revolutionary innovation. The Czech, the Pole, the Magyar, and the ugoslav have all cause to wonder, even if prudence forbid them to give their thoughts expression, whether their lot under the House of Habsburg was not preferable to that they have obtained by following the advice of those too confident persons who have taken upon themselves in our days to put the world to rights.

There were other matters in agitation in the last phase of the Palmerstonian era besides that of the unification of Italy or the expulsion thence of the Habsburgs. The relations between the Anglo-Saxon races in England and the United States and the contention of Dane and German over Schleswig-Holstein were alike calculated to attract attention and provoke war's alarms. The prevention of hostilities in the one case owed much to the Prince Consort who in his last days exhausted himself so as to temper a despatch to the requirements of peace and owed much in the other case to the resolution of Victoria herself, who was determined not to allow her two aged but powerful Ministers to jockey the country into another conflict.

Derby, with particular reference to the Polish Question, aptly described Russell's foreign policy as one of 'meddle and muddle'. In the famous case of Mason and Slidell—emissaries respectively to England and France from the Confederates of the Southern States of America, who, contrary to international usage, had been forcibly removed from the British steamer, *Trent*, by a certain Captain Wilkes in the Federal Government's employ—Russell, however, was, indeed, forced to meddle, yet was evidently under as urgent an obligation not to muddle. His intended despatch was calculated to exacerbate the dispute; and Palmerston was not the man to mollify the written word. Albert happily spotted the point, where an alteration of language might lead to an accommodation of the quarrel. Wilkes, though praised in America for his deed, had lacked any apparent authority to do it. Albert suggested that he might have acted without instructions or alternatively might have misunderstood those that were given him; while, at Washington, Lyons, the British Ambassador, pressed the case for the release of the two Confederate emissaries with all the skill of the old diplomacy, in which he shone as a master. Lincoln yielded to the demands of a justice in which he concurred, and braved the criticism of a public which he was not the man to fear. By the time a settlement was reached, however, the Prince Consort was dead. The prodigious power of quarrelling possessed by mankind permits of no close season and rarely affords the human race more than the briefest opportunity to follow the precept to weep with those that weep. The death of Albert left Victoria a widow too sensible of her grief, as has been said, to allow her sorrow to be proud. She was a pathetic figure, all too ready to allow her abiding sense of irreparable loss free and frequent expression, all too slow to invest the feeling of solitude, rendered the more moving by her exalted isolation, with its tragic splendour. Let the words she addressed to Derby represent the burden of lamentations, again and again repeated. 'To express what the Queen's desolation and utter misery is, is almost impossible; every feeling seems swallowed up in that *one* of unbounded grief. She feels as if *her life* had ended on *that* dreadful day . . . She sees the trees budding, the days lengthening, the primroses coming out, but she *thinks* herself still in the month of December.'[1]

Nevertheless, if in a seclusion bound in time to excite adverse comment, where the solitary is in occupation of a throne, Victoria continued to discharge her political functions as distinct from her social duties with a resolution and a judgment that probably owed much to the twenty years and more of close contact with Albert's wiser mind. This strength and sagacity became fully apparent in the case of the Danish Duchies. Not one Briton in ten thousand could perhaps have given any clear account of the complications involved in that affair at the time; and still fewer could give it to-day. Indeed, but for Palmerston's epigram, the vexed question might be pretty nearly forgotten. In the original version the Prime Minister appears to have said that only three men in England had ever understood the Schleswig-Holstein question: the Prince Consort, who was dead; Mellish,[2] who was mad; and himself, who had forgotten it. The Prince's view was doubtless sufficiently reproduced in Victoria's attitude. Though she did not like the Treaty of London in 1852 which approved, without guaranteeing, the sovereignty of the Danish King over the Duchies, one of them (Holstein) predominantly, the other (Schleswig) partially German in population, she thought this settlement should stand, since it had the signatures of all the Great Powers of Europe and of Denmark as well. In return for the acceptance of an arrangement by means of which the Duchies remained attached to the Danish Crown, though the Danish King had inherited through the female line, the legal male heir—the Duke of Augustenburg—had received the sum of £350,000, and the King of Denmark had promised, what he did not perform, at any rate to the satisfaction of the Germans, a constitutional system safeguarding the rights of his German subjects in the Duchies. Instead, he had been on the point of incorporating Schleswig in Denmark and separating off Holstein, whilst retaining it under his rule, when death made away with him. His nephew and successor, Christian IX, who had become, just before his accession, the

[1] Queen's Letters, February 17th 1862.
[2] A clerk in the Foreign Office.

father-in-law of the Prince of Wales, reluctantly assented to the proposed arrangement; and thereupon the smouldering indignation of Germany, with Bismarck fanning the fire, burst into flame. Austria agreed with Prussia; and the forces of these Powers, as representative of the Germanic Federation, occupied Holstein without meeting with resistance. At this point the Duke of Augustenburg revived his claim and set up his Court at Kiel.

Victoria's sympathies lay with the Duke and, also, in a general way with Germany, where her eldest daughter had become Crown Princess of Prussia; and her reason told her that, if Britain interfered in the business, it should be as an arbitrator between the Germans and the Danes, and not as a partisan of Denmark. Granville gave her some support in the Cabinet and had, it seems, ground for supposing the smaller fry among Ministers were with him, though, as he tells her,[1] he thought the policy of the Prussian Government suicidal. But Palmerston alarmed her by his bluster; and Russell was, if anything, more disposed to intervene than Palmerston. At the close of the session of Parliament in 1863 the Prime Minister made so bold as to declare that, if Danish independence and Danish rights were threatened, 'it would not be Denmark alone' with which those who threatened them would have to contend. Characteristically strong words, and not less characteristically unwise ones!

These tendencies became accentuated in 1864. Granville, however, pursuing his mediatorial way between the Crown and 'those two dreadful old men', as the Queen, exasperated beyond measure by their conduct, styled them about this time in a letter to Leopold,[2] contrived to drag from Palmerston an admission in Cabinet, of what he had already privately confessed, 'that there was no question of our going to war singlehanded'.[3] Oblivious of the impression which his own treatment of Greece and China, to say no more, had once made upon the world, he was energetically representing to the Queen that 'the Germans were acting like a strong man who thinks he has got a weak man in a corner and that he can bully and beat him to his heart's content'.[4] Victoria was surely right in observing that no good could come of her debating with him the respective merits of the rival policies of Germany and Denmark.[5] She had much cause to complain of Russell's simultaneous assurance in conversation with the Prussian Ambassador that Great Britain would aid the Danes in resisting the occupation of Schleswig by Prussian troops—an assurance reported, and not repudiated, by Russell himself in his despatches to English Ambassadors abroad.[6] And, when, some few weeks later, a German army crossed into Schleswig and not so much as

[1] Queen's Letters, February 24th 1863.
[2] ibid., February 25th 1864.
[3] ibid., January 14th 1864 (Granville to Phipps).
[4] ibid., January 8th 1864.   [5] ibid., January 10th 1864.
[6] ibid., January 10th 1864.

an English platoon was there to oppose them, Her Majesty's Government, at least to a spectator behind the scenes, must have looked a trifle foolish, whilst the policy of Palmerston's administration with its Italian sympathies might have qualified as a fine example of a Spenserian word of Anglo-Italian composition—braggadocio.

The issue between the Queen and the Prime Minister is one of still living interest and importance. As the Queen and many of her Ministers saw things, her duty was to keep her country out of war, unless British interests were concerned. It was a simple rule and a clear one; and the substitution of any other introduces incalculable difficulties of which we have now had some experience. Ministers in fact should behave as the trustees of their country, not as knights-errant righting wrongs everywhere without discrimination. 'Lord Russell knows', Victoria wrote to him in February 1864, 'that she will *never*, if she can prevent it, allow this country to be involved in a war in which *no English interests* are concerned.'[1] Russell in reply put up a plea that, whilst the Queen might be averse from involving her country where its interests did not require, she would doubtless wish to defend its honour. The answer he received on this score was as sharp as anger could make it: 'The Queen . . . does not require to be reminded of the honour of England which touches her more nearly than anyone else.'[2] People should bear in mind, in reconsidering these Teutonic questions, a remark of John Morley's that 'the German Confederation of the Congress of Vienna was a skilful invention of Metternich's . . . inert for offence, but extremely efficient against French aggression'.[3]

The Queen's good sense was resolute; and with it went, though not so resolutely nor so far, the judgment of a number of rather inarticulate Ministers. 'A large portion of the Cabinet', Granville wrote to Russell in May 1864, 'have all along wished to keep for ourselves perfect liberty to act how, and when we like, but to avoid committing ourselves to any threat of definite action, particularly action of an isolated character.'[4] A ministerial crisis was, however, the last thing the Queen wanted; and she caused Granville to be instructed to keep matters as smooth as possible. But the Prime Minister did not make things easy for her. Sir Charles Phipps told her that 'he did not believe that Lord Palmerston had any intention of being offensive, but that he had a singular want of knowledge of what may or may not be said'.[5] This did not, however, go far towards mollifying her feelings towards one who in old age was again displaying those self-assertive and bellicose tendencies that had marked him in earlier life. Converting his name, in the familiar family fashion they used with one another, into German, the Queen

---

[1] Queen's Letters, February 13th 1864.   [2] ibid., February 15th 1864.
[3] Morley, *Life of Gladstone*, Vol. II, p. 319.
[4] Queen's Letters, May 5th 1864.   [5] ibid., May 11th 1864.

let Leopold see the very next day the depth of her indignation. 'Pilgerstein is gouty and extremely impertinent in his communications of different kinds to me.'[1] Once again she expressed to Clarendon her earnest wish that her Ministers would try to be impartial and free themselves in their negotiations from that Danish bias which encouraged the Danes and angered the Germans. Still, though her policy of non-intervention was sound in the circumstances, she can scarcely herself be acquitted of some leaning towards (in her own words) 'that country from which *everyone* nearest and dearest to the Queen has come and to which she is bound by every possible tie'.[2] She clung indeed to the distinction which so many others have since striven to establish between the Germans on the Rhine and the Danube and the Germans on the Spree. 'Prussia', she wrote a year later to Leopold, 'seems inclined to behave as atrociously as possible, and as she *always has done*. Odious people the Prussians are, *that* I *must* say.'[3] She had, none the less, married her eldest daughter to one of them, and to no insignificant one either. Perfect consistency in our disordered world is hardly to be expected and the absence of it perhaps deserves less animadversion in the narrow circle within which royalties, conditioned in their choice by German etiquette and Protestant principles, were at that date expected to seek their partners.

Bismarck, the Brandenburger, had, meanwhile, been strengthening his hold upon his intended prey; and Austrian policy, in face of the development of Prussian designs, was well calculated to bring to mind the Great Frederick's immortal epigram on Maria Theresa—'*Elle pleurait, mais elle prenait toujours.*'

Under the Convention of Gastein, Prussia had occupied Schleswig and Austria Holstein, threats and protests from the British Prime Minister and Foreign Secretary receiving such attention as their impotence invited. When at length an armistice was proclaimed in May 1864 between the Germans and the Danes, the Queen once more exhorted her Ministers, if England again attempted to intervene, to display 'a true spirit of impartiality' instead of the decidedly Danish bias so far characteristic of British policy;[4] and she made a strong point by urging that the course pursued in respect of the Duchies should be in conformity with that pursued in Italy, where the aim had been to satisfy the wishes and to consult the feelings of the locality.

Enough, however, of these diplomatic entanglements! An essay cannot pretend, and should not attempt, to follow in detail the meanderings of long and complicated negotiations, such as arose in Italy, which was in process of being united, the U.S.A., which had all the appearance of dividing, and in China, where Podsnappery in Palmerston's time had more than one innings. It must be sufficient to say that, although with little distinction, England

---

[1] Queen's Letters, May 27th 1864.
[2] ibid., May 27th 1864.   [3] ibid., August 3rd 1865.
[4] ibid., May 9th 1864.

escaped from futile hostilities and that by the end of June 1864 the Prime Minister was not far from seeing eye to eye with the Queen. Victoria in her Journal of the 21st day of that month says she found him 'very sensible, wonderfully clear-headed and fully alive to the extreme dangers of the situation', but more apprehensive of France dragging us into a war to get the Rhine frontier than of Germany uniting against us. All the aid England could hope to give the Danes lay in the direction of naval assistance; and that only as was reckoned, for the duration of three months. Such very limited help was worse than useless; and in his newly found impotence Palmerston was to be heard calling the Danes 'the most obstinate people he knew' and accusing them of lack of intelligence and narrow-mindedness.[1] A day later the Queen pointed out to the Prime Minister that Cowley's letters from the Paris Embassy showed the French to be eager to get us into the quarrel in the hope of finding an opportunity of getting back the frontier of the Rhine, and that this fact gave us the better reason for keeping out of it. And the day after that she advised Russell that the total rejection by the Danes of our mediation or arbitration gave us an excellent reason for warning them that they must look for no aid from us if hostilities were resumed. 'Great as are the difficulties of the present crisis', she wrote, 'far greater are sure to arise from allowing this country to get entangled in a war in which its interests are not concerned.'

By the end of June General Grey was writing to Victoria that 'Your Majesty may justly take to yourself a principal share in the maintenance of peace.' Gladstone, Granville and Gibson, the men of peace, were gaining ground in the administration over the men of war, but the Sovereign's firmness had had a good deal to say to their success. It was the last round in the long battle with Palmerston and perhaps the greatest of Victoria's victories over him. Her policy had prevailed, partly because the weight of the Cabinet was with her, partly because the Prime Minister had opposed his old policy of bluff and bluster to the as yet unrecognized genius of Bismarck, working ever within his strength, a strength careless of bloodshed and firm as iron. In a while, and a very little while, the star of the Third Napoleon would fall and the Martian planet of the German *junker* be soaring into the European sky.

If in foreign affairs the sinking sun of Palmerston seemed to forebode 'ills to come, woe and unrest', it did hardly less in domestic matters. A generation had passed since Grey's Reform Bill; and some extension of the suffrage had begun to preoccupy the minds of the very able pair of combatants who were on the road to party leadership. The last eighteen months of Palmerston's life produced an epoch-making speech from Gladstone which roused alike the indignation of the Sovereign and of the Prime Minister and showed their

[1] Queen's Letters, June 21st 1864.

minds on this matter to be in close accord. Without consulting his Chief, the Chancellor of the Exchequer told the House of Commons that 'every man who is not presumably incapacitated by some consideration of personal unfitness or of political danger is morally entitled to come within the pale of the Constitution'. In the correspondence which followed Palmerston told his colleague that the speech laid down the doctrine of universal suffrage which he himself could never accept; whilst Gladstone took his stand on the point that he had only advocated the enfranchisement of all who can be given the vote 'with safety'—a distinction no doubt of so elastic and indefinite a kind as to enable the speech to signify almost everything or next to nothing according to the interpretation preferred.

The Prime Minister's vigour, however, was not yet quite spent. The Budget of 1865, which of course was of Gladstone's making, reduced the income tax from 6d. to 4d. and the tea-duty from a shilling to sixpence; yet, while Gladstone lost his seat at Oxford, Palmerston came romping in with an increased majority at the General Election in the summer. The return of the administration was reckoned to have been due in the main to the personal hold on the country of its head. Had Palmerston not been there, Derby might well have won and many things have turned out otherwise than they did.[1] As it chanced, he only survived his great victory by a month or so; and on October 18th died at Brocket Hall, an old man more than eighty years of age.

With Palmerston there passed away, so far as any such division can be precisely established, the Early Victorian era. By an odd coincidence it had opened with the premiership of his brother-in-law and now closed with his own; and it might be said that he had proved no less acceptable to the soul of the English people than Melbourne to that of the young Queen. They were both of them English gentlemen of the olden time, though Melbourne of finer clay than the other—much more cultivated in mind, more charming in conversation, and more penetrating in thought. But Palmerston excelled his brother-in-law in energy and by that very quality, which provoked among the elect the charge of Philistinism, fastened his hold on the imagination of his compatriots. He was not a very great man nor a very good one. He had not read much, nor thought deeply, nor dreamed at all of higher things. But his path led where every man of the true John Bull breed was ready to follow, and his jokes and repartees had just the quality the Englishmen of the time liked best. His advice to the deputation from Rugeley which came to him in distress because the name of their town had become associated with a murderer of the name of Palmer and they desired some new appellation is classic: 'Well, Gentlemen, I am very sorry for you, and the only thing I can do is to suggest that you call it "Palmerston".' To Rowcliffe, the

[1] Low & Sanders, *The History of England during the Reign of Victoria*, p. 196.

butcher of Tiverton, who regularly appeared to heckle him at his meetings in that place, he gave rather better than he got. His interlocutor, who accused him of being a downright Tory, proceeded to pester him with questions, and among them how far he would go with manhood suffrage. 'I will give a straightforward answer to that', rejoined Palmerston, 'I will not tell him.' The Minister went on to add that he hoped that the political differences between him and his friend would not affect their private relations. He was sorry to disagree with him, but no one could agree with everybody, and the man who did so did not merit having anybody to agree with him.

There was nothing very brilliant in this, but it was easily understood of the people and roused all the cheers and laughter required. 'Pam' was a clever but a commonplace man; and the public of that day was very well satisfied it should be so. Fortunate in the decade of his premiership, he was also lucky in the hour of his death. He had reached fourscore years without any great sense of labour and sorrow. He did not exactly diffuse the odour of sanctity befitting one whose exit from this life could not be long deferred, but his coat was still so gay,[1] his spirit still so game that he might be reckoned an outstanding disciple of John Peel, as well as of John Bull. The scent of the chase was as the breath of his nostrils; and the sound of his horn, when it no longer roused the politician from his slumbers, lingered in the memory like the echo of a strain regretted. Horace Vachell has well said that in those days a Master of Hounds seemed a much greater man than a Master of Balliol. And 'Pam', when he passed, seemed to the common man more notable by virtue of his firm seat and easy bluster than men of immeasurably abler mind and manoeuvre who had bestridden for a time the destiny of their country.

Various were the judgments passed upon this versatile Victorian; and from them, for they are not contradictory, we can reach the measure of his merits and defects. King Leopold's is the most complimentary. In November 1863 he wrote to Victoria: 'I have had from Lord Palmerston . . . a most admirable letter. How clear and strong that mind remains; may he be long preserved to (be) a Minister.'[2]

Victoria's own estimate, when, at the close of Palmerston's life, she gathered her feelings together, and wrote to the King of the Belgians, makes a generous allowance for his view and does credit to her sense of justice: 'The death of poor Lord Palmerston, alias Pilgerstein . . . is very *striking*, and is another link with the past—the happy past—which is gone, and in many ways he is a great loss. He had many valuable qualities, though many bad ones, and we had, God knows! terrible trouble with him about foreign affairs. Still, as

---

[1] I am aware that the correct version of the song is 'his coat so grey', but I must be excused for using the more familiar form.

[2] Queen's Letters, November 24th 1863.

'rime Minister, he managed affairs at home well and behaved to me well. But I *never* liked him, or could ever the least respect him, nor could I forget his conduct on certain occasions to my Angel. He was very vindictive, and *personal* feelings influenced his political acts very much. Still he is a loss!'[1]

The most distinguished of Palmerston's colleagues, who had understood better than the then Archbishop of Canterbury the effect upon the nation of Palmerston's Divorce Bill of 1857 and had opposed it with untiring resolution, is witness to his chief's statement to him that in his public life he had had two principal objects in view—the abolition of the slave-trade and the defence of the country:[2] and it is Gladstone, too, who gives evidence for the fact that of this Prime Minister it was correct to say that he read war and foreign office papers, but left the rest 'to rust and rot'.[3]

Another critic, and one whose opinion, as the reader will have guessed, I rate very high, has passed a more sweeping judgment on the broad influence of this remarkable man. 'When Lord Palmerston was first made Leader of the House', says Walter Bagehot, 'his jaunty manner was not at all popular, and some predicted failure. "No," said an old member, "he will soon educate us down to his level; the House will soon prefer his Ha! Ha! style to the wit of Canning and gravity of Peel."' 'I am afraid', Bagehot continues, 'that we must own that the prophecy was accomplished. No Prime Minister, so popular and so influential, has ever left in the public memory so little noble teaching. Twenty years hence when men inquire as to the then fading memory of Palmerston, we shall be able to point to no great truth which he taught, no great distinct policy which he embodied, no noble words which once fascinated his age and which, in after years, men would not willingly let die. But we shall be able to say "he had a genial manner, a firm sound sense; he had a kind of cant of insincerity, but we always knew what he meant; he had the brain of a ruler in the clothes of a man of fashion . . . The House of Commons, since it caught its tone from such a statesman, has taught the nation worse and elevated it less than usual".'[4]

On that note, however softly struck, any just appraisal of Palmerston as a man, to be worth consideration, is bound to end. The estimate of him as a Minister is not so easy to determine. In the long struggle with the Crown for the mastery in the department of foreign affairs, it might be difficult to maintain that he was worsted. The Queen might, I think, have argued that, as representing the whole nation in a way to which no Prime Minister could pretend, she had come off best in the conflict. She held her right to be kept fully informed of the course that policy was taking; she won on the specific issue of Schleswig-Holstein and, in spite of the Prime Minister's menacing

---

[1] Queen's Letters, October 20th 1865.
[2] Morley, *Life of Gladstone*, Vol. II, p. 45.   [3] ibid., p. 465.
[4] *The English Constitution*, Chapter V.

pledge, kept the country out of war; and, after Palmerston was dead, in 1868, for some reason not fully ascertained, she vetoed Clarendon's reappointment to the Foreign Office and preferred Granville in his place. This royal interposition does not stand alone. Granville, though for a long while intimate with the Sovereign, eventually fell from favour; and in 1886 Rosebery was put in his stead. Thus the Queen seemed to have tacitly established her right to have a Foreign Secretary to her liking and, therewith, an undisputed continuity of policy.

Mr. DISRAELI

BENJAMIN DISRAELI, 1st EARL OF BEACONSFIELD
born 1804 died 1881

Entered Parliament (Member for Maidstone) 1837

Chancellor of the Exchequer
  (First Derby administration) February to December 1852
  (Second Derby administration) February 1858 to June 1859
  (Third Derby administration) June 1866

Prime Minister February 1868 to December 1868
          February 1874 to April 1880

THE EARL OF BEACONSFIELD
From the portrait by Sir John Millais

CHAPTER X

MR. DISRAELI

'TO the present writer', the late Lord Rosebery tells us in his *Napoleon: the Last Phase*, 'Lord Beaconsfield once explained why he wrote *Count Alarcos*; a drama nearly, if not quite forgotten. It was produced, he said, not in the hope of composing a great tragedy, but of laying a literary ghost.'[1] The explanation does not quite tally with the account of the genesis of the book presented in Disraeli's official biography; but let that be. It affords, at least, a suggestion why people still continue to supply studies and essays on Beaconsfield himself. The story of his life, with its curious circumstance and its singular sort of pomp—very well symbolized by the peacock which adorns the best edition of his novels—is not likely ever to be given better or more fully than in Monypenny and Buckle's admirable six-volume biography; nor probably will any greater brilliancy ever be imparted to his portrait than was attained by Froude in an almost contemporary monograph. Yet still the ghost of Disraeli walks, haunting the Victorian scene in a way that is achieved by no other figure of the age, and cannot be laid. Still the spectator seeks to lay hold of its significance, asking himself like Hamlet whether he looks upon a spirit of health or a goblin damned, so questionable is the shape he sees. Gladstone has no such power; nor any other of 'the Ten'. They yield to close inspection and tell their tale; but Beaconsfield remains a mystery, Asian if you will, English if you prefer, but certainly a riddle as baffling as any propounded by the Sphinx. He was a man of his time, or else would not have been able to master it or even mix with it. But he was a man of other times no less, wandering, as his creation, Contarini Fleming, does, at the outset of the novel called by that name, by the banks of the Nile, conjuring up visions like the mirage of the adjacent desert and meditating the composition of 'a book which shall be all truth'. No wonder that, when other characters in the company assembled at Jerusalem coin appropriate inscriptions before they set out from the city over which Solomon had held sway, Contarini Fleming wrote *Time*. No wonder that Heine declared: 'Modern English letters have given us no offspring equal to *Contarini Fleming*. . . . It is . . . one of the most original works ever written: profound, poignant, pathetic; its subject the most interesting, if not the noblest imaginable—the development of a poet; truly psychological; passion

[1] *Napoleon: the Last Phase*, p. 222.

and mockery; Gothic richness, the fantasy of the Saracens, and yet over all a classic, even a death-like repose.'[1]

Beaconsfield was born in 1804 and was, as everyone knows, the child of that strange man, Isaac D'Israeli who lives still a little by virtue of his *Curiosities of Literature* and whom his greater son compared to Oliver Goldsmith. Isaac was just remarkable enough for Byron to feel that he was worth getting to know; and this connection of his father's was clearly a definite element in the making of Benjamin. The portrait of Byron in *Venetia* under the title of Lord Cadurcis is pleasing—more pleasing than that of Shelley—imagined in middle age, which forms its companion in the novel. Psychologically the book deserves attention, for here is to be seen the young Disraeli setting sail under the influence of the Byronic legend with d'Orsay and Lady Blessington, as shipmates, not to speak of Melbourne on board as Monteagle. The book came out a month or so before Victoria's accession and before Disraeli entered Parliament as member for Maidstone, where he had professed devotion to the Crown, faith in the balance of the Constitution and in the national Church as the guardians of civil and religious liberty, and special regard for the interests of agriculture and for those who followed that calling. It was already by then some few years since he had wandered about the coasts of the Mediterranean after the manner of Childe Harold and that, 'standing upon Asia and gazing upon Europe', he had conceived the idea of a 'Revolutionary Epic' as a pendant to the epic of the siege of Troy, with Napoleon clothed in such glory as fell to Achilles and himself as the Homer of the tale. But that dream had faded, leaving behind it only the baseless fabric of a vision; and he had emerged from the experience a politician, but not a poet; a Tory and not a revolutionary. It might be interesting to pause and compare Disraeli meditating on the site of Troy with Gladstone pursuing his Homeric studies in a library and from that to go on to suggest that, whilst the former started with the temperament of a romantic, the latter, about whose impressions of Athens we know so little,[2] was of a classical disposition from the first; but this inquiry would entail a preliminary disquisition, for which there is neither time nor place on the validity of the distinction between romanticism and classicism. Still, as the two men were to end in an historic and significant antagonism in spite of a great deal of conservatism in both, the disquisition might not be altogether waste of time. The outcome for Victorian England of the clash between these two strong personalities was certainly momentous. Could their minds have met, as Disraeli at one time was ready enough they should do, surprising results for their country might have followed.

[1] Quoted from Monypenny's *Life of Beaconsfield*, Vol. I, pp. 192-3. Monypenny confesses he had failed to find the original quotation in Heine.

[2] Morley's *Life of Gladstone*, Vol. I, p. 605.

That however, was not to be. Disraeli set to work to create a Tory democracy; and Gladstone a democratic commonwealth wherein aristocracy had a great part to play. But in both men regard for old institutions stood high, and in neither was change a synonym for improvement.

We are concerned here, strictly speaking, only with Disraeli. Politics makes strange bed-fellows; yet no stranger trio ever sprung from the blend of character and circumstance than Disraeli, considered, as his biographer considers him, in conjunction with Newman and Carlyle. All three in their different ways were intellectually at war with the spirit of the Revolution; all three were men of marked genius; all three were engaged in sustaining 'aids to reflection', not apparent to such teachers as Bentham and Mill. Newman rested his thought upon the logic of a conscience craving for and convinced of a divine revelation and found the development of his expectation in the evolution of the Christian Church; whilst Carlyle put his trust in the exceeding, bitter cry of the human heart for God. Disraeli, however, characteristically looked for light to the ethos of the Hebrew race. His father had broken with the Synagogue. He, in his racial pride, restored this broken link by acknowledging the God, become incarnate at Bethlehem, as the very genius of his people. It was a bold, and indeed a masterly stroke of thought; for it put him in line with the local religion of the English and enabled him to produce in the very heart of the Oxford of 1864, with Bishop Wilberforce as his sponsor, a phrase that of all his many phrases is the best remembered. It was introduced at a meeting in the Sheldonian Theatre for the better endowment of small livings and less casually than repeated repetition has made it appear. He led up to it in fact through some talk about 'the age of faith', coming not so ill from the author of *Contarini Fleming*, with its description of the Catholic service of Benediction. He passed to consider the charge of 'craving credulity' which was brought against the period. He elaborated Sidonia's theme in *Coningsby* that 'man is made to adore and to obey'. He considered how it would fare with a national Church, sustained by clerical controversy relying on personal eloquence and dependent on second-hand learning. He went on to draw his reflections into line with the 'mighty movement popularly called the French Revolution, which has not yet ended', which seemed to him (so he said) to be 'certainly the greatest event that has happened in the history of man', to be compared only with the fall of the Roman Empire, and which had had the effect of subverting the foundations of our society, leaving Sinai and Calvary to reappear amidst a waste of waters, like beacon-heights beckoning mankind back to the way of truth, long since discovered by a people chosen to be the recipients of Divine revelation.

So Disraeli's memorable discourse moved on before an audience intently listening, until, as it attained its climax with the dissection of the up-to-date science of that time, it set all Oxford rocking with laughter at one arresting phrase: 'I hold', said the speaker, 'that the function of science is the interpretation of nature, and the interpretation of the highest nature is the highest science. . . . Man is the highest nature. . . . What is the question now placed before society with a glib assurance the most astounding? The question is this—Is man an ape or an angel? My Lord, I am on the side of the angels.'

As a refutation of the argument against Christianity derived from Darwinian biology, Disraeli's thesis could hardly be bettered even to this day. Wilberforce had indeed, attempted to crush the biological critic some four years earlier at a meeting in Oxford of the British Association, but had only succeeded in giving a demonstration of sophistry and bad manners. Disraeli's thought in general, though it is sometimes dismissed as that of a charlatan, went far deeper.

Disraeli seemed to know by a kind of racial instinct where to believe and where to doubt; and both his faith and his scepticism were rooted in the very soil of things. But the Young Oxford of the time was not quite so confident. The politician—and not all politicians were accounted angels—might have been merely mocking. He was good at that, and a thorn in Gladstone's flesh in consequence. If they wanted to make sure of Disraeli's cogitations over the riddle of the universe, they might have been well-advised to make a close study of Sidonia in the pages of *Coningsby*. For 'Sidonia', we are told, 'was a great philosopher who took comprehensive views of human affairs and surveyed every fact in its relative position to other facts, the only mode of obtaining truth'. And Sidonia, too, found 'one source of interest . . . in his descent and in the fortunes of his race. As firm in his adherence to the code of the great Legislator as if the trumpet still sounded on Sinai, he might have received in the conviction of divine favour an adequate compensation for human persecution'.[1]

There, then, lies the key to what Disraeli really thought. And, though as all know, one of his later characters is made to say that all sensible men are of the same religion and, when pressed to tell what religion that is, adds 'sensible men never tell',[2] Waldershare, the character in question, is meant for Smythe, not for Disraeli himself; and his words are as those of jesting Pilate. Baron Sergius, reflecting faintly, perhaps the talk of Metternich, which Disraeli listened to at Brighton in 1849 with such unfeigned admiration as to call it, in a letter to his wife, 'divine'[3] gave more truly the considered judgment of his mind: 'No man will treat with indifference the principle of race. It is the key of history.'[4]

---

[1] *Coningsby*, Book III, Chapter i and iv, c. 10. Both chapters throw a great deal of light upon the psychology of Disraeli.

[2] *Endymion*, c. LXXXI.   [3] *Life of Beaconsfield*, Vol. III, p. 130.

[4] *Endymion*, c. LVI.

If one is in pursuit of the key-stone of Disraeli's politics as well as of his religion, it is wise to hunt for it in the same direction. 'The Jews', says Sidonia to Coningsby, 'are essentially Tories.'[1] Toryism, indeed, is but copied from the mighty prototype which has fashioned Europe.[2] And along this line of thought the writer manages to work until he has given that peculiar twist to English history which is associated with his name and which fulfilled his project of turning Toryism back to its earlier sources—to St. John Boling-broke and Shelburne. Tory-democracy has to be presented in opposition to Whiggery with its 'progressive' affiliations, as the truer development of the national genius. This was done with extreme ingenuity and largely through the mouth of Sidonia, 'descended from a very ancient and noble family of Aragon' which, in spite of having produced an Archbishop of Toledo and a Grand Inquisitor, had remained loyal to the law of Moses and the God of Sinai. Where exactly the colony of Arabians to which Sidonia belonged had originally sprung from is not clear; what alone seems certain is that they had preserved a fine culture and had displayed a magnificent resistance in time of persecution. Sidonia, if in some respects too much of an aristocrat to be identified with Rothschild, emerged from the Peninsular War, rich in a fortune to be reckoned by millions and possessed, not only of the wealth, but of the wisdom of the Hebrews. Widely travelled and wisely read, he puts an interpretation on history not by any means uncongenial to the attentive ear of Coningsby, and puts it with an arresting originality and an abundance of epigram that, like greater dialogues, is calculated to serve the interests of political philosophy better than a treatise. 'You will observe one curious trait', he says, in speaking of England, 'in the history of this country; the depository of power is always unpopular; all combine against it; it always falls.' The Barons, the Church, the King, the People; and finally Parliament, which for the last sixty years has been growing more and more unpopular and, to which, though in 1832 it tried to renew its strength, had, by so doing, merely made itself more odious. What, Sidonia proceeds to examine, is the cause and the significance of this. He does not find them in economic circum-stances. These may, indeed, have precipitated a catastrophe, but they can hardly be said to have provoked it. Physical comfort was well diffused in 1640; the population was of a manageable size; agriculture was improving; commerce was flourishing. Yet still 'the imagination of England rose against the Government'. The proper inference from what happened is that political institutions are not the cause of change, but that 'the motive power is the national character'. Utility is, therefore, no principle of reconstruction. We ought not to despise it, for every rational foundation in political thought should be welcomed. Yet the reason of man has not been at the root of the great movements of society; not at the root of the Siege of Troy; not at the

[1] *Coningsby*, Book IV, c. 15.   [2] ibid.

root of the Saracenic invasion or of the Crusades; not behind the rise of monasticism or of the Jesuits; 'above all it was not Reason that created the French Revolution'. 'Man is only truly great when he acts from the passions; never irresistible but when he appeals to the imagination. Even Mormon counts more votaries than Bentham.'

This mixture of sophistry, satire and sense is both amusing and instructive. It was, however, to be given a sharper edge when the theme which it introduces of the Whigs as the sponsors in England of a Venetian constitution, with the King in place of a doge and the Whig Aristocracy as the equivalent of the merchant princes of the maritime Republic, is further developed a year later by the publication on May Day 1845 of *Sybil or The Two Nations*. The 'two nations', as all the world knows, were 'The Rich and the Poor'; and Disraeli's design was now fully disclosed. He was engaged in an attempt to revive the Tory Party on, to use his own language in *Coningsby*, a 'conservative', and not a 'concessionary' basis. The closing pages of *Sybil* set out the Disraelitish conclusion that 'In the selfish strife of factions, two great existences have been blotted out of the history of England, the Monarch and the Multitude; as the power of the Crown has diminished, the privileges of the people have disappeared; till at length the sceptre has become a pageant, and the subject has degenerated again into a serf.'[1]

This was the historical thesis upon which the enterprising young Jew, in the fateful years involving the Repeal of the Corn Laws, proposed to reconstitute the Tory Party. It contrasted sharply with the ways of Canning and Peel who had been content by giving here a little and there a little, to come to terms with the spirit of the times, so that Tadpole and Taper, perhaps Disraeli's most effective creations in fiction, display opportunism as an applied science in the practice of politics. 'An affectionate pressure of the hand', observes Taper, 'will sometimes do a great deal; and I have promised many a peerage without committing myself, by an ingenious habit of deference which cannot be mistaken by the future noble.' . . . 'I had sooner be supported by the Wesleyans', said Mr. Tadpole, 'than by all the marquesses in the peerage.'

So, we are required to suppose, the Peelites plotted and planned under the influence of middle-class morality.

The weakness of Disraeli's argument lies in the fact that it postulates a Philistinism of ethics in the middle-class which has no assured foundation and a high-principled affinity between the nobility with the squirearchy on the one side and the proletariat, if that be a civil term to use, on the other, which is no better established. Predisposition is treated as proof throughout the argument. The worth of the middle-class was in truth never better vindicated than under Victoria—intellectually, no less than commercially.

[1] *Sybil*, c. XIII and last.

Of course, if one is looking for black sheep, one can find them in every flock; but the Gradgrinds and the Bounderbys, the Tapers and the Tadpoles are not really more damaging to their kind than the disciples of Alcibiades or of Thersites. There is, as has often been argued, no more combustible commonwealth than one in which the middle-class is lacking, so great a service can it do in reconciling Disraeli's 'two nations'. But the middle-class in general is not romantic even when it can boast of Cobden and Bright, and Disraeli was in search of romance, which meant little or nothing to Peel, like Guizot in France the middle-class minister *par excellence*. The *Young England* of George Smythe and other of his contemporaries afforded Disraeli an aristocratic ambush whence he could stalk both the bourgeois and the oligarch, and in George Bentinck he found presently a leader under whose guidance he could conveniently conceal his manoeuvres. It would no doubt, after Russell had been given the opportunity of forming a Free-Trade administration which he had been unable to seize, have been a more generous and graceful act on Disraeli's part to recognize Peel's difficulties and to come to his aid; and a nobler mind than that of a politician, bent on political success, might have preferred this course to that which a consistent championship of the agricultural interest offered him or to attacks on the Conservative leader which lacked nothing in sarcasm or savagery. However, Disraeli's conduct, if it was hardly that of a gentleman, can derive a good deal of support from the logic of argument, from the policy pursued by Peel, and from the final outcome of the situation. 'Only those', say Low and Sanders in their history of the period, 'will call (Disraeli's) speeches flippant who have not read them'.[1] The charge of apostasy from the creed of Protection, which lies against Peel, can only be pressed by those who find Disraeli not guilty on a similar count, in respect of parliamentary reform, round about twenty years later. And the plea that necessity knows no law will hardly be urged by those who reflect that the duties were under Peel's proposals to last three years more, and that already, with the protective system still prevailing, the tide of disaster seemed to have turned, foreign trade to be increasing, wages to be higher, labour to be in greater demand, and the price of food—beef, mutton, and flour—to be falling. Cobden's reasoning was unanswerable, if the world was going to follow a British lead and if peace was thereby going to be made perpetual; but his arguments were too much in the nature of assumptions needing to be proved. His fervour, and the fervour of his supporters, was very persuasive; and it was long after Disraeli's death as well as after his own that the country began to wonder whether there was not something to be said for List's[2] view, published in Germany in 1841, no less than for Adam

[1] *Political History of England*, p. 59.
[2] Friedrich List, 1789-1846, was a German economist whose chief work *Das Nationale System der Politschen Okonomie*, 184, advocated protection by tariff until national industries were firmly established.

Smith's, published three-quarters of a century before. So puzzling is the right road to find, when politics, economics and sociology meet at the cross-ways !

Lie justice where it may, Disraeli had managed to remove Peel from his path to power in 1846; and Bentinck, a hard worker but no genius, was removed by Providence from his path suddenly some two years later. Two obstacles to his rise to supreme power were, therefore, gone: there remained, as Melbourne had pointed out to him, the greatest of them all—Derby. Him Disraeli could not hope, nor perhaps wish, to oust from the field or pass in the race; and he was anyhow wise enough never to attempt it. Contarini Fleming, as we have said, wrote *Time* across the map of life. And *Time* cleared Disraeli's way, but not before Derby had made a great refusal of office in 1855.

'The Monarch and the Multitude'—those were the words, potent as 'Open, Sesame' with which Disraeli had planned that the doors of supreme political success should fly open before the Tory Party. Bolingbroke, Shelburne and the Younger Pitt had assumed in his eye a slightly fanciful rôle as patriarchs or protagonists in the struggle of the nation against the Whig or Venetian Oligarchy which had dominated the politics of the eighteenth century in England; and his relations with the royal and the popular elements in the State supply a convenient division under which his own actual achievements may be considered.

A prelude of discontent with things as they were had been sounded in *Coningsby* in 1844; and then in 1845 followed the clarion-cry of *Sybil*. From 'a palace in a garden', where 'youth and innocence and beauty' were to be seen enthroned, the reader is transported to the north of England and into the neighbourhood of the ruins of Marney Abbey, where an Earl of Marney was reigning in place of the Abbot and the Monks. Unaware as yet that the time would come when, at the Monarch's express solicitation,[1] he would pass the Public Worship Regulation Act of 1874, described by the Archbishop of Canterbury of the time (Tait) as the most important ecclesiastical statute since the Reformation, and when, moreover, he would himself ridicule the Ritualists by stigmatizing the Eucharist, in the manner in which they celebrated it, as 'the mass in masquerade', Disraeli, still much of a novelist in 1844-5, did not hesitate, as we have seen, to throw out the suggestion in *Coningsby* that 'it was the fall of the Papacy in England' that had laid the foundation of 'the Whig aristocracy';[2] whilst in *Sybil* he built his story round the figures of two Catholic devotees—Sybil and Trafford— and his argument round the ancient care or charity of the Church for the poor. It is in *Sybil* that, I believe, the only Disraelite allusion to Thomas à

---

[1] Queen's Letters—Disraeli to the Queen, July 11th 1874: 'If this blow is dealt against t he Sacerdotal School, it will be entirely through the personal will of the Sovereign.'
[2] Chapter V.

Kempis is to be found,[1] as it is in *Coningsby*[2] alone that Pascal is recognized as 'the greatest of Frenchmen'. Such casual remarks are reminiscent of the 'Young England' period of Disraeli's life. When they appear no more, we may conclude that he has abandoned any attempt to attach to himself the leadership of the High Church Party, which passed, therefore, much to the advantage of the Liberals, into Gladstone's keeping.

In this respect the cult of the Monarch may, perhaps, be said to have prevailed over the cult of the Multitude. The pull of thought in *Sybil* is the communal, or, as we might say, the socialistic idea; and the book came out on May Day (1845). 'The writer speaks of circumstances within his own experience' is a statement in the novel;[3] and witness is born to the truth of this claim by visits paid by Disraeli to the north of England in the autumn of 1843 and 1844. His sympathy with the distress occasioned by the well-intended, but nevertheless harshly operating Poor Law Amendment Act of 1834 was older and can be traced back to the year 1837, when a series of bad harvests had begun to increase the sufferings of the agricultural districts. He recognized that there was a good deal of rude truth in what the Chartists were saying, although truth in need of far more subtle treatment than the Chartists were likely to have the intelligence to give it. Here, therefore, was the gate of opportunity.

These things being so, it follows that the year 1837 must be regarded as an important date in the development of Disraeli's interest in 'the Multitude'. It needs no saying that his interest in 'the Monarch' as something more than a symbol dated from the same year, which was also the year, as it chanced, when he took his seat in Parliament and which has, therefore, the effect of an outstanding milestone on the path of his career.

When he introduced the famous passage in *Sybil*[4] on the Queen's accession, which owed much to Lyndhurst, Disraeli looked full at Victoria and thought, as to do her justice, she had already thought herself, of the inspiration she might prove to her subjects. 'Allegiance to one', he wrote, 'who rules . . . over a Continent of which Columbus never dreamed: to the Queen of every sea and of nations in every zone! It is not of these that I would speak: but of a nation nearer her footstool and which at this moment looks to her with anxiety, with affection, perhaps with hope. . . . Will it be her proud destiny at length to bear relief to suffering millions. . .?'[5]

Victoria, however, looked shyly at Disraeli himself and did not particularly like what she saw. Here is what Derby repeated to him of the Queen's reaction in February 1851 to the thought of his having high office: 'He (Derby) told me that Her Majesty had inquired of him to whom he proposed to entrust the Leadership of the House of Commons, and he had mentioned

[1] Book I, Chapter X.   [2] Book III.
[3] *Sybil*, Book VI, Chapter vii.   [4] Book I, Chapter vi.   [5] ibid.

my name. The Queen said: "I always felt that, if there were a Protectionist Government, Mr. D. must be the Leader of the House of Commons: but I do not approve of Mr. D. I do not approve of his conduct to Sir Robert Peel." Lord Derby said: "Madam, Mr. D. has had to make his position, and men who make their positions will say and do things which are not necessary to be said or done by those for whom positions are provided."

' "That is true", said the Queen. "And all I can now hope is that, having attained this great position he will be temperate. I accept Mr. Disraeli on your guarantee." [1]

There was obviously a gulf to be bridged before the Minister would be acceptable to the Monarch; and it took fifteen years to bridge it. Not until 1866 can one mark some change of feeling (in an entry in the Queen's Journal on November 25th): 'Saw Mr. Disraeli after tea. . . . He was amiable and clever, but is a strange man.' Then in May 1867 General Grey, the Queen's Private Secretary, tells her that he shares her opinion that 'Mr. Disraeli is evidently the directing mind of the Ministry and . . . the person to whom any representation can now be most effectually made.' In 1867 the passage of the Reform Bill, which offended some old Conservatives by its palpable dishonesty was not displeasing to the Monarch.[2] In her own way she pursued her grandfather's ideal of 'the Patriot King'; whilst Disraeli, whose mind, as we have seen had been also powerfully affected by Bolingbroke, aimed at making her the patriot Queen. Five or six years of Gladstonianism were needed before she was ready for that rôle. The most unpopular years of the reign, however, were passing—the year (1866) when John Bright, no advocate as he reminded his audience, of Courts or Crowns, felt an obligation to stand out and defend the Sovereign's undying grief as the guarantee of a great and generous heart and of sympathy for all her subjects; the year (1871) when Dilke to his lasting discredit characterized the cost of maintaining the Throne as 'moral mischief'; and the year (1872) when Dilke's bosom friend, Joseph Chamberlain, announced, with all the ignorance of a revolutionary mind still unaware of the place that tradition held in any living constitution, that a republic must come in Britain. These years had gone by when early in 1874 a revulsion of public feeling swept Disraeli back into power with a majority of fifty behind him. His hour had come at last; and the man, now almost seventy years of age, had had ample time to make ready. The Prime Minister, indeed, lost no time in putting his, so to say, 'Monarch and Multitude' policy into force. To preserve chronological order, it is better to reverse their sequence. The implementation of social improvements was mainly left to lesser men; but the mind, which had made its mark with *Sybil*, was at work at the highest level. Cross's Public Health Act,

[1] M. & B., *Life of Disraeli*, Vol. III, p. 290.
[2] Queen's Letters—to Lord Derby. May 8th 1867.

consolidating and elucidating a long series of measures for the betterment of the poorer members of the community was supplemented by an Artisans' Dwellings Act, empowering corporations of towns containing twenty thousand inhabitants to buy buildings condemned as unhealthy by medical officers of health; and these two Acts may be treated as notable examples of Disraeli's characteristic motto *'sanitas sanitatum, omnia sanitas'* in practice, if, indeed, the Act of 1870, making education compulsory, does not also claim inclusion under that head.[1] Cross went on to limit the cases in which trade combinations could be charged with conspiracy—a most important measure in the growth of trades-unionism. Breaches of contract were, thenceforward, removed from the category of crimes and treated as actionable wrongs, unless they endangered public health or safety by withholding the supply of gas or water. Cairns,[2] as Lord Chancellor, countenanced the trend of this legislation by carrying into law a definition of 'picketing' which permitted the 'peaceful persuasion' of potential strikers without the commission of any political offence.

The Lancashire lawyer at the Home Office found an active colleague at the Exchequer in a Devonshire squire. Northcote[3] helped the philanthropic movement of the time by an act to encourage the submission of the accounts of friendly societies to the inspection of the Government; whilst Richmond's Act, giving a tenant compensation for agricultural improvements, was another case that could be cited to prove that fortunate persons were not indifferent to the welfare of the less-fortunate. 'Labour' as such had just begun to be represented in the House of Commons; and it is from one of the two Labour Members of Parliament between 1874 and 1880 that there comes a testimonial more telling than the enumeration of any amount of Acts bearing on the welfare of the poorer classes. 'The Conservative Party', said Alexander Macdonald in 1879, 'have done more for the working classes in five years than the Liberals have in fifty.'[4] The good faith and good sense of Tory-Democrats and their power of marching with the times does not deserve, in face of that testimonial, to be challenged; nor does Disraeli's part in them. His had been real and fruitful imagination distinguishing itself from what, in *Sybil*, he had styled the 'coarse specific for our social evils' of the Chartists.

In all this social energy on behalf of 'the Multitude' the part to be played by 'the Monarch' was not overlooked. In a manner indeed the Prime Minister may be said to have caused them to fuse. The real multitude of Victoria's

---

[1] R. A. Cross, afterwards first Viscount Cross, Home Secretary in Disraeli's second administration, 1874–80. Home Secretary, first Salisbury administration, 1885–6. Secretary for India, second Salisbury administration, 1886–1892.

[2] Hugh MacCalmont, first Earl Cairns.

[3] Sir Stafford Northcote, Chancellor of the Exchequer 1874–80, afterwards first Earl of Iddesleigh.   [4] Quoted from Buckle's *Life of Beaconsfield*, Vol. V, p. 369.

subjects was to be found overseas among the teeming millions of India. Disraeli was enough of an Oriental to see that representative institutions could never play, at any rate within any time that Englishmen could measure, such a part in the governance of Asiatics as it may have done in that of Europeans. The names of Asoka and of Akbar afforded to India as much inspiration as Gibbon had found in recalling the names of the Antonines. India was Tennyson's dream:

> but while I groan'd,
> From out the sunset pour'd an alien race,
> Who fitted stone to stone again, and Truth,
> Peace, Love and Justice came and dwelt therein,
> Nor in the field without were seen or heard
> Fires of Suttee, nor wail of baby-wife,
> Or Indian widow:
> So then:—
> Here, till the mortal morning mists of earth
> Fade in the noon of heaven, when creed and race
> Shall bear false witness, each of each, no more,
> But find their limits by that larger light,
> And overstep then, moving easily
> Thro' after-ages in the love of Truth,
> The truth of Love.

There was the dream of the Victorians, as they gazed at the distant continent which 'the expansion of England' had thrown into their keeping. It was a dream that the romantic Disraeli was to call into potential life.

As early as 1851 Disraeli, after his manner had found a phrase which embodied his policy of Empire. He did not indeed quote it correctly, but, as Bacon had done before him, he rather improved it by misquotation. In a happy age, Tacitus had declared, the Emperor Nerva had mingled the Roman Principate with Liberty, two things formerly thought incompatible. For *principatus* Disraeli substituted, by accident or design, the word *imperium*. *Imperium et Libertas!*—the association was free of the vulgar error generally accepted a century later, despite Lecky's effort to check its growth, that democracy and liberty meant the same thing. The great ages of the world— the age of Pericles, the age of Augustus, the age of Charlemagne, the age of Elizabeth, the age of Louis Quatorze—were ages when the human mind enjoyed, if we are to judge by results, a sufficient range of freedom, but not as a result of anything that can be truly called democracy. The extension of the suffrage was in Disraeli's eyes no more than an incident. 'Liberty', Burke had said (though Disraeli's regard for Burke was halting and uncertain), 'such as deserves the name, is an honest, equitable, diffusive and impartial principle. It is a great and enlarged virtue, and not a sordid, selfish and illiberal vice. It is the portion of the mass of the citizens and not the haughty licence of some potent individual or some predominant faction. If anything ought to be despotic in a country, it is its government; because there is no cause of constant operation to make its yoke unequal.'[1] Descriptions or definitions of this subtle, elusive mercurial thing that we, all of us, have more or less in mind when we speak of it, invariably escape us, for it encourages no such treatment. A Jew had, in fact, said the last word about it when, eighteen hundred years before Disraeli, he was writing to some Greeks: 'Where the Spirit of the Lord is, there is Liberty.' In England, in India, that was the context in which it had been sought.

Some such cogitations, at any rate, must be supposed behind all the Victorian conception of the Government of India; behind the thoughts evoked by the memory of Clive—behind the 'Clive' of Browning's Poem, even more perhaps than of Macaulay's essays—behind Warren Hastings; behind the line of proconsuls that followed after them; behind all the heroes of the Mutiny. In the map of time the English in India occupy no more than the space of two centuries, but in the work of integrating India their contribution had been stupendous and, had sagacity prevailed in British counsels, that achievement, crowned by the British Sovereign's assumption of the Imperial title, should have stood like stone and not have ended in froth and bubble, or worse. The apex of the Indian adventure was reached with singular propriety, whilst the only British Prime Minister with any title to be regarded as an Oriental swayed the House of Commons and stood high in the counsels and consideration of the Queen.

These years of destiny in India, during which the policy of Empire took shape, followed swiftly upon and, indeed, pretty nearly coincided with the fateful years of social reform in Britain; and they included 'the terrible year of 1877, when famine was raging.' The road to India became indeed a pre-occupation of the British mind, and of no British mind more than Disraeli's. Late in 1875 Frederick Greenwood, the editor of the *Pall Mall Gazette*, intimated to Derby that the Khedive of Egypt, owing to financial embarrassments, was endeavouring to dispose of his interest in the Suez Canal; and this circumstance became almost simultaneously known to Disraeli, very probably through Baron Lionel de Rothschild, a personal friend. Derby seems at first to have recoiled from, but Disraeli at once to have jumped at the opportunity. It was a question of moving quicker than the French, who were already in negotiation with the Khedive. Disraeli, with a swiftness in a politician akin to that of lightning, managed to secure the assent of his Cabinet and, what was almost as important, the consent of the Queen. The Khedive was in such financial difficulties that he had almost agreed to let a

[1] Letter to Richard Burke, Esq., 1793.

French syndicate take over his 177,000 shares—nearly half the total issue of 400,000—on conditions beneath their proper value. Fortunately, however, France lay under a recent obligation to Britain; and Decazes, at the Quai d'Orsay, was anxious not to antagonize his British neighbours. More easily, maybe, than at another time, the French Government listened to Derby's representations to the effect that the Suez Canal was the Queen's highway to India and that the shipping passing through it was predominantly British. The French deal was called off; and before the end of November the British had acquired the Khedive's share for £4,000,000. This considerable sum was raised through Rothschild. In less than half a century the shares were valued, not at four, but at forty millions. If, however, we had known in 1875 that by 1950 the English would have abandoned India, the project might have called for pause.

Nothing, however, was further from all men's minds at that time! The Prime Minister had resolved to place the Imperial Crown of India firmly on the British Sovereign's head, where indeed it had been loosely resting since the close of the Mutiny. The Suez Canal deal went through the Commons by the end of February 1876; in the following May the Royal Titles Bill was introduced, though with less tact than the case required. Neither was the Opposition informed, nor the Prince of Wales consulted; and both resented the omission. In other respects the resistance to the Bill had the look of being factious, since the Queen approved the conversion of the courtesy title of empress into a formal style, which seems to have been acceptable enough in India, where Lytton, the Viceroy, made it the occasion of a brilliant Durbar on New Year's Day, 1877.

Whilst the Prime Minister was effecting the exaltation of the Queen in the order of monarchy, the Queen was considering the elevation of the Prime Minister in the scale of society. From her in June 1876, came the suggestion that Disraeli should take a peerage and so relieve himself of the fatigue incidental to the Leadership of the Commons. Nobody, who has glanced at his intimate correspondence about that time can doubt that, whatever pretences he might put up his strength was consciously failing him: and Victoria's timely proposal told him only what he knew, that he should resign from the conduct of public affairs altogether, or else carry them on from the sheltered purlieus of the House of Lords. There are persons, he was to observe a month or so later in one of the most entertaining of his sallies, who have retired from business, and there are persons from whom business has retired. He consulted some of his colleagues how it should be with him. Opinion was clear as to the loss he must inflict on his party if he left the Commons; and this view was confirmed by the lamentations of Lucy,[1] over the dullness that followed his withdrawal. But, if no one could replace him in debate

[1] Sir Henry Lucy, *Diary of Two Parliaments*, Vol. I, p. 218.

it was still more certain that no one could take his place in counsel. So he accepted the Queen's offer and carried the Sword of State on February 8th 1877 when Victoria, now proclaimed Empress of India, opened Parliament in person. He had always been an actor. This was the climax of his triumphs. In the drama which he had planned, he had fulfilled his rôle. He had shown himself in the Commons as a tribune of the people; and now in the Lords, as he stood 'with all the dignity of pose and lack of facial expression that distinguished him on great occasions',[1] he seemed to have wafted the Monarch to her place in history.

Beaconsfield had still to make the Multitude understand what the Monarch stood for; and again he left his countrymen with a phrase to ponder, and a very telling phrase. It was possibly suggested to his mind by some casual words dropped by Lobanoff the Russian Ambassador, to the Court of St. James's.[2] Anyhow, if so, it had to lie dormant till Beaconsfield was closing his book of life and was within two months of the end. He was arguing that Candahar should be retained, but he did not for that lose his sense of realities. 'There are several places which are called the Keys of India. There is Merv . . . there is Ghuznee; there is Balkh; then Candahar. . . . But, my lords, the Key of India is not Herat or Candahar. The Key of India is London.'

This is perhaps the point in any study of Disraeli where some further allusion should be made to the antithesis which existed between him and Gladstone and in which a later age may perceive a contrast no less striking than that between Pitt and Fox, both of them Whigs at the start. 'Disraeli', in Monypenny's estimate, 'was in English politics the embodiment of the counter-revolution, the political creed which does not shrink from demo- cracy, nor even from the revolution on its salutary, constructive side, but which opposes to the destructive tendencies of both a fuller and wider reconstruction';[3] and though this terminology had been bettered by Joseph de Maistre, it confirms and explains the sense of obligation to Metternich from whom Disraeli, on his own showing, learnt much. But if there was a fundamental political difference needing to be emphasized between his fully developed politics and those of Gladstone much more deserving still of notice is their difference of temperament. The two men could never prob- ably have understood one another, even in the sense which is open to most antagonists. For each at heart regarded the other as a fraud. Both were superb actors on the stage at Westminster—so good that no other pair of actors has perhaps ever countered one another's arts more effectively. Yet, when we say this we must restrict the term 'actor' to its acquired meaning. Unfortunately they themselves did not. They seemed, each in the eyes of the other, to be

[1] Buckle, *Life of Beaconsfield*, Vol. VI, p. 519.
[2] ibid., Vol. VI, p. 605.
[3] ibid., *Life of Disraeli*, Vol. VI, p. 643.

hypocrites. Gladstone, on being told that Disraeli, after a speech at the Academy banquet, praising the grace and originality of the exhibits, had confessed to Stratford de Redcliffe that he had seen nothing original there, is said to have observed: 'Even within those sacred walls, he could not forget to play the hypocrite.' And Disraeli, writing to Lady Bradford in 1877, when circumstances in the Near East were tending to develop fast their mutual antagonism of opinion, remarks: 'My theory about him (i.e. Gladstone) is unchanged: a ceaseless Tartuffe from the beginning.'[1] This was the theme that, we cannot doubt, he had intended to develop in his last unfinished novel where Falconet affords us a study of Gladstone as he appeared in Disraeli's eyes. Perhaps we have reason to be grateful to the hand of death for staying the itch of penmanship in this final thrust at an opponent who to men as eminently just as Dean Church could appear a model of sincerity.[2] All the ferocity of the Hebrew, indeed, entered into Disraeli's estimate; and it was a ferocity which demanded a full accompaniment of ridicule to give it point and penetration. Tenniel's well-known cartoon, depicting Gladstone, with *Lothair* in his hand, murmuring 'Flippant!' whilst Disraeli, a little way off at his back, dismisses a volume entitled *Juventus Mundi* with the observation 'Prosy!' is a happy hit. For Gladstone could never be brought to see the merit of Disraeli's novels.[3] 'The spirit of whim in them, the ironic solemnity, the historical paradoxes, the fantastic glitter of dubious gems, the grace of high comedy . . . in union with a social vision that often pierced deep below the surface'—All this was hidden from the great Oxonian, who saw so much, but never that. As for Disraeli, many casual allusions to Gladstone's incapacity to write bespatter his letters and betray his opposition of temperament and his difference of technique in approaching the problems of life. Here, indeed, all is clear enough. It is a much nicer problem to determine what it was that rendered the Sovereign so much more susceptible to Disraeli's influence than to Gladstone's. The latter had much about him that the Queen might have been expected to prefer. He exemplified the rise to power of the middle-class which had been so patent in Peel and had found so ready a response in Victoria. Disraeli, on the other hand, it is irresistible to say, particularly in view of subsequent associations, pursued a primrose path of dalliance reminiscent of the Byronic age. By the time, indeed, that he became familiar with Victoria he had shed his showy waistcoats and shaken off the smell of Gore House;[4] yet his language remained flowery and his flatteries were blatant. Or at least they would seem so, had Victoria not manifestly enjoyed them. She was a queen, and could play that part with great dignity and distinction; but she was no

---

[1] Buckle, *Life of Disraeli*, Vol. VI, p. 181.
[2] *Life and Letters of Dean Church*, p. 305.   [3] *Life of Gladstone*, Vol. I, p. 588.
[4] Lady Blessington's, where she and Count D'Orsay entertained the fringe of Regency society.

fairy queen, whatever he might pretend. Still, only an unwomanly woman would find a harangue more to her liking than a succession of fulsome compliments. Into Victoria's preference for Disraeli, however, there entered considerations more valid than those of sex. Disraeli's conception of a monarch giving leadership to 'the multitude' appealed to the Queen who perceived more and more, as time went on that Gladstone, whatever might be his devotion to herself, was a menace to her Empire. The trouble in the Balkans, which preoccupied Disraeli's administration in its later phase, was made much worse by Gladstone's inflammatory speeches. To the Empress of India and to her Prime Minister at home it appeared of immense consequence that Russia should gain no hold over Britain's route to Hindustan. Russia must remain within her boundaries and, more especially, within her Asiatic ones. In Europe England might expect to command the aid of Austria, of France, and perhaps of Germany, in repelling the supposed policy of the Tsar. In Asia she had to depend on herself with such modest aid as the Turks and the Afghans might afford her.

For the British Empire her Occidental and Oriental policies required some sort of fusion in 1878; and this was what the Beaconsfield administration effected after Salisbury passed from the India Office to replace Derby at the Foreign Office. The Russo-Turkish Treaty of San Stefano was to be submitted in detail to a European Congress; and the 'big Bulgaria', which it contemplated, was to be split into two divisions, Russia dominating through her ally, Bulgaria, the region north of the Balkans, and Turkey retaining some sort of hold over the territory south of the Balkans (Eastern Rumelia) under a Christian Governor. So much appears to have been agreed between Salisbury and Schouvaloff before the British Envoys proceeded to Berlin; and so much was betrayed by a Foreign Office auxiliary clerk of the name of Marvin to the *Globe* newspaper. Another secret agreement between Britain and Turkey, which went by the name of the Cyprus convention, placed Cyprus in British hands in return for a promise of British support for Turkey in Asia, if Batoum, Kars and Ardahan, or any of them, were surrendered to Russia. India's share in the negotiations was emphasized by the despatch of seven thousand native Indian troops to Malta under orders from the Crown.

Bismarck's line in promoting the policy of a European Congress to determine the Near Eastern imbroglio had made a great point of insuring its success[1] and the previous Anglo-Russian and Anglo-Turkish Agreements promised to further this purpose. The critics of the British Government, however, after the revelation of the negotiations going on behind the scenes, were no doubt in a position to say that the Congress had become little more than 'a chamber of registration'. The forum provided for the deliberations

[1] See the footnote to p. 288 of Buckle's *Life of Disraeli*, Vol. VI.

of Europe had really become a stage on which the statesmen of the time might strut and fret. To take a leading part in such drama the ageing Beaconsfield seemed to be cut out. His colleagues were agreed that he, and he alone, possessed prestige adequate to represent his country; and no one was firmer than Salisbury in advocating it.[1] The Queen, once she got over her anxiety about the strain his presence at a Congress so distant as Berlin would put upon the Prime Minister, was consenting to the plan; the Prince of Wales was insistent upon it; Beaconsfield was perhaps more than ready to go; and Bismarck put the sentiment of Europe into a classic phrase which has survived: 'Der alte Jude, das ist der Mann.'

The old Jew made his way out slowly to his destination by train in the early June of 1878, his suite accompanying him, but not the colleague on whom most of the detailed work of the mission was expected to devolve. There were already understandings with Russia, with Turkey, and with Austria. A harmony of purpose had still to be reached with Bismarck; and to the attainment of this Beaconsfield devoted his endeavours as soon as he arrived in the German capital. On the very evening—June 12th—of setting foot in Berlin, he was invited to a conversation with the German Chancellor. The two men had not met for sixteen years; and Bismarck had become much rounder and redder with the lapse of time. He did not, however, appear to the English Prime Minister any the less well-disposed to work for a peaceful outcome to the Congress than his assent to a pre-Congress understanding between England and Russia had indicated. 'The interview', as Beaconsfield wrote to the Queen, 'was not unsatisfactory'; and it was settled that the Bulgarian Question should have the first place on the agenda.

Bismarck's method as President of the Congress was tersely described by Beaconsfield to his Sovereign in the following words: 'All questions are publicly introduced and then privately settled.' There were two problems to which the Prime Minister devoted his energies in particular. He was resolved to make sure that Bulgaria, south of the Balkans, should remain in Turkish hands; and it was when the Russians endeavoured to modify the Anglo-Russian understanding by excluding Turkish troops from Southern Bulgaria that Beaconsfield, after hinting to the Italian Ambassador for communication to Bismarck that he would not yield this point, ordered a special train with a view to the departure of himself and his mission. Bismarck came running round to see whether 'the old Jew' meant business and, finding that he did, brought such pressure to bear upon the Russian plenipotentiaries that the Tsar's surrender was available within an hour.[2]

There was another matter where it was Beaconsfield's intention to make his influence felt—the destiny of Batoum and the delimitation of the Russo-Turkish frontier in Asia. There had been some obscure mention of Batoum

[1] Buckle, Life of Disraeli, Vol. VI, p. 307.   [2] ibid., Vol. VI, p. 326.

in the preliminary Anglo-Russian negotiations; and it was not unreasonable
that Russia should take what had passed to mean that this port on the Black
Sea should be left in her hands. Beaconsfield was resolved to see it converted
into a free and merely commercial harbour and, though his health was just at
the time at its worst, he twice visited Gortchakoff[1] in private and carried his
point in Congress. As to the frontier-line there was a more serious tussle.
A difference appeared on the respective maps of the plenipotentiaries and,
whether Gortchakoff had made a muddle or whether there was deliberate
trickery, tempers rose at the Congress and the business had in the end to be
taken from Beaconsfield and Gortchakoff and handed over to settle to Salisbury and Schouvaloff,[2] by whom it seems to have been determined to the
British advantage.

The broad result of the Berlin Congress, at least, it is generally agreed was
the rehabilitation of British prestige in the eyes of Europe, the vindication of
the British claim to stand out as a great Oriental Power, and the emergence of
Disraeli as the embodiment, at least theatrically, of British capacity in foreign
affairs. His presence at Berlin had set the ladies reading *Henrietta Temple*, a
novel at once the most romantic and the least political that came from his
hand. What we know of the book confirms the choice of its cosmopolitan
readers at the Congress. An entry in Disraeli's Diary in 1846 runs: 'Parted for
ever from Henrietta. Returned to Bradenham at the latter end of August;
concluded *Henrietta Temple*.' Who was she, the lady of classic beauty who
recalled a 'nymph tripping over the dew-bespangled meads of Ida or glancing
amid the hallowed groves of Greece'; who inspired the famous description
of 'love at first sight' beneath the cedar tree at Armine; who moved Guedalla
to declare that in this more than in any other part of Disraeli's work 'the
rustle of real petticoats' is audible; who set all the Congress at Berlin gossip-
ing, forty years after and more. If tradition is to be trusted, one may hunt for
the mention, in such books as provide this kind of knowledge, of a Henrietta
Villebois who married a certain Sir W. F. Sykes of Basildon in 1821 and died
in 1846.

Towards four in the afternoon of July 13th the treaty which preserved
Europe for some thirty years and more from a fresh revolutionary convul-
sion, was signed at the Radziwill Palace in Berlin. Beaconsfield had re-
integrated that Concert of Europe, which had served as a master-card in
Metternich's hand and had doubtless been displayed to the younger apostle
of the counter-revolution when the two men talked at Brighton in January
1849, and Metternich gave Disraeli that 'most masterly exposition of the
present state of European affairs and said a greater number of wise and witty

---

[1] Prince Michael Alexandra Gortchakoff was Russian Minister to Vienna during the
Crimean war.
[2] Count Peter Schouvaloff, Russian Ambassador to Great Britain 1874–79.

things than Disraeli ever recollected hearing from him on the same day'.[1]

The signature of the Berlin Treaty brought the performance of the great actor to its penultimate act, and indeed to the close of its cosmopolitan demonstration. All the eyes of Europe had been fixed upon Beaconsfield as he carried his policy to its conclusion; and he stood out by virtue both of his shining abilities and his oriental ancestry as the Briton best fitted to make good the claims of one, who was not merely Queen of England, but whose imperial dominions now spread eastwards. Monarch of one of the largest of Moslem communities, Victoria seemed to be acting not out of character, as her chief minister steadied the toppling throne of the caliph of Islam and also took steps, not apparently disagreeable to the Sultan, for the reform of the administration of Anatolia and the protection of the Christians resident in those parts by the appointment of Sir Charles Wilson as military consul-general— an appointment resulting in effective changes for the better, so long as Beaconsfield remained in office and Layard continued as Ambassador at Constantinople. One feature of Beaconsfield's dramatic success calls, perhaps, for notice. He seems to have intended to address the Congress in the French language. His French was far from good; and his pronunciation of that language would, perhaps, have provoked ridicule. The British Ambassador—Odo Russell—saw that this reckless adventure must be averted; and he represented to the Prime Minister that it would be a sad disappointment to the assembled company of eminent statesmen if they were not allowed to hear so eminent an orator speak to them in his mother-tongue. Whether or not Beaconsfield saw through this manoeuvre, there is nothing to tell us; but at all events, if so, he took the hint. The English Prime Minister addressed the Congress in English.

So then the curtain dropped upon the gorgeous pageant; but it remained still to celebrate the return of the conquering hero. Though Salisbury had a constitutional dislike and distrust of such epilogues, some demonstration of achievement was entirely congenial to his chief and not uncongenial to Victoria, who estimated highly Beaconsfield's success in restoring the prestige of England in Europe. She offered him a dukedom, which he was wise enough to refuse; but she gave him the Garter which, on condition that Salisbury, to whom, in the Prime Minister's phrase, had fallen 'the labouring oar', had it also, he accepted. A popular acclamation of the two plenipotentiaries had preceded these acknowledgments; and, in returning thanks from a window in Downing Street, Beaconsfield had revived the phrase 'peace with honour'. Revived !—because it was subsequently found to have been used by the first Robert Cecil in the reign of James I.

Disraeli—to resume the name which must always serve to recall him

[1] To Mrs. Disraeli. See the *Life of Disraeli*, Vol. III, p. 130.

better than the title he chose, first for his wife, and then for himself—had now climbed to the apex of his fortune and, if he cared still for power, which he did in spite of failing health, he should have gone straight to the country. But, in those days of septennial parliaments, his term of office had still two years to run; and he risked the prolongation of his popularity. We can see now how ill-judged was his action; yet there were no warning signs that his star was waning. Bye-elections looked not unpromising; nor did the Zulu and Afghan Wars seem to portend defeat. So the brilliant old player played on. It had become his habit even before the great stage-performance in Berlin to dramatize situations to the uttermost and so to give his genius full scope. The episode of Pigott's appointment, when he was supposed to have perpetrated an outrageous job in favour of a young member of the Civil Service, whose father had been clergyman at Hughenden, is well known. The Prime Minister had in fact a complete answer to the accusation; but it amused him to make people think he was at a loss, and he walked down to the House of Lords as if he were the very picture of dejection. Then, when he rose to speak, he began in a minor key, reserving his thunder for the crushing rejoinder which he kept for the close of his speech.[1]

It was, I suppose, between 1878 and 1880 that this habit of dramatization so took hold of him that there occurred a little incident, of which I have heard in my family circle, but which has not, I believe, been put on record by anyone else. The administration had got into a patch of rather rough water and was making headway with difficulty; and it was during these anxieties that the Prime Minister happened to pay a call on the then Lady Salisbury. He described the political situation in melancholy terms, and finally wound up his lament with the observation: 'And, my dear lady, in these circumstances, we have nothing to dispose of but one Garter and the Bishopric of Durham.' Had there been ten Garters to give, and the sees of London, Durham and Winchester to fill, it is improbable that it would have made the slightest difference to the fate of the Government. But Beaconsfield liked to think it would, and so to find himself back in that old world of his youth and before his youth, when such things counted among the assets of an administration. Those were the days from which his novels had taken their spring— the days of 'young dukes'; of 'phantoms of a past but real Aristocracy'; of 'an Aristocracy that was founded upon an intelligible principle', claiming 'great privileges for great purposes', with hereditary duties keeping it in the eye of the nation and maintaining its pre-eminence by constant illustration;[2] in fact, of the days of Lord Monmouth and Lord Steyne. The Monarch and the Multitude represented his political principles: the Aristocracy represented the company he kept.

[1] The whole story is to be found in Buckle's biography, Vol. VI, pp. 194-7.
[2] *Coningsby*, Book VI, c. 2.

Monarch and Multitude furnished a useful piece of political alliteration and was no despicable phrase, if you had set yourself to do battle with a 'Venetian oligarchy'. But Beaconsfield's social tastes, as opposed to his political theories, must be looked for in the society with which he consorted; and, when *Lothair* had come out in 1870, with its dedication to the duc d'Aumâle, its description of the Abercorn family, and its adoption of the then Lord Bute, a man of such colossal wealth as to set all the mothers-of-eligible-daughters thinking, it became pretty evident where the magnet lay that this artist in ambition found most attractive. Froude, indeed, ranked *Lothair* very high as a picture of the great world of its time; and the introduction of Cardinal Manning (or it may be, Cardinal Wiseman) and of an Anglican bishop, who can hardly be other than Wilberforce, adds spice to the comedy of manners.

In April 1880 Beaconsfield appealed to the nation for a verdict on his six years' administration of the country under the banner of Tory-Democracy. Political prophets are only a little less unfortunate than weather prophets; and hardly any prophet of that time seems to have anticipated any emphatic verdict. The appeal, however, proved quite decisive. The majority in Parliament was almost exactly reversed. Where there had sat 351 Conservatives, there now took their seats 349 of their opponents; and where there had sat 250 Liberals, there now were seated 243 Conservatives. There had been in fact a Conservative *dégringolade*. Beaconsfield was staying at Hatfield as the results came in. Report affirms that he behaved with admirable stoicism, for he cherished no illusions. To the eldest son of the House, who long remembered his words, he observed, 'This is the beginning of your political life, but it is the end of mine'. He had in fact only some twelve months to live. Victoria, who was dismayed at his disaster and hoped for his early return to power, showered on him attentions, exceeding perhaps by a little those befitting a constitutional Sovereign. She sent him pretty compliments. He had been, she wrote, 'the kindest and most devoted as well as one of the wisest Ministers she had ever had'; he must write to her no longer in the third person, for that was too formal for their kind of friendship; he must advise her on family matters and, not alone upon these, but 'about great public questions'; 'she should take no notice of Mr. Gladstone, who had done so much mischief'; he must not regard their separation as a real parting; she would always let him hear how she was, and he must promise to do the same about himself.

The Queen wrote from abroad. The situation was one of peculiar, perhaps of unexampled difficulty, for the Sovereign. There were three outstanding Liberals who might be invited to form an Administration—Granville, Hartington, or Gladstone. To anyone of these she might correctly turn; but Gladstone, whom she immoderately disliked, was by far the most powerful in the country. Beaconsfield, summoned to Windsor to dine and sleep before he resigned office, advised the Queen first to inquire of the Leader of the Opposition whether he would undertake to form a new Government. Hartington, thus indicated, met the Queen's approach by replying that no administration could stand without Gladstone as a member and that in his own opinion, Gladstone himself would accept no place but the greatest. A day or two later the Queen informed her late Prime Minister that Gladstone had accepted office as his successor and had kissed hands. The Monarch had been completely defeated by the Multitude.

Beaconsfield, meanwhile, went for a day or two to Hatfield, where he was becoming more and more acclimatized, and so on to Hughenden to 'find repose in its woods'. A final leavetaking at Windsor was required of the fallen Minister as such: but three times during the remainder of the year he visited the Sovereign as a friend, the third visit being the last time they ever met. Informal letters continued to pass between them, though prudence might perhaps have curtailed a correspondence from which politics were by no means excluded.[1] But the Queen never forgot all his help had meant to her. Let the reader turn up her diary for April 19th 1891, and he will see, 'Ten years since Lord Beaconsfield, that kind, wise old man was taken'. The lapse of a decade showed no vanishing sense of obligation; nor was even that the end. In the Queen's Journal six years later still is to be read 'Cimiez, 19th April 1897—sixteen years since my kind friend, Lord Beaconsfield, died'. And yet again at the same time and place in 1898 'Already seventeen years ago that good Lord Beaconsfield died.' Fidelity could ask no more. In truth he had more to do, perhaps, than any man with that new efflorescence of the reign which was marked by the consolidation of the Empire of India, by the acquisition of Cyprus, by the advent of Indian Princes at the Jubilee, and by the association of Indian troops with English in the First World War. The Queen, who perceived the trend or end of Beaconsfield's policy better than some of her advisers, recognized that touch of imagination, near allied to genius, in his work, 'The French Revolution', Beaconsfield makes Walder-share say to Endymion in the latest of his novels, 'introduced the cosmopol-itan principle into human affairs instead of the national, and no public man could succeed who did not comprehend and acknowledge that truth'.[2] To find the true internationalism is the real problem that the Victorians left to those who came after them.

In one of the boldest and most brilliant of his literary excursions, Lytton Strachey brings to an end his monograph on Victoria with an imaginary retrospect of what the Queen might have thought about as she lay dying. Its only defect is that it is pure fiction: we dare not affirm that it contains any

---

[1] Buckle, *Life of Disraeli*, Vol. VI, p. 542.
[2] *Endymion*, Book I, Chapter XXIV.

word of truth. But of her much loved Minister, as he spent his last summer in the peace and solitude of Hughenden, we know for certain that the strange story of his life passed before his eyes like a piece of dramatic pageantry and that the figures which had played their part in its development came crowding in upon his fancy-like airy creations. *Endymion* is not a particularly good novel, though one or two of the author's colleagues praised it in pleasing terms. But, treated just as a pageant, it conveys very well all the fantasy of his own career. The moon-struck youth, dreaming away in days of old as a shepherd on the slopes of Mt. Latmos, was by tradition the nightly recipient of the embraces of the moon; and, as Lady Bradford's name was Selina, we may suppose that a little more was meant than met the eye in the choice of the title. The derivation of the strange name emphasized in the novel itself and attested by Lord Rowton, carries the mind back to Endymion Porter, a Caroline courtier: whilst circumstances in the novel lend themselves to a comparison with the circumstances from which Disraeli sprang.

There was in the background what all the critics have identified with Isaac Disraeli's old manor-house at Bradenham on the slopes of the Chilterns. And the comparison is countenanced also by the close of the book when, after many vicissitudes, Endymion rises to be Prime Minister. But these similarities by no means satisfy the demands of autobiography; and indeed Disraeli in a letter to the Queen, expressly repudiates any wish to make Endymion a hero or even a character of interest. He confesses him to be a man devoid of imagination and with passion held under severe restraint. His qualities are said to be those of 'a plodder'—'patience, perseverance, judgment and tact, which qualities, with good looks, have, before this, elevated men in your Majesty's Councils'.[1] I thought him, the author adds, 'quite good enough to be a Whig'. The theme of the book is in fact not altogether remote from autobiography, being as it is that of the influence of women upon the fortunes of man. 'You will find friends in life', says his sister, Myra, to Endymion, 'and they will be women.' 'Everything in this world depends upon will,' Lady Montfort tells Endymion. 'I think', he replies, 'everything in this world depends upon women.' 'It is the same thing', Berengaria replies.[2] The beams of moonlight are, then, the high lights of the book—the moonbeams that find their way to the side of Endymion and point out to him his path through the night. Myra's power of will is foremost in this work; and her marriages to successive husbands, who are portraits beyond question of Palmerston and Napoleon III, show the range of her ambition. But there are other women engaged in beckoning Endymion on. The Queen supposed that she had rightly identified Louise, Duchess (in those days) of Manchester, with one of these. But according to

[1] *Queen's Letters*, February 10th 1881.   [2] *Endymion*, Chapter LXIV.

the author's statement which he declared 'he would admit to no one else but
your Majesty' Lady Montfort is a blend of Lady Palmerston in her younger
days with 'some traits of devotion drawn from someone else', whom we are
probably correct in supposing to be Lady Bradford, as Disraeli knew her
late in his life. Lady Jersey, a famous hostess in his early days, appears as
Zenobia; and Melbourne's friend, Mrs. Norton, maybe, lends a touch or two
also to that portrait.

The gorgeous figures that strut and fret upon the stage are reminiscent of a
world that had wandered by and left the scene pictorially the poorer. King
Luitprand may be Louis Philippe, Baron Sergius may be Metternich, Count
Ferrol is undoubtedly Bismarck. The novel is a wonderful *bal masqué*; for the
author was writing of what he had seen and known and even now and again
of those he had himself crossed swords with. And, as in a theatre the eyes of
men, after a well-graced actor leaves the stage, are idly bent to see who enters
next, so do we strain our vision to see who follows as that long specatcle
pursues its way from the London of 1827 to the London of 1855 and as much
further, perhaps, as we care to watch Disraeli's moving finger pass and point.
In that year of its appearance the Victorian conception of statecraft was
approaching its apogee, though it was to the Queen and Salisbury that the
steering of the ship of state into smoother waters was to be entrusted. This
essay will have been written all in vain, however, if it has not been made
evident that Disraeli had a rare gift of vision; that, as Monypenny maintained, his politics realized the Pauline admonition to forget the things which
were behind and to reach forward to the things that lay before.[1] 'I am neither
Whig nor Tory', he had cried at the beginning of his career, 'My politics are
described by one word, and that word is England.'[2] But beside distant visions,
such as that of Britain, 'if ever Europe by her shortsightedness fell into an
inferior and exhausted state',[3] turning her back on the Continent and setting
her face towards the New World which shared her laws, language and
religion, there came among his *obiter dicta* occasional flashes of insight which
give one pause. Such a flash is that which enters, as early as 1849, into a letter
to Frances Anne, Lady Londonderry: 'The fact is the elements of government
do not exist in the greater part of Europe, and we are destroying them pretty
quickly in England. Russia alone develops herself and will develop herself
still more in the great struggle which is perhaps nearer than we imagine.
Once destroy the English aristocracy and enthrone the commercial principle
as omnipotent on this island, and there will be no repelling force which will
prevent the Slavonians conquering the whole of the south of Europe.'[4]
Disraeli, when he wrote this, had just seen all Europe shaking under the

[1] Monypenny, *Life of Disraeli*, Vol. I, p. 245.   [2] ibid., p. 210.
[3] Buckle, *Life of Disraeli*, Vol. IV, p. 231.
[4] Monypenny & Buckle, Vol. III, p. 195.

impact of the Revolution of '48, whilst England and Russia alone remained stable. There is enough penetration in the forecast to make it worth quoting, but not enough precision in the detail to lift his words out of the class of clever conjecture. To return, however, to *Endymion*!

For two women, indeed, who played important parts in Disraeli's career, the pageant provides no place—Mrs. Wyndham Lewis, a wealthy widow, years his senior, with a house in London and an income during her life of from £4,000 to £5,000 a year, whom he made his wife; and Mrs. Brydges Willyams, another widow of some means, who was a staunch admirer of the Tory-Democratic leader and had in some degree followed the development of his thought, being racially a Jewess and having become confessionally a Christian. When I was very young, I committed the impropriety of describing Lady Beaconsfield in an article as 'a funny old woman'. The editor took exception; and I substituted 'singular old lady'. My father, who had been acquainted with the character in question, consoled me by saying—'That was just what she was—a funny old woman!' Disraeli had told his sister in 1833 that he had no intention of marrying for love 'which', he added 'I am sure is a guarantee of infelicity'. Whether by 1839 he had changed his views, there is, so far as I know, nothing to say, but certainly he never failed to treat his wife with superb courtesy and devotion and certainly, on her side, she gave him, to convert a phrase from its customary use, as good as she got. 'Dizzy married me for my money', she would declare, 'but, if he had the chance again, he would marry me for love.'[1] To a young lady about to be married, who many years later told me the story, she volunteered advice on matrimony; and the advice (and I believe I recall it aright), came to this: 'My dear, everything in marriage depends on tact. Look at this locket. I wear it continually. It was given me by my first husband. Dizzy has never alluded to it.' So, thus, the two pursued the uneven tenor of their days; and, when the time came for parting, no husband could have felt himself more desolate.

As for Mrs. Brydges Willyams, she too, at the age of seventy or more when she came to know Disraeli, had all the making in her of a figure of fun. No one can doubt it who has studied the caricature of her and her two dogs on the promenade at Torquay. She was, as has been said, of the House of Israel; and her legacy of some £30,000 to Disraeli seems to have been given him in recognition of his services to his race.

To have introduced either of these strange figures into *Endymion* would have been difficult without turning fancy into falsity or perpetrating a tasteless joke at the expense of the dead; but both women had beyond doubt no small influence over Beaconsfield's career. Yet, if he did not altogether disdain the main chance, it would be unfair to say that he went after riches. Some of

[1] Monypenny's *Life of Disraeli*, Vol. II, p. 53.

his early embarrassments came of recklessly backing bills for friends; and his offer to return part of the money (£10,000) which he had received for *Endymion* to the publisher, for fear the firm should lose on it, shows how far he was from holding on to a financial advantage even when equal chances made it fairly his. However judgment may go in these matters, the last months of Beaconsfield's life are hardly less material to his fame than the seventy-six that went before them. He had clearly run his race; yet time was needed for an assessment of his complete achievement; and the prolongation of the struggle with indifferent health was calculated to attract to him that modicum of sympathy which is needed to remove all bias from the mind of an onlooker. The Monarch had long learnt to see his merit; the Multitude was to come nearer perceiving it, as he played out the last act of life's drama to its moving, melancholy close. The Commons had seemed to some eyes to go dull some years earlier, when he left them; in the Lords, as time went on, he was compelled to galvanize his tired body into a semblance of strength at the appointed hours of effort. Then, as the spring returned, and, as it chanced, when the season of primroses was reached, a last decline set in and he lay prostrate in that gaunt house at the end of Curzon Street (No. 19) which used to seem to me, contemplating it curiously in a now distant past, as if it would suffer no other occupant to reside there. He guessed rightly enough that he had reached the end of the journey, though the doctors kept up a pretence of recovery and discouraged the Queen from coming to see him lest her visit should overtax his strength. Flowers she could send him; and they came in abundance; spring flowers, his beloved primroses amongst them. Intimate friends—Rowton, Barrington, Rose—were constantly at his bedside. On all who ministered to him in his last illness, his gentleness and consideration for others made a deep impression. Death had no terrors for him; he had taken his fill of life; he had made history. More than most of us he had felt with Jaques the profound truth that lies behind the words from Petronius, newly inscribed in Shakespeare's day over the Globe Theatre, 'All the world's a stage' (*totus mundus agit histrionem*). Not to see the world around as the stage of some great drama is to see it without any great design. He had been conscious from the first of possessing poetic talent; then in time he came to see that his gift was really histrionic. And so he grew into the man he was. 'Kings love him that speaketh right', the Queen caused to be set on the memorial she put up in the Church at Hughenden. And, perhaps, her epitaph was rightly chosen; at all events no other seems to satisfy better all that comes to mind in connection with this baffling character and career.

Mr. GLADSTONE

The Right Hon. WILLIAM EWART GLADSTONE
born 1809 died 1898

Entered Parliament (Member for Newark) 1832

Junior Lord of the Treasury (First Peel administration) 1834

Under-Secretary for the Colonies (First Peel administration) 1835

Secretary at War and for the Colonies (Second Peel administration 1846

Chancellor of the Exchequer (Aberdeen administration) 1852 to 1855

Chancellor of the Exchequer (First Palmerston administration) February 1855 to February 1858

Chancellor of the Exchequer (Second Palmerston and second Russell administration) 1859 to 1866

Prime Minister 1868 to 1874
                1880 to 1885
                1886
                1892 to 1894

CHAPTER XI

MR. GLADSTONE

'IN political matters,' commented Walter Bagehot, 'how quickly a
leading statesman can change the tone of the community! We are most
of us in earnest with Mr. Gladstone; we were most of us not so earnest
in the time of Lord Palmerston.'[1] The reader of these pages must now be
content to become serious, and for a great while to come. The asides of
Disraeli, in so far as they can be heard across a stage echoing with what he
styled the inebriating exuberance of Gladstone's verbosity, may afford some
occasional relief, but we have to surrender and without demur to the prospect
of much high thinking and also of far less plain speaking. There is another
consideration that needs to be stressed at the outset. Though Victoria liked
none of her Prime Ministers so little as Gladstone; though his conclusions,
both religious and political, failed increasingly to satisfy other highly influential and deservedly distinguished leaders of the age—Newman, Huxley,
Ruskin, Tennyson; though some part of the nation was as little moved by
his eloquence as the Queen, when she complained that he talked to her like a
public meeting; though all this was true, still, more than any other man,
Gladstone was representative of the spirit of his time. Preoccupied with
theology and morals, persuaded that 'Reason governs and has governed the
World', convinced, if possible, more profoundly than Hegel, that 'in the
Christian religion God has revealed Himself . . . has given us to understand
what He is, so that He is no longer a concealed or secret existence', and
eventually almost as well satisfied as Hegel that 'the History of the World is
none other than the progress of the consciousness of Freedom',[2] Gladstone
was to an extraordinary degree able, thanks to the swelling torrent of his
language, the passionate enthusiasm of his conviction, his astounding mastery
of detail in exposition, and perhaps, too, to the compelling force of his, not
mild but magnificent eye, to give conviction to the hopes and beliefs of many
thoughtful members of the middle-class, now in a fair way to become and
throughout his time to remain the dominant power in the State.

I have quoted Lecky before as saying that at no time and in no country has
there existed a better constitution than England possessed between the
Reform Bills of 1832 and 1867.[3] It might, if so, be true to add that at this

---

[1] From Bagehot's *Physics and Politics*.
[2] Hegel's Introduction to his *Lectures on the Philosophy of History*.
[3] *Democracy and Liberty*, Chapter I.

period Britain enjoyed more nearly than at any other date what Aristotle seems to have regarded as par excellence a polity,[1] that is, a combination or fusion of the two principles distinctive respectively of aristocracy and democracy—virtue and freedom. Into this fusion the modern idea of equality as a mark of justice can hardly be said to have entered at all. The seat of political influence, not the distribution of wealth, was the main matter at issue; and, throughout Gladstone's time, nobility, which in the Aristotelian view represented an amalgamation of 'ancestral virtue and wealth', still exercised its magic on the mind, so that in the result the constitution presented many salient features of an aristocracy.

Seldom, then, if ever, can the lot of any statesman have fallen in a fairer ground than when, with the resignation of Russell, Gladstone succeeded to the leadership of what we must henceforth call without qualifying clauses the leadership of the Liberal Party. Two circumstances, as it chanced, coincided at this time to modify old loyalties and open the way to new adventures. The tradition of Palmerston and the representation of Oxford University had alike combined to hold Gladstone to the pursuit of ancient paths in politics. Almost simultaneously, however, these restraining influences were removed. On July 18th 1865 Oxford cast him out: rather later, on October 18th, Palmerston died. The intervention of the short Whig administration of Russell is hardly worth recalling, though it produced an abortive reform bill. Gladstone had been released by circumstances from the Oxonian, and now too, the Palmerstonian, as well as the Peelite, ties that held him to his former moorings. To himself, indeed, at the time, and even later, the change seemed no more than a fuller development of the belief in faith and freedom. 'I have never swerved', he told a Lancashire audience in July 1865, 'from what I conceive to be those truly conservative objects and desires with which I entered life. I am, if possible, more attached to the institutions of my country than I was when, as a boy, I wandered among the sandhills of Seaforth or frequented the streets of Liverpool.' And, long after this, in 1890, as his life was drawing to a close, he explained once again that he had had no love of change for its own sake, but had adopted it as a policy only where it gave promise of something better; that he revered antiquity, wherever it merited reverence; and that his 'Liberalism' was based upon the love of liberty for himself and all others, in proportion to their several means and opportunities. In short he professed himself an indefatigable learner in the school of life.[2] But some onlookers thought they could see much more in it than that. There is the curious record in Morley's *Life* of a conversation at Hawarden in 1878 between the then ageing statesman and Ruskin, which throws much unfamiliar light on the minds of both the speakers. Ruskin

[1] Aristotle's *Politics*, Book VI, Chapters 8-29.
[2] Morley, *Life of Gladstone*, Vol. II, pp. 178-9.

WILLIAM EWART GLADSTONE
From the portrait by S. P. Hall

boldly accuses his host of being a 'leveller'. 'You see', he pursues, 'you think one man is as good as another and all men equally competent to judge aright on political questions; whereas I am a believer in an aristocracy.' Gladstone meets this with a stout denial: 'Oh! dear no! I am nothing of the sort. I am a firm believer in the aristocratic principle—the rule of the best. I am an out-and-out *inequalitarian*.' Ruskin, so Morley says,[1] was delighted and clapped his hands in triumph.

So stated, there might be found few genuine lovers of the English way of life who would question or condemn Gladstone's creed. Yet it would be idle to deny that his application of it split his party, alienated his Sovereign and excited widespread distrust among friends and foes. If in these circumstances we wish to study a contemporary portrait of him as he looked to those who had lost faith in the integrity of his mind, we can hardly do better than read the pages in the later edition of *Democracy and Liberty* which Lecky devoted to an estimate of his character and career. 'An honest man with a dishonest mind' is there suggested as the solution of a riddle which reached its climax of difficulty when in 1885 he went to the polls, to the best belief of colleagues such as Bright, Hartington, and Chamberlain, a convinced supporter of the Anglo-Irish Union, and emerged some weeks later, after the General Election had failed to give him an over-all Liberal majority, a convert to Home Rule for Ireland. He was, in Lecky's view, by nature a casuist of the casuists; but casuistry is one thing when it merely reflects the operation of an intellect of great subtlety, and another when it works or appears to work miracles of party advantage for the possessor. Gladstone's youthful resignation over the matter of the Maynooth Grant discovered in him an exceptionally high, if not excessive sense of honour; but in his later years nothing similar is to be discerned. An inexhaustible power of distinction in the presentation of a case had become with him a frequent asset in debate and reached its climax in his description of Gordon at Khartoum as 'hemmed in but not surrounded'. The simplicity of his private life, full as it was of charity, courtesy and courage, satisfied in every respect Salisbury's posthumous description of him as 'a great Christian statesman': yet in his conduct of public affairs the ramifications, dexterity and obscurity of his language, when he did not wish to commit himself, were out of line with the thinking of plain men. One example of this especially attracted public attention. To enable his attorney-general to qualify for appointment to the Court of Appeal, he promoted him previously, for a day or so only, to the Bench and thus fulfilled the letter of the law requiring that the nominee must be a judge, whilst patently ignoring the spirit of this proviso. There were other shadows which Lecky's portrait shows. Yet still does the sunlight stream on his close association with such men as Peel and Aberdeen, on his

[1] *Life of Gladstone*, Vol. II, p. 582.

I

command of faultless phraseology on high occasions, on the fact that, in public as in private life, he showed himself, in Lecky's words, 'pre-eminently a gentleman', on his hatred of cruelty and oppression, on his ready, ingratiating charm in reminiscent conversation, on his indefatigable industry, and on his incomparable gift of affording interest to financial expositions. We might, as Lecky remarks, stand before portraits of Burke or Pitt or Fox and fail to guess that these men were great beyond the ordinary. In Gladstone's case, however, it is impossible. The face, though no single picture could show its infinite play of expression, could not fail to arrest the eye by its power or to inform the observer that he stood before the likeness of some extraordinary being.

Lecky was admired by Gladstone himself for his clear insight into the practice of politics as it presents itself to the politician. His conclusions, both favourable and adverse, respecting their most distinguished practitioner in his time, are the more worthy of attention. He passed judgment, however, just after Gladstone's career had closed, when the play, so to speak, was to its last syllable all played out, when the actor, full of years, had entered into his last sleep, and when his monument seemed only to await its epitaph, if a just man might find it. Here, then, was a study of final ends.

Another and a more brilliant historian had interested himself in Gladstone's first beginnings; and the student of Gladstone's place in history might do worse than consult Macaulay's impressions for an idea of how he appeared as he first rose to fame.

The first contact, or at least conversation, between these two eminent Victorians was, scenically speaking, as dramatic as even such a master of narrative as Macaulay himself could desire. Both alike had chanced to be spending part of the winter of 1839 in Italy: it was Christmas Eve in Rome and the two men separately wandered into St. Peter's. There, in the heart of the Temple which the fiercest prejudice can hardly deprive of its claim to represent the conception of a united Christendom, they met: or rather, there Macaulay caught sight of Gladstone in the crowd, made for him, though no previous formal introduction had occurred, and entered into a conversation which the time, the place and the immense intellectual virility of the speakers must have combined to render memorable. 'We talked and walked together', records Macaulay, 'in St. Peter's during the best part of an afternoon', and then adds that he found his companion 'both a clever and an amiable man'. Some temporary defect in Gladstone's eyesight had limited for the time his powers to go sight-seeing; and, with Wiseman as a guide and Manning as a companion, he was devoting much of his time to the hearing of a multitude of sermons. The young member for Newark, it appeared, was a very ecclesiastically-minded young man, much more than had been Peel, who was now his leader and in whom there was much to tempt comparison, once allowance has been made for the initial fact that their families sprang from different sides of the border—Peel was a Lancastrian by descent, Gladstone a Scot on either side. Still, both were northcountrymen, born and bred. On the far horizon of Gladstone's vision, as in old age he looked back over his career, lay the sandhills of Seaforth, the streets of Liverpool, a little city then of perhaps no more than a hundred thousand souls, and the borough of Bootle abloom in summer days with wild roses. Then, in the foreground of the scene stood the house at Seaforth where John Gladstone—or Gladstones as the name was at that time spelt—with Anne Robertson, a Highland lassie out of Dingwall and of the kinship of the Mackenzies and Munros, had settled and whence he had guided and improved a paternal venture in the marketing of corn until it expanded into an East India house, and led on to an investment in sugar and coffee plantations in the West Indies, incidentally involving slave labour and inviting at a later date, when the campaign against slavery had gathered strength, the eloquent, if tempered, advocacy of his son. This shrewd and capable Scot, for all the wrong he did to humanity by trafficking in a servitude, which is to-day represented as far more indefensible than the conscription of labour for military service or other forced labour, though not so very greatly estranged from them, was a man greatly beloved by the ablest of his children and conducted his household on lines of unaffected, evangelical piety. He became a Member of Parliament; he fostered in his son the veneration for a statesman of which we can catch an echo in the reference in the younger Gladstone's *Gleanings*[1] to 'the light and music' of Canning's eloquence; and he was rewarded for his labours with the honours of a baronetcy.

If, however, such a career and rise of fortune appear too common to suggest any striking analogy with that of the Peels, the similarity will force itself on the mind as we watch this fourth son of Sir John's, William Ewart, the subject of our study, entering like Peel, Wolsey's foundation at Christ Church and leaving Oxford, as Peel had done, with a double first to his credit. The upper-middle class were fast equipping themselves to fill the rôle which had once fallen to the squirearchy, to the Pitts and the Foxes, and their elect representatives, before the Victorian era was well up on its way, would be sitting in the seats of the mighty, not apologetically or absurdly, but with the full assurance of conscious capacity and high distinction. It was in fact to be part of the work of the Coburgs to restore that aristocracy of intellect which the Tudors had destroyed by striking down the second estate of the realm—the Clerks who in the old dispensation had represented, not merely an acknowledgment of Divine priorities, but a tribute to intellect and education.

Peel and Gladstone, it is true, had begun their learning on rival playing-fields—Peel at Harrow and Gladstone at Eton—but they had completed it

[1] In 'A Chapter of Autobiography'.

alike at the University destined to take a decisive lead in the thought of the Victorian era; and they stand out as superb examples of what the upper middle-class was already able to give the country.

It was in the spring of 1832 that Gladstone, a young man of twenty-three at the time and rich in the splendour of his newly-won academic honours, first stood before the fane of St. Peter's and felt mixed emotions of wonder and regret. He had not before experienced the mysterious sense of Christian unity embodied in the thought of the Universal Church; nor had he previously mourned over the breach which had torn Christendom in two. But here in Rome the vision, which in a very little while was to set all Oxford thinking, and England in its wake, was shown him.

Keble may have blown smouldering embers into flame by his Assize Sermons of 1833 as he had before loosed hidden waters from their rockbound cavity by the publication of his *Christian Year*, but, as Dean Church rightly asserts, it was Newman's resolve to throw into public notice, with a clarity permitting of no evasion, 'the great article of the Creed—I believe one Catholic and Apostolic Church'—which constitutes the true inception of the Oxford Movement.[1] It was Newman's genius for disentangling an essential thought from the subsidiary accretions of time that set ideas, new to his time and country, though old enough in themselves, sweeping through the land with the speed of a forest fire or the force of a foaming flood.

The sight of that historic figure, as he appeared in the first days of his leadership, demands, even compels, a slight pause in a study devoted to Gladstone; for largely through Gladstone's interest in the Oxford Movement, itself in the best sense of the word conservative, Liberalism was able to attract to itself religious influences that we can hardly associate with the philosopher or publicist of Ferney or the elect circle of Whigs that carried on the work of Voltaire and the Encyclopaedists at Holland House.

Let this essay pause, then, for a moment to take a look at Newman in his prime and see him as he had seemed to a critic, little, at the time of reminiscence, disposed to favour his ideas. 'Greatly as his poetry struck me', wrote Froude recalling early associations at Oxford, 'Newman was himself all that the poetry was and something far beyond. I had then never seen so impressive a person. I met him now and then in private; I attended his church and heard him preach Sunday after Sunday; he is supposed to have been insidious . . . he was on the contrary the most transparent of men . . . He could admire enthusiastical.y any greatness of action and character, however remote from his own. Gurwood's *Dispatches of the Duke of Wellington* came out just then. Newman had been reading the book, and a friend asked him what he thought of it. "Think?" he said, "it makes one burn to have been a soldier" . . . He, when we met him, spoke to us about subjects of the day, of literature,

[1] Church, *The Oxford Movement*, Chapter II.

of public persons and incidents, of everything which was generally interesting. He seemed always to be better informed on common topics of conversation than any one else who was present. He was never condescending with us, never didactic or authoritative; but what he said carried conviction along with it. . . . Prosy he could not be. He was lightness itself—the lightness of elastic thought.'[1]

What eventually happened to Newman was, if we reflect, only what happened to Gibbon at a much earlier age and in a far more intellectually indolent Oxford. Gibbon's mind, untouched, so far as we can judge, by any of those gracious influences and profound attachments which have made the story of Newman's conversion so moving an apologia, grasped at the age of sixteen the intellectual strength of the Catholic argument and caused its owner, untampered with, as he records, by priest or parson and merely directed to the address of an ecclesiastic by a Catholic bookseller, to be received into the Church that took all its theology from Rome. The change of faith, in this case a purely rational affair, was easily altered afresh by an intolerant parent into complete unbelief; but it remains an interesting example of intellectual reflection in the mind of a born historian, untouched by human affection or divine devotion.

Two, if not more, of Gladstone's early friends were in due course to surrender to the force of the Roman argument. Manning, after the loss of his wife, to whose abiding influence on his life he was to pay tribute on his death-bed, resigned the archdeaconry of Chichester to become, at long last, Cardinal-Archbishop of Westminster; whilst Hope, in comparison with whom Gladstone declared that he had always felt and known his 'mental as well as moral inferiority',[2] may be said to have completed the Waverley saga by marrying the heiress of Abbotsford and adding the name of Scott to his own. It was from him, at Chelsea Hospital, somewhere about the year 1836, that Gladstone by his own account derived a vastly greater interest in the Oxford Movement than he had before possessed.[3] These contacts, these intimacies, these ardent communications from souls in travail with new ideas, seem never to have shaken a mind striving for that slow, fragmentary but firm method in theology which he takes to be the particular genius of Bishop Butler as opposed, in his judgment, to Newman's 'impatience of doubt and premature avidity for system'.

This indeed, if he is right in supposing it to be Newman's defect, was also noticed by a loving and well-qualified observer to have been at times his own. 'Mrs. Gladstone', records Morley, 'said to me (1891), that whoever writes his (i.e. Gladstone's) life must remember that he had two sides—one impetuous, impatient, irrestrainable, the other alls elf-control, able to dismiss all

---

[1] Short Studies—*The Oxford Counter-Reformation.*
[2] Lathbury, *Correspondence on Church and Religion of W. E. Gladstone,* Vol. I, p. 227.
[3] ibid., p. 226.

but the great central aim, able to put aside what is weakening or disturbing; that he achieved this self-mastery and had succeeded in the struggle ever since he was three or four and twenty, first by the natural power of his character, second by incessant wrestling in prayer—prayer that had been abundantly answered.'[1]

'The great central aim' in Gladstone's theology was indisputably belief in God—and there Butler satisfied all his need. 'James Mill and John Mill', he observes to a correspondent, 'both said no one, from the Deist's point of view, could answer Butler: any such, any beginning with belief in God, he compels to be a Christian.'[2] Here Gladstone stood on ground of the firmest. Ecclesiastically he was less secure in his footing; and in fact his feet were destined to slip. '. . . that great idea, that good idea, of a National Church, which was born with the Reformation',[3] he wrote in 1837. And again in the same year: 'I yet hold and feel that kings ought to be nursing fathers of the Church, and that the road from *separation of Church and State* to atheism is, if indirect, yet broad and open.'[4]

In the years since he passed from the Schools at Oxford with his honours thick upon him, Gladstone's mind had been much occupied with matters of Church and State and the relation that lay between them. Indeed, the young man's fancy turned for a moment from the 'fascinating' (it is his own word) lure of politics towards a more direct participation in 'setting before the eyes of man, still great even in his ruins, the magnificence and the glory of Christian truth'. The ardour of youth has not seldom kindled with this desire of sacrifice. Although, however, the embers of that early enthusiasm never ceased to glow, and will be seen at many turnings in his long career, politics carried the day; and within a twelvemonth of his leaving Oxford, thanks to the influence of the Duke of Newcastle, whose son was one of his friends, Gladstone was representing what John Morley styles 'the rather rotten borough' of Newark.

No more suitable year could perhaps have been found than that of the Reform Bill for the entry into Parliament of one who was to be the boldest innovator of his time; yet it was in defence of such a dying institution as negro slavery that he was to make his début. The Church, however, was still engaging his attention and earnest application; and in these years under the influence of Hope's and Manning's growing Anglicanism and of William Palmer's *Treatise on the Church*, published in 1838, he was busy shaping his views on the complex relationship of Church and State. His book indeed had just come out when Macaulay met him in Rome, and in the April following there appeared in the *Edinburgh Review* the well-known essay by that

---

[1] Morley, *Life*, Book II, Chapter VI.
[2] Lathbury, *Correspondence on Church and Religion of W. E. Gladstone*, Vol. II, p. 101.
[3] ibid., Vol. I, p. 31. [4] ibid., Vol. I, p. 39.

famous hand. The political architecture of Holland House, if such figures of speech may be permitted, stood ranged against the spire of St. Mary's and the quadrangles of Wolsey's foundation at Christ Church, reformed by the Eighth Henry's hard and horny hand.

The principle at issue—in Gladstone's own words—was supposed to be whether the State had a conscience, though, as he adds, the real point of controversy did not lie so much in respect of its existence as of its range.[1] The Established Churches of England and Ireland had not ceased with the Reformation to lay claim to distinguish between truth and error; and it was the operation of this claim, more particularly in respect to Ireland, that Gladstone had set out to vindicate. The propagation of religious truth in fact appeared to him at the time he wrote his book as one of the principal ends of government.

This thesis was one which Macaulay's genius was admirably constituted to probe, pierce and buffet; and the thrusts of his sword and the blows from his mace are seldom seen to better advantage than in his dissection and pummelling of the Gladstonian argument. Observing that 'it is evident that many great and useful objects can be attained in this world only by co-operation' and 'equally evident that there cannot be efficient co-operation, if men proceed on the principle that they must not co-operate for one object unless they agree upon other objects', he draws a highly entertaining picture of the Battle of Blenheim, had it been fought on the principles recommended by Mr. Gladstone for the conduct of affairs in Church and State. The obligation to maintain religious truth being assumed paramount among the purposes of the State, it would have followed that Eugene would have had to give up his command for being of Catholic convictions and that the Dutch and Austrian colonels would have had to be cashiered for failing to subscribe to the Thirty-Nine Articles, with the result that Marshal Tallard's position must have been so vastly improved, by the withdrawal of a large section of the opposing army through its supposed defects in the tenets of true religion, as both to give him victory and to lose Europe its liberties.

Gladstone's case had in fact been too little qualified by caution and too much embellished by rhetoric. As he admitted in his 'Chapter of Autobiography', published some thirty years after, 'the line was left too obscurely drawn between the wilful and wanton rejection of opportunities for good and the cases in which the state of religious convictions, together with the recognized principles of government, disable the civil power from including within its work the business of either directly or indirectly inculcating religion . . .' But also, as Macaulay remarked in his essay with prophetic insight, 'Mr. Gladstone's rhetoric, though often good of its kind, darkens and perplexes the logic which it should illustrate . . . He has one gift most

[1] *Gleanings*, 'A Chapter of Autobiography'.

dangerous to a speculator, a vast command of a kind of language, grave and majestic, but of vague and uncertain import; of a kind of language which affects us much in the same way in which the lofty diction of the Chorus of Clouds affected the simple-hearted Athenian.

ὦ Γῆ τοῦ φθέγματος, ὡς ἱερον καὶ σεμνὸν καὶ τερατῶδγς

Holy, reverent, portentous !' This 'dim magnificence' assuredly played a part in the Gladstonian legend, bewitching some, bewildering others. Was Macaulay wrong in alleging thus early, that one whom he rightly calls in the same essay 'a very able and a very honest man', would have been saved from almost all his mistakes by 'a barren imagination and a scanty vocabulary'? With Macaulay's aid we can detect in this early venture of the eminent Victorian the qualities and defects that Lecky was to diagnose some sixty years later.

Neither the 'rising hope of the stern, unbending Tories' of 1839 nor the Whig apologist had, perhaps, really fathomed the depth of the question that lay between them. The latter was soon to write—or maybe had already written—a sentence in the opening chapter of his *History of England*, which must have enraged some of his contemporaries and delighted others, but which will be useful to reflect upon in plumbing the matter which he and Gladstone were debating—'It is difficult to say', Macaulay wrote, 'whether England owes more to the Roman Catholic religion or to the Reformation.' And he went on to point out that to the one England is chiefly indebted for its union of races and emancipation from serfdom, to the other for its individual freedom in both Church and State. The statement invites a great deal of comment; but it is, broadly speaking, true to say that Catholicism created the social tissue, and that the Reformation in its last effects shaped the social organism of our Society. Both elements are required in the formation of the State and for its maintenance. Gladstone's speculative mind was still busy with the one, Macaulay's practical intelligence preoccupied with the other. Yet, as Morley observed, 'not the least wonderful thing about Macaulay's review is that he should not have seen how many of his most trenchant considerations told no more strongly against Mr. Gladstone's theory than they told against that Whig theory of establishment, which at the end of his article he himself tried to set up in its place.'[1]

But was it really wonderful? Does not every party in power see its creed as, potentially at least, the last word in wisdom? The Catholic, possessed as he believes of the true and traditional revelation of God, has not always reflected that a real religion of Love can only be established by the methods that Love approves. The Whig, well satisfied that he is the rightful guardian of the liberties of man and the conclusions of common sense, penalized

[1] Morley, *Life of Gladstone*, Vol. I, p. 178.

severely the Irish peasant who had been so obtuse as not to recognize in
Whiggery the considered counsels of the Almighty. The Liberal or the
Latitudinarian, persuaded that a common denominator can be found by the
wisdom of Parliament to fit the multiple vagaries of Christian doctrine, had
no hesitation in fining the believer in clearer views and dogmatic definitions
in order to subsidize an undenominational omnium gatherum of a creed.
And since all politics run back into some sort of religion or negation of it the
Communist, who dances to the tune of an ill-defined dialectical materialism,
excites the alarm and invites the repression of the Socialist who has lately discovered that Communism, so far from being the new civilization of which he
was in search, is the deadly foe of the religion of humanity he professes to be
establishing. Each and all of these worthies has discovered, or is in process of
discovering that no body politic or religious can in the last resort afford to
have the pure milk of its word contaminated by error. Macaulay's theory,
on the other hand, that the essential aims of a society are satisfied by the
protection of the persons and estates of the citizens and that the propagation
of religious truth, though not to be ruled out of statesmanlike considerations,
is a secondary matter and wholly dependent on circumstances, can only be
the comfortable doctrine of a State, whose metaphysical and moral foundations have been so well and truly laid that they have survived shocks like
that of the Reformation and fissures as wide as those that gape between the
catholicity of the Anglican liturgy and the calvinism of the Thirty-Nine
Articles.

Gladstone, ten years younger than Macaulay and born and bred in another
political camp, could hardly fail, with an intelligence so theologically alert
as was his own, to see that the historian's theory of a State sustained by about
as much religion as a Whig gentleman liked, was unequal to the rising
requirements of a University, whose eager Youth was in full cry after a
Christian society that, with at least some semblance of probability, might be
described as one, holy, catholic and apostolic, and sought unity of being, not
only in confessing one Lord, but also one faith and one baptism. His political
genius, however, conditioned his religious fervour. The development of his
ideas, the satisfaction of his soul was not, as in many of the Oxford men of
the time, a search for personal salvation. 'It was', as John Morley observes,
'at bottom more like the passion of the great popes and ecclesiastical master-
builders for strengthening and extending the institutions by which faith is
spread, its lamps trimmed afresh, its purity secured.'[1] Here, however, Gladstone recognized, as time went on, that his way was barred; and the fact
appears clearly in his letters to Manning, and perhaps in the following
sentences above all: 'It is the essential change now in progress from the
catholic to the infidel idea of the State which is the determining element in

[1] Morley, *Life of Gladstone*, Vol. I, p. 323.

my estimate and which has, I think, no place in yours. For I hold and believe that when that transition has once been effected, the State never can come back to the catholic idea by means of any agency from within itself: that, if at last, it must be by a sort of re-conversion from without.'[1]

'A pregnant passage' indeed! as John Morley observes, and, written as it was in the spring of 1846, closely coincident with the secession of the Peelites from the main body of Conservatives. Gladstone's mind was in labour for twenty years with that 'pain of new ideas' of which Bagehot speaks; and the labour was not the less painful that it involved for him the exchange of a loftier for a lower conception of the State. 'I never held', he wrote in his 'Chapter of Autobiography', 'that a National Church should be permanently maintained except for the nation; I mean either for the whole or at least for the greater part, with some kind of real concurrence or general acquiescence from the remainder.' It came to him, then, as a startling surprise when he found about the middle of the century that Nonconformity had outstripped in chapel-building the growing increase of churches responding to the great agitation for holiness which was shaking the Establishment out of its languor and routine. The difference, so he wrote some thirty years after his controversy with Macaulay, was 'that his theory was right for the practical purpose of the time, while mine was wrong'. He detected that Macaulay's theological affinity was to Paley's *Evidences* as it is clear his own must be sought in Butler's *Analogy*. Paley's light is hard and dry—the noonday light of a mind that sees few shades and has all its lines cut clear and all its colours strong and sharp. Butler's light, though neither soft nor radiant, is alive with the sense of mystery. Macaulay's brilliant pages scintillate with the marmoreal confidence of Paley: Gladstone's complex and qualified phrases bear some analogy to Butler's laboured manner. Neither theologian satisfies the desire for certitude which is sensible in the style of Newman, so unassuming, limpid and subtle as to invite comparison with Pascal's perfect fusion of thought and language. Paley is too cocksure; Butler too conscious of the difficulty of things and the infirmity of the human mind.

Gladstone could neither touch Memnon's harp at morning nor draw its music from departing day. But he had seen the significance of St. Peter's; he listened ever and again to the voice of Dante; he thought along the lines of Christendom. And, if he surrendered to what he styled the 'infidel' State, he was yielding to circumstances which to his eye appeared inexorable. The crisis, so far as politics were concerned, came during Peel's administration, from which he resigned on the occasion of an increase in the grant to the Catholic College of Maynooth. He had already come round to the view that the State must no longer refuse to subsidize what, on Anglican principles, was error; but he recognized the inconsistency between what he had taught

[1] Morley, *Life of Gladstone*, Vol. I, p. 324.

and that to which he was become a party. The world did not find it altogether easy to understand the scholastic theologian. Newman understood and wrote to him; and Gladstone commended the explanation as admirable. It can be read in Morley's *Life*.[1] One or two sentences may with advantage be extracted.

'I say, then,' writes Newman, 'Mr. Gladstone has said the state *ought* to have a conscience, but it has not a conscience. Can *he* give it a conscience? Is he to impose his own conscience on the state? He would be very glad to do so, if it thereby would become the state's conscience. But that is absurd. He must deal with facts. It has a thousand consciences, as being in its legislative and executive capacities the aggregate of a hundred minds; that is, it has no conscience. You will say, "Well, the obvious thing would be, if the state has not a conscience, that he shall cease to be answerable for it." So he has—he has retired from the ministry. While he thought he could believe it had a conscience . . . he served the state. Now that he finds this to be a mere dream, much as it ought to be otherwise, and as it once was otherwise, he has said, "I cannot serve such a mistress" . . . I really cannot pronounce, . . . nor can he perhaps at once, what is a Christian's duty under these new circumstances, whether to remain in retirement from public affairs or not . . .'

'Compared to the supreme case of conscience indicated here, and it haunted Mr. Gladstone for nearly all his life', comments Morley, 'the perplexities of party could be but secondary.'

Thus obliquely do we stumble upon a possible explanation of the charge that Gladstone was 'an honest man but with a dishonest mind'. Had he retired from politics, he might have preached from pulpit or platform a theory of the State entirely consistent with his innermost convictions. That man, his contemporaries might have said, does not move with the times, but his views have the force of a conviction which at another date might have given him the power of a Hildebrand or the eloquence of a Savonarola. But not even his force of intellect and character could triumph over the spirit of the age; and this, within a little while of the publication of his book, he perceived himself. 'Scarcely had my work issued from the Press', he wrote, 'when I became aware that there was no party, no section of a party, no individual person probably in the House of Commons who was prepared to act upon it. I found myself the last man on the sinking ship.'[2] He might, to shift the metaphor, have retired to his tent and left his panoply to rust, the victim of an age which was losing little by little, not so much as yet the ethics as the convictions of Christianity. He chose to fight on but under a different flag. In the retrospect he was disposed to see his conduct in the light of a willing surrender to the value and growing feasibility of freedom in politics. But the critic is likely to feel here that the subtlety of his thought

[1] Vol. I, p. 632.
[2] From 'A Chapter of Autobiography' in *Gleanings of Past Years*, 1843-70.

fell short of the truth. Burke had as great a regard for liberty; Salisbury believed in it as tenaciously as he did himself. The importance of personal liberty was not really in dispute among the best minds of that time, though the best way to obtain it seemed to some of them to lie far from any pursuit of the doctrine of Rousseau. What Gladstone therefore surrendered to was rather Liberalism than liberty—a surrender, that is, for practical purposes to an extended suffrage, to the sentiment of nationality and in economics to the so-called doctrine of *laisser-faire*. The last end of Liberalism is to be seen in the fate of the Liberal Party, now no more than the shadow of a great name. Democracy has again issued over half the world in such despotisms or oligarchies as in Caesar's time and Napoleon's it gave birth to. Nationality has ended in a distress and division of nations which the wrangling organizations of Geneva and Lake Success do their poor best to repair: and a free economy, untutored and unrestrained by the infusion of Christianity, has produced a violence and hatred in respect of the distribution of wealth which would have shocked no man more than Gladstone himself. In all these matters the spirit of Liberalism, which was anathema to Newman's searching eye and clearer vision, led Gladstone forwards towards something far adrift from that 'impregnable rock of Holy Scripture', to which his craft had first been moored. Yet, for all that, his own foundations of belief were so well and truly laid, that, whilst he lived, his sole, unswerving faith gave to his party the ground on which to stand. People do not find it particularly convenient to-day to recognize how unstable society quickly becomes without a belief in God and the Devil to sustain it. But the fate of the Liberal Party compels the veriest sceptic to think. The Gladstonian tradition survived to sweep Liberalism once more into power after he himself was dead. Never had administration looked more powerful, never had Cabinet shone with a greater galaxy of talent than in the year 1906 when Asquith, Haldane and Grey, Morley, Birrell and Bryce were conjoined in counsel whilst two brilliant swashbucklers stood waiting in succession at the Board of Trade and the Colonial Office for time and opportunity to bring a greater measure of power within their reach. Yet within less than fifty years all this lustre of Liberalism was gone and a drab Socialism has taken its place as the creed of self-styled progressives. Mr. Churchill, it is true, still remained in politics, but he had resumed his conservative tendencies and led the Tory-democratic Party. Liberalism had in reality been stricken at the heart when Gladstone died. His political creed, for all its late florescence, had been rooted in his personal theology and, when his personality was withdrawn, a swift decay set in. But we must get back to 1850.

That was the year in which Hope and Manning, Gladstone's closest friends, 'went over', as the phrase has it, 'to Rome'; and it serves as a milestone upon his road of change, from abandonment of the ideal of a Christian

State to the acceptance of a State, neutral, tolerant, devoid of other public conscience than the *vox populi*, too optimistically expected to identify itself, under the influence of an expanding freedom of action, with the *vox Dei* heard by Gladstone himself in the oracles of Augustine, in the cantos of Dante, in the Analogy and Sermons of Butler and in those writings of Dean Church which reflect the finest contemporary thought and feeling of the Anglican Communion.

There, then, we must take leave, except for some casual references, of Gladstone in the first, pre-eminently ecclesiastical phase of his public life. Its importance, in any finished estimate of the man, can hardly be exaggerated; and the student who would give it its proper place will supplement Morley's *Life* here with Lathbury's extensive collection of Gladstone's Letters on religious subjects and with George Russell's study of him as a leader of the English Church. But already by 1850 a later Gladstone—the Gladstone of finance—was well upon his way to supplant the Gladstone preoccupied with matters ecclesiastical.

✶   ✶   ✶   ✶   ✶

Considering the talent he possessed for, and, according to most good judges, displayed in financial affairs it is remarkable for how small a degree of competence to deal with them, Gladstone, at the outset, should have given himself credit. He was almost dragged by Peel to the Board of Trade, where, from 1841 as Vice-President and from 1843 as President, he distinguished himself. Theologians, perhaps, like poets, are born; economists made. At any rate, if genius signifies in the final diagnosis an infinite capacity for taking pains, Gladstone had it in finance. If he worked himself like a Trojan, he worked his subordinates (or at least so it seemed to them) like a Tartar—amiable, it is true, but untiring as Napoleon when engaged in civil administration. The Conservative Ministry of Peel in which he served his apprenticeship—so he told Victoria many years later[1]—surpassed any other he had ever known in its observance of 'many of the most important rules of public policy'. Among these was the inauguration of a new system of public economy destined in conjunction with other favourable circumstances, to yield—in his own phraseology—an 'almost intoxicating growth of wealth'.[2] No biographical essay, of course, can hope to deal adequately with so vast a subject as Gladstonian finance. It must be studied in Northcote's almost contemporaneous commentary, in Morley's massive biography, in Mr. Hirst's supplementary monograph, in Courtney's criticism written for T. H. Ward's *Reign of Victoria*; and even then authorities innumerable will still be left for the purposes of amplification, elucidation and, of course,

[1] Morley's *Life*, Vol. I, Appendix, p. 642.
[2] ibid., Vol. II, p. 66.

general discussion of the principles upon which a sound political economy should be based.

Gladstone was fortunate in that the tide both of public sentiment and private experience had been for somewhile past making in his direction. The essayist must therefore be pardoned if he pauses to glance in the direction of Samuel Smiles and John Stuart Mill. The former had a name to attract the attention of the punster, and to establish itself in the memory of the public. Moreover, Smiles's comely platitudes afforded as much genuine pleasure to the sagacious Victorians as they have provided malicious pleasantry to the Edwardians and neo-Georgians who came after them. Samuel Smiles, to give him his due, was, however, no kinsman of Martin Tupper. He did not suppose himself to be setting forth any new ideas or conceive that he was discovering the secrets of a novel philosophy. He merely sought to suggest that the old roads to the celestial country, and even to secular success, were not worn out and that it was still possible to walk profitably in the ancient ways. It was characteristic of the mid-Victorians that they thought there might be a good deal in what he said. Some enterprising young men, resident in the north of Great Britain, of modest means but of much faith in the worth of knowledge, invited him to address them on winter evenings in 'a large dingy apartment . . . which had been used as a temporary cholera hospital'. He was touched by and responded to the request. He spoke to his hearers of what he called 'self-help', enforcing his point by some account of the resolution and pertinacity that had brought men success in the working out of inventions, in the perfecting of arts, and in the accomplishment of public service by land and sea. The theme would seem to have had little attraction for such as felt that they had been victims of circumstance. But this was not the mood of the time. What others had done good mid-Victorians supposed they might do also; and Smiles fostered their innate determination to make good in face of difficulty. He was giving the real reply of the old Humanist Society of Christendom to the new violence of the Revolution of 1789, of which, a century after Smiles's time, we are still constrained to say that it has not been able, for all the many forms and fashions of government it has fostered, to find one that meets the needs or retains the affections of the French people. Some ingredient has always seemed to be wanting and a fourth or fifth adventure in popular government is no more likely, by the look of it, to succeed than the rest.

Wellington, as might be anticipated, moves rather like a presiding genius through the pages of Smiles's book, appearing, retiring, returning again, a master in rectitude and common sense. But it is significant of Smiles's thesis that he is presented above all as 'a first-rate man of business', strict, straight, and as careful of detail as becomes the hero of a people ridiculed by his defeated rival as a nation of shopkeepers. There were cads enough among the

kings—such as Frederick the Great, such as Bomba[1]—but there had been
more cads in the ranks of the revolutionaries; and Smiles was shrewd enough
to appreciate the significance of the fact. The title of his final chapter couples
his key-word 'character' with the redundant phrase 'The True Gentleman'.
At the very date when Thackeray was busy emphasizing the prevalence of
snobs in a society which as yet he did not perhaps very intimately know,
Smiles was thus stressing, with reference to such men as Francis Horner,
Robert Peel and the two Grants, who were supposed to have served Dickens
as a model for the Brothers Cheeryble, that manners were the property of
no class, the product of no fashion, the perquisite of no wealth, but lay well
within the reach of all. Metternich once said something to the effect that in
England the aristocracy were, not the nobility, but the gentry, and that the
code, of which these last were especially the guardians, permeated to a
greater or less degree all ranks of English society. Smiles, without probably
being aware of the remark, had seen the force of it; and all those follies of the
time that amuse us in novels and shock us in memoirs, do not alter the broad
fact that in the great body of the nation Gladstone had material of the best to
work upon—a generation of men to whom honour and honesty meant more
than probably they have ever meant at any time of our history. And he
agreed very closely indeed with Smiles's diagnosis of the human situation.
In a memorable speech delivered in the full maturity of his powers in 1871
at Blackheath before a huge and, it is said, sympathetic audience, will be
found the following passage: 'It is the individual mind, the individual conscience; it is the individual character on which mainly human happiness or
human misery depends. The social problems that confront us are many and
formidable. Let the government labour to its uttermost, let the Legislature
spend days and nights in your service; but, after the very best has been
achieved, the question whether the English father is to be the father of a
happy family and the centre of a united home, is a question which must
depend mainly upon himself.' The speaker goes on to denouce the 'spurious
philanthropy' which deludes the public with 'phantasms', and then repeats:
'No, gentlemen, what we have to ask ourselves are questions which it
depends upon ourselves individually in the main to answer.'[2]

Character—personal character—as the basis of the State postulates freedom
—individual freedom—as the cornerstone of society. It was all to the good
from Gladstone's standpoint that, not only was Smiles stressing the moral
obligation of 'self-help', but that Mill was expounding the economic advantage of liberty. Mill's famous essay in favour of freeing human beings from
the meddlesome interference of the State ultimately carried the argument
to a point which must give all but the most temerarious pause. But some

---

[1] The last Bourbon king of Naples.
[2] A. Tilney Bassett, *Gladstone's Speeches*, p. 423.

ten years before that—in the very year which goes by the name of 'the year of Revolution'—he had, through the medium of his *Principles of Political Economy*, put forward a case, very dispassionately debated and carefully safeguarded, for confining the provinces of government in respect of the wealth of the nation to the uttermost. A single sentence will serve to show the nature of his position. '*Laisser-faire*', he says, 'in short, should be the general practice: every departure from it, unless required by some general good, is evil.'

If that terse canon be allowed, if men are really the best judges of at any rate their immediate interests, then the statesman is left with little more to trouble him in economics than the incidence of taxation. Mill, though he deprecates the inheritance of great fortunes in a way that could hardly have approved itself to those entrusted with large landed estates or even to the master of Hawarden (as Gladstone was destined for a short time in 1874-5 to become) shows no malice in his treatment of rich men. 'To tax the larger incomes at a higher rate than the smaller', runs an illuminating sentence, 'is to lay a tax on industry and economy; to impose a penalty on people for having worked harder and saved more than their neighbours. It is partial taxation, which is a mild form of robbery. A just and wise legislation would scrupulously abstain from opposing obstacles to the acquisition of even the largest fortune by honest exertion.'[1] It is to be feared then that no benediction would fall from Mill's lips, any more than from Gladstone's, on the egalitarian school of economics which claims so glibly, what Christ disclaimed, to have been appointed the judge and divider of other men's heritages. The 'saint of rationalism', as Gladstone on one occasion styled Mill, stood in economics not far removed from Adam Smith whose four famous canons of taxation are equality, certainty, the convenience of the taxpayer, and economy in the collection instilled in rules. Only equality calls for fuller definition. Here Mill discloses the single modification he conceives to be required by justice in a sentence which deserves to be quoted. 'To tax all incomes in an equal ratio would be unjust to those, the greater part of whose income is required for necessaries; but I can see no fairer standard of real equality then to take from all persons, whatever may be their amount of fortune, the same arithmetical proportion of their superfluities.'

Such, anyway, was the ethical and economic soil upon which Gladstone had to raise his financial structure. Few men can ever have had one more promising; and few men, to judge by the results achieved, can ever have used the disposition of the place and the climate of the time to better advantage. Not only was the growth of wealth almost intoxicating;[2] but he drew

[1] From the chapter on 'General Principles of Taxation' in Mill's *Principles of Political Economy*.

[2] See Morley, *Life of Gladstone*.

contentment from the reflection that, while the rich had been growing richer, the poor had become less poor.[1] He had not made the mistake of supposing these two sections of the community to be as irrevocably divided as two nations, nor, had he in championing, as in some respects he did, the cause of the under-dog, made the political stage into a dog-fight. This was partly due to the fact, which Morley signalizes with great emphasis, as 'the fundamental fact of his career',[2] that 'all his activities were in his own mind one'—that all his politics ran back into religion, that God stood out over-shadowing all His creatures at the very centre of the human scene and as the source of all the humanities. 'Gladstone was not only a fervid practising Christian (I am quoting again from Morley); he was a Christian steeped in the fourth century, steeped in the thirteenth and fourteenth centuries.'[3] That sort of historic Christianity cannot logically combine with a socialism based upon the idea that man is to remake the world after his likeness or in conformity with his ideals. Upon all the suppositious ultra-democracy of Gladstone's thought, in fact, Christian Humanism or, if we prefer, Hellenic Christianity imposed a barrier. We have already mentioned the illuminating colloquy at Hawarden in 1878 between Gladstone and Ruskin; it may be reviewed as a commentary on some conclusions that have been advanced here.

Quite apart from this, however, Gladstone's economics were too scientifically conceived to admit profligate bribery or patent malice. The best known of all his phrases registers his conviction that money should be left to fructify in the pockets of the people; while the promise that came nearest to a piece of electioneering was that given in 1874 to the effect that, if he were returned to power he would get rid of the income tax. There could be no plainer indication of his belief that taxation was in itself an undesirable thing and should be regarded as an unhappy necessity. As a headline for the chapter in his biography dealing with the spirit of his finance his biographer has chosen some words of Lecky's which have behind them the ethos and experience of history.[4] 'Nations seldom realize till too late how prominent a place a sound system of finance holds among the vital elements of national stability and well-being; how few political changes are worth purchasing by its sacrifice; how widely and seriously human happiness is affected by the downfall or the perturbation of national credit or by excessive, injudicious and unjust taxation.'

Gladstone came first to the Exchequer in December 1852 when Aberdeen formed that Cabinet of All the Talents (except for Derby's and Disraeli's) which had so bright a morning but whose sun sank 'weeping in the lowly West', as in the East the storm-clouds gathered over the Crimea. The admini-

---

[1] Morley, Vol. II, p. 60. [2] ibid., Vol. I, p. 200.
[3] ibid., Vol. I, p. 201.
[4] ibid., Vol. II, p. 54.

stration owed no small part of its inaugural splendour to Gladstone's presence at the head of its finances. He took office whilst the prestige he had won by smashing Disraeli's Budget of 1852 lay thick about him; and he brought to his office all the advantage of having served at the Board of Trade and under Peel. His Budget of 1853—in Mr. Hirst's view 'the most memorable, certainly the most brilliant of his Budgets'[1]—constituted incidentally the deferred revenge of the Peelites upon the Tory Protectionists who had brought their leader down, destroyed the chances of conservative change under well-considered guidance and compelled the Country Party, for near thirty years after, to wander in the wilderness of Opposition with nothing more than occasional sights of the land of promise. Never did Tory numbers stand in greater need of conservative brains.

The most considerable parliamentarian of the time, if as yet unrecognized as such, stood hesitating throughout the decade we are traversing; already a man of between forty and fifty, with his political abilities plainly of the highest order, but neither an independent nor a partisan. It was an extraordinary chance which put him precisely at this hour in charge of the finances of the nation, long in need of drastic reconstruction and of a mind *sine ira et studio* to work out a design neither oblivious of familiar use, nor blindly refusing to recognize the claims of time and change.

The Budget of 1853 is admittedly epoch-making, embodies the best thought of the period, and merits the same kind of praise which, as Gladstone notices in the course of his speech, was given by Mallet du Pan to Pitt's treatment of the Budget of 1798 when he declared that this represented 'a complete course of political economy'. The dominant feature of Gladstone's first Budget is, as some critics affirm, the extension of the Succession Duty, which had hitherto fallen only upon personal property, to freehold tenures of land and houses, and also to personality passing under settlement. The landed interest had secured the exemption of real property from a proposal of a similar nature in 1796; but national interests were now strong enough to insist upon a more equitable arrangement. What, however, was more controversial in the Budget and afforded Gladstone a striking opportunity to display his persuasive talent and financial tact, lay in his long disquisition on the origin and aim of the income tax. A hundred years ago, when reason could still hold its own with passion, a financier was concerned to justify the maintenance of an impost that Pitt had very properly introduced in time of war but which Peel had temporarily re-introduced in conditions of peace. Gladstone had his audience with him when he argued that the continuance of this tax (as undesirable owing to its encouragement of fraud as it was unwelcome owing to its inescapable inconvenience) must be explained by a state of emergency. The emergency, however, he argued, might arise in the

---

[1] Hirst, *Gladstone as Financier and Economist*, p. 137.

piping times of peace no less than to the accompaniment of the drums of war. The emergency he was facing was the need to release trade from its last fetters, to complete the policy, so far as possible, of free exchange, to reduce indirect taxation to the utmost at the cost of maintaining the income tax a little longer. There were alternatives to this; and he dealt with them in detail but so as to leave no doubt in the mind of his hearers that they would like them even less. In conclusion he carried, so to speak, the income tax across the Irish Sea, so as to equalize more nearly the taxation of the two kingdoms of England and Ireland. And, with that, he rose to the summit of his subject. To use his own poetic simile, he had brought his hearers from height to height of a journey comparable to the climbing of the Alps, and he now bade them survey the prospect before them—fair as the plains of Italy when, after that tremendous ascent, they fell upon the traveller's gaze. With a prophet's hand he indicated the remissions of excise and customs he had become in a position to make. The public was to be relieved from indirect taxation falling upon no less than a hundred articles of food, from the duty on soap, and, by degrees and to a substantial extent, from the duty on tea, from great part of the taxes on life-assurance, on indentures of apprenticeship, and on advertisements, and from some part of that on hackney carriages. This was not all, but it is enough to stress that the retrospect appeared almost as pleasing as the prospect. For, as the moving finger of the prophet pointed forward to the plain soon to be freed from a hundred barriers and excrescences upon its surface, the darkest feature in the scene behind began to disperse. The hated income tax, which stood in 1853 at sevenpence in the pound, was to fall to sixpence in 1855, to fivepence in 1857, and to disappear altogether in 1860.

It was an astonishing Budget, seeming as it did to scatter largess on every side. But even this work of wonder was not altogether to escape from the vanity of human wishes. Within a little while, and a very little while, came the war in the Crimea, and with it the retention of the income tax, not as a temporary expedient in view of hostilities or as a vanishing impost to avert less tolerable troubles, but as an evil that would be always with us, magnified many times as the years went on, multiplied indeed so much at length as to send the monumental country-houses the way of the monasteries and, despite the increasing wealth of the world, to deprive them of their grace and meaning of beauty, to render them no better than museum pieces, attracting the attention of a curious eye, yet lacking in all that glory of human habitation with which they had ministered to successive generations.

Had the Peelites prevailed over the voices counselling ill-considered intervention and calling noisily for war, had Aberdeen and Gladstone been able to defeat Palmerston and Russell, the Budget of 1853 might have stood out yet more than it does as an achievement without parallel, as a promise crowned by accomplishment, as an example of patriotism set free from party. But, even as matters turned out, it remains a marvel of financial reconstruction, an administrative *tour-de-force* matching the claim that Gladstone made for Aberdeen that of all the men he had known, this Prime Minister ranked highest in 'the love of exact justice'.

That fair, fine balance of mind, that golden modesty (shall we say, since mediocrity has other connotations) of thought which the Peelites possessed could not in the nature of things be expected to endure in a country committed by custom, if not constitution, to the governance only of two rival parties. It represented an adjustment of political thinking too delicate for the rough tussle of politicians with eyes pre-occupied by party or personal preferment, and it could only be congenial to Ministers like Aberdeen, like Graham, like Sidney Herbert, like Gladstone himself, who were moulded of finer clay than the rank and file of their associates. Age and infirmity could be trusted to make away with most of the Peelites; but Gladstone was still in the full vigour of manhood; and the rare chance which brought about the short-lived coalition under Aberdeen and incidentally placed him at the Exchequer had raised his reputation to a height that made his adhesion to either of the traditional parties a matter of the utmost interest and concern. From the fall of Peel in 1846 to the day in March 1869, when he removed his name from the Carlton Club, it was anybody's guess where exactly he would end. He clung himself for a long while to the belief that the temper of mind he had found in Peel and reverenced in Aberdeen still represented practical politics. 'There is a policy', he told Elwin, the editor of the *Quarterly* in December 1856, 'going a begging; the general policy that Sir Robert Peel in 1841 took office to support—the policy of peace abroad, of economy, of financial equilibrium, of steady resistance to abuses, and promotion of practical improvements at home, with a disinclination to questions of reform, gratuitously raised.'[1] That was doubtless the policy for which wise men might well have wished—conservative in the best sense of the word, a policy of development on traditional, and therefore national lines. If Aberdeen could have held the fort against the jingoes, if Lansdowne had been some years younger and Gladstone himself had been willing in 1855, as later on he thought he should have done, to serve under him, then it is possible things might perhaps have turned out differently. But, as it was, Gladstone for all his talent had as yet no effective following, nor was recognized as potentially an effective leader. The parliamentary protagonists were Palmerston and Disraeli; and Gladstone had less than nothing in common with either. He had crossed swords with the former in 1850 when, to Palmerston's famous invocation of *Civis Romanus sum* in the Don Pacifico case, he had inquired whether it became a Christian nation to defy 'the law of nature and of God'

[1] Morley, *Life of Gladstone*, Vol. I, p. 553.

by arrogating to itself the privileges of caste and conquest, once asserted by Roman imperialism. And, when in 1857 Palmerston introduced legislation affording through the machinery of the law-courts instead of, as hitherto, by costly private legislation facilities for divorce, Gladstone had come down upon the old pagan—to borrow Morley's words—'with a holy wrath as vehement as the more worldly fury with which Henry Fox, from very different motives, had fought the Marriage Bill of 1753'.[1] But though he was at issue with the ethics of Palmerston at home and abroad, the pupil of Peel could hardly be expected to look with a kindlier eye upon the subtle Oriental who had compassed his master's fall and whose merits both as a humorist and a political thinker wholly escaped his understanding.[2] This was not altogether Disraeli's fault. Those who see him merely as an ambitious and unscrupulous politician will find in the confidential letter he addressed to Gladstone in 1858 an incident not altogether consistent with their conception. It is as frank and generous a communication as perhaps one political antagonist ever addressed to an uncongenial rival. The opening words, which furnish the key to the rest, are in the grand manner of the time. 'I think it', wrote Disraeli, 'of such paramount importance to the public interests that you should assume at this time a commanding position in the administration of affairs that I feel it a solemn duty to lay before you some facts that you may not decide upon a misapprehension. Our mutual relations have formed the great difficulty in accomplishing a result which I have always anxiously desired.'[3] Derby had already intimated with what pleasure he would place Gladstone at the head of the Indian Board of Control, just vacated by Ellenborough, or alternatively at the Colonial Office. Disraeli went out of his way to assure him of the utmost consideration in Parliament and to suggest that, even if circumstances rendered it difficult at the moment for himself to resign the leadership in the Commons—a not impossible contingency ('I may be removed from the scene, or I may wish to be removed from the scene')—yet that Gladstone might stand in the same relation to himself as Canning had been content to do in respect of Castlereagh.

'Don't you think the time has come when you might deign to be magnanimous?' The appeal falls upon the ear even still with a curious sense of pathos and excites an idle wish that Gladstone had seen his way to try the proposed combination. Perhaps there was something in what Manning said to Disraeli and Disraeli repeated to Northcote, that he knew Gladstone well and thought him the most revengeful man he had ever known.[4] Or perhaps Disraeli, in his old age, had given force to a casual observation. At

[1] Morley, *Life of Gladstone*, Vol. I, p. 570.
[2] 'None of us, I believe, were ever able to persuade Mr. Gladstone to do justice to Disraeli's novels . . .' ibid., Vol. I, p. 588.
[3] Buckle, *Life of Disraeli*, Vol. IV, p. 157.
[4] ibid., Vol. VI, p. 584.

any rate there was no moment in their long antagonism in which these two great rivals stood so close to one another; and Gladstone's refusal to cooperate left Disraeli with the *beau rôle*. But neither Graham, nor Aberdeen, could quite bring themselves to advise acceptance; indeed Aberdeen, though Gladstone regarded his opinion as indecisive, leaned towards a reply in the negative. Graham did, however, go so far as to point out that, whilst the abdication of Disraeli could not be made a condition precedent to the association, yet Gladstone's pre-eminence in the Commons would be certain, nevertheless, to come about.

As we pause to consider the rejected overture and the consequent final severance, the observer may well allow himself to be carried forward perhaps twenty years later to contemplate Disraeli in conversation with one of Gladstone's daughters, at one of those resplendent parties which marked the London of Victoria. A personage of evident distinction and foreign appearance was noticeable amongst the crowd; and Mrs. Drew, if it were she, asked Disraeli who he was. 'That', came the characteristic answer, 'is the most dangerous man in Europe—except, as your father would say, myself, or, as I should prefer to say, your father.' Probably the two could never have run in harness, either side by side or in tandem: perhaps Gladstone was right and perhaps Dizzy's grand and graceful gesture was futile. Still it was made; and, had it met with a response, might conceivably have issued in a conservative or Tory-democratic combination of unparalleled strength and immeasurable possibilities. Derby might have formed the link between the two men. Churchmanship was as strong in him as in Gladstone; and, moreover, it had been from Stanley, as he then was, that Gladstone had received congratulations of the warmest and most appreciative kind of his maiden speech in the House a quarter of a century before. Anyhow Derby showed himself reluctant to bolt and bar the door to the return of the great Peelite to the Conservative camp. In the autumn of 1858 the Derby administration offered to send him on a special mission to the Ionian Isles; and he agreed to go. It had no particular success; and ultimately these islands were returned to Greece. But naturally people had pricked up their ears at Gladstone's acceptance of the offer and had begun to see him returning to the tents of his former allegiance. There was nothing, however, in the idea. In June, 1859, the nation learnt that he had joined Palmerston's newly-formed administration as Chancellor of the Exchequer. The Prime Minister and his new lieutenant were, after all, both old Canningites; and Gladstone did not then know, what he presently found out to his discomfiture, that Palmerston counted the re-armament of the country among the two great purposes of his life. At the moment of decision, moreover, the affairs of Italy occupied all thoughts; and here Gladstone's mind was moving along the nationalist lines agreeable to Palmerston, and not in accord with those of his old chief,

Aberdeen, who stood by the Treaty of Vienna. He felt too that, in the state of Europe, the Queen's Government needed to be as strong as it could be made; and he joined the administration of his old enemy without a sigh or a resistance. The Rubicon had been crossed at length.

Gladstone's Budget of 1860 is almost as memorable as his budget of 1853; and the references to the commercial treaty with France have the same sort of place in its structure as the treatise on the income tax in the earlier one. Nothing, however, lends itself less to a racy or even interesting treatment than old finance; and the reader has already endured enough in the way of apologetics on its account. One can say that, apart from some small charges on timber and corn, the Budget left nothing in the way of protective or differential duties to offend the eye of the free-trader. Cobden, who negotiated the actual agreement with Napoleon III, had lived to see a realized ideal, and he merited Gladstone's tribute which was couched in no niggardly terms. 'Rare', said the Chancellor of the Exchequer, 'is the privilege of any man who, having fourteen years ago rendered to his country one signal and splendid service, now again within the same brief span of life, decorated neither by rank nor title, bearing no mark to distinguish him from the people whom he serves, has been permitted again to perform a great and memorable service to his Sovereign and to his country.'

Though the wealth of the nation was rising by leaps and bounds, as reflected in the returns of income tax, the year 1860 had nevertheless arrived without the disappearance of that impost. 'With justice', said the Chancellor, 'may it be demanded of me—what has become of the calculations of 1853?' The answer, he replied, was to be found in the growth of national expenditure. 'In 1853 the whole amount voted for Supply and Services of every description . . . was £24,279,000 . . .' But in 1860–61, instead of £24,279,000, these charges amounted to £39,000,000, showing an increase in expenditure of £14,721,000. This increase is, as nearly as may be, representative of what would be in itself an income tax of 13½d in the pound. 'I ask Sir, . . . whether I have not redeemed my pledge?' So, whilst the relief from indirect taxation was about £4,000,000, the income tax on incomes above £150 a year, which were less severely taxed, was to be tenpence in the pound; and tea and sugar must still pay something.

The fundamental principles, latent or perhaps rather patent, in all Gladstonian finance were admirably epitomized in a letter written some three years later to Gladstone by the astute and penetrating publicist of Lombard Street. 'Indirect taxation', Bagehot wrote, 'so cramps trade, and heavy direct taxation so impairs morality that a large expenditure becomes a great evil.'[1] 'Economy', Gladstone wrote himself, 'is the first and great article (economy such as I understand it) in my financial creed. The controversy

[1] Quoted by Morley, *Life of Gladstone*, Vol. II, p. 63.

between direct and indirect taxation holds a minor though important place.'[1]

Ruskin, whose reflections on the problems of wealth and poverty were, about 1860, beginning to appear under Froude's aegis in the columns of *Frazer's Magazine*, came nearest perhaps of any man of that time to reaching the centre of a problem of which the solution can clearly never be effected except through the most perfect balance of heart and mind. No man, as a long footnote in *Unto This Last* makes clear beyond dispute, had less belief in the socialistic creed, of which he is now strangely supposed to have been one of the foremost apostles. But, on the other hand, no man stressed more that stewardship of personal wealth which any votary of the religion of beauty discards at his peril. Maecenas—and many like him—must be there to complete the personnel of a polity, at least where Aristotle has any say in its making. The Megalopsychos, the magnificent man, cannot be spared, where beauty is reckoned a value and grace esteemed an adornment. In a great society the patron is pretty nearly as much a condition of great art as the painter; and it would be an astonishment to find a Turner without an Egremont. Ruskin could well imagine what the arts would have lacked, if the cities of Italy, or for the matter of that of England, had been shorn of their petty grandees. Gladstone's great Budgets disclose perhaps the largest belief in the value of individuality and the lowest in that of State competence that our history offers in the record of public finance. Yet he was certainly no doctrinaire. Though in 1841 a Committee of which he was chairman reported against State-ownership of the railways, he made a reference in a speech of 1844 to the possibility of their nationalization at a future date.[2] He realized what a socialist finds it so hard to do, that time, circumstance, and in fact expediency, in all its wide, ranging irregularity, must be the final arbiter in all such decisions.

One other detail of the Budget of 1860 still calls for some allusion. Gladstone was resolved to sweep away the paper-duties as mischievous obstacles to knowledge. Metternich had possibly the best grasp of the matter when he freed pamphlets of a certain length from censorship but retained some control over newspapers. Anyone who will take the trouble to read a pamphlet through, may be presumed to be in serious search of knowledge: most of those who scan a paper or glance at a headline may be as plausibly suspected of seeking to save themselves the trouble of thinking out difficult subjects thoroughly. However that may be, Gladstone was for the cheapest Press that the removal of the paper-duties could bring about. Not so Palmerston, the Prime Minister! That shrewd old worldling could not see, as Melbourne, would have phrased it, why you should not let things alone. The House of Lords was of the Prime Minister's mind and the repeal of the paper-duties

---

[1] Morley, *Life of Gladstone*, Vol. II, p. 62.
[2] F. W. Hirst, *Gladstone as Financier and Economist*, p. 89.

was consequently rejected in the Lords; and the Chancellor of the Exchequer had to content himself with resolutions condemning the peers for meddling with finance Bills.

Two things came of this ill-timed and ill-judged conflict between the Houses. Thenceforward measures of finance were sent to the Upper House all together, and no longer in separate Bills. The peers must either take all—or else reject all, as they did with disastrous results to the constitution some fifty years later. And in the second place Gladstone, if Morley reads him aright, moved a long way towards Liberalism under the influence of the rebuff the Upper House had given him. The people, seeing what was done, came for the first time to regard him as their champion. For the first time in his career he became a popular figure; for the first time the winged words that wandering breezes bear might, to an attentive ear, have seemed to mutter the fond nickname of 'the People's William', someday with age and admiration to be changed again into that of 'the G.O.M.'—the Grand Old Man.

The lustrum between 1860 and 1865 was, as we have seen, of great psychological significance for one who was now himself past fifty. Aberdeen died at its beginning; then in 1861 both Graham and Sidney Herbert, both deeply in his confidence; and, before the close of the same year, the Prince Consort, temperamentally a Sovereign (in all but name) with whom he might have worked in much greater ease and sympathy than with Victoria. Newcastle, the close and early friend to whose father he had owed his entry into Parliament, went in the autumn of 1864; Cobden, whom he was inclined to rate as the simplest, noblest and most unselfish character he had met in public life, in the spring of 1865. He was conscious of growing loneliness. And then, in the July of 1865, Oxford, the mother whom he had loved so well and for whom he had on the whole laboured so wisely, even though men as different as Jowett and Pusey were highly critical of his Oxford University Reform Bill, cast him out. His growing doubts on the subject of the Established Church of Ireland had been too much for the common rooms where Keble had once talked and the pulpits where King Charles enjoyed the reputation of a martyr. Repudiated in the glades and meadows of that city which still was eloquent at every turn of the way with the thought of things he loved and honoured, Gladstone made his way to South Lancashire, where industry was at full blast, where progress was identified with the production of material things, and where dreams found exit through gates of horn. Each milestone on his political journey took him further from the ivory palaces, the ivory portals, the ivory towers of the south. He never looked back, yet he never forgot; and in those two facts lay much of his strength in the years that were yet to come.

The country meanwhile was waiting perhaps unconsciously for an occurrence which could not be long deferred and which in its nature must, when it came, wind up an epoch. Palmerston, stormy petrel as he might appear abroad, was in home affairs as little a lover of change as Derby; and as we have seen, in the October of this same year of transition, he died at Brocket. He was past eighty and as a small child had known the world before the Revolution in France. It is not altogether suprising that this long-lived disciple of Canning was not eager to see it changed in his immediate English surroundings. Abroad revolutions aroused in him not a little interest, excitement and even sympathy. It was rather fun, whatever the Court might feel about it, to hear of Marshal Haynau, reputed guilty of certain brutalities of which nowadays, with fuller knowledge of what has been perpetrated on the Continent by democratic dictators, we should not think much, being tossed in a blanket and pursued by draymen with broomsticks. It made life more colourful to welcome Garibaldi in his red shirt and applaud him as the hero of an Italian nationalism, which in its day did away with some indifferent governments only in our day to breed a new dictator, who substituted scorpions for whips.

Gladstone had watched Palmerstonian policy in Italy in the full conviction that he was beholding the birth of a nation and perhaps in the fond expectation that the Romans were about to be born again. Such expectations, if he had them, were as illusory as those which Byron had entertained regarding the revolt in Greece. Enthusiasm is often pleasing; but cynicism is seldom misplaced. In domestic, if not in foreign affairs, Gladstone, however, had all his wits about him. Remembering Peel's close supervision of all departments of his administration, he could not but distrust Palmerston's easy-going indolence, whilst, as the Prime Minister more and more showed his open hand in respect of expenditure upon defence, the Chancellor of the Exchequer betrayed increasingly his distrust of a policy that cut right across his own confidence in preserving peace by means of the development of international trade. The head of the Government by something perilously like a breach of faith, had in 1860 obtained two millions for use upon fortifications; and it was little less than a marvel that by the close of the Palmerstonian era— in 1866—his tenacious Chancellor of the Exchequer had managed to bring expenditure back to the level of 1857.[1] 'It is a characteristic of the mischiefs that arise from financial prodigality', Gladstone said, 'that they creep onwards with a noiseless and a stealthy step; that they commonly remain unseen and unfelt until they have reached a magnitude absolutely overwhelming.'[2] He had seen to it, however, that, for all Palmerston's pressure, the old man's prodigalities did not prevail.

And now the road, but for one stumbling-block, stretched clear before him. The country was not urgent for Reform; nor was he himself, as he made

---

[1] Morley, *Life of Gladstone*, Vol. II, p. 51.   [2] ibid., p. 53.

clear to Denison (the then Speaker, and later Lord Ossington), anxious to
bring it on before the time was fully ripe. But for Russell, the new Prime
Minister, the sands were fast running out; and he was consumed by a wish
to associate his name with some further extension of the suffrage. So a measure of reform was introduced. A franchise qualification of £7 in the
boroughs and £14 in the counties was proposed. 'We may smile', as John
Morley observes, 'at the thought that some of the most brilliant debates ever
heard in the House of Commons now turned upon the mighty puzzle
whether the qualification for a borough-voter should be occupancy of a ten,
a seven, or a six pound house;—nay, whether the ruin or salvation of the
State might not lie on the razor-edge of distinction between rating and rental.'

Of the Reform Bill of 1866 that failed—and failed naturally enough in a
Parliament elected in support of Palmerston, who wanted no reform at all—
the thing best remembered, if not the only thing now worth remembering,
is the peroration of Gladstone's speech in its support. A few words from it
may be recalled as an example of the kind of elegance of which he was
master. ' . . . This Bill', he said, 'is in a state of crisis and of peril, and the
Government along with it . . . We stand with it now; we may fall with it a
short time hence. If we do so fall, we, or others in our places, shall rise with
it hereafter. . . . You may drive us from our seats. You may bury the Bill
that we have introduced, but we will write upon its gravestone for an
epitaph this line, with certain confidence in its fulfilment: "Exoriare aliquis
nostris ex ossibus ultor." You cannot fight against the future. Time is on our
side. The great social forces which move onwards in their might and majesty
and which the tumult of our debates does not for a moment impede or
disturb—those great social forces are against you; they are marshalled on our
side; and the banner which we now carry in this fight, though perhaps at
some moment it may droop over our sinking heads, yet it soon again will
float in the eye of heaven, and it will be borne by the firm hands of the united
people of the three kingdoms, perhaps not to an easy, but to a certain and to a
not distant victory.'[1]

This was rhetoric of course, but rhetoric of a fine quality; and Disraeli,
as he listened did not need to be told that it contained a large quantity of
truth. Sooner or later the suffrage, whatever Lowe or others might feel,
would have to be extended. The only question was whether a Tory-democracy could be created quickly enough to snatch the prize out of Gladstone's
hands. Disraeli believed that it could. Whether he also saw that something
falling not far short of the subtlety of the serpent would be needed to achieve
it is matter for speculation. Of that unattractive quality he was, anyhow,
himself possessed. With the aid of all the so-called Adullamites—of all the
distressed, that is, and all the discontented—with the help especially of Lowe;

[1] April 27th 1866.

by the use of manoeuvres which drew from one Conservative the observation that no single division at this time was taken in good faith,[1] Russell's administration was defeated on an issue of taking rateable as against rental value as the basis of the proposed £7 franchise and resigned, when they should probably in their own interest have dissolved Parliament and appealed to the country. Derby regained power and Disraeli seized his opportunity. Conjuring with the telling phrase 'household suffrage' he introduced another Reform Bill, adding something like a million new voters (as against the four hundred thousand proposed in the Russell Reform Bill) to the electorate; and carried it through Parliament without breaking up his party and for the loss only of a few colleagues. Before the next year was out, however, Disraeli had resigned; and Gladstone had been charged by the Sovereign with the formation of his first administration. The General Election had given him a majority of 112 in the House of Commons. His star, perhaps never rose higher; his opportunity never at any time perhaps, was greater. 'Progress' was a word on all lips. Only Disraeli, and a few men like-minded with him, asked questioningly, 'Progress—whence?' 'Progress—whither?'

'The session of 1870', wrote Herbert Paul, 'may challenge comparison with any which preceded or have followed it for the extent and variety of its achievements.'[2] This was no idle boast and indeed might, perhaps, be more extensively applied to the work of that famous administration of 1868–74, subject to the reservation of a careful student of the period that there was a fall in the energy and ability of the administrators when its first two years were over.[3] With a speed calculated to alarm, not only those who walk habitually in ancient ways, but those whose dispositions are best met by hastening slowly, Gladstone had disestablished the Irish Protestant Church, the deepest and most daring assertion of the English overlordship of Ireland, but further, in defiance of Palmerston's dictum that tenant-right meant landlord's wrong, had reconstituted the relationship between the land-owner and the land-occupier by giving the tenant, if evicted, compensation for his improvements. In England, too, Gladstone had made drastic, if not equally momentous changes. He had introduced the ballot at elections and thus checked the power of electoral intimidation: he had swept away the time-honoured system of selling commissions in the Army and had brought in the plan of short-term enlistment with the Colours and of a subsequent period of service in the reserve. The Civil Service had been opened to general competition, though Clarendon had contrived to keep the Foreign Office still outside the operation of the new arrangement, and, what was a greater change than all of these, education had been made free and compul-

---

[1] Morley, *Life of Gladstone*, Vol. II, p. 205.
[2] Paul, *History of Modern England*, Vol. III, p. 238.
[3] Hammond, *Gladstone and the Irish Nation*, p. 109.

sory; and religious education, though here the Prime Minister was at heart a dissentient, was to be given in State-schools under the Cowper-Temple clause,[1] on the supposition that a common denominator could really be found for all Christian denominations and that all confusions of creed could be conveniently blended into cloudy infusions of ethic. Here was a plan indeed to please the English mind which fancies that theology is no science and can do very well on words, rather designed to conceal thoughts than to clarify ideas.

The Irish, to whose problems of higher education Gladstone had begun to think of applying treatment not altogether dissimilar from that so vague and popular in England in respect of elementary schools, were, unfortunately from his point of view, less accommodating. His idea was to consolidate the Irish Universities, not indeed by a sort of pooling of Catholic and Protestant tenets but by a kind of gentlemen's agreement between the authorities of the two religions not to tread on one another's toes. The Chairs of Moral Philosophy and History were to disappear and, by virtue of what Fawcett called the 'gagging' clauses of the scheme, a teacher was to respect, by absence of comment, the religious opinions of his pupils.

The plan was full of difficulties, both latent and patent. It was but a few years before that Newman had advanced the view that 'religious doctrine is knowledge in as full a sense as Newton's doctrine is knowledge'; that 'University Teaching without Theology is simply unphilosophical'; and that 'Theology has at least as good a right to claim a place there as Astronomy'.[2] Newman's argument that 'the omission of theology from the list of recognized sciences is, not only indefensible in itself, but prejudicial to all the rest', would perhaps be even harder to refute to-day, when science seems in doubt about the very existence of matter as distinct from energy; but, even in his own day, it was cogent enough to give any clear thinker pause. And, though Manning gave some countenance to Gladstone's scheme, Cardinal Cullen, all powerful in Catholic Ireland, proved uncompromisingly hostile. A University after all, it may be said, does exist to teach; and a University has so much the more reason to be sure of its own mind. It needs to make proof of all things, but yet to hold fast to that which is true. But this, it is not at all likely to be able to do, unless some metaphysical foundation of thought is found behind the physical.

No one was much better aware of all this than Gladstone; and no people was less disposed to a solution on indeterminate lines than the Irish. Hibernian

---

[1] The Cowper-Temple clause was moved as an amendment to Forster's Education Bill of 1870 which originally left the matter of religious instruction to the discretion of the individual School Boards. The Cowper-Temple amendment, which was adopted, confined religious instruction to the reading and exposition of the Bible and forbade the use of any specific Catechism.

[2] Newman, *Idea of a University*, passim.

theologian joined forces with English rationalist to defeat the Liberal States-man. The administration had spent its strength. In 1872 Disraeli had com-pared Ministers poetically, but a little prematurely, to a range of exhausted volcanoes. In 1874 he declared in jingling oracles that the nation was resolved to put an end to this ministerial career of 'plundering and blundering'. The phrases, though they could scarcely be called true, were telling. The glamour of the Great Gladstonian administration was certainly passing; and Gladstone, defeated in the House by an adverse majority of three, resigned. Disraeli, however, declined to take over the work of governance; and in the end the Liberals returned to office, though hardly to power. Selborne's Judicature Act of 1873[1] cast a dying glow upon the extensive work of the administration; but the settlement in 1872 of the Alabama claim at Geneva in favour of the U.S.A. lent an air of justice but no lustre to its record in foreign affairs. At home and abroad the country wanted change; and Gladstone, who had replaced Lowe at the Exchequer, scored no advantage by promising, if he were returned to power, to abolish the income tax. The hour was adverse, not only to Gladstone, but to Glad-stonian finance. It had been the theory of Pitt and of Peel to hold the income tax in reserve for cases of national emergency; and Gladstone had, as we have seen, planned his budgets in harmony with this idea. Democracy, however, as the event has shown, cannot resist the temptation of making use of a method so convenient for penalizing the richer members of the community; the year 1874 and the return to power of Disraeli sounded, little as people realized it, the knell of Gladstonian finance; and the country, without in the least understanding what it was doing, embarked on a sea of expenditure, of which no man can yet perceive the bounds. 'The election of 1874', ob-serves Morley, 'was the fall of the curtain; the play that had begun in 1842 came to its last scene. It marked the decision of the electorate that the income tax—re-introduced by Peel and continued by Gladstone for the purpose of simplifying the tariff and expanding the trade—should be retained for general objects of government and should be a permanent element of our finance. It marked at the same time the prospect of a new era of indefinitely enlarged expenditure, with the income tax as a main engine for raising ways and means.'[2] To discuss whether Peel and Gladstone at one end of the change of policy or Dalton and Cripps at the other, were the better financiers is only to debate whether men who imagine they can borrow more cheaply than the credit of the Government really permits, or who boast many times over that money will not be devalued, but in the event are compelled to propose a drastic devaluation, are better qualified for their work than those whose

[1] The Judicature Act 1873 united the eight superior courts of justice into one supreme court: the judges of one division were enabled to sit in any other.

[2] Morley, *Life of Gladstone*, Vol. II, p. 496.

administration of public finance causes the country to advance from strength to strength on a great wave of freedom and on a great faith in leaving money 'to fructify in the pockets of the people'. The wise historian will not allow his mind to be entangled in such webbing. Any modern economist, however, afflicted with doubts on this subject, might do worse than refresh his memory of Mill's observations in his Political Economy on the limits of the province of government and in particular to recall to mind Mill's quotation from Dunoyer on the effect of the meddling of the inspectors and commissaries of the *ancien régime* with the processes of trade in the France of the Eighteenth Century. There he will find the answer, unprejudiced by any views entertained of the broad results of the Revolution, to the critics of Gladstonian finance and much reason besides to reflect that human ideas have a way of moving in a circle, according as people perceive the particular evils of any system in vogue at the moment. There exist economic laws, but none so infallible that they cannot be contested or challenged. Gladstonian finance, however, will stand many hard knocks before the rock on which it rests can be effectively chipped.

So too, maybe, will Gladstonian theology; though that we have yet to consider. Gladstone, as things turned out, was to be Chancellor of the Exchequer again from 1880 to 1882, in which year he put Childers in charge of national finance; for after 1874 his mind was seeking new pastures. 'I was most anxious', he wrote many years later, 'to make the retirement of the Ministry (of 1868–74) the occasion of my own.' There were from his standpoint greater things to be done even than those in the sphere of political economy. 'I am convinced', he wrote to his wife in 1874, 'that the welfare of mankind does not now depend on the state of the world of politics ; the real battle is being fought in the world of thought, where a deadly attack is made, with great tenacity of purpose and over a wide field, upon the greatest treasure of mankind, the belief in God and the gospel of Christ.'[1] This was searching diagnosis; and it was not surprising that one, whom Huxley credited with 'the greatest intellect in Europe',[2] should perceive it. During the Midlothian Campaign Gladstone, in giving his address as 'Lord Rector of the University' at Glasgow in 1879, defined, more or less, the lines along which his defence of Christianity would presumably have run.

'The thing to do', he said, 'is to put scepticism on its trial and rigidly to cross-examine it: allow none of its assumptions; compel it to expound its formulae; do not let it move a step except with proof in its hand; bring it front to front with history; even demand that it shall show the positive elements with which it proposes to replace the mainstays it seems bent on withdrawing from the fabric of modern society.'[3] 'Thought', he cried aloud,

[1] Morley, *Life*, Vol. II, p. 500.   [2] ibid., Vol. III, p. 536.
[3] ibid., Vol. II, p. 591.

'is the citadel.'[1] 'Renan's *Life of Christ*,' he wrote in private, 'I thought a piece of trumpery.'[2]

As things turned out, Gladstone was diverted from the execution of his theological programme by the course of events in Ireland, but, admirably conceived as it was for the defeat of the particular enemy he had in view, it is doubtful whether a British public would ever have allowed him to pull his full weight as a professional combatant in the struggle. It would have been far too easy to disparage his opinions as those of an amateur, though an article on 'The Courses of Religious Thought', which Morley characterizes as 'one of the most remarkable he ever wrote',[3] shows how well-equipped he was to lead such a religious movement as he had outlined.

It may indeed astonish many to-day, when physical science has before our very eyes performed a *volte-face* as complete as the accomplishment of any acrobat and no more easy to follow in detail than acrobatics, to have it claimed that Gladstone made as good a business of the theological case for believing that Scripture was founded on an impregnable rock as the best trained professional advocate might have done; but, if people would remember Dean Church's advice not to assume that a position assailed is a position lost, they would find his polemics easier to follow. He did not ask of Genesis the phraseology of a scientific text-book; he understood that religious poetry must be allowed the licence allowed to poetry in general as a medium of truth; and, this much conceded, he dealt with the then new conception of evolution, new at least to all who had never noticed that the scriptural account of creation had started, not from the appearance of man, but of a world already supposed reeling from a fall in the celestial hierarchy, had suffered a crushing blow from which, rather by divine than mortal aid, it might hope to recover. Everything individually might be denominated as in itself a marvel and very good of its kind, yet the whole collectively might lack the look of harmony latent in the original design. Let that be, however, as it may. There was nothing much to be made out of the consideration that some first intimation of certain phenomena credited to events at the close of creation could, maybe, be detected at an earlier date.

Gladstone's intervention in the controversy supposed to be raging between the Bible and Physical Science was valuable as a corrective to critics who could not easily discern the distinction between a profound and a pettifogging criticism. The impress of a mind, whose power could not be denied, and the intervention of a man, trained by experience in great affairs to seize on the essentials of a subject and to make probability the guide of life, had at that time no small value in steadying controversy and checking shortness of thought. Like Disraeli, Gladstone had come out on the side of the angels.

---

[1] Morley, *Life of Gladstone*, p. 590.   [2] ibid., p. 476.
[3] *Contemporary Review* of June 1876 (*Gleanings*, Vol. III).

His strategy was good; his tactics were clever. Even at this distance of time, they are not to be despised. But what would have come of it, if he had pursued his way, can be little more than a fascinating speculation. Whether this student of Dante and Joseph Butler could have given to the world of his time such a work as could have arrested the movement advancing towards the quagmire of dialectical materialism, into which Karl Marx and his pupils in Britain were leading mankind, must have depended, to some extent at least, upon the receptive qualities of the British public at that time. Froude was maintaining, or was soon to maintain, that we were afraid to look into each other's minds for fear of what we might find there; and the reply of the sceptic who, after asserting that he professed the religion of all sensible men, proceeds, upon further interrogation, to declare that 'sensible men never tell' what that is was gaining ground, no doubt aided by the currency which Disraeli gave it, if he did not originate it, in *Endymion*. Speculation upon what Gladstone might in his own chosen sphere and in his last phase have done can only represent, therefore, a passing, if very permissible diversion from the main tenour of his course. All that can safely be said is that his diagnosis of the international situation was correct; that to such a political idea as Christendom the truth of Christianity is fundamental; that the question of Ireland, however urgent, must be classed as a side-issue which breaks in a little roughly upon reflections as to a finished education in the humanities such as possessed Gladstone's mind and is set forth in his letter of 1861 to Lord Lyttelton;[1] that the essay of his great friend, Acton, written in 1862, effectively disposes of the argument from 'Nationality'[2] by holding up the British and Austrian Empires as more perfect political entities by reason of their mixture of races; and that Gladstone's decision to give his last years to the solution of the Irish problem may well be regarded as 'the great refusal'. For Gladstone, after all, had seen so clearly that Christianity in its purest form had from the first run counter to every disintegrating tendency whether of Jew or Greek, had occupied with surprising ease the metropolis of the civilized world and had caused its best adherents to lose all their local affinities in the thought of 'one Lord, one faith, one baptism, one God and Father of us all'.

National politics are apt, however, to be blinding. Both Gladstone and Disraeli had vision penetrating enough to show them from what direction the nearer storm, as opposed to the more distant cosmic typhoon, was advancing upon mankind. 'Ireland, Ireland! that cloud in the west, that coming storm, the minister of God's retribution upon cruel and inveterate, but half-atoned impulse. Ireland forces upon us . . . great social and religious questions. God grant that we may have courage to look them in the face and

---

[1] Printed in Morley's *Life*, Vol. II, Appendix (p. 646).
[2] Acton, *History of Freedom and Other Essays*, IX, 'Nationality,' p. 298.

K

to work through them'.[1] So Gladstone had written to his wife as early as the autumn of 1845. And, as he left his official residence in Downing Street after the disastrous election of 1880, Beaconsfield, never so loquacious as his rival, and now grown sardonic with age, replied to the gloomy vaticinations of a friend, anticipating trouble in the Near East from the change of Ministry, by the single word, uttered with solemn emphasis, 'Ireland' ![2]

Disraeli, it may be, deserved some share of the blame for the state of the neighbouring Island. He had written of it with much insight in his *Life of Lord George Bentinck*; he had diagnosed the causes of discontent there as a starving population, an absentee body of landlords and an alien church. But, when at last in 1874 he came into real power, he did nothing in particular for the distressful country. Perhaps he would have defended himself by pointing out that Gladstone had in the meanwhile dealt with the problems raised by the land and the Church; nor would that have been altogether special pleading. The Irish Protestant Church had been disestablished in 1869; and the Ulster system, giving the tenant credit for improvements to his holding had been extended in 1870 to the rest of the country. Something, however, still remained to be done to capture the goodwill of the people. That had evidently not been impossible in the early part of the century, for all England's ignorances and negligences in the centuries before. There was a wonderful wealth of loyalty to be tapped if the Sovereigns of Great Britain had cared to be Sovereigns of Ireland too. Consider, for example, a passage in Mrs. Arbuthnot's recently published diaries where we read that in May 1821, 'Lord Londonderry was received in Ireland with the greatest possible applause; one man was heard to say to another in the midst of a crowd that were loudly hurrahing him, "But after all it was he who carried the Union", to which another replied, "Never mind, Honey, he has brought us the King".[3] And that King was only George IV, with Lady Conyngham in hiding behind him. It was no hopeless quest to try, with some small measure of understanding, to keep Ireland politically an integral part of the British Isles.

Still no doubt here was an opportunity missed as decisively as had been that of 1703, before the Union of England and Scotland; which wise men have thought might, if seized, have changed the course of history.[4] The hour for a royal intervention, even though Prime Ministers continued to play with the notion of setting up the Prince of Wales with an establishment in Ireland—a notion not at all encouraged by Victoria, who did not regard her heir as well suited for any such occasion—had, however, possibly gone by.

[1] Morley, *Life of Gladstone*, Vol. I, p. 383.
[2] ibid., Vol. III, p. 47.
[3] Journal, May 21 1821.
[4] See for example Lecky's *Leaders of Public Opinion in Ireland*, Vol. I, p. 5.

But, in the light of that strange episode of the association of Arnold Toynbee[1] and Michael Davitt[2] (of an Oxford don, under the influence of T. H. Green, and of an Irish labourer, who had had much to say to the foundation of the Land League), can anyone assert with confidence that an Anglo-Irish understanding, rooted in common humanity, was really quite out of the question? No darker hour could have been chosen for this attempt to find, behind the politicians, some firm ground of friendship than the year in which the ghastly Maamtrasna Murders had followed close upon those, much better remembered, of Cavendish and Burke in Phoenix Park; yet Toynbee and Davitt seem to have understood one another well and to have elicited, each from the other, that goodwill towards men which was in both their minds. But Toynbee died early in 1883; and Davitt was put back in prison near the same time.

The Irish Question was in fact too difficult for the politicians. It might, perhaps, be said that each side in the contention had an unanswerable case. After long years the problem has been settled, if not solved, with the unwilling consent of both parties, by the separation of north-east Ulster from the rest of Ireland. But no one dreamed of such a settlement when, after a bad season and the failure of the crops in 1879, Gladstone came into power in 1880. Irish tenants were back, as Gladstone said, where they had been before his Land Act of 1870. Evictions for non-payment of rent were many; and murder stalked abroad. In these circumstances the Government concentrated its attention on saving the Irish people of Ireland from starvation; the Conservatives on saving the Irish landlords from expropriation; and the Irish Party on getting free from English mismanagement. The subsequent sweeping reductions of rent in the Land Courts show, as Hammond observed,[3] that the case of the Irish peasantry was just enough. The murder and rapine that the champions of the people failed to stop, called loudly for the preservation of law and order. The failure of Gladstone's remedies of ten years before invited the criticism that the English had no talent for the governance of Ireland.

In times deranging to that 'really historical consideration' of the Irish case, for which Gladstone earnestly appealed to Hartington in 1885,[4] there is often a tendency in the public to seek a short road to decision through the medium of old saws or smart sayings. Many people, accustomed to the law of contract as it existed in England, doubtless felt that Palmerston's all too characteristic epigram to the effect that tenant-right was landlord's wrong did all the thinking that was necessary.

[1] The memory of Arnold Toynbee is perpetuated in the East End settlement which bears his name, Toynbee Hall.
[2] The reader will find a sympathetic account of the case in Hammond's *Gladstone and the Irish Nation*, pp. 322-3.
[3] ibid. p. 180.   [4] ibid., p. 405.

The essential need was to insure compensation to the tenant if, owing to hard times, he had failed to pay his rent. This case the Act of 1870 had not envisaged, unless the rent could be regarded as 'exorbitant'; nor was Forster, the Irish Secretary, disposed to take steps which in his view must render all rent capricious. Ultimately, however, the puzzled Minister gave way, only to find the House of Lords taking up his first position and rejecting the measure. Crime, meanwhile, was increasing under the encouragement given it by Parnell. This was the time when Capt. Boycott, Lord Erne's agent, added a word to the language by finding himself abandoned by all his staff, the kind of punishment Parnell had explicitly advised in dealing with political opponents being meted out to him. The English were at their wits' end what to do. In the circumstances Forster resorted to a new Coercion Act, which put it within the power of the Irish executive to clap into prison without trial any person suspected of treason or of agrarian crime until the end of September 1882. No one with English traditions could like such a measure; and Salisbury, leading the Conservative Party in the Lords, disliked it perhaps as much as any man outside Ireland.[1]

The history of that time, far too complicated for an essayist even to survey at all adequately, gives the idea of an almost indescribable confusion of mind and policies. Some phrases that survive preserve, however, the memory of its tension. These were the days when John Bright, though a supporter of coercion in the Cabinet, declared that 'force was no remedy'. These were the days when the same Minister used the term 'prairie value' to bring home the state of a tenement, stripped of all tenants' improvements. These were the days when Gladstone, rigid economist though he was, banished political economy to Saturn, after Professor Bonamy Price[2] had proposed to maintain it in Ireland. These were the days when, just before Parnell's confinement in Kilmainham Gaol, Gladstone announced at Leeds that 'the resources of civilization were not exhausted'. And these, too, were the days when the Speaker of the House of Commons—Brand—confronted by Parnell's policy of interminable obstruction won golden opinions by extricating the House from a hitherto unknown dilemma by introducing from the Chair the closure of debate.

Other circumstances arose to swell the tide of confusion. The Bessborough Commission, to Gladstone's astonishment, reported in favour of an acceptance for Ireland of what were known as the 'Three Fs.'—fair rent, fixity of tenure and free sale; and in the same month there appeared the Minority

---

[1] See his *Life*, by Lady Gwendolen Cecil, Vol. III, p. 43.

[2] Bonamy Price was Drummond Professor of Political Economy at Oxford, 1868-1880 and served on the Duke of Richmond's Commission on agriculture. Gladstone said of him that he was the only man who had the resolution to apply 'in all their unmitigated authority, the principles of political economy to the people of Ireland as if he had been proposing to legislate for the inhabitants of Jupiter or Saturn'.

Report of the Richmond Commission—a commission which had been set up by the Beaconsfield administration, to its credit, to study agricultural conditions generally—recommending much the same policy, with all the emphasis that could be added to it by the subscription of the name of Carlingford, who, as Fortescue, had had a great deal to say to Gladstone's discredited Land Act of 1870. Gladstone very wisely yielded to this consensus of expert opinion; and the result was the Irish Land Act of 1881, to which Gladstone's official biography encourages the critic to give the first place among his legislative achievements.[1]

The Prime Minister, when he started ten years before to deal with the Irish Question, had known little about it; nor indeed did he ever know much from personal observation of Ireland, which he only visited once in his life (in 1877) and for three weeks only.[2] But his wonderful intellect, excelling in concentration, enabled him to acquire a great mastery of the Irish problem; and, though by 1880 he had passed the psalmist's classic climacteric of three score years and ten, nobody questioned his ability, even if, perhaps, his wisdom, in dealing with the main preoccupation of his thoughts.

All parties to the bitter struggle of the 'eighties of last century were on the alert to suspect the worst of their opponents; and plausible theories were readily advanced to prove a lack of scruple in men who would have been as certainly blamed if they had failed to explore every possibility of settlement that offered itself. The Irish members after 1879 and under Parnell's guidance ceased, indeed, to play the political game with that regard for the dignity of Parliament that had characterized the nobler leadership of Isaac Butt;[3] and this fact conditioned all attemps to meet them on their own ground. Consequently, when in 1882 Parnell was released from prison, into which some six months earlier Forster, the Irish Secretary, had thrust him without any form of trial, or of a term of detention under the powers of coercion of which the Gladstonian administration had lately been ill-advised enough to possess itself, the liberation invited attention. A bargain, giving the Irish leader his freedom in return for the assumption by England of the arrears of debt incurred by impecunious Irish tenants, and possibly, too, for some aid in working the new Land Act, was suspected. Belief in this so-called 'Kilmainham Treaty' can derive some support from Parnell's suppression in a letter he read aloud to the House of Commons of a passage about working with the Liberal Party;[4] from Hartington's admission that probably the affair, though no pledge was given, had assumed in the end 'something of the character of a negotiation';[5] and from Balfour's rash overstatement that

---

[1] Morley, *Life of Gladstone*, Vol. III, p. 56.
[2] Hammond, *Gladstone and the Irish Nation*, p. 159.
[3] Isaac Butt was leader of the Irish Parliamentary party before Parnell.
[4] Hammond, *Gladstone and the Irish Nation*, p. 288.
[5] ibid., p. 287.

it stands in our political and parliamentary history 'alone in its infamy'.[1] To such a height of suspicion and hatred could party feeling rouse the Conservatives. The Liberals discovered little more in respect of political charity After the fall of Gladstone's administration, under the united weight of the surrender in South Africa on the morrow of Majuba, of the death of Gordon at Khartoum, and of a tension in Ireland, so alarming that John Morley quotes 'an Irishman of consummate experience and equitable mind' as saying to him that in 1882 Ireland had seemed 'literally a society on the eve of dissolution',[2] suspicions of political intrigue shifted to the short-lived Salisbury administration of 1885–6 where Carnarvon, as Viceroy of Ireland, made for himself by his charm and temerity such a position as had not probably been enjoyed by by anyone since Fitzwilliam in 1795. Flushed by success and haunted by the seeming insolubility of the Irish problem, Carnarvon went on to explore the question further by means of a private meeting, proposed by Parnell, in London. To that interview Salisbury assented with no particular enthusiasm and on the assumption, afforded him by Carnarvon, that Ashbourne, the Irish Lord Chancellor, would be present.[3] To his 'dismay', however, the presence of this third party was in the event dispensed with; and two different accounts of what passed at the interview were given by Parnell and Carnarvon. The latter, though Carnarvon seems to have done all a man could to make it clear that he spoke only for himself, was alleged by Parnell to have offered him, on behalf of his Conservative colleagues, an Irish Legislature in Dublin. This pledge neither the Prime Minister, whose line on Home Rule had been steadily negative, nor the Cabinet, which did not even hear of the supposed offer until in June 1886 Parnell announced the fact across the floor of the House of Commons, had authorized Carnarvon to give. The student of history, having first taken into account that Carnarvon was the soul of honour and that Parnell, whatever he may deserve to be called, could never, in view of the details afforded by the subsequent O'Shea divorce case, be styled that, can take his choice which of the two men he prefers to believe. Herbert Paul, the Liberal historian, inclines to credit Parnell's story. 'Whatever responsibility', he adds, 'Lord Carnarvon incurred, was shared by Lord Salisbury in the fullest degree.'[4] Against any such complete participation Carnarvon, however, himself bears witness. 'I informed you', he writes to Salisbury, 'of my intended interview with Parnell before it took place and, though you urged me, most properly, to be extremely cautious in all that I might say, you did not, as head of the Government, interpose to prevent the meeting.'[5] This is obviously a very different instruction than a charge to

[1] Hammond, *Gladstone and the Irish Nation*, p. 290.
[2] Morley, *Life of Gladstone*, Vol. III, p. 70.
[3] Lady Gwendolen Cecil's *Life of Salisbury*, Vol. III, p. 157.
[4] *History of Modern England*, Vol. V, p. 7.
[5] Quoted from Salisbury's *Life*, Vol. III, p. 158.

make Parnell an offer of Home Rule. Had the Prime Minister refused to allow the Viceroy even to explore the ground with the Irish Leader, every hostile historian would have dwelt on his supposed Conservative bias against so much as looking into the Irish case. Salisbury, refusing in a later letter to so old and intimate a friend as Carnarvon, to enter 'on the dangerous path of Cabinet revelations' observes 'if all I had said was known, no one could suggest that I coquetted with Home Rule'.[1]

There, perhaps, the obscure relationship of the Conservatives and the Irish in that critical autumn of 1885 is best left. No one saw clearly; everyone was more or less waiting upon opportunity and upon developments. All that seems certain is that the three party leaders, whilst all alike disinclined to show their hands, were reaching strong conclusions. Parnell's hopes of playing off his two opponents against one another and snatching from them for Ireland the prize of a successfully engineered auction were rising. Salisbury's mind was, if possible, strengthening in the view that the Union must be at all costs preserved and the Protestant minority in Ireland protected. And Gladstone's belief was growing that some sort of local legislature in Dublin would have to be conceded, if the Irish problem was ever to be solved at all. His wish was undoubtedly that this concession might be made by the Conservative and Liberal Parties acting together. Only a year before the country had seen the unfamiliar sight of the party leaders consulting in private at the Queen's request for an agreed settlement of the proposed new franchise for Great Britain, giving in effect household suffrage in the counties, and for a concurrent, drastic redistribution of seats; and in this negotiation Salisbury had to some eyes assumed the rôle of the innovator and Gladstone that of the conservative. It was not, then, altogether unreasonable to hope that something of the same sort might come to pass in respect of Irish affairs.

Internal differences in the Liberal Party were, meanwhile, rendering Gladstone's policy of delay more difficult. The Whig element under Hartington, who would have no truck with Home Rule, was pulling one way: the Radical, not to call it Socialist, element under Joseph Chamberlain, with his politics at that time embracing a so-called 'unauthorized' programme, was pulling another.

Into an atmosphere thus charged with electricity soared, just before the Christmas of 1885, what became known as 'the Hawarden Kite'. The General Election of a few weeks before had given the Liberals a majority over the Conservatives of 82[2]—a majority owing more to the new agricultural voter,

---

[1] *Life*, Vol. III, p. 161.
[2] I take the figure from Dr. Gooch's *Annals of Politics and Culture*, p. 444; but some slight difference of reckoning will be found, if other authorities, e.g. Morley's *Gladstone* (Vol. III, p. 25), are consulted.

much taken as he was at the time with the idea of 'three acres and a cow', than to the enfranchised townsman of an earlier date. The eighty-five Irish representatives could approximately, therefore, cancel out the Liberal advantage; and, when Herbert Gladstone, without his father's concurrence, let fly 'the Hawarden Kite' through conversations with the editor of the *Leeds Mercury* on December 15th and with the National Press Agency on December 16th, the excitement of the political world rose to fever-heat. It was in vain that Gladstone made it known that the announcement of his conversion to Home Rule was no more than a speculation published without his authority. Nothing but a plain denial would in the circumstances serve; and that, he was too far gone towards Home Rule to give. He had, in fact, within the knowledge of his intimates, and of course of Herbert Gladstone, been moving towards the Home Rule solution of the Irish problem for some time; and rumour was ruthless as when in Virgil's immortal lines[1] it sped with gathering strength through the cities of Libya; her feet still trampling the earth, her head buried in the clouds, she played havoc with Gladstone's reputation. I find with regret some reflection of that *monstrum horrendum ingens*, in the too confident observation, reminiscent probably of some generally credited report at the time, in Lady Gwendolen Cecil's *Life* of her father,[2] that Parnell had visited Hawarden in that critical autumn of 1885; whereas all the evidence goes to show that he went there first in December 1889, just four years later.[3] This, like the story that Gladstone went to the theatre on the night he received the news of Gordon's death at Khartoum, appears to be a legend of contemporary manufacture to which no credence whatever should be attached.

If Lecky was right in supposing that the ultimate verdict of history on Gladstone's character would be based upon his conduct at this period, then everything asserted of it deserves as close an examination as the allegations that led to the writing of Newman's *Apologia*. His mind, like Newman's, was too subtle in its operation to be understood by the plain man; and he was, moreover, reaching conclusions from two sets of premises—a fact that in a way he realized, when he diagnosed the movement of his thought as one from a faith in authority to a growing belief in liberty.[4] It is this double conviction—this reverence for old institutions underlying a readiness to welcome change, after the manner of Hegel, as an evolution into greater freedom—that gives its significance to the Liberalism of his time, which was in reality a very transient thing and, to a degree seldom admitted, dependent on his peculiar character and personality. Behind Gladstone lay Whiggery, with its embodiment in Hartington; before him a Radicalism that could

---

[1] *Æn.*, Vol. IV., Chap. 11 pp. 173–198.   [2] Vol. III, p. 282.
[3] See Morley's *Life of Gladstone*, Vol. III, p. 420, and Hammond's *Gladstone and the Irish Nation*, p. 438.   [4] Morley, *Life*, Vol. II, p. 179.

only eventuate in a prolongation of Chamberlain's views into Socialism. He alone had the credentials for leading the Liberal Party. As Morley observes: 'One of the strangest things in Mr. Gladstone's career and growth is (the) unconscious raising of a partially Rousseauite structure on the foundations laid by Burke. . . .'[1] There is nothing surprising, then, in finding among the entries in his diary for December 18th 1885, and for the early days of the following January (that is, during those very days we have just recalled, when 'the Hawarden Kite' soared into the sky and all England was agog with speculation) what political philosopher had primacy of place in Gladstone's thoughts at that time: 'December 18—Read Burke; what a magazine of wisdom on Ireland and America. January 9—Made many extracts from Burke—sometimes almost divine.' John Morley, lest the reader should regard these extracts as extravagant, reminds us that Macaulay had written in *his* diary 'I have now finished reading again most of Burke's works. Admirable! The greatest man since Milton'.[2]

It was, I suppose, that underlying sympathy with Burke's outlook on life which enabled Salisbury to say later of Gladstone in words of generous praise that his had been 'the most brilliant intellect ever devoted to the service of the State since Parliamentary Government began'.[3] For all that, he did not carry the best English intellect of the time with him. That sort of 'aristocracy', as Herbert Paul points out,[4] was in the main opposed to him. Lecky, Froude, Seeley and Goldwin Smith; Spencer and Jowett and Martineau; Huxley and Tyndall; Tennyson and Browning; even Swinburne—all these, though of Liberal leanings, were against him. They set more store by keeping the British Isles united than by satisfying the major fraction of the Irish people, 'nationalists' though they were.

There the critic might be glad to end, if he could, a tale already overburdened with the weight of the chance and change attending a life prolonged to three score years and five. But Gladstone could not stop. He had pledged himself to find the solution of the Irish problem; and, when overtures to Arthur Balfour during a visit to Eaton in December 1885 for a non-party settlement of the question proved fruitless, he took office again himself in February 1886. His administration included Joseph Chamberlain, who presided over the Local Government Board, but who resigned before March was out, and in April declared for a federative system in which Ireland was to find a place. Gladstone's Home Rule Bill of 1886, which gave the Irish no seats at Westminster, whilst requiring Ireland to provide a sum amounting to one-twelfth of the British revenue, was defeated in the Commons in June by a majority of thirty. The Prime Minister dissolved—'an old man in a

---

[1] Morley, *Life*, Vol. I, p. 203. [2] ibid., Vol. III, p. 280.
[3] Quoted from Paul's *Modern England*, Vol. V, p. 258.
[4] ibid., Vol. V, p. 57.

hurry', as the famous epigram declared. But the country would not be hurried; and in the July Election the Conservative and Liberal Unionist opponents of Home Rule were returned with a majority of more than a hundred. Gladstone resigned, and, at seventy-seven years of age, retired into the wilderness, his self-imposed mission to settle the Irish problem still unfulfilled. He held on to the leadership of his policy of dis-union whilst his opponents put into practice once again that of coercion. Arthur Balfour, as Irish Secretary, proved an adept at enforcing 'resolute government'; and his courage and dexterity, combined with a certain measure of generosity, eventually won some recognition even from his opponents. Parnell, as John Morley remarks, 'knew and often said that of course strong coercion must always in the long run win the day'.[1] Gradually Balfour, wise enough to temper justice with grace, gained ground; and, as he gained it, Gladstone lost it. Still *The Times*, by fighting the famous law-suit over 'Parnellism and Crime', gave some aid to Parnell, against whom it was felt that evil had been too readily believed.[2] The O'Shea case, however, more than drove back this current of opinion. The full facts of the matter were not, indeed, yet available; but it is doubtful whether, even had they been known, the 'Church' in Ireland or the 'Nonconformist' conscience in England would have given Parnell's politics their blessing. Anyhow, Gladstone's course seemed clear. The rump of the Liberal Party under his leadership could not ally itself with the Irish Nationalists under Parnell. In the circumstances the Irishmen, on Gladstone's representations, split their forces; and he came back to power in 1892 with a majority of forty behind him. It was enough to enable him to introduce another Home Rule Bill, under which the Irish would have been represented at Westminster; but it was not enough to enable him both to carry it through the Commons and compel the Lords to bow to their verdict. He was eighty-two; he had not got England and Scotland behind him; Great Britain remained beyond doubt 'the predominant partner' in the Union of Great Britain and Ireland; and his appeal to the sentiment of nationality did not meet that of the then Argyll, when he spoke of the cabins of Antrim aglow with the light of the setting sun, as they might be perceived from the west of Scotland, and claimed that his country and that of Ireland, thus seen, *mutatis mutandis*, from the opposite coast, were united by a proximity which no minority could overrule. It was felt that the action of the Lords in throwing out the Home Rule Bill of 1893 had spoken for the British Isles. Gladstone,

---

[1] Morley, *Life of Gladstone*, Vol. III, p. 369.

[2] In 1888 Frank Hugh O'Donnell, a Parnellite M.P., brought an action for libel against *The Times* arising out of charges made against the Irish members in that newspaper for a series of articles published under the title 'Parnellism and Crime'. He lost his action, largely because Sir Richard Webster, Counsel for *The Times* produced a number of inflammatory letters alleged to have been written by Parnell. The letters were obtained from an Irish journalist named Pigott, who afterwards declared that they were forgeries, though he subsequently reiterated that they were genuine. Pigott fled the country and committed suicide.

with all his greatness and fighting to the last with rare skill and temerity, had
lost the game for any time he could look forward to.

Home Rule, it is true, came at last, but in circumstances and on conditions
to which its great Scottish champion (for Scotch he was) would have hated
to yield. He had lived and laboured only to lose at the end the confidence of
his countrymen and what seemed, if possible, sadder, that of the Crown.
The Queen had not always disliked him. Kindly tributes to him are scattered
among her letters. But a sound instinct told her that his policy tended towards
the disintegration of her Empire. We know now that, when Gordon was
killed, she wired to him at Holker *en clair* 'You have murdered Gordon.
Victoria'.[1] And, when he resigned on March 3rd 1894, she was too honest
to feign regret or to find any pretty speech with which to ease the parting.
He had utterly lost her love and had to forgo her gratitude. He felt it
keenly, for none of her Ministers had desired to serve her more loyally than
he. The event is not merely pathetic, but has in it all the making of tragedy.
Perhaps, as has already been suggested, if he had followed his more oecumenical impulse in 1874 and devoted the remainder of his days to the
apologetic of Christendom, he would have satisfied the needs of the next
century better than by promoting 'nationalism' in these islands and giving
it countenance all the world over. No man of his race and allegiance had
anything like the power to put the political case for Christianity; and no man,
perhaps, cared for it more or could have pressed home the cosmic argument
for it with a richer eloquence of conviction. The actual resignation, according
to the account of it that has recently been made public[2] from Rosebery's
memoranda, lacked all the grace of parting. Gladstone's colleagues could not
subdue their emotion; and Gladstone himself, a true Victorian in this appears
to have disliked this absence of restraint, to have responded coldly to it, and
to have spoken of his too susceptible colleagues ever after as 'the blubbering
Cabinet'. Gladstone lived on a few years, tasting again the joy of old friendships and the delight of familiar foreign travel. Presently he found himself on
the Riviera at Lord Rendel's villa. There Victoria sent for him to come and
see her at Cimiez. He noticed that she gave him her hand, a thing which in all
his experience she had never done before. Yet he found her changed; and
much of the old vitality was wanting. The sands were, indeed, fast running
out—for him even more swiftly than for her. It was the winter of 1897. He
was to reach the May of the following year. Rosebery and John Morley
went down to see him at Hawarden. The latter has left a record of the scene
within and the scenery without, which in its contrasting, simple irony has
long seemed to me strangely moving: 'Without a struggle he ceased to
breathe. Nature outside—wood and wide lawn and cloudless far-off sky—
shone at her fairest.'

[1] See a letter in the *Daily Telegraph* of April 18th 1950.
[2] In *History To-Day*, January 1952 *Mr. Gladstone's Last Cabinet*, Part II.

LORD ROSEBERY

ARCHIBALD JOHN PHILIP PRIMROSE,
5th EARL OF ROSEBERY
born 1847 died 1929

Entered House of Lords on succession to the title in 1868

Under-Secretary for the Home Office (Gladstone's administration) 1881. Resigned 1883

Lord Privy Seal (second Gladstone administration) 1885

Foreign Secretary (third Gladstone administration) 1886

Foreign Secretary (fourth Gladstone administration) 1892 to 1894

Prime Minister 1894 to 1895

CHAPTER XII

LORD ROSEBERY

THE official life of Lord Rosebery published in 1931 fell into the world of books at an acceptable, if not in every respect a fortunate time. The society that it recalls, not less than the statesman that it portrays, is admirably calculated to afford all the pleasures of contrast to those who desire to exchange, even though only in review, the spectacle of an England war-torn and weary for that of an England easy-going, prosperous, and confident of strength, or to hear, even though only through the medium of the printed page, voices of an eloquence more subtle and suggestive than that to which, with Democracy now blowing at full blast, our ears have grown familiar. The rugged grandeur of our present stage and the size of our contemporary actors are replaced by smiling scenery and statesmen equal to their situation. Our parents, it is true, distracted overmuch by the presence in the background of a proper complement of villains, idiots, and buffoons, skulking, gibbering, and jesting—though no more, and perhaps even less, than at any other time in history—scarcely rated at its correct value this aspect of the political drama of their time. Yet for us it stands out, witnessing to a tradition of Parliamentary government so finished that, if finality were part of our lot, the institutions of that period might well have seemed final, but, change being inherent in political as well as in other concerns, suggesting rather the melancholy reflection that climax is the sure forerunner of decline.

Two statesmen illustrate to a pre-eminent degree this elegance of the late Victorian and Edwardian periods—both of them Lowland Scots born within little more than a year of one another (and that year the famous 'year of revolution'); both of them Etonians; both of them young men of capacity undiscovered by academic honours; both of them men of means and leisure and influential connections; both largely shaped for political life by the study of Macaulay's *Essays*; and both very definitely pushed forward by the interest of highly-placed personages, in one instance the Prime Minister, in the other the Queen; both of them destined to become foreign secretaries of merely modest achievement and prime ministers so transient and embarrassed that in each case the immortal *capax imperii, nisi imperasset* rises to the lips; both making their major contribution to the constitutional history of their country by their respective shares in the creation of the Committee of Imperial Defence; and both, to conclude, challenging comparison with any of their contemporaries as the most interesting and—to attach a French meaning to an English word—'intriguing' men of their generation.

There, however, the tempting parallel terminates. Lord Balfour and Lord Rosebery, illustrating in common the peculiar, finished perfection of their age, differed as much as any two men of shining ability, with their heads turned in the same direction and with the world from the first at their feet, could well be expected to do. The cool dialectic of the one lies no nearer to the gorgeous rhetoric of the other than the Poles to the Equator; nor does Lord Balfour's philosophic regard for fine ideas compare more easily with Lord Rosebery's humanistic admiration for remarkable people than the serene mind of Prospero with the bruised and brooding soul of Hamlet. As it was with both men at the core, so also on the surface. Whilst the one was clad in a coat of light, impenetrable mail, the other had nothing but the thinnest of thin skins to oppose to the slings and arrows of fortune. No one knew his own advantage better than Lord Balfour. Nothing, he declared, would induce him, if he were Lord Rosebery, to remain in political life, since it meant being made miserable twice in the day—when the papers came in the morning, and when they re-appeared at night. Rosebery noted the same fact about himself, but with the aid of a more dubious terminology. In his latest days he marked down pride as his master-failing. Hamlet—for it is to the character of Hamlet that his son-in-law and biographer, Lord Crewe, rightly points as the clue to this investigation—had similarly thrown it into prominent relief in the course of that strange conversation with Ophelia where the light of self-analysis is flashed into other obscure recesses not to be overlooked in the study of complex natures. Yet pride in the proper sense was no more Rosebery's prevailing weakness than what we call a proper pride was his prevailing virtue. Pride as the last solemn sentence upon a career is the property of the fallen Archangel, of the Lost Apostle—at least, as Rubens depicted him in that absorbing portrait in the Brera which contrasts so oddly with Leonardo's more famous but meaner conception of him hard by—and of all the troop of souls who fall either to some dark grandeur of defiance or to the final silence of despair. A lesser, lighter word meets Rosebery's case.

It is perhaps enough to say that Rosebery was profoundly sensitive as he was preposterously self-conscious and that in all his self-regard there was to all appearance no disposition either towards that mystical losing of life which is identified on the highest authority with the finding of the soul or towards that bold losing of the soul which is symbolized in the Faustian pact with Evil. Nevertheless, as his most elaborated writings show, it was precisely natures capable of such things that most deeply stirred his curiosity— Chatham, who could sublimely merge his own being in that of his country; Napoleon, who could observe that to a man like himself the lives of a million

THE EARL OF ROSEBERY
From a photograph by Elliott & Fry

of men were of no account. Here were subjects which the artist in Rosebery
had the skill to depict, but the statesman in him no strength to emulate,
divided from them as he was, obviously enough, by a vast inferiority of
power and purpose. A moment's reflection, indeed, is enough to show us
that, not in majestic performance, but in the pathetic failure to perform, lies,
at any rate for us, the supreme interest of his personality; and thus are we
forced back upon the thought of Hamlet. Beyond doubt he was of Hamlet's
school; a man of infinite mood and much hesitation, conscious both of the
lure of opportunity and the vanity of attainment, possessed of brilliant talent
and penetrating insight, yet bringing no fruit to perfection; subtly whim-
sical; fond of incisive jest; irritable, incalculable, autocratic, alarming, and
yet in turn abundant, if he pleased, in charm and courtesy; responsive to the
swift thrill of the racecourse, yet moved beyond measure by the tears of
things, so that we may catch him gravely comparing the departure of his
schoolboy sons at the opening of the Lent term to the parting of Louis Seize
with his family at the same season of the year, or surprise him making a sudden visit to Birmingham to look the last upon the face of Newman and,
overcome by the romance of the 'strange, brilliant, incomparable end' of
one who had begun life in such different surroundings, paying his homage
to the dead Cardinal with a kiss.

To paint the portrait of so subtle and versatile a being was not an easy
undertaking, and where the son-in-law was the biographer the task presented
features of peculiar difficulty. The great example of Lockhart proves indeed
what can be done from this unique angle of vision; only Lockhart had the
luck to be dealing, not only with one of the most lovable of men, but with
a man still in love with life, even in life's decline and after fortune's failure.
Pleasure and pathos, joy and its sister, sorrow, blend in truth in the story of
Scott so as to give the teller every conceivable assistance. But of Rosebery's
life his biographer warns, almost in the last words of the envoy, that it
would be untrue to state that it was very happy. Gifts and graces seemed,
indeed, to be his in more—much more—than common measure; yet something was plainly lacking, and for that something, through all the passage of
Lord Crewe's book, we, not incurious, search. Crewe, indeed, was satisfied
to let him remain 'when all is said and done . . . something of an enigma to
those who knew him best'. Yet a riddle requires to be read, though a relation
is not perhaps always the readiest reader.

To suggest that Rosebery's biography does not achieve that vivid, gradually unfolding, finally illuminating revelation of its subject by close companionship, which is the genius of Lockhart's work and Boswell's, which
Morley tried for in his *Gladstone* but perhaps failed to get, and of which a
modest example is afforded by Festing Jones's life of Samuel Butler, is not to
affirm a failure. As Wilfrid Ward used to maintain, there is an objective as

well as a subjective element in the art of biography; and the biographer must first make sure of such a portrait as every one will recognize and every one consent to, before he dare attempt that subtler study of his subject, as seen particularly by himself. Crewe painted this indispensable likeness, and painted it with just such distinction as might be expected from him—with scholarly allusions befitting his father's son, with a knowledge of the great world born of long acquaintance, with an understanding of political situations enriched by experience of what Bacon calls 'great place', with the wisdom of one upon whom there had been set the choicest mark of an English diplomatic career. The book in a word was a work of piety, weightily authenticated and warily discharged.

It is probable, however, that another hand will some day attempt a slighter, bolder sketch; and it is possible that, when that attempt is made, chronology will be less exclusively considered. Science teaches us—or taught us till lately—that we come nearer to the heart of reality by seeking a dimension that is neither that of time nor space, but compounded of them both. In the notion of the 'interval' a student may find some analogy to the best expression of biographical truth and some comprehension of the particular difficulties of biographical art. Between the minutes, hours, days, months, and years, 'passing over to the end they were created' and measuring with steady beat the passage of the individual through time, and that spacing of larger issues which, like the incidents of Towton field, breaks in upon the sensuous life of men, and most of all of statesmen, it is no easy matter to establish any just relation. And least easy is it when the individual life embodies in addition all the interest of the Hamlet-motif—all the interest of a mind, not merely buffeted by fate, but tormented by conscience or its self-conscious shadow, and cursing the spite which has mingled the process of the intellectual soul with the play of forces beyond its power to guide.

Drama alone, it may be, is adequate to deal with the character and career of one who was not last nor least an actor—drama, that is to say, which would give us not merely dramatic treatment, but dramatic distance. An official biographer can but intermittently afford to remember that the play's the thing; and Crewe stood very close to his subject. Let the piece be staged, and the spectator in the auditorium will see both less and more.

In this manner of presentation the curtain would rise, not as is generally the case with English political biography upon a scene of family life, but of national circumstance. No spreading pedigree nor table of descent would meet our eyes, but just a tableau of the Court of Victoria in the early 'sixties with 'those two dreadful old men' of the Queen's correspondence standing like supporters beside the throne. Behind Russell and Palmerston would be seen the figures of Gladstone and Disraeli. The piece, in other words, would open with the last Whig Ministry in power and Democracy, both Liberal and Tory-democratic, awaiting its dissolution. Then, after this stage-effect, there would enter in due course the hero—well-named 'Prince Charming'[1] —privilege in his bearing, distinction in his speech, largess in his hands. Is he, as we say, 'too late for the fair', or will the political markets delay to close in face of that engaging presence, that brilliant address, that, at least potentially, well-filled purse? He wants, said one watching him, 'the palm without the dust'. Was he to have it, as not a few had done, by virtue of talent alone? And there's the play!

Through his mother's second marriage with the Duke of Cleveland[2] and the extensive hospitalities of Raby, the young Rosebery became acquainted at an early age with the rising political protagonists. They seemed curiously calculated to appeal to a nature, of which the elements were strangely mixed, and to a mind, already signalled by the ever-memorable William Cory as possessed of the finest combination of qualities that he had ever come across. No boy with histrionic tastes could fail to appreciate a meeting with Disraeli, nor a boy of religious, not to speak of political, disposition, a meeting with Gladstone; and Rosebery was a little theatrical and more than a little religious.

Spangled with all the glories of 'Pop' and a star performer in its debates, the young Etonian walked in the great park of Raby besides the eminent Hebrew statesman and talked of Corn Laws and of kings, of great speeches in Parliament, and doubtless of other matters also. The two got on capitally, but, as Mrs. Disraeli, of whose singular, sometimes very singular, conversation there appears to be some record in the young man's diary, informed the boy the evening after, the elder had not failed to remark that his companion was a Whig. He might, perhaps, have added that the old Whig Ministry was gone or going, and that it was no time for young Whigs to be born.

Rosebery's particular cast of political thought had been of interest not only to accomplished statesmen. An uncle of mine, who was his fag-master at Eton, used to tell the story of a schoolboy-conversation in which the future Liberal Leader was subjected to the ignominy of being assured by the lineal heir of Lord Eldon that he was no more a Liberal than his interlocutor. The accused, according to the report of the accuser, could find no better reply than to admit the justice of the impeachment, but extenuated its effect by pleading that he had a better chance on the Liberal side. Cynicism at school, and for some while after, is not, of course, a faith, but a fashion; and besides, if one is rudely ambushed, one must be allowed the free use of methods of escape. But, if Rosebery had wanted to meet the charge with

---

[1] I have borrowed the name from Mr. A. G. Gardiner's *Life of Sir William Harcourt*.
[2] Lord Rosebery's mother was Catherine, daughter of the 4th Earl of Stanhope and great-niece of William Pitt. After the death of Lord Rosebery's father in 1850 she married the 4th Duke of Cleveland.

proper solemnity, he should have answered, as Disraeli answered for him, that he was neither a Tory nor a Liberal, but precisely a Whig.

The Whigs were—for they are now, alas, for practical purposes extinct— a peculiar people, though doubtless, as Lady Frances Balfour rejoined when Lord Balfour taunted her with the charge, 'zealous of good works'. Their peculiarity, indeed, lay precisely in the fact that they were tenacious at once of their social privileges and their political philanthropies, that they wanted to be perennially eminent and at the same time perpetually benevolent. The difficulty here is obvious enough. The contents of every purse are eventually expended; and a long series of *beaux gestes* and electoral benefactions will exhaust the finest inheritance. When Lord John Russell announced political 'finality' it was plain that the resources of the Whigs were running out; and, when Lord Russell died, the Whig purse was all but empty. Yet Whigs, if Whigs they were to remain, must still be giving; for their philosophy was based upon popularity and not, as with the Tories, upon function and degree. Disraeli, seeing their weakness, accused them, as every reader of his novels knows, of being no better than a Venetian oligarchy, and tried to revive the old direct connection of the Crown and the people which the Whig Revolution of 1688 had impaired and George III, in conformity with the ideas of Bolingbroke's *Patriot King*, had temporarily and unskilfully restored. Within a year or so, in fact, of his conversation at Raby with young Rosebery, Disraeli contrived to pass the Tory-Democratic Reform Bill of 1867. This stroke of statecraft, unhealthy in its incidental accompaniments, resulted in the dishing, and ultimately in the death of the Whigs. They became a picturesque but moribund survival; the Liberals took over their inheritance; while the bog-oak of Ireland eventually supplied them with a coffin.

It is, however, the fortunes of Rosebery, not the fate of the Whigs, that we have to follow. What merits notice is that the Whig in his blood caused him to miss the Tory in Tory-Democracy. In that admirable monograph of his on Lord Randolph Churchill, which Lord Crewe places high among his writings, both for charm and symmetry, he finds the Tory-democratic idea, after much critical examination, no better than a base amalgam of conservative men and liberal measures. Doubtless it lends itself effectively enough to this damaging analysis. Yet, for all that, there is in this cavalier treatment of it some lack of philosophical penetration. For in the last resort this at first sight self-stultifying creed rests upon the notion that Democracy, or English Democracy at all events, had not fallen out of love with the principle of honour. 'Man', Sidonia warns Coningsby in some memorable words, 'is born to adore and to obey'; and to the Liberal doctrine of *la carrière ouverte aux talents* Toryism opposes a less coldly rational, perhaps we might say more actually cordial conception of civic life, dominated from top to bottom by the courteous principles of place and function and the graceful

precept of *noblesse oblige*. Tory-Democracy was in its way an attempt—a not
wholly unsuccessful attempt—to retain or recover for the enfranchised
populace a world of romance, of duty, and of vision; and when we have
laughed to our hearts' content at all Randolph Churchill's quaint chivalry,
careering as knights and dames and what-not along their primrose way,
when we have observed with all the required Radical acidity of soul that
England dearly loves a lord and Englishmen more dearly still to be belorded,
when if so we please, we have recalled Rosebery's own vigorous attack upon
the Royal Titles Act of 1875, and have refused in spirit to assist the imagination of three hundred million Indians by the creation of an Imperial overlord,
we may yet be compelled to confess that, human nature being as it is, and the
British people what they are, the Tory inheritance was really more adaptable
to new conditions than the Whig.

Whiggery, if the truth be told, as it has been told by Prof. Butterfield in a
remarkable essay,[1] rested upon a version of history too lightly accepted.
That essay must speak for itself. Its postulate, in Mr. Butterfield's words, is
that 'when we organize our general history by reference to the present we are
producing what is really a gigantic optical illusion', and its argument is that
the Whigs did so organize their historical studies. Political, not to speak of
religious, liberty became with them a magnificent gesture made in the stately
homes of England by persons whose opulence and enlightenment afforded
to their fellow-citizens the direction and discipline without which these
latter, to quote Burke's frank exposition of the matter, 'can scarcely be said
to be in civil society'.

That Lord Rosebery drew his political temperament from the victorious
Whigs of the English Revolution will never be in doubt amongst those
who have noticed the infinite patience with which he unravels the intrigues
and dissects the characters of the Whig society that beset the path of
Chatham. His book upon the early life and connections of that famous man
is, indeed, the least of his important works; and Crewe, unmindful of Basil
Williams's biography, unwarrantably excused its lack of power and perspective by observing that 'Chatham's *Life* has never been written at full
length'. The mark of the Whig is, however, as subtly and as surely stamped
upon its pages as upon Rosebery's deliberate acquisition at a later date of the
earldom of Midlothian for, apparently, no graver reason than a wish to
prevent so distinguished a style from being adopted by some undistinguished
person.

If the 'Chatham' book discovers the trend of Rosebery's disposition, the
little volume, earlier published, upon the younger Pitt reveals the process of
his reflection. The Whig idea of history, as Mr. Butterfield would doubtless
point out to us, is indeed there perceptible enough—as, for instance, in the

[1] H. Butterfield, *The Whig Interpretation of History*.

casual comparison of Luther and Fox, and the loose sentiment for a liberty that means little, if it be not left undefined—yet, behind it, can be detected the presence of a judgment largely emancipated from party considerations. It is a high point of interest in Crewe's biography that this aspect of the 'Pitt' is placed beyond a doubt. In a letter to a mother whose Stanhope descent[1] may, perhaps, have caused her to fix too vigilant an eye upon her son's political vagaries, Rosebery alludes with glee to the mistake she had made in supposing that his sympathies, when he wrote, had lain with Fox. They were, he assures her, 'wholly and entirely the other way'.[2]

This is not to say that Rosebery was, as his Eton fag-master had suspected, no more than a veiled Conservative. Pitt, we need to remember, would have called himself, a Whig, and for the possession of Burke's philosophical estate political protagonists do battle even to this day. What the admission shows is that Rosebery's mind marched with that of one whose thoughts were so near the poise of political equilibrium that we may say of him pretty much what we please—that he was, as against North a Whig, as against Fox a Tory, that he was neither in servitude to the English King nor in sympathy with the French Revolution. Pitt—and this, surely is what constitutes the supreme fascination of his career—lived in one of those rare moments of our national life when the patriot soul can take its seat without discomfort upon party benches. Rosebery, to give him his due, was made for such a time as that, but the lot had fallen to him in far different ground.

'To be or not to be'—there precisely for the brilliant young Oxonian, whose love of racehorses had cost him his degree, was in the second act of our imaginary drama the question. Should he content himself with all that two Continents have—or had—to offer to a young peer in fitful pleasure and second-rate success, or should he, as the phrase is, go in for politics, and, if so, under what banner? He hesitated long. He had the chance in 1872 of figuring, though in a very modest capacity, amongst the personnel of Gladstone's first administration; he had the offer a year later of the Lord-Lieutenancy of Linlithgow; he had the Under-Secretaryship at the India Office pressed upon him in 1880. A prey to sensitiveness and hesitation, he declined these various occasions. So brilliant a talent was not, however, to be lightly lost. Mr. Gladstone continued his flattering attentions; and Harcourt, as in face of subsequent developments we do well to observe, was yet more urgent to the same end. 'Rosebery', wrote Sir William to the Prime Minister, 'should join the Government, for all reasons and particularly on the ground of my great personal regard for him.'[3] Eventually in 1881 he was prevailed upon to become Harcourt's Under-Secretary at the Home Office, with particular charge of Scottish affairs. This disposition of business had its inconveniences;

[1] See footnote p. 275. Crewe's *Life of Lord Rosebery*.
[2] ibid., p. 481.   [3] ibid., p. 144.

and Rosebery, as he was fully entitled to do in view of the provisional character that Mr. Gladstone had assigned to it, presently insisted upon an alteration. He carried his point against a body of reluctant colleagues. The creation of a Scottish Office was decided upon; and he was invited, not once but three times, to become its head. It was all in vain. Hamlet had returned to his hesitations. And at this point the curtain drops for the second time.

When the next act opens a figure, already some while visible in the background, is seen to have moved to the front of the stage. It was in 1878—in that great year of his administration—that the most famous Jew of the century assisted at the marriage of Rosebery and Hannah Rothschild. Lady Rosebery was of Disraeli's race; and Disraeli's own marriage had set an example of matrimonial devotion raised upon a similar, if much less magnificent, basis of financial obligation. The bridegroom left the church completely equipped for the rôle of a great Whig magnate with large and liberal ideas: and, for the rest, nothing in his book is more pleasing than Crewe's unqualified tribute to the bride:

'Divine wisdom warns "How hardly shall they that have riches enter into the Kingdom of Heaven"; but if that kingdom is a place into which unkindness, and petty self-love, and lack of charity cannot penetrate, and where only things of good report abound, those who knew Hannah de Rothschild either in her girlhood or through her married years could never doubt that she was one of the happy souls for whom its gates are always standing open. It was indeed a very noble character . . .'

With this character—with its ultimate absence as well as its immediate presence—we have from this time forward to reckon in the survey of Rosebery's career. We catch a not unamusing glimpse of the devoted wife contending with Mrs. Gladstone about the Scottish Office affair; and, again, in relation to her husband's resumption of a post in the Government and admission into the Cabinet, she is to the fore. It was to her that Mrs. Gladstone addressed the warning in 1884 that if Rosebery refused to rejoin the administration, from which he had resigned over a year earlier, he must imperil his political future; it was upon her that the then Prince of Wales impressed his conviction that patriotism might, as things then were, require his old friend to accept the little-esteemed post of First Commissioner of Works. Eventually Rosebery complied, the dignity of Lord Privy Seal being associated with the duties of the First Commissioner. The Government, discredited as it was by differences of policy in Ireland, had little life left when he joined it; and six months later it perished. In those six months, however, assisted to no small degree by a private friendship with the Bismarcks and a tactfully executed visit to Berlin, he acquired both contact with foreign affairs and consideration with the Queen. He greatly impressed those who knew him with his grasp of diplomacy. I have in my possession a letter from J. A. Spender in which he says that, looking back, Rosebery seems to him the one man of his time who understood Europe and the European system. He might have proved powerless to stay the trend of events, but he would at least have seen what it was, and I think he would have been as slow as Salisbury proved to abandon the Victorian or pre-Victorian tradition.

Upon the return in 1886 of the Liberals to power with the Irish vote behind them, foreign affairs underwent a significant change of personnel. Granville, three times Foreign Secretary, had in the end lost caste both with the Queen and the Country, and, as Crewe shrewdly observes, 'in the practical conduct of public life statesmen have to be treated as being what common opinion judges them to be'. Kimberley, acceptable as Foreign Secretary to Gladstone, was unacceptable to the Crown. Rosebery pleased all parties; and according to the Queen, his was 'the only really good appointment' in the administration.

Thus began a relationship between a Sovereign, old even for her age in experience, and a Minister, young, as things were, for his office. It was a relationship that contained for Victoria possibilities of quasi-parental interference and quasi-parental disappointment; but it worked for a time well enough, and had enabled Salisbury, as Lord Crewe conjectures,[1] even as early as 1885, to give valuable assurance both to Germany and Austria that there would be no change in the continuity of British foreign policy, should the Liberals regain power. For of the merits of continuity in the conduct of foreign affairs Rosebery was fully convinced—of a continuity, that is, which satisfied, as he considered that Salisbury's did, the conditions of success. About the actual issues in the Balkans and in Egypt he was agreed with his predecessor; there was no marked difference between their respective attitudes towards France and Russia; and Rosebery, when at a later date he declared that 'you should never put your foot forward further in diplomacy than you can keep it down' was speaking all Salisbury's mind on that crucial test of method. He passed creditably through the ordeal of a six-months' administration and reached, as perhaps one might say, the apex of his fortune, if not yet the crux of his fate. The Queen informed him privately of her contentment; Mr. Gladstone called him publicly 'the man of the future'; and he himself declared that he had 'attained much more than the highest summit of his ambition'.

A change of Government in July 1886 brought with it the partial eclipse of six years in opposition, and when the curtain rises again upon the penultimate act of our drama Rosebery is a widower. The restrained dedication of his monograph upon Pitt enshrines the memory of a grief, tinged as so many of our saddest griefs are tinged by the pity of idle words and lost opportunities. The most intimate letter, however, that finds a place in this biography

[1] Vol. III, p. 224.

reveals what others, more observant, had guessed—the situation beneath the surface. 'I dearly loved my wife', he assured the Queen, 'and our home was happiness itself; but I only now know what I have lost, and each new day represents a new desolation.' Thenceforward, Crewe tells us, 'he remained a lonely man'.

The tragedy of Hamlet, as Andrew Bradley told us half a century ago, turns upon no inherent, ineradicable weakness of will in the hero, but upon the fact that, at the particular conjunction of events which called upon him for the highest energy, the shock of his mother's second marriage had paralyzed his active, and promoted his reflective powers. Something analogous, perhaps, happened to Rosebery when Death struck down untimely the good companion of his days. It was in the autumn that he lost her; and in the spring that followed we catch a glimpse of him walking amidst the gloom and splendour of the Escorial—'the most expressive church', he writes, 'I have ever entered; with its cruel grey granite and its crushing silence . . . the very valley of the shadow of death.' Brief as it is, this swift vision of a stricken spirit against the background of a palace that is all personality, and that personality perhaps the greatest and gloomiest which ever ruled in Spain— of a spirit constrained by suffering to confess its conviction that here stood 'one of the most interesting and wonderful things in the world'—is, perhaps, the most haunting, the most Hamlet-like episode in all the drama of his life.

Then, once again, Rosebery is back in England, and, under the pressure of the aged Prime Minister, of colleagues fearful lest the reins of the premiership should pass into the hands of the rough-riding Harcourt, and of the Prince of Wales, voicing the sentiments of the apprehensive Queen, once more at the Foreign Office. Victoria, it is true, had marked a change in him— a new 'radical', nay, as it seemed to her, 'almost communistic', trend in his speeches—but had found an explanation in the fact that 'poor Lady Rosebery was not there to keep him back'. Yet, even so, he remained the most acceptable of those, to her eye dare-devil, Gladstonians, who in the fifty-fifth year of her reign seemed to be pulling her Empire about her head; and the reprobate was still her candidate as Foreign Secretary. 'You know', she told him—'quite maternally', so he records—'I have always given you good advice.' And the Garter, at Gladstone's suggestion, was given him also.

Pushed forward in this manner by the political parent who counted still so much upon his help, Rosebery found himself in instant conflict with the one-time political sponsor, whose rival for the approaching vacancy in the Liberal leadership he had plainly become. In the character of a Little Englander, on the occasion of trouble in Uganda, Harcourt made plain his opposition to the Foreign Secretary's imperialist leanings so effectively that resignation from office nearly followed upon the heels of acceptance. The matter was, however, compromised; and Rosebery remained to score a modest diplomatic triumph over France in Siam and to contract a strong distrust of French methods all the world over. Then in 1894, some eighteen months later, Gladstone resigned, and the moment arrived for the Queen to claim the price of her continued favour. Circumstances had played into her hands. John Morley, within the last year or so had shifted from Harcourt's side to Rosebery's—a matter mainly of temperament. Two of the most sensitive men in politics had thus joined forces against the most insensitive of politicians. Reluctantly, at least in appearance, and certainly under pressure, Rosebery agreed to form an administration. He had no illusions. The Queen would fall foul of him on account of his views, Harcourt on account of his promotion.

In the event everything went as badly for him as is easily conceivable. Victoria, to judge from the entertaining correspondence that has been made public in her Letters, treated him much like an opinionated schoolboy; and Sir William seized every occasion to make him feel that he was anything but master in his own house. The Queen took vigorous exception to the brave menaces of wrath to come that he addressed to a now predominantly Conservative House of Lords, should it dare to exercise its political judgment in accordance with its constitutional powers; whilst Harcourt as Chancellor of the Exchequer would have none of the Prime Minister's protests against a Budget[1] well calculated to promote the continuous and constitutionally disastrous secession of Liberal peers. Two passages from the Queen's Letters serve to show all the depth of Rosebery's plight. 'Fifty-seven years ago', Victoria wrote to him, with the distant, majestic ceremony of a Sovereign addressing a subject, 'the Constitution was delivered into her keeping and . . . right or wrong, she has her views as to the fulfilment of that trust'.[2] And he had already confessed to her that 'he himself is only able to guide this tumultuous party through a leader bitterly hostile to himself and ostentatiously indifferent to the fate of the Government'.[3]

Yet this was not the sum of all his sea of troubles. The Liberal Party complained of his acknowledgment, platitudinous as it might appear, that Irish Home Rule must wait upon the will of the English 'predominant partner'; the Nonconformists criticized his racing-stable, and, so much the more because, precisely in those two years of his premiership, Fortune excelled in irony and made him twice over the winner of the world's most famous race; the German Government, to say nothing of the French, caused him to rescind the deal that Kimberley, his Foreign Secretary, had made with the King of the Belgians by arranging for a lease of the Bahr-el-Ghazal

---

[1] The principal feature of this was the drastic changes in the death duties which were made to yield an additional £4,000,000 per annum.

[2] Queen's Letters, III Series, Vol. II, p. 449.

[3] ibid., p. 399.

district in exchange for a strip of territory in the Tanganyika and Albert Nyanza region and the consequent advance of Rhodes's dream of a British dominion or domination running from the Cape unbroken up to Cairo.

The unhappy man suffered as best he might the expostulations of the Queen, the truculence of the Chancellor of the Exchequer—who complained that, contrary to stipulation, he was kept in the dark as regards foreign affairs —and the unnatural confederacy of Little England opinion with the German Imperial opposition to his African policy. But he was miserable and sleepless and longed to be released. Deliverance came at last. An adverse vote on the supply of cordite blew up the frail fabric of his administration. Two days later appears in his journal as perfect an envoy for that tumbledown Government as the historian could desire:

'June 23. Harcourt came to me spontaneously before dinner: the first time since I have been P.M.'

As for an epitaph, had he not already written an opinion adaptable for that purpose some years before?

'It would be too much to maintain that all the members of a Cabinet should feel an implicit confidence in each other; humanity—least of all political humanity—could not stand so severe a strain. But between a Prime Minister in the House of Lords and the Leader of the House of Commons such a confidence is indispensable.'[1]

At London dinner-parties half a century ago it was rare for Rosebery to be mentioned without some allusion being made to his three declared, and by that time realized ambitions—to marry an heiress, to own a Derby winner, to be Prime Minister of England. Crewe gives no countenance to the story, but, apocryphal or not, it gives, if not Rosebery's measure as a man, yet certainly the measure of him by the men of his time. The three wishes, like wishes in a fairy-tale, had all been granted him, yet, as each came and passed, there was to be heard that 'laughter of gods in the background' of which George Meredith warns us. For a little while Rosebery remained the leader of his party. Then—a final irony—Gladstone took up the cause of the massacred Armenians and dealt him—the expression is his own—the *coup de grâce*. As an experienced Foreign Secretary, accustomed in Cabinet discussions of the affairs of his department to find himself in a minority of one, and never at all addicted to what can only be adequately, if irreverently, described as indulgence in anti-Turkish delight, he was incapable of following his old master in a new crusade. He had thus the occasion, for which, perhaps, he was seeking, to lay down leadership; and against the advice of his best friend[2] he took it. With that event, to the great loss of his countrymen, his political career passed into its ultimate phase.

Crewe unfortunately states that Rosebery's book on that same aspect of

[1] *Pitt*, p. 24.   [2] Who? A.J.B.

Napoleon's life was 'first published in 1908'. The printer, if the printer be to blame, has done the student a bad turn. *Napoleon: the Last Phase* was actually published in 1900, and though written, 'to lay a literary ghost' that had long haunted its author, may presumably be attributed to the three years that passed between Rosebery's retirement from leadership and the real date of its publication. It contains, therefore, as we may feel pretty sure in the case of one who was a more accomplished littérateur than he was a letter-writer, the key to this period, and we shall miss some part of its meaning if we do not detect, even amidst the distant blare of trumpets and the echoing tramp of ghostly legions, a note of personal lament faintly sounding: 'Does not history tell us that there is nothing so melancholy as the aspect of great men in retirement—from Nebuchadnezzar in his meadow to Napoleon on his rock?'[1]

Rosebery was not great as these, nor perhaps great at all, but he had held, if only for some fleeting months, the greatest office in one of the greatest of empires at what may well prove to have been its greatest hour. He had still thirty, or almost thirty, years of life—years of inevitable anti-climax, unless he were to be content to let his self-created St. Helena suffer a sea-change, lose its ocean splendour, and turn into an Elba within reach of a realm not altogether lost. On the political mainland change was proceeding, and change which tended to remove his more personal difficulties. The highly critical old Queen, the Grand Old Man, had left his passage clear when the new century got on its way. The situation in its more positive aspects was not less to his advantage. The Liberal Imperialists who were his natural adherents included Asquith, Grey, and Haldane, some of the ablest men of the party and his personal friends. Once or twice he seemed on the point of putting to sea, but in the end the island-furrow, along which in imagination he ploughed his lonely way, held him prisoner. Though the will to tempt fortune afresh was wanting, the mind was still busy with politics. As occasion called, he condemned the Entente policy of Lords Lansdowne and Grey, castigated in drastic terms the Budget associated with the name of Lloyd George, criticized the provisions of the Parliament Act, and finally, after all power of public protest was spent, delivered his soul—a very caustic soul indeed!—on the subject of the Peace of Versailles; and in all these things, as earlier in the case of Home Rule, he showed a clarity of insight and a balance of judgment the more remarkable that it ran counter to the temper of the time. Yet there the matter ended. He who might easily have displaced a leader more remarkable than most for avoiding division by dividing counsel—Campbell, as the squib declared, severing himself, when convenient, from Bannerman; he who might perhaps have resumed for the asking the direction of foreign affairs, and thus forestalled the perils he foresaw; he who might certainly, if

[1] *Napoleon: the Last Phase*, p. 222.

Lord Spencer's evidence goes for anything, have had the Colonial Office and thus given a new impetus to the spirit of Empire; he whose presence in the administration of 1906 might have tempered plunder, and calmed passion, and in that of 1916 might have allayed vengeance; he who must have exercised, had he chosen, in 1910, a large influence upon the then Prime Minister in respect of the question of a reform of the House of Lords, was in every case found wanting. He had left, indeed, some telling phrases. He had said at Adelaide in 1884 that the Empire was 'a commonwealth of nations' and that consequently no nation, however great, need leave it; and, ten years later, he had boldly asserted that Home Rule for Ireland was an issue, whose decision must rest with 'the predominant partner'. But words seemed with him increasingly to do duty for action; and action, at least in respect of his votes upon the Budget and the Parliament Bill, to eviscerate words. Hamlet's famous dilemma might almost be said to have ended in Hegel's hardly less famous delusion; and the problem, whether to be or not to be, to have resolved itself into the persuasion that being and not being were one and the same thing. He who had made 'efficiency' the legend on his banner had become in fact the outstanding example of ineffectiveness.

And yet when all has been said that should be said about this tragic loss of power, it is still in place to speak in praise of Rosebery. Though his strength —impaired, as we ought in justice to remember, by sleeplessness as well as by sensitiveness—had abated, his eye was not dimmed. His criticism fixed with unerring precision upon the three points which History will in all probability indicate as the main causes of British decline during the last half century— the diplomatic consequences of the Entente; the moral, or, if we will, the immoral effect of the 1909 Budget; and the international results of the Peace of Versailles. Crewe, as a loyal member of the Liberal Government of 1906 and a former Ambassador to France, was not perhaps in the best position to give his father-in-law credit in these directions, and indeed tends a little to minimize their consequence. A casual or careless reader, for instance, might easily conclude from Crewe's treatment of the subject that Rosebery's disapproval of the Entente policy was related only to the squabble in Morocco. It needs the more to be emphasized that Rosebery's mind appears to have moved along parallel lines with Salisbury's, to have favoured 'neighbourliness' but not entanglements in foreign relations, and, in short, to have approved an English policy that held the balance and not an English policy that weighted decisively one or other of the scales. A friend,[1] who enjoyed more than one opportunity of private discussion with him on the subject of the Entente with France and on one occasion was present at Dalmeny when he discussed it with Lord Grey, is good enough to allow me to say that these conversations had, to the best of his recollection, no special

[1] Sir Richard Lodge.

reference to Morocco, and that there was certainly no limitation put upon his general condemnation of the Entente policy as tending to involve England in war with Germany. In my informant's recollection the substance of Rosebery's criticism was conveyed in his concluding words to Grey. 'Well! all I have to say is that it will lead to war.' It did; and under Grey's guidance.

The Entente of Lord Lansdowne had, as time tends more and more to emphasize, one all-important difference from the Entente which his famous ancestor (for Talleyrand is now generally admitted to have been Flahaut's father)[1] concluded with Lord Aberdeen. The France of the Orleans Monarchy was free from other entanglements; the France of the Third Republic was already bound by her Russian alliance. The older and firmer bond held her more tightly than the newer and more flexible one; and England thus became, rather innocently, enmeshed in the web of Russian diplomacy and made subservient to the recovery of Russian prestige. The causes of any war are old as time and wide as life; yet the Macaulay of the future may presently affirm with no little show of rhetorical plausibility that, because an Austrian Foreign Minister got the better of a Russian Foreign Minister in a discreditable deal at a Moravian country-house, and because an Austrian Archduke with Slav sympathies and Slav ideals fell a victim to Yugo-Slav animosities and Yugo-Slav ambitions, British and German soldiers massacred one another upon the banks of the Somme, British and German sailors sank one another off the coast of Jutland, Indians fought in the fields of France, and Englishmen marched between the rivers of Mesopotamia.

Rosebery, when the whole matter came thus at length to its grim conclusion, gave of his best to the cause of his country—gave his splendid eloquence and the life of a dearly-loved son. His voice uttered no uncertain sound; the note was fierce and strong; to ruthlessness for better or worse he would have caused ruthlessness to be opposed. Yet there was no man living in Great Britain who had a better claim to say that he had striven in the day of visitation to teach his countrymen the things that belonged to their peace, no man who had sought more earnestly to save them from the Pyrrhic victory, which was all they could ever hope to win. In the day of diplomacy he had remembered his praise of Pitt's long effort to keep out of war; yet in the day of battle he pressed England as of old to save herself by her efforts and Europe by her example.

As Rosebery's mind penetrated the fallacies of a foreign policy which took from England the security of independence without securing to her the advantages of alliance, so did it tear away the sophistries of Mr. Lloyd George's

---

[1] Lord Lansdowne, the 5th Marquess, was the son of the 4th Marquess and his second wife, Emily Jane Mercer Elphinstone de Flahaut, the eldest daughter of the Comte de Flahaut and the Baroness Nairn and Keith. Flahaut, who was Ambassador to England in 1842, was rumoured to be the son of Talleyrand.

finance. To expose a measure of which the central project was presently swept away by its own author after a million and a half of revenue had been raised at a cost estimated at five, requires, perhaps, no profound effort of intellect, but Rosebery's attack was turned as much against the implications of the Budget as its actual taxes. There seemed at the time a certain extravagance in declaiming against it as socialistic and taking occasion to declare that socialism was 'the end of all, the negation of faith, of family, of property, of monarchy, of Empire'. But the old student of Adam Smith was not at fault, and had reason enough to warn his old Liberal colleagues that they knew not what spirit they were of. Plunder—in the sense of a capricious transfer of wealth from one class to another—turned quickly to profligacy; and profligacy after twenty years into the wildest waste. Rosebery did not live to see the extraordinary *dénouement* of 1931—the credit of England in decline; a Prime Minister taught, no longer at school, but in Downing Street, the elements of economics; all the nation roused afresh to nobility; and all the wordy battles of party strife merged for the moment in a policy of common sense—but no conceivable passage of events could have served to raise his reputation as a prophet higher.

The Entente dissolved in war and tears and was replaced by wider misunderstandings; the Budget of 1909 paled to insignificance as War and Socialism piled up their vast commitments; but of the provisions of the Treaty of Versailles it had long to be said that they were always with us. The old statesman, exhausted by his war-time efforts, was a stricken man by the time when the Peace was made; but he lashed in private that singular eirenicon no less forcibly than he had publicly lashed its companions in mistake. Nothing certainly was wanting to the vigour or comprehensiveness of a criticism which called upon the ghost of Brougham to come and deliver 'one of his huge seven-hour speeches crushing the Treaty of Versailles in gross and in detail'. For the last time in that long life he had put himself in line with the best English tradition. As he had resisted diplomatic entanglements, as he had protested against penal taxation, so he rejected an international settlement which surrendered to the pleasures of revenge the old moderation in victory that had marked the British policy of a hundred years before. He was consistently wise beyond, or, if we please, behind, his generation.

Puzzled by his restlessness in party-harness, dazzled by and a little distrustful of his fine paces, much too ready to believe that any solid roadster or spirited colt can reach the goal as well, if not as quickly as the best-bred hunter, the public never clearly saw how wise Rosebery was, how excellent was his sense of direction, and how skilfully his judgment took the fences that separate past and future. To no man of his time or since his time can a new generation be more safely recommended for an example of the spirit, if not the stuff of which National Governments are made and by which they must be sustained, for none, perhaps, had so perfectly assimilated the two leading lessons of history—that no nation can afford to sever itself from its past and that nothing, or at best very little, in the political sphere is ever done at the right time. He had, in fact, shaken himself free from the scrimmage between Liberal and Tory, and climbed beyond the wisdom of the Whigs into a serener air. It was observed that his political as well as his other speeches reached their loftiest level in the year in which he finally decided to lay down the burden of party-leadership. Not, of course, that he ever spoke imperially in the grand manner of Burke! For so ardent a Scotsman he cared curiously little for abstract ideas. His genius lay—and at this point we may conveniently exchange the metaphors of the racecourse for those of the studio—in the portrayal, with magic brush and patriotic hand, of the lively features, paramount traits, and enduring fascinations of Britain's remembered worthies—of the statesmen first and foremost, sometimes, as in the case of Pitt and Peel, at full length, or sometimes, as with Fox and Shelburne, in incomparable vignettes, but also of those who, like Burns and Johnson, strike still deeper chords of feeling and move the mind to yet more spacious artistry.

After this manner, then, though in a way as remote from Disraeli's as a Whig is remote from an Oriental seer, Rosebery may be said to have commended to his countrymen ideas of *imperium et libertas*, perceiving in their combination, as Disraeli had done before him, the particular genius of his fellow-citizens. And, as we turn from the portraits he has painted to look our last upon his own, we may reflect in passing that it was from this assiduous tending of the twin torches of liberty and empire that he won his outstanding place in our annals.

It is, however, the enigma of a striking personality and not the portrait of a great Prime Minister that rivets the eye. Since the London neighbour whose likeness Rosebery drew with so much care—the famous 'Jesuit of Berkeley Square'—was dead, there has been, with the single exception of Disraeli, no figure in English politics that lends itself so much to mystery as his own. Certainly he took himself no pains to read the riddle for us; rather, perhaps, the contrary. To 'peep and botanize' around his political grave may lead us at first sight to speculate with Hamlet that 'here might lie the pate of a politician'. And yet who is there that, rising from the study of his literary remains, will refuse to him Fortinbras's epitaph on Hamlet's self: 'He was likely, had he been put on, to have proved most royally'? The actual event doubtless disputes this title to regard, but how if, as with Hamlet, circumstance was only in a temporary ascendancy over character?

Over their wine, then, it is likely that men will someday debate the final significance of this delicate connoisseur—a man much like a crystal with many gleaming facets and behind them some mysterious pools. They may speak of him as a born citizen of the Republic of Letters, or as a Whig magnate of a dying type, or as a collector of Napoleon's relics, all too sensitive to Napoleon's charm. They may notice that his confession of liberty seemed to be balanced in practice by something perilously like an autocratic temperament. They may perceive that politics was to him as a mistress whom he could neither live with nor yet without. They may quote, if they have ransacked informing sources, Mr. Spender's suggestion that the premiership, too swiftly attained and too gravely embarrassed, had left him 'like a burnt child dreading the fire' and resolved to resume office only on terms so exacting as to be impracticable, or Mr. Spender's complaint that 'no one could discover what he wished or what he would do';[1] as well as the complementary opinion of the same high authority that he seemed 'more likely than any one else to steer a prudent course' as Foreign Secretary.[2] They will pass on perhaps to discuss his brilliant talent for conversation and perhaps to challenge—for it can, within my knowledge, be effectively challenged— Mr. Spender's assertion, doubtless in general accurate, that 'his epigrams came to him on the spur of the moment'. They may make mention of his passing fancy for a villa at Posilippo;[3] of his careless courage at sea; of his strange nocturnal drives, inevitably reminiscent of King Ludwig of Bavaria, though, as every one knows, imposed by insomnia. They may recall his close friendship with 'hang-theology' Rogers, the lovable and latitudinarian incumbent of St. Botolph's, and, perhaps, also the fact that Rosebery wrote, and Rogers delivered from the pulpit of St. Paul's a sermon on the text, 'This one thing I do, forgetting those things which are behind and reaching forth unto those things which are before, I press toward the mark for the prize of the high calling of God in Christ Jesus.' Then, in a yet graver vein, they will perhaps refer to his visit to Newman's corpse, to his distress at the intrusion upon his grief of a different religious faith at the time of Lady Rosebery's obsequies, to his attendance at Holy Communion on the morning before he accepted the premiership.

[1] J. A. Spender, *Life, Journalism and Politics*, Vol. I, p. 57.   [2] ibid., p. 107.
[3] The Villa Delahante, which he bought after he resigned the leadership of the Liberal Party in 1896.

L

speak of him as a benefactor of the Republic of Letters, or as a Whig magnate,
or a dying Czar, or as a collector of Napoleon's relics, all too sensitive to
Napoleon's charms. They may notice that his confession of liberty seemed to
be balanced in silence by somewhat perilously like an autocratic propensities. They may perceive that politics was to him as a mistress whom he
could neither live with nor yet without. They may quote, if they have
ransacked informing sources, Mr. Spencer's suggestion that the premiership
too swiftly attained and too gravely embarrassed, had left him, like a burnt
child dreading the fire, and anxious to resume office only on terms so exacting
as to be impracticable, or Mr. Spender's complaint that 'no one could
discover what he wished or what he would do,' as well as the complementary opinion of the same high authority that he would 'more likely than
any one else to steer a prudent course' as Foreign Secretary. They will pass
on perhaps to discuss his brilliant talent for conversation and perhaps to
challenge—for it can, within any knowledge, be effectively challenged—
Mr. Spender's sonorous, hopeless, in general sentence, that 'his epigrams
came to him on the spur of the moment.' They may make mention of his
passing fancy for a villa at Roehampton, of his careless conduct in seat of his
strange nocturnal drives, of his visible faintness of King Ludwig of Bavaria,
though, it seems, one knows nothing by anecdote. They may recall his
close friendship with 'immaculate' Rogers, the lovable and inquisitorial at
incumbent of St. Neot's yard, perhaps also the fact that Rosebery wrote,
and Rogers delivered from the pulpit of St. Neot's a sermon on the text.
This one ranged the foregoing three things which are behind and reaching
forth unto those things which are before, I press toward the mark for the
prize of the high calling of God in Christ Jesus.' Then, in a yet graver vein,
they will perhaps refer to his visit to Newman's corpse, to his distress at the
intrusion upon his grief of a different religious faith, at the time of Lady
Rosebery's obsequies, to his attendance at Holy Communion on the morning
before he accepted the premiership.

¹ A. Spender, *Life, Journalism and Politics*, Vol. I., p. 87. ² *Ibid.*, p. 107.
³ The *Villa Delahante*, which he sought after he resigned the leadership of the Liberal
Party in 1896.

LORD SALISBURY

ROBERT ARTHUR TALBOT GASCOYNE-CECIL,
3rd MARQUESS OF SALISBURY
born 1830 died 1903

Entered Parliament as Lord Robert Cecil (Member for
Stamford) 1853

Secretary for India (as Lord Cranborne) (third Derby
administration) June 1866 to March 1867

Secretary for India (second Disraeli administration) 1874
to 1878

Foreign Secretary 1878 to 1900

Prime Minister and Foreign Secretary*
July 1885 to February 1886
August 1886 to August 1892
June 1895 to November 1900

Prime Minister   November 1900 to July 1902

He was Foreign Secretary only from January 1887 onwards.

CHAPTER XIII

LORD SALISBURY

THERE can be few more regrettable incidents in the annals of recent biography than Lady Gwendolen Cecil's[1] failure to complete the life of her father. She seemed to have every qualification for the work—a powerful style, a profound understanding of the political problems of his time, the deepest admiration of his powers combined with a very remarkable talent for detaching her judgment from her affections, and, in a word, an intimacy with the subject of her task which no future or supplementary student can have any hope of possessing or obtaining. Yet, just as her narrative reaches the summit of its difficult ascent, just as Salisbury's character attains the plenitude of recognition and influence, just before he gathers into his last, long administration all the outstanding forces of his era—the Conservatives of the Peel tradition, the Tory-Democrats of the Primrose League, the Whigs of the Devonshire allegiance, and the Radical Imperialists of the Brummagem brand—the pen falls from the tired hand and the book, which some of us had watched advancing from its first inception forty years before, shuts with the finality of fate and the significance of a tale that is told. She thought, indeed, herself that she had dealt with all in her father's life that was of paramount importance. It was useless to press on her the contrary view. It is proper to add that her opinion in this matter derived some support from her father's abiding conviction that his real work lay in the sphere of foreign affairs, not in the direction of home policy, and not, had Devonshire or another been willing to act as Prime Minister, in the control of a Cabinet resting on a coalition. Possibly she stood a little too near him herself to take the full measure of his personality or to appreciate all that he had given in the way of inspiration to the men who grew up in his time. Anyhow the book leaves on the mind the impression of some splendid torso—or, perhaps rather, of a series of brilliant studies for a portrait, each of which discovers a mass of fine strokes, of vivid colour and of close observation. And those who knew the author well will see in them the mirror of a mind rich in reflection on and in contact with human life and its conditions, and of a nature profoundly influenced in reflection and method by association with a father preoccupied by just those problems of politics and religion which had also a great attraction for herself. There was always, in talking to her, the feeling

[1] Lady Gwendolen Cecil was the daughter of the third Marquess of Salisbury. The first volumes of her *Life* of her father were published but the work was never completed. She died in 1945.

that she grasped every question at issue, not through current conventions or familiar criticisms, but freshly, with a free mind, and a great independence of judgment. It was so her father had looked at the world; and it was so also that she saw it.

What stood in the way, I used to feel, of the completion of her work, was her perfect assimilation of the truth of Pascal's well-known remark that nothing can compare in value with a drop of charity. She seemed always at the disposal of others. What she was, as one of her great friends and admirers once said to me, was so much more important that what she accomplished that any regrets one might feel over her unfinished book were reduced to insignificance by the recollection of her personality. It is not too much to make use of the well-worn phrase and to say that to know her was an education, at least in any considered approach to political or religious questions. In her retreat within the confines of Hatfield Park she qualified for the name of Egeria, which an old friend of the family did in fact bestow upon her; and when I think of her, it is as of one who might be mentioned in the same breath with Mme de Sévigné, Mme de Stael, or Mme Swetchine, or with our own English Margaret Godolphin and Dorothy Osborne—women who needed no vote to make them a power in the land, and who would have coveted none.

From what has just been said it might be guessed that the biography is a little lacking in architectural design; but this is on the whole a thing to be glad of. For some matters that a more conventional biographer might have reserved for a final chapter, she dealt with on her way as they came into her mind. This is noticeably the case with Salisbury's views on religion which are treated in the fourth chapter of her first volume as a necessary introduction to the life. It would indeed be as difficult to understand him without this prefatory excursus as to understand Gladstone if one refrained from stealing a glance at his Scottish ancestry and at the contemporary movement of religious thought which took its name from, and had its origin in Oxford. Salisbury's unfaltering confession of Christianity as expressed in the Established Church of his country occupies from the first a central place in his thought, though it did not escape, any more than his other opinions, from that critical distrust of the views of experts discovered in a highly entertaining and characteristic letter, addressed to Lord Lytton, in the year 1877: 'I think', he writes, 'you listen too much to the soldiers. No lesson seems to be so deeply inculcated by the experience of life as that you never should trust experts. If you believe the doctors, nothing is wholesome; if you believe the theologians, nothing is innocent; if you believe the soldiers nothing is safe. They all require to have their strong wine diluted by a very large admixture of common sense.'[1]

[1] *Life*, Vol. II, p. 153.

It might be difficult to find among Salisbury's writings any passage illustrating more forcibly his independence, originality, or humour than this sally. The mind almost instinctively takes up a position challenging the commonplace. The great religious issue of the time was of course that of the Newmanites; but here, instead of the familiar charge that Catholics place themselves, so far as thinking goes, in the power of the priests, we are confronted by a far more searching objection. 'Roman Catholics', Salisbury maintained, 'rationalize' too much. It was, he would doubtless have added, of the very essence of religion for us to be content to see through a glass darkly; and any great clarity of reasoning invited suspicion. 'We live', he told the British Association in his presidential address on Evolution in 1894, 'in a small bright oasis of knowledge surrounded on all sides by a vast unexplored region of impenetrable mystery.' His own religious opinions approximated, then, in the last analysis to something near akin to personal mysticism; and, if some governing sentences are to be looked for in his biographer's account of his theological views, the choice should, perhaps, fall on those which follow:

'It would probably be impossible—it would certainly be beside the point —to attempt an analysis in logical form of his (i.e. Salisbury's) acceptance of the Christian revelation. It rested upon a spiritual vision which had an existence altogether apart from his intellectual processes and which was more compelling of conviction than any evidence which they could produce.'[1]

Such an outlook rendered him very little disposed to be critical or censorious regarding the paths taken by others. A distinguished contemporary— James Anthony Froude—I think among the *obiter dicta* in his *Short Studies*— stresses the impression left upon his own mind in early youth by the verse 'Thy word is a lantern unto my feet and a light unto my paths'. The foundation of Salisbury's unfaltering faith, laid early in life and never abandoned, seems, if we search for its cornerstone, to have approximated intellectually to the familiar warning that we have to make our journey through this world by faith, and not by sight—by night, and not by day. 'Salisbury declared', his biographer tells us, 'that, while he had never known what it was to doubt the truth of Christian doctrine, he had all his life found a difficulty in accepting the moral teaching of the Gospels.'[2]

That, as it seems at least to one critic, is a difficulty bound to arise, where a national outlook on religion displaces a cosmopolitan one. It is to be clearly seen in actual operation in the passage in Salisbury's 'Essay on Castlereagh' when he treats of the use of bribes in bringing about the Irish Union in 1800. No Christian can, without grave difficulty, persuade himself that he is justified in achieving a desirable end by encouraging another man to yield to wholly undesirable means. To bribe a man with a peerage or otherwise is

[1] *Life*, Vol. I, p. 113.　　　　　[2] *Life*, Vol. I, p. 102.

in such circumstances no doubt, as Salisbury points out, on a par with the action of a general on active service who rewards a spy for betraying his country. There is surely no plainer case than this of the end being used as a justification of the means; and Salisbury appears to shrink slightly as he presses the point home . . . 'We cannot refuse', he says, 'to admire the skill with which Castlereagh effected the Irish Union. But still we should prefer to dwell on any other display of administrative ability than that which consists of bribing knaves into honesty and fools into common sense . . . In the supreme struggle of social order against anarchy, we cannot deny to the champions of civilized society the moral latitude which is by common consent accorded to armed men fighting for their country against a foreign foe . . . No casuistry, however subtle, can draw a tenable line of distinction between the two cases, so that the weapon, which is lawful for the soldier, shall be forbidden to the statesman.'[1]

With such uncompromising clarity of thought and vision, it is easy to see why a reconciliation between the dogma and the ethic of Christianity appeared difficult to the statesman. But it is not easy to see, if so much be allowed to soldier and politician, why the philosopher, though he be Thrasymachus or Machiavelli himself, should not also receive some benefit from a similar extenuation. Things evil, we say in desperation, are providentially overruled for good. And assuredly the Victorians also, before they reached the fullness of their thought, were bound to say so. There was not only the Irish Union; there was the conquest of India. Certainly Seeley found some comfortable words to say, when he declared that England had expanded into Empire 'in a fit of absence of mind'. But Salisbury had not got it in him to colour hard truths with telling phrases. All his criticism of life postulates a fearless acknowledgment of facts; and his ultimate place in the estimation of his countryman came as the reward of looking resolutely at things as they really were. It was, however, no easy business at first to make his particular kind of merit understood. 'Lord Robert Cecil',[2] Palmerston wrote to the Queen in the last year of his life,[3] 'never loses an opportunity of saying or doing an unhandsome thing . . .' The subject of the Prime Minister's strictures was by then thirty-four; and Palmerston's caustic observation is not altogether out of line with Salisbury's later description of himself about that time as an Ishmaelite with his hand against every man and every man's hand against him.[4] Palmerston's harsh words came, it must be remembered, after Cecil had sat for over ten years as member for Stamford, a small

---

[1] *Biographical Essays*—Castlereagh, p. 8.

[2] Lord Salisbury entered the House of Commons as Lord Robert Cecil in 1853; he was the second son of the 2nd Marquess, but owing to the death of his elder brother in 1863 he was known as Lord Cranborne until 1868 when he succeeded his father and became 3rd Marquess of Salisbury in 1868.

[3] Queen's Letters, April 18th 1864.   [4] *Life*, Vol. I, p. 123.

borough in the pocket of his distant cousin, the Exeter of that time, and one that he never had occasion to contest. The country was at that date to its great contentment, in the hands of an old septuagenarian whose Whiggery rendered him disposed to govern on conservative lines. Cecil's speeches, however, and perhaps still more his anonymous, but for all that correctly ascribed articles in the *Quarterly Review*, in those times a powerful periodical, attracted attention. Disraeli was leading the Conservative Party; and to Disraeli's vision with its eye upon Bolingbroke and Shelburne, the value that Cecil set on Castlereagh and the younger Pitt as examples of statesmanship was temperamentally opposed. His leader was, however, too old a hand at factious opposition to be troubled by one of his junior adherents, bent, according to Disraeli's apprehension of the parliamentary game, upon attracting notice. A story, said to rest upon Cecil's own authority and, if so, presumably authentic, tells how, after violently attacking his chief, Robert Cecil found that Disraeli formed part of the company, with whom he himself was expected by his father to associate during a visit to Hatfield. Appalled at the prospect suddenly disclosed, he wandered miserably about the grounds of his home, wondering whether or not to take flight from the approaching, awkward encounter; and, then, as he turned a corner fell straight into the arms of Disraeli. Quite literally so; for Disraeli's tactics were no other than to clasp the young rebel to his breast! 'Before the horrified young Englishman could make even a gesture of protest', declares his biographer, Disraeli 'enfolded him in his embrace' with the words 'Robert, Robert, how glad I am to see you!' Disraeli was a very difficult man to get the better of. Not Gladstone alone found that his opponent's resources were many and versatile.

The main matter in dispute during Derby's short administration of 1866–8 was the extension of the franchise, which Gladstone had attempted to introduce in the former year on very moderate lines. The basis of the county franchise in the Gladstonian plan was to be a rental value of £14 and in the case of the borough franchise a rental value of £7. Out of these proposals had come a greater debate than ever arose between the Houses of Argyll and Airlie. Lowe had spoken from the viewpoint of one who took his stand on the intellectual excellence, hardly to be improved upon, of the existing House of Commons; Gladstone had asked, on the other hand, why any man should be excluded from political power. Both cases were arguable, and were argued with great brilliancy. The Conservatives, assembling at Lord Salisbury's[1] house in Arlington Street, with Derby in the chair, had decided to stand by the existing constitution; and the Russell Government, assailed by Lowe and Disraeli at the same time, received a mortal wound. In this encounter Cranborne had fought. What, then, was his political position when in 1867, only a year later, Disraeli himself proposed a franchise based upon household

The second Marquess.

suffrage; the 'compound householder', who did pay his own rates, becoming almost as enigmatic a figure as *la femme incomprise* or *la chambre introuvable*. The Conservative confusion which resulted from this unscrupulous manoeuvre, ended in the resignations from the administration of Cranborne, Carnarvon and General Peel, Sir Robert's brother; whilst the sentiments of those who retired rather than associate their names with so dishonourable a piece of chicanery are preserved in an article in the *Quarterly Review* for October 1867 under the title of 'The Conservative Surrender', of which everyone seems to have known that Robert Cecil was the writer. The withering sarcasm of those pages has lessened with the lapse of time, but their language remains as scorching as it is searching. No one, however, should attempt to read them who has not first bathed himself, so to say, seven times in the *Politics* of Aristotle and regained recollection of the fact that 'the master of those who know' regarded democracy as being as much a perverted form of government as tyranny or oligarchy. 'The Democrats', Aristotle says, 'hold that justice is equality; and so it is, but not for all the world, but only for equals. The Oligarchs hold that inequality is just, as indeed it is; yet not for all the world, but only for unequals. Both put out of sight one side of the relation, viz. the persons who are to feel the equality or inequality, and consequently form a wrong judgment. The reason is that they are judging matters which affect themselves; and we are all sorry judges when our personal interests are at stake.'[1]

As it happened Cecil's judgment lay open less than almost any man's to this disparaging accusation. He came of an ancient house and, upon the death of his elder brother in 1865, had become heir to great estates. But circumstances had already enabled him to show that he was profoundly indifferent to these things. At a time when, as his father pointed out to him, it lay within his brother's power to cut him out of his probable inheritance,[2] he had made a marriage admirably suited to his own intellectual and other requirements, but inacceptable to his father.[3] 'The persons', he wrote to his father, 'who will cut me because I marry Miss Alderson, are precisely the persons of whose society I am so anxious to be quit. My marriage, therefore, cannot entail upon me any privations. I have considered the matter for very many months anxiously and constantly. I have come to the conclusion that I shall probably do Parliament well if I do marry, and that I shall certainly make nothing of it if I do not.'[4]

---

[1] Aristotle, *Politics*, Book III, Chapter IX.   [2] *Life*, Vol. I, p. 61.

[3] Lord Salisbury married in 1857 Georgina Caroline Alderson, daughter of Sir Edward Alderson, last Baron of the Exchequer. Salisbury's father, the 2nd Marquess, disapproved of the match and refused an allowance, so that Lord Robert Cecil as he then was became for a time largely dependent upon his writing. Out of these circumstances largely came the famous series of articles in the *Quarterly Review* which powerfully impressed public opinion.   [4] *Life*, Vol. I, p. 59.

The younger Pitt, of whose high-mindedness Salisbury's essay on him shows that he entertained an appreciative opinion, had suffered his affection for Eleanor Eden to be vanquished by poor circumstances; and the episode is one of the least attractive in his life. Cecil for a few years faced with equanimity the difficulties of narrow means and of a family for whom he could not hope to provide, if anything happened to himself. Then, of course, after 1865 his fortunes mended; and in 1868 he succeeded to the family estates. Even so, it is arguable that these brought him the very minimum of satisfaction. The duties involved in the possession of large acres were not congenial to him, as they had been to his father; and he discharged them rather from duty than with pleasure. His disbelief in democracy was, therefore, no outcome of personal advantage, masquerading as disinterested patriotism; and the familiar portrait of him as a patrician is all askew.

What he saw, and saw clearly, is that an acceptance of democracy was in effect a repudiation of education, at least in the French, if not the English sense of that term. 'A clear majority of votes', he wrote, 'in a clear majority of constituencies has been made over to those who have no other property but the labour of their hands.' One can, of course, maintain that all men are free and equal; and also that all women are equally so. But whether one can really believe this is quite a different matter. One can, of course, sentimentalize about the common level of humanity. But whether one can rationalize one's thought to the same result is much more doubtful. Hardly anybody could in 1867! Not Gladstone who proposed a £7 rental value in boroughs and a £14 rental value in counties as affording a proper qualification for exercising a vote; not Disraeli, who advised the creation of certain so-called 'fancy franchises' (dropped, however, later on) as a safeguard against the evils of democracy, the franchise having once in 1851 been in his opinion 'the privilege of civic virtues' and no universal right;[1] not John Bright, who just at this time affirmed that the nation included 'a residuum' unfit to possess a vote! To all these the possession of property seemed to carry with it some guarantee of responsibility. Cranborne, though he recognized that, as he said, 'it was the duty of every Englishman and of every English party to accept a political defeat cordially',[2] though he recognized also that 'the spirit of innovation always must exist' and that 'the world would grow very stagnant, if it disappeared',[3] recognized no less, and even, perhaps, rather more, that changes must be effected in such a way as to preserve their agents from the reproach of want of principle such as the opponents of Gladstone's Reform Bill of 1866 must of necessity incur by the passage of their own far further-reaching Act of 1867. It was, indeed, not so much the measure in itself that shocked him as the means by which it was carried. And, in due

---

[1] See Monypenny & Buckle's *Life of Disraeli*, Vol. III, p. 285.
[2] *Quarterly Review*, No. 246, p. 534.   [3] ibid., p. 557.

course, the Conservative leaders admitted that, as early as 1859, they had decided to introduce 'household suffrage'—a development of which Disraeli had been sharp enough to appreciate the popular appeal, though he had been less sharp in proclaiming at Edinburgh the educational value for the minds of Conservatives. As Cranborne argued in his *Quarterly* article, no nation had yet entertained the idea of 'placing a great empire under the absolute control of the poorest classes in the towns'.[1] 'The issues of this conflict', he wrote, 'are far more momentous. The very conditions under which our institutions exist, have been changed; the equilibrium of forces by which they have been sustained is shaken . . . Those who have trusted to the faith of public men or the patriotism of Parliamentary parties or the courage of aristocratic classes must now find other resting places on which to repose their confidence.' 'Then', he goes on, 'if the Conservative surrender of 1867 be considered, not in its results, but in the state of things that it reveals, it is a phenomenon of tremendous import. The evils of the measure itself, dangerous as we think it, are not necessarily irremediable . . . The hopelessness, if hopelessness there be, lies in the spirit and feeling on the part of the Conservative classes which the vicissitudes of this conflict have disclosed . . . To understand what a headlong rout it has been, we must take into view the earlier as well as the later movements of the struggle, the manifestoes that were put forth, the claims that were made, the positions that were occupied during the years which preceded and led up to this last fatal campaign.'[2]

Lowe's remembered phrase to the effect that, once the Act of 1867 was passed, they must set to work to 'educate their masters' is more apposite here than Disraeli's phrase about educating the Conservatives. Lowe was, as Gladstone himself allowed, the most formidable of the opponents of Parliamentary Reform; and there is, perhaps, little in Cranborne's argument that is not to be found in Lowe's speeches at the time and that was not vindicated, a quarter of a century after, in Lecky's *Democracy and Liberty*. Still Gladstone was in one sense right. Time was on the side of the extensionists of the suffrage; and all the arguments on the other side were no more than bulwarks with as much chance of stopping the tide of 'reform' as Mrs. Partington's memorable mop. It does not, of course, follow that Gladstone was right, so to say, in the abstract. A student, as assiduous as himself, of Dante's great poem and one disposed to think out the problems of life, political as well as personal, at a far deeper level than politicians as a rule attempt, has remarked that 'passion', not 'place' corresponds with the true law of love; that 'anything else is democracy intoxicated with itself, the moon-lunacy of equality without degree, as without equality degree is only a sun-madness'. 'Existence', the same critic goes on to say, 'is equal, function hierarchical; at every moment the hierarchy alters, and the functions re-

---

[1] *Quarterly Review*, No. 246, p. 534.   [2] ibid., p. 553.

ladder themselves upward. To know both—to experience and to observe both—is perfect freedom.'[1]

At this depth of thought men can afford to exchange views; nearer the surface they are in peril of wrangling to little purpose. Who dare yet feel sure that Democracy has not fallen into the pit of ineptitude that Cranborne feared and foretold? Plebiscites had been used to propel the First Napoleon along the paths of his ambition. Plebiscites were to be the playthings of the Third Napoleon in his rise to power. And plebiscites, or something like them, have served to steady the seats of other despots, whose malignant qualities have earned them the hatred of their fellow-men. Democracy is not so much in love with liberty that it can defend a constitution which is the embodiment of rational discussion against a constitution where one ruler does in fact claim to represent the 'general will' of all. 'If you will have democracy', Cranborne wrote in 1866, 'you must have something like Caesarism to control it.'[2] England, as he thought, anyhow prematurely, had reached the end of that 'exquisitely delicate' system of constitutional checks and balances which had won for English institutions the adoring admiration of Burke, 'when true to himself', as Acton declared at the close of his inaugural lecture as Professor of Modern History, 'the most intelligent of our instructors'.

Cranborne, although he regarded the actual consequences of the 'Conservative surrender' as trivial,[3] by comparison with the blow dealt to the politicians' claim to integrity believed that it would inaugurate an unscrupulous spoliation of the richer by the poorer part of the community.[4] The best part of a century had, however, to elapse before that forecast would be verified; and there was still time for wisdom to get to work. As it seemed, however, to the Cranborne of 1867, the old English constitution had suffered a mortal blow; and Salisbury (as he became through the death of his father in April 1868) regarded his own career as closed. 'My opinions', he wrote to a friend, 'belong to the past; and it is better that the new principles in politics should be worked by those who sympathize with them heartily.'[5] Things did not, as has just been indicated, move with the speed he expected. They seldom do; for neither does the nature of man encourage, nor his mind permit it. The 'pain of new ideas', as Bagehot called it, is too great for that. Salisbury, for all his opinions, was himself destined to serve his country for the space of another generation, and, not only to serve it, but to lead it. '*Nous ne voyons point le dessous des cartes,*' as Mme de Sévigné wisely says.[6]

---

[1] Charles Williams, *The Figure of Beatrice*, p. 197.   [2] *Life*, Vol. I, p. 139.

[3] Robert, Lord Salisbury, *Essays—Biographical*, p. 121. 'There is nothing abiding in political science but the necessity of truth, purity and justice.'

[4] See the first paragraphs of 'The Conservative Surrender' in the *Quarterly Review* of October 1867.

[5] *Life*, Vol. I, p. 294.   [6] To Bussy-Rabutin (August 13th 1688).

The political career we are following seems, however, to pause in 1868: then, in 1874, after Gladstone's famous administration between those years, it resumes its way. For this a reconciliation with Disraeli, who had replaced Derby as Prime Minister, was evidently necessary. It was not, however, urgent until the Conservatives (if that be the right name by which to speak of them) came within sight of taking office again under Disraeli's leadership. Meanwhile Salisbury, removed by his father's death to the House of Lords, grew in stature and in strength of sarcasm. Of one of his last speeches as Cranborne in the Commons—in March 1868—Disraeli had written to the Queen that it lacked nothing in malignancy but something in 'finish'.[1] A *rapprochement* between the two men was bound to be slow, and, as Salisbury put the matter to his wife in February 1874: 'The prospect of having to serve with this man again is like a nightmare. But except intense personal dislike, I have no justification for refusing. There is no temptation to him to be Radical in this Parliament—for his majority cannot be less than 50.'[2]

The party desired, moreover, to see the breach healed; and Salisbury's stepmother, who in 1870 had been married to the new Lord Derby,[3] was indicated by circumstances as the natural mediator. Under her auspices, after some approaches had been made, the two men exchanged letters and telegrams; but neither the biography of the one, nor of the other, throws much light upon what passed. It was probably a case of 'least said, soonest mended'. Church matters were rather tricky. Salisbury wanted to make as sure as he could that, if he took office, he would not become involved in an attack on the Ritualists; and Disraeli 'professed himself a High Churchman'.[4] When the list of Ministers was submitted for the Sovereign's approval, the Queen made an entry in her memorandum of the interview, presumably upon information given her by the Prime Minister, that Salisbury 'had quite readily consented to join the Government'.[5]

So then Salisbury found himself once more at the India Office. Though he appears to have earned golden opinions in his capacity as Indian Secretary, a detailed account of his departmental work is hardly, as Lady Gwendolen expressed it, 'remunerative biographically'. Indian policy was moving from the influence of Lawrence to that of Northbrook and Lytton—from a policy of 'masterly inactivity', as it has been called, and by Salisbury himself, towards one of advance on the North-West Frontier. Russian aims and ambitions needed to be closely watched; and for the student of Salisbury's career it is pertinent to notice that it was through those windows of the then British Empire, which at that date gave from India on the Middle East and where the view was well-designed to set to work some of the most subtle and

[1] Queen's Letters, March 1868. [2] *Life*, Vol. II, p. 46.
[3] See p. 10.
[4] *Life*, Vol. II, p. 50. [5] Queen's Letters, February 18th 1874.

searching calculations of diplomacy, that he gained his first glimpse as a statesman of foreign affairs. The situation looked, early in 1876, as if the troubles of the Turks in Bulgaria and Roumania might give Russia an excuse for gratifying her age-long ambition to reach Constantinople. Salisbury had no bias against the Russians. If he belonged in this matter to any school of thought, it was to that of Aberdeen. One of his most remarkable and original essays in the *Quarterly* is in fact a defence of the Russian attitude towards Poland; his point being that, if one only carried investigation into the past far enough, the Poles could be proved to be the first aggressors. He was in this way an exceptionally fit and proper person to represent the Cabinet at an international conference on the European situation, which assembled at Constantinople in December 1876; and even Gladstone, who was trumpeting, at his loudest, denunciation of the infamous Turks, thought so. In a word 'the appointment', he wrote, 'of Lord Salisbury to Constantinople is the best thing the government have yet done in the eastern question.'[1]

On the way out Salisbury visited some of the principal Courts of Europe and saw Decazes in Paris, Bismarck in Berlin, Andrassy[2] in Vienna; but, as he wrote to Derby, 'in the course of my travels I have not succeeded in finding the friend of the Turk'.[3] The Russian Ambassador awaited him at Constantinople. Ignatieff was amiable, conciliatory, but an unblushing rogue. When Salisbury called his attention to the fact that a frontier-line, agreed upon at a previous sitting, had been shifted on the map, he merely rejoined with a beaming smile, '*M. le Marquis est si fin—on ne peut rien lui cacher*'. All Salisbury's indignation melted into uncontrollable amusement. The incident, it may be assumed, served to confirm his unfavourable estimate of his fellow-creatures as political animals.

Salisbury had not, indeed, gone out, expecting that much would come of the Conference; and not much did. The Turks, like the House of Lords and the wicked man in the Psalms, had no wish to be reformed and cherished the comfortable belief that in the last resort Britain would sustain them as they were. The agitation which Gladstone was leading in Britain had reactions tending rather to fortify them in this view; and Salisbury betrays his embarrassment with regard to the Prime Minister's scheme of reforms, in a letter where the sentence will be found, 'Whether I shall be able to make these stupid Turks accept this scheme, I do not know'. In a communication to Carnarvon on the same day the epithet 'idiotic' is substituted for 'stupid'. Elliot, the British Ambassador, inconvenienced him with good intentions almost as much as Midhat, the Grand Vizier, with perversions of truth; and,

[1] Morley's *Gladstone*, Vol. II, p. 560.
[2] This was Count Julius Andrassy, 1823–90 who represented Austria at the Congress of Berlin, 1878. He was the father of the Count Julius Andrassy who, in 1918, tried to negotiate a separate peace with President Wilson.
[3] *Life*, Vol. II, p. 107.

as Elliot took a favourable view of the mendacious Midhat, Salisbury found
his mission encompassed on all sides with difficulties. By the middle of
January 1877, the Conference, having failed to achieve anything, was plainly
breaking up; and on the 22nd Salisbury sailed for home.

A year of doubts and discussions now followed. Very possibly Colonel
Wellesley's Christmastide despatch of 1877 from St. Petersburg, in which he
alleged that Russia was somehow getting intimate information of what
passed in the Cabinet and advised making war at once, added in both its
aspects to confusion in counsel, though historians have not dwelt upon this.
Quite possibly, without any treacherous dealings, but merely by taking note
of conversational indiscretions in Derby's immediate circle, Schouvaloff, the
Russian Ambassador, was getting to know things not intended for his ears.
Quite possibly, too, Colonel Wellesley fancied himself as a statesman even
more than as a military attaché. Anyhow his despatch may have given the
Cabinet, which had been looking long to Derby for a lead, a good deal to
think about. Divided counsels in high places were certainly apparent. Derby,
able as he was and logically as he reasoned, had not been helpful, whilst
Salisbury was trying to clear his own thought beside the waters, so full of
oriental fascination for the Prime Minister, of the Golden Horn. As Salisbury
saw things, a great mistake had been made by the Palmerstonian School in
trying conclusions with Russia in the Crimea. The Turkish Empire was as
ready to collapse then as the Spanish Empire of a hundred and fifty years
earlier; and a policy of partition has been clearly indicated at that time as the
policy of commonsense. The hour for this had, however, been missed by
Aberdeen, who was not, as we have seen, master in his own house. Russell
and Palmerston, with Stratford de Redcliffe[1] dominating the situation in
Constantinople, had rendered the overtures of Nicholas I futile, and, as a
result, the country had drifted into hostilities which terminated in the Peace
of Paris of 1856, with its three-Power guarantee of the Turkish Empire by
England, France and Austria. Upon that settlement British policy had since
been based. 'The commonest error in politics', Salisbury wrote at this time,
'is sticking to the carcasses of dead policies . . . We cling to the shred of an
old policy after it has been torn to pieces; and to the shadow of the shred
after the rag itself has been torn away. And therefore it is that we are now in
perplexity.'[2]

So far as Derby's administration of foreign affairs can be said to have had
direction, it appears to have aimed at neutrality, to have leaned towards

---

[1] Viscount Stratford de Redcliffe, the British Ambassador at Constantinople, was a
man of great influence throughout the near East and he was passionately pro-Turk.
He regarded Russia as England's most formidable potential enemy and desired to inflict
upon her a diplomatic or even a military reverse, in spite of the fact that Aberdeen, the
Prime Minister and Clarendon, the Foreign Secretary were trying to keep the peace.

[2] *Life*, Vol. II, p. 145.

co-operation with Austria, and to have concerned itself only with British interests, of which Derby has been credited with saying, what in reality was first said by Wellington in 1840,[1] that peace was the greatest of British interests. He favoured peace, however, if such a thing be possible, inordinately. His hatred of hostilities exceeded even that of Salisbury, of whom his daughter declares that it rendered 'a crusader almost as antipathetic to him as a jingo'.[2] Beaconsfield, on the other hand, admired both Palmerston and the Jews too much to be either radically or racially pacific, and perhaps never considered how completely lacking in the New Testament is any instance of Christ's countenancing the use of force to advance that unity of heart and mind to which he was seeking to persuade mankind (the scene in the Temple with the money-changers being recorded in one Gospel alone, and then with the obvious implication that the scourge of small cords was intended for use or menace against the cattle introduced into the Temple for sale). For the rest, the Cabinet can hardly be said to have had any common opinion, so various were the angles of vision it afforded. When Derby, together with Carnarvon, resigned in the January of 1878, as a result of the British Fleet being ordered to send ships up to Constantinople and of the prospect of military preparations in the immediate future, there was consternation in the Cabinet; but the tension was quickly relieved by the news that the Turks were suing for peace. The British instructions to the Fleet were rescinded; and Derby was induced to return to the Foreign Office. The jingo-Press blamed Salisbury for encouraging inaction, though in fact he became aware of the change of policy which brought Derby back only after it had been put into effect, and then disapproved of it as mischievous vacillation.

Confusion became worse confounded in the months that followed; and it was plain to everyone that the Cabinet was distracted by conflicting counsels. British ironclads moved again to the mouth of the Golden Horn; whilst Russian troops, under the terms of the armistice with Turkey, advanced within thirty miles of the gates of Constantinople. The situation, it need not be said, was highly explosive; and by the end of March 1878, Derby had resigned again. Beaconsfield lost no time in replacing his old pupil in politics by the bitterest of his former conservative critics. It was a bold move, but in the event it justified itself entirely. These two men—Beaconsfield and Salisbury—who had once seemed incapable of making any contact in home politics came now to an almost complete agreement in foreign affairs. Both were courageous in decision; and this quality, perhaps more than anything else, enabled them to work together.

Salisbury, as has been seen, had no particular liking for the Turks; but the ex-Indian Secretary did not conceive it to be in the interests of the Indian Empire, which, with the adoption of the Imperial title by the Queen, may

[1] See the D.N.B. on Wellington.   [2] *Life*, Vol. II, p. 92.

be said to have come formally into being under his Indian administration, that Russia should dominate a Bulgaria reaching from the River Danube to the Ægean Sea. Britain had need of something more than Malta on the route to India. Everything was quickly set in train for the meeting of a European Congress. On the night of March 29th, between the hours of 11 p.m. and 3 a.m. on the 30th, Salisbury composed the memorable circular, which may perhaps be said to have established his fame in Europe as a diplomatist. It emphasized the reasons for bringing every proposed change in the Treaty of Paris of 1856 before the signatory Powers which had originally guaranteed it, for discussion, not in this item or that, but as a carefully considered entity. Only with such confirmation could the recently-concluded Russo-Turkish Treaty of San Stefano be generally recognized. A big Bulgaria under Russian influence was not in British interests; nor was an Ottoman Empire dominated by Russian control. Such changes as had been proposed at San Stefano were clearly of importance to all Europe. The circular bore witness to the activity of a firm, determined hand in British counsels. It was followed by a secret agreement between the British Foreign Secretary and the Russian Ambassador, under which Bulgaria was to be divided and the southern province, no longer bordering on the Ægean, to be placed under a Christian Governor, but not withdrawn from Turkish suzerainty. The British interest in Turkey in Asia was also recognized. Through the malpractice of one, Marvin, a copying clerk, this preliminary settlement was made public, contrary to intention, in the columns of the *Globe*. Or so it was said. Salisbury himself, however, seems to have suspected a more eminent hand than Marvin's in the business—the hand of Schouvaloff himself.[1] Challenged in the House of Lords, he described the publication as 'wholly unauthentic and not deserving of the confidence of your Lordships' House'. It was, in fact, inaccurate in one important point, though hardly one so important as to constitute a good reason for calling it 'wholly unauthentic'. The only adequate defence for a denial in such a case is the casuist's argument that all statements in private or public must be treated as subject to the safeguard of 'secrets apart'. Otherwise no pledge of secrecy could be worth anything. A statesman under cross-examination must assume then, that his tongue is tied as really as that of a priest in respect of things heard in the confessional or of a doctor to whom confidences have been revealed in the course of his practice. This rule, doubtless, presents difficulties in application, where the examinee is answering in a legislative body, but it is not easy to find any better when to refuse a reply is tantamount to an admission.

The revelation in the *Globe* is commonly said to have rendered the collocutions at Berlin more or less of a farce. For the protagonists—England and Russia—had come to an understanding before the Congress opened; and

[1] *Life*, Vol. II, p. 285, note, and p. 289.

Bismarck, the self-styled honest broker, had not much brokerage to do. This view is plausible enough; but it has the effect, not always noticed by historians, of depriving Beaconsfield of all but dramatic opportunities at Berlin and of fortifying Salisbury's own observation, in a letter to Lady Salisbury, that 'what with deafness, ignorance of French, and Bismarck's extraordinary mode of speech, Beaconsfield has the dimmest idea of what is going on—understands everything crossways—and imagines a perpetual conspiracy'.[1] This result, if it was correctly discerned, may have been not inacceptable to the Prime Minister who loved acting, was fertile in imagination, and doubtless played his part after the manner of Henry Irving, to whom he was not unlike in appearance.

Play-acting, however, had no charm for Salisbury, except in so far as it made for comedy. There is a characteristic entry in his letters to his wife, which reads that: 'B(eaconsfield) and I had to go and see (the Empress) Augusta to-day in evening dress! She was very foolish, and B's compliments were a thing to hear.' Little as Salisbury is generally supposed to have noticed the faces of those with whom he had to do, often as the story, apparently true, has been told of his asking who W. H. Smith (at the time his lieutenant in the Commons) might be, he seems to have observed pretty closely the make up of his principal colleagues at Berlin. He notices in his correspondence that Beaconsfield has grown a beard and that Bismarck has removed one.[2] He watched closely, too, the interplay between Gortchakoff and Schouvaloff, and how the Russian Ambassador handled his vain, irascible old chief, Gortchakoff, and carried through the Bulgarian agreement, despite Gortchakoff's protests. But he deplored Beaconsfield's development of the drama into a final epilogue on British soil; the organized demonstration when he and the Prime Minister arrived in London bringing, in the latter's famous phrase, 'peace with honour'; the acclamations; the wreaths of victory; the Garters, one of which he had to accept, lest, by not doing so, he should cause his chief to suffer the chagrin of refusing the other. The wire-pullers, he declared, were mismanaging the affair and would 'find it out at the polls'. He did not see what had been accomplished as a great achievement. 'I never wish', he declared, in the retrospect, 'for my foreign policy to be judged by my action in '78. I was only picking up the china that Derby had broken.'[3] And his thoughts ran back to his old admiration, Castlereagh, who returned, undecorated, from the Congress of Vienna.

All these considerations have force, but, in remembering them, it does not do to forget that Rosebery, an able student of, and practitioner in, the art of

---

[1] *Life*, Vol. II, p. 287.
[2] 'Bismarck has shaved—and sits upon the Turks mercilessly' is the exact phrase. The beard may, therefore, have been of the slightest.
[3] *Life*, Vol. II, p. 231.

diplomacy, has placed Salisbury's work at Berlin at the summit of his achievements; that this raised Salisbury's reputation at home as high as it raised British prestige abroad; and that without it, his subsequent succession to Beaconsfield as head of his party, would have been much more uncertain. Prime Ministers, with few exceptions, have been chosen from successful Foreign Secretaries or successful Chancellors of the Exchequer; and the Congress of Berlin was the occasion of Salisbury's spectacular success. This is in a way the more remarkable that the result of the General Election of 1880 reflected in the main, as competent criticism avers, a judgment of the nation on the foreign policy of the Conservative Party. The country, as we have seen and as Salisbury's own very English instincts told him, had not much liked 'the roaring and the wreaths' that celebrated the return of Ministers from Berlin; and it had been goaded by Gladstone's Midlothian campaign into a belief that British foreign policy should aim rather at the 'Balkanization', as we have learnt to call it, of the Near East or, which was the same thing, at the disintegration of the Turkish Empire. This aim was a reversal of the policy Gladstone had stood for between 1852 and 1858, when in fact, in Salisbury's view, it should have been pursued. As things had worked out by 1878, the maintenance, and, if possible, the reformation of Turkish rule, was the only practicable policy, if we were not to assist the larger ambition of Russia to establish satellite States round Constantinople. The Congress had the effect of bringing British European policy into line with its Asiatic interests as trustee for India in Afghanistan and Persia. Here, however, lay the beginnings of a long-term purpose which Salisbury did not expect his fellow-countrymen to discern. 'Diplomacy'—it was one of his maxims—'cometh not by observation'. As Lady Gwendolen records, when he came back to the Foreign Office, five years after, in 1885, he looked into the record of what had passed to see what had become of his labours at Constantinople and then, referring to his policy and its fate, observed 'They have just thrown it away into the sea'.

Victoria had a good understanding of foreign affairs. She had relations and connections in many of the Courts of Europe; and she believed that the Monarchy, so long as it did not cross the will of the people in domestic matters, had still some duty of direction in foreign policy. She saw that Gladstone was possessed, if not obsessed, by the thought of small nationalities struggling to be free, and that he had no good eye for diplomacy; whereas her well-beloved Beaconsfield had had a deep perception of the imperial idea and its implications. What actually passed between her and Salisbury in 1885 is a matter of speculation; but this much is certain, that Rosebery replaced Granville at the Foreign Office in the Liberal administration of 1886; that Salisbury conveyed both to the Courts of Berlin and Vienna in the preceding summer (1885) that they had no need to fear a change in

British foreign policy, if the Liberals should be returned to power; and in short that the unfortunate uncertainty that had prevailed in foreign affairs, owing to the personal antipathy of Gladstone and Beaconsfield, could and would be thenceforward replaced by political continuity in this department.

In due course we shall have to return to foreign affairs upon which, more than anywhere else, Salisbury left his mark; but the impression of his personality is also very distinctly stamped on the domestic history of the time. No man, as we have seen, could have been more sensible than he of the dangers of democracy; but it is also true that, once democracy was adopted by the nation, no citizen could have striven more patriotically to avert its perils. His succession to the family peerage in 1867 had done a good deal to facilitate his new rôle as a Conservative leader. From the rough and tumble of the Commons which he was distressed to leave, he was removed by circumstances to the remote, but still potentially powerful House where distance from the battle combined with aloofness of spirit served to give his utterances weight and secure for them attention. Critics, like Hammond,[1] have marvelled at 'the contrast between Salisbury's conspicuous wisdom and address as a Foreign Minister and his recklessness and his taste as a party combatant'. This is more understandable if one reflects that the former was associated with the work he much preferred and the latter was connected with work in the value of which his faith was very limited. Had Devonshire or another been willing to take the Premiership, he would have readily stood aside. The old 'Quarterly Reviewer', the great master of 'gibes and flouts and jeers',[2] as Disraeli called him, would re-appear now and again in what his critics called 'blazing indiscretions', especially when he spoke of domestic affairs about which feeling ran high, and would not be controlled. Still at the back of all his home policy there remained a firm, independent foreign one. If this was secure, he felt that domestic difficulties could be dealt with.

Not, of course, that Salisbury's conservative and constitutional mind was capable of entertaining Utopias! The real road to improvement, as he saw things, was Christianity in practice—personal Christianity unhampered by the promises of politicians, with every man, high and low, fortunate and unfortunate, seeking to do, and to be good in the state of life in which he found himself situated. The two central articles of his social creed were, as his biographer puts it, 'corporate charity and individual liberty'.[3] Such progress as would follow this philosophy put into practice must clearly be slow—as slow as the regeneration of the human race. For the rest, the keyword in his political thought was 'integration', just as the word of fear was

---

[1] Hammond, *Gladstone and the Irish Nation*, p. 469.
[2] Disraeli's phrase. See *Salisbury's Life*, Vol. II, p. 60.
[3] *Biographical Studies of The Life and Political Character of Robert, Third Marquis of Salisbury*, p. 82 (privately printed).

that, which he used for the title of his concluding contribution to the *Quarterly*, 'disintegration'. Another phrase in his vocabulary, equally unfamiliar to the politicians of to-day as a term of reproach, was 'optimism'. When he spoke of 'the essential cowardliness of optimism', there was, as his biographer tells us, always a presumption of an irrational or unproved foundation underlying what was said.[1] He expected facts to be faced fearlessly and frankly, as it was his own nature to do with them. The times were full of menace, if these considerations were not borne in mind; and there is a certain psychological significance to be suspected in the fascination which all publications bearing upon the French Revolution possessed for him.[2] To his eye, the preservation of the rights of property went far beyond any justice owing to a class, and reached the foundation of any society which sought to escape the fate of those oriental communities which, as a result of insecurity of possession, showed great wealth and sordid poverty associated in dangerous proximity; wealth spending itself lavishly because there was little point in saving where risk had become excessive, and poverty associating itself with plunder because the significance that Christianity set upon the 'true riches' had been lost sight of in a shameless struggle to get hold of the false wealth of the world. To his eye the Radical Party fed upon and fostered discontent. 'Of course', he argued, in a speech made in 1882, 'I have no doubt that they (the Radicals) will tell you that their mission is to hear of grievances and to obtain their redress. Yes! but a party whose mission it is to live entirely upon the discovery of grievances are apt to manufacture the element upon which they subsist.'[3] Like all the thoughtful men of his age; like Gladstone; like, if it comes to that, Ruskin, he could not persuade himself, as has been done by some of the lesser minds of a later time, that by robbing the rich, you could relieve the poor: yet his words are not lacking in penetration of the problem which Disraeli had in his imaginative way styled the problem of 'the two nations'. Only he thought about it, not imaginatively, but practically and honestly. 'Depend upon it, in the long run it is the class that lives by industry that will be the sufferer, whenever Government departs from the right way . . . If the property of the rich could be divided among the poor, how little value would it be to each individual workman or shopkeeper in this country. What is of all things important to them is that capital should flow, that employment should exist, that wages should fertilize the channels of commerce . . . In order that capital may flow, that employment may exist, enterprise must be free and enterprise must be secure.'[4]

There then lie economic foundations of the Victorian way of life and of the Victorian inheritance; and every little Liberal or Conservative grew up with the idea that they were soundly laid, whatever Herr Marx, spinning cob-

---

[1] *Life*, Vol. III, p. 19.   [2] *Life*, Vol. II, p. 13.
[3] *Life*, Vol. III, p. 65.   [4] *Life*, Vol. III, p. 66.

webs in the British Museum or elsewhere, might think about it. The difference between the Conservative and the Radical lay, as Salisbury saw things, in the fact that, whereas the former looked forward to an increase of production to alleviate or do away with distress, the Radical looked back upon the wealth already created, and advocated its division and subdivision; so that his policy really resolved itself into a struggle for riches already garnered, but very perishable.[1] 'The Conservative', Salisbury argued, 'points the working-man forward to obtain wealth which is as yet uncreated. The Radical—at least the Radical as shown by recent discussion—on the contrary turns his eyes backwards, does not tell him to create new sources of wealth, but says that the wealth which has already been obtained is badly divided, that some have got something, that others have got nothing at all, and that the real remedy is to look back and fight among yourselves for the wealth that has already been obtained.' 'Now', he went on, 'I am not here speaking for the rich man. He will defend himself, and you will find him a very hard nut to crack. I am not defending him. I am speaking of the benefit of the community, and especially of the provision of work and of wages for the working man. And I say that the fatal defect of this Radical finance which asks you to think of "ransom" and "restitution" instead of looking forward to reaping new wealth by carrying your industry into new markets and making the community richer as a whole—its fatal defect is that it will prevent that development of industry . . . for the sake of the wretched morsel which, by disorder, by departing from all the traditions of good government, by destroying all confidence, you may be able to divide.'[2]

Politics presented in this manner were as deeply rationalized as those of its opponents were sentimentalized or, if one likes the word better, mystified. It was characteristic of Salisbury's mentality that he instinctively used the rational approach in the problems of politics, the mystical approach in those of religion, the places where each in the first instance belongs in the map of human thought. But, though he was the last man to offer a stone where bread was the prime necessity; it would be a sad mistake to see him as a man unmoved by the material distress of men. The housing problem had a large place in his thoughts; and, when in 1885 he brought forward, as Prime Minister, a Bill to emphasize the liability and give effect to the compulsion of landlords for the condition of houses in their possession he is said to have had the radical Sir Charles Dilke for an associate in framing its recommendations. They had sat together on that famous commission of 1884 on the housing of the poor, for which he had moved in what Herbert Paul terms 'a wise and humane speech',[3] and which included among its members, besides the two public men just mentioned, 'Albert Edward Prince of Wales', as he

[1] *Life*, Vol. III, p. 263.
[2] *Life*, Vol. III, p. 264.   [3] *History of Modern England*.

then was, 'Henry Edward', Cardinal Manning, Bishop Walsham How, Lord
Shaftesbury, the philanthropist, Henry Broadhurst, 'a representative of the
working-classes', and greater than them all in this connection, the soul and
spirit, though not the bodily presence on the board of Octavia Hill, an
authority, perhaps without an equal, upon problems of poverty and the
proper way to treat them. The personnel, indeed, afforded an admirable
example of how such an advisory commission should be constituted by the
inclusion of people capable of throwing their minds into the common stock
and seeking, not a solution agreeable to a class or a party, but to the whole
nation, so far as circumstances allowed of arriving at any such thing. The
underlying design lay far as the poles asunder from that approach to social
questions to be made familiar later on by the harangues of Lloyd George, and
later still by those of another Welshman of similar exuberance of diction. It
was a real attempt to bring together men of goodwill in a cause far above
party and, if such inflammatory material ever allowed of it, into the united
service of the poor. Even so, its admirable intention did not enable Salisbury
to escape criticism from the purist of economic individualism. The Lord
Wemyss of that day was a character notably marked by independence of
thought and expression as well as by other striking characteristics; and he let
fly from his bow the suggestion that Salisbury was a socialist. This singular
shaft drew from its target the objection that terms needed to be defined—
that 'socialism' might be a synonym for spoliation, but in the case under consideration could mean no more than 'the application of the power and
resources of society to benefit, not the whole of society, but one particular
class, especially the most needy class of that society'. 'The main command-
ment of the gospel preached by my noble friend', Salisbury added, 'is "Thou
shalt not use the public resources to benefit the poor".'

This argument perhaps lacked rigid logic but lay in line, as the user pointed
out, with the constitutional acceptance by the State for three centuries past
of responsibility for the support of the pauper. It was, let it be observed,
entirely characteristic of Salisbury's mind not to be fettered by any narrow
consistency, where some urgent action was evidently called for by the dictates
of commonsense, even though a strict rationalist might characterize the
policy adopted as the thin end of the wedge. Let Macaulay be quoted against
him, as was in fact done in this instance, and Salisbury would make reply
that he was no disciple of his. He exemplified in fact that *via media* in politics,
so congenial to the Englishness of his disposition. There was no room in his
outlook upon life for the Utopian visions which were in the coming century
to possess the minds of his countrymen. What his contemporaries saw in
him, as they saw also in the then Duke of Devonshire, was a man who cared
so little for place or power that he thought for himself and was content to go
into political exile rather than be untrue to his convictions. In 1867 he would

have been a bold man who foretold that the Cranborne of that day would
become Prime Minister three times—from July 1885 to February 1886;
from August 1886 to August 1892; and from June 1895 to July 1902, and on
this last occasion would be the triumphant head of a coalition, comprising
Conservatives as distinguished as Balfour, Liberals as different from one
another as Devonshire and Joseph Chamberlain, and in command at the
start of a majority in the House of Commons of over 150 votes.

This situation could never have arisen but for the predominance in politics,
once Gladstone had declared for 'home rule', of the Irish Question. To that
for a moment, then, we must turn. The disintegration of the British Isles
seemed to Salisbury, as to the rest of his contemporaries, Gladstone not
excepted, an idea not to be entertained for a moment. Gladstone in February
1882, when 'Captain Moonlight', to borrow Parnell's symbolism, was in
control in Ireland and Parnell himself under arrest, repudiated the allegation
that his policy was making for separation and declared that he would concede
in Ireland nothing in the way of local government that he would refuse
in Scotland.[1] But Salisbury, with clearer vision, felt that Ireland should be
thought of rather in the same way as India and had written in the *Quarterly*
ten years before—in 1872—that 'on Tory principles the case (of Ireland)
presents much that is painful, but no perplexity whatever. Ireland must be
kept, like India, at all hazards: by persuasion, if possible; if not, by force'.[2]
That utterance should be regarded as a basic conviction; the ambiguous
utterance in his Newport speech of 1885, when Carnarvon, his friend, was
at the time Viceroy of Ireland, may be thought of rather as musing in public
over one aspect of the Irish problem which should not be lost to view in any
general project of decentralization. What is clear is that he was conscious
that what Time had joined together, it was unwise for men to put asunder.
So precious in his eyes were the influences that made for integration; so
dangerous, those that made for the reverse! In unity lies strength; in diversity,
in nationality, lies too often weakness. As Acton[3] was teaching as early as
1862, Britain and Austria-Hungary represented at that time 'substantially the
most perfect' States, in so far as they included various distinct nationalities
without oppressing them, thus promoting a rare richness of character in the
resulting people; and so no doubt it might be said of America to-day.
The Balkans, although most Englishmen had a way of falling foolishly in
love with one or other of the Balkan races—maybe the Serbs; or the Bul-
gars; or even the Albanians—should be accounted the modern replica of the
Tower of Babel. Above all, however, Salisbury seems to have been actuated
in his Irish policy by considerations of honour. 'The original and determining personal factor', to use his biographer's words, 'in Lord Salisbury's

[1] See Hammond's *Gladstone and the Irish Nation*, p. 255.
[2] *Life of Salisbury*, Vol. II, p. 40.   [3] *History of Freedom and Other Essays* p. 298.

opposition to Home Rule was his overmastering sense of an honourable national obligation towards the minorities in Ireland—landholding, Protestant, Loyalist—who depended on England's protection.' So long as Salisbury lived, and for a little while after, the intelligence of 'the predominant partner' to the Union kept the British Isles united. Then statesmanship of a lower order came into fashion; and the Liberalism of Lloyd George, after attempting the coercion of Ireland with the Black-and-Tans, split the country into two, whilst the Unionism of Neville Chamberlain, to the great danger, as was presently proved, of Western civilization, went on to abandon the British hold on the Irish ports—Queenstown and Berehaven, as well as the base in Lough Swilly, which even Michael Collins had been statesman enough to see that Great Britain should retain the right to re-occupy.[1]

In Salisbury's presentation of the case against Home Rule there are ambiguities; and Gladstone cannot altogether be blamed for seeing, in the much-canvassed Newport speech of 1885, an occasion for an overture designed to effect a non-party settlement of the Irish Question. The overture, made through Balfour, was, however, indignantly rejected; but any settlement that can claim to represent the agreed assent of the Nation is so obviously more desirable than one which has nothing but party—and party more than likely hot from the polls—to back it, that even a rejected address must always be praised by the sagacious historian. It was, after all, in 1885, little more than a year earlier, that an unprecedented consultation had taken place between the party leaders at the express instigation of the Sovereign with reference to the extension of household suffrage to the counties and the attendant redistribution of seats.[2] Gladstone, so Morley tells us,[3] was much struck at this conference 'with the quickness of the Tory leader and found it a pleasure to deal with so acute a man'. Salisbury, so it seemed to Gladstone as they discussed the issue, 'proved' (again in Morley's words) 'to be entirely devoid of respect for tradition, and Mr. Gladstone declared himself to be a strong conservative in comparison.' In these circumstances, then, conference worked. Only once was there danger of a breakdown; and then again another woman—not the Queen—rushed in to the rescue. Salisbury was resolved not to allow University representation—that bulwark of education in the best sense—to be abolished; but the Liberals were only a trifle less resolved to sweep it away. A fatal deadlock appeared full in view. Lady Salisbury, a daughter of one of the last 'Barons of the Exchequer' and an extremely clever woman, though scrupulously careful as a rule to keep free from meddling, resolved to break her general rule of abstention. For the one and only time on record she drove down to Downing Street about tea-

---

[1] See for a short account of this notable affair Churchill's *Second World War*, Vol. I, p. 215.

[2] Morley, *Life of Gladstone*, Vol. III, p. 137.   [3] ibid., p. 138.

time and asked to see the Prime Minister. She was admitted; and then, introducing all the common memories of Oxford after the Movement as being dear to Gladstone as to her own husband, warned the Liberal leader that, if he declined to yield, the conference was doomed. Gladstone gave way 'and told her that it was owing to her intervention that he had done so'. Two great women between them had saved the State from being lost on the rocks of party-strife, as the rising tide of democracy began to beat upon the ship. Morley, oddly enough, makes no mention of the incident, but it is beyond question authentic[1] and ended gracefully with a return visit from Gladstone to 20 Arlington Street.

It is impossible not to speculate whether, if the Irish Question had not arisen to divide them and if Beaconsfield had not been there to transfer the heritage of the Conservatives into the hands of the Tory-Democrats, these two old sons of Christ Church, these two sometime adherents of Peel, these two disciples of the Oxford Movement, these two temperamentally strong antagonists of Disraeli in his earlier phases, might not have found their 'loves' and their 'hates' compelling them into a unity of patriotic purpose. Neither in all probability would the distinction in domestic or foreign policy which marked their careers have widened into so great a difference as presently appeared, had they chanced to be earlier associated. Both men were in their way accommodating; and both sought earnestly to serve the Queen. It was the wisdom of Salisbury that, in the matter of democracy, he had no disposition to attempt to reverse the decision of the country in '67; and it was the strength of Gladstone that he was willing to let his foreign policy, discredited by his misfortunes in the 'eighties, pass from Granville's hands into Rosebery's.

The dissension that divided the two leaders was not without its humours. It is on record that once, when Gladstone was staying at Hatfield, Hugh Cecil —Salisbury's youngest son and subsequently Lord Quickswood—came upon him in the Armoury and rebuked him with childlike vehemence, telling him plainly that he was a bad man. Gladstone defended himself as best he might, under this sudden attack, and with what weapons he could. 'If I were a bad man,' argued he, 'your father would not have me in his house.' The child would not allow his rebuke to be thus disposed of and proceeded to reinforce it with an assurance that fell rather short of veracity. 'He is coming', he replied with conviction, 'to kill you in a quarter of an hour.' 'Mr. G.'s' stout heart was proof against even this circumstantial information; and he hurried upstairs gleefully to the Gallery to retail his adventure. Where political opponents can enjoy such exchanges, the nation to which they belong is sound in wind and limb. To change, where the need for it was patent, Salisbury was the last man to be opposed; yet he was well aware that change

[1] See *Salisbury's Life*, Vol. III, p. 124.

should not be forcefully hastened, but should gradually grow. He was in fact ahead of conservative opinion in wishing for a reform of the House of Lords. He had supported Russell's Bill of 1869, giving the Crown the right to confer a few peerages for life; and in 1888 he brought in, himself, a Bill which enabled fifty such peerages to be created, but which even his prestige, as Prime Minister, was insufficient to carry. The peers, unfortunately, resembled the wicked man in the Psalms and would not be reformed. They consequently kept their hereditary privileges and lost their powers. Had they been willing to abandon the pitiful satisfactions of precedence and place on high occasions, they would after all merely have returned in principle to the historic constitution of their House which, under the medieval dispensation, was an aristocracy of intellect, comprising, when Henry VIII came to the throne, 108 representatives of the higher clergy, as against only 36 temporal peers with hereditary titles.

To regard Salisbury, then, as the prop of the 'stern, unbending Tories'— the classic description of the young Gladstone which Macaulay made famous —is totally to misconceive him. He accepted loyally, though with misgivings, the decision of the Electorate at the mid-century in favour of democracy; and his pursuit of a political career was directed towards mitigating the evils attendant upon the adoption of that way in politics. It was an entirely honourable and patriotic course to adopt; and it secured the statesman who had taken it the esteem of all such as value a fearless independence associated with political gifts of no mean order.

Salisbury proved in fact a very capable leader both in the Cabinet and the Country. No better testimony to this can probably be found than what has been written by Mr. Winston Churchill in the Life of his father: 'In all that concerned the management of individuals Lord Salisbury excelled. No one was more ready to sacrifice his opinion to get his way. No one was more skilful in convincing others that they agreed with him, or more powerful to persuade them to actual agreement. His experience, his patience, his fame, his subtle and illuminating mind, secured for him an ascendancy in his Cabinet apart altogether from the paramount authority of First Minister. The Leader of the House of Commons, triumphant in Parliament, almost supreme in the country, found himself almost alone in the Cabinet.'[1]

The memorable clash with Randolph Churchill to which these words refer occurred in 1886, and behind it we may perhaps discern the last stand of the Peelites against the growing power of Disraeli's Tory-Democracy. For a time Randolph had been able to restrain those pugnacious impertinences which had marked his treatment of Stafford Northcote, when leader of the House of Commons. But, like Joseph Chamberlain at a later date, he supposed

[1] Churchill, *Life of Lord Randolph Churchill*, p. 602.

in 1887 that he understood foreign affairs better than the sagacious Salisbury and the not so sagacious Iddesleigh (Northcote) who for a few months (August to December) was entrusted with the 'Foreign Department', as his office had formerly been styled. Salisbury watched and waited, counselling patience and prudence to his restive lieutenant in the Commons. Gradually, however, he saw that he would have to try conclusions with the brilliant young man, attractive in one way, exasperating in another, whose political talents far surpassed those of most of his colleagues. Matters were drawing to a head when, in accordance with custom, Salisbury spoke at the Lord Mayor's Banquet on November 9th. His biographer, who may have been his companion on the occasion, marked his attitude at the time.[1] I recall her giving me in person and, in consequence, with more vivid impressionism than is felt in her written description, her recollection of the scene—his supporters urging the Prime Minister to grasp the nettle resolutely, and the sinister-sounding remark that rose to his lips, as he sat back in his carriage and tersely observed—'The time is not yet.' Cranbrook—a Minister now forgotten, but then of some note—urged him to use his authority to guide the deliberations of his colleagues in his capacity as head of the administration, blamed him for an excess of self-renunciation, and drew from him an admission that, but for fear of the fall of the Government, he would have earlier abandoned the attempt to, as he phrased it, 'lead an orchestra in which the first fiddle played one tune and everybody else, including himself, wished to play another.'[2] In public he said, however, but little; only remarking to an assembly of City Conservatives that 'the Conservatives were quite as conservative as ever'. Then at length, when the forthcoming Budget came up for discussion, the time arrived to let Randolph measure his strength and learn his weakness.

The Chancellor of the Exchequer joined issue with George Hamilton and W. H. Smith over the size of the estimates required for the proper maintenance of the fighting departments—the Admiralty and the War Office. Randolph, writing most ill-advisedly on a sheet of notepaper bearing 'Windsor Castle' as its superscription, presented the Prime Minister with an ultimatum. The 'chief of the Army and Lord of the Fleet'[3] must give way, he urged, before the economic restrictions of the Chancellor of the Exchequer or he would himself resign. Salisbury consulted one or two of his

[1] *Life*, Vol. III, p. 325.   [2] *Life*, Vol. III, p. 327.

[3] The allusion is to a forgotten squib, which ran, if I remember, thus:
> The Chief of the Army, and Lord of the Fleet
> Went out to visit both Cyprus and Crete
> The natives, delighted to see such fine stars,
> Christened one of them Neptune, the other one Mars.
> They erected a temple to Neptune forthwith:
> And put up a book-stall to W. H. Smith.

colleagues and considered for a day or so. Then came the reply that he was in favour, himself, of the views of the defence Ministers. They were in fact the very last men to deserve the suspicion of war-mongering. So Randolph resigned on an issue, which was oddly opposed to the demand for adequate rearmament destined some fifty years later to make the fortune of his son. The insight, or perhaps rather the judgment, possessed by that son, was wanting in the father; and, for lack of it, the meteoric career of the elder man flashes across the sky of history and leaves no mark behind. Randolph indeed failed even to secure a Cabinet triumph by his challenge. 'I forgot Goschen' ! —the words have become famous. For, by offering the Chancellorship of the Exchequer to Goschen, Salisbury countered Randolph's blow effectively; whilst the appointment of his own nephew, Arthur Balfour, to the Irish Office about a month earlier, had been almost an act of genius, so little political consideration did Balfour at that time possess, so much did he ultimately attain. It may indeed be said of Salisbury's Cabinets, what can be said of very few others, that, as time passed, they grew in strength. Goschen was the first Liberal-Unionist to join him, but in 1895 there was added the co-operation of Devonshire and Chamberlain who had long been opposed to Home Rule in Ireland and who in the ten years that followed became more and more closely associated with Conservative policy, both assimilating and modifying its tenets. With Devonshire coalescence was easy enough; his political honesty met and matched the loyalty which was so marked a feature of Salisbury's political technique. With Chamberlain contact was less easy and not perhaps so successful. Nevertheless, the fact that, from 1895 onwards, Joseph Chamberlain, whom Randolph Churchill had wished to take for a guide in internal politics,[1] sat in two Salisbury Cabinets is, perhaps, the most impressive tribute to Salisbury's powers of management and the most telling justification of Churchill's remark to Stephen that 'to argue with Salisbury is like arguing with a rock'; that 'he had a mighty intellect'; and that he 'might have made what he pleased of me'.[2]

These considerations help to explain how one, so contemptuous of all that is cheap and tawdry in politics, retained for so many years the confidence of the country. There was, however, another quality in him which told in that respect, perhaps, more than all the rest. He was equipped to take, and he took, the office that beyond all the rest, beyond the expert direction of public finance, beyond the care of public health, is calculated to enable a nation to grow from strength to strength. As the Temple of Janus served in the Roman, so should the Foreign Office have served in the British Empire. If the Foreign Secretary was master of his business, the doors of the Foreign Department closed almost automatically to the entry there of Mars and his minions with all their costly panoply of war. 'There are twin gates of war,' Virgil had

[1] Salisbury to Stephen, *Life*, Vol. III, p. 337.   [2] ibid., p. 336.

declared in the famous passage: . . . '¹ a hundred brazen bolts close them, and
the eternal strength of iron, and Janus, their guardian, never quits the thresh-
old.' There have been janitors of these portals, who did not altogether grieve
to see them opening and peace slipping out past the widening gap, whilst
war pushed in. For Salisbury, neither personally nor politically, had war the
smallest attraction. The letter to his father in which he had early rejected the
offer of the colonelcy of the Middlesex militia, then in the gift of the Lord
Lieutenant of the county, is significantly amusing.² 'Your proposition', he
wrote, 'gave me a stomach-ache . . . I detest all soldiering beyond measure.
As far as taste goes I would sooner be at the treadmill. But I do not intend
to burden my conscience by deciding this question on a point of inclination
. . . I understand your wish in putting me into Parliament to be that I should
learn to speak if I could . . . It will be impossible that I should both attend
in Parliament with any shadow of regularity, and also be subject to a military
routine of duty.' Politically, as we have already seen, a jingo was in the last
degree repellant to Salisbury's mind. His acceptance of war as in the last
resort an unavoidable concomitant of effective statesmanship had, however,
been manifest in 1878; and, in tracing his conduct of foreign affairs, this
acceptance has to be borne in mind, not less than Lady Gwendolen's statement
that 'it would be difficult to exaggerate his horror of war'.³

The Gladstone administration of 1880–85 represented in the eyes of its
opponents a widespread policy of 'scuttle'. Peace, Beaconsfield had assured
the country in his Election manifesto, rests on the presence, not to say the
ascendancy, of England in the Councils of Europe. At Maiwand, at Majuba,
and finally at Khartoum, the Liberal administration suffered reverses which
caused much searching of heart amongst a people unaccustomed to such
misadventures. Salisbury had to regain for his country, if he could, its old
prestige. 'Diplomatic work', says his biographer in an audacious paradox,⁴
'attracted him for its essential sincerity'. The pertinent facts, she means,
cannot be buried from view, as in much other political effort, by means of
phrases. It was no matter to him that he lived in the age of Bismarck and
Crispi,⁵ some of the aptest pupils Machiavelli has ever had. They had eyes
for the facts; and he could accommodate himself without difficulty to such
realism as theirs. The reader has already been made familiar with the way in
which he damned an optimism without foundation in fact; and he was
equally contemptuous of quixotry as the betrayal of a trust placed in the
keeping of Ministers by their fellow-countrymen. 'Reverence for truth and

¹ Æneid, vii, p. 607.   ² Life, Vol. I, p. 50.
³ Biographical Studies of the Life and Political Character of Robert, Third Marquis of
Salisbury (privately printed), p. 66.
⁴ Life, Vol. III, p. 201.
⁵ Crispi was the Italian republican nationalist who enlisted Garibaldi to 'liberate'
southern Italy and Sicily.

reality as the testing touchstone for what is admirable in statesmanship was the note recurrently struck.'[1]

In 1870, as the memorable epigram puts it, Europe exchanged a mistress for a master. In the combinations and permutations to which that predominant fact gave rise, Salisbury's foreign policy was forged and moulded into shape. The disciple of Castlereagh (inasmuch as that eminent Foreign Minister endeavoured to see to it that in every European crisis Britain should be found 'in her place' in the counsels of Europe) Salisbury sought to work, as well as might be, through the medium of a concert of Powers. So far as his discernment went, the German Chancellor, during those critical years when Boulanger dominated the politics of the French Republic, was extremely anxious to get Russia entangled in the meshes or lost in the mazes of the Balkans, perhaps through the Bulgarian issue;[2] and this aim of Bismarck's seemed to point to a wish to bring on another Franco-German War, with Russia otherwise engaged. We cannot be sure; and Dr. Gooch in his diagnosis[3] of the relations of France and Germany at that time, gives no conclusive answer. The one thing, however, that was plain in January 1887, was that all Europe was arming. 'It is curious', Salisbury wrote to Sir Augustus Paget,[4] 'that everybody should be arming, if there is no real danger, and yet there is no shadow of a pretence for it.'[5] The complicated situation, out of which, however in the end no war came, had enabled Salisbury to clear his own thought and to define British policy. Very noticeably it had shown him the value of Austria, whose importance as 'a counterpoise to France and a barrier against Russia' he had been inclined to dismiss in 1876 as an exhausted tradition.[6] It was not in the British interest in 1886 to acquiesce either in the absorption of Bulgaria or the domination of Turkey by Russia, nor to fight another Crimean or similar war for the convenience of Bismarck; and, that being so, Austria had to be brought by slow degrees to the point of opposition to the aims of Russia.[7] This was accomplished by the end of that critical year; and the Austro-Hungarian Ambassador intimated that the occupation of Bulgaria by Russia would provoke a remonstrance from the Dual Monarchy and that an enduring occupation would end in hostilities.

---

[1] *Life*, Vol. III, p. 20.

[2] General Boulanger, erstwhile military governor of Tunis, captured the public imagination in France about 1886, when a succession of diplomatic set-backs and financial scandals had shaken the prestige of the Third Republic at home and abroad. Boulanger became Minister of War under Jules Grévy and France hoped for, and Europe feared, a coup d'etat. But Boulanger allowed his chance to slip by and the emboldened administration decided to arrest him for treason. He fled to Brussels and ultimately committed suicide.

[3] G. P. Gooch, *Studies in Diplomacy and Statecraft*: Franco-German Relations.

[4] *Life*, Vol. IV. p. 8.

[5] *Life*, Vol. IV, p. 16.   [6] *Life*, Vol. II, p. 85.

[7] *Life*, Vol. IV, p. 9.

THE MARQUESS OF SALISBURY
From the portrait by Sir George Richmond at Hatfield House

Victoria had watched the European situation with an anxious and intelligent eye and had kept the Prime Minister informed of what reached her through private sources. In January 1887, after she had received from her Prussian son-in-law[1] a warning that Bismarck considered that the chance of war was growing, she wrote, reminding Salisbury that it was said that Clarendon, though a weaker man than himself, would, had he lived, have prevented the Franco-Prussian War, and urging her Prime Minister and Foreign Secretary to devise measures to put an end to the advancing menace of war. Salisbury had already reminded her in the preceding August that she must be indulgent towards servants set to make bricks without straw and required 'without money, without any strong land force, with an insecure tenure of power', to counterwork the activities of three Empires not similarly embarrassed; and in January 1887 he repeated the confession of his impotence to intervene between France and Germany, whilst all the strength he had at his disposal must be given to the maintenance of British interests in South-Eastern Europe. Moreover, as Alfred Austin, not without some countenance from Salisbury, was urging at this time in the *Standard* under the title of 'Diplomaticus', England could not take the part of France against Germany without renouncing the main purpose of British policy everywhere.

The obligation (not, in Derby's view at least, to be reckoned several, however, but joint) to defend Belgium under the Treaty of 1839, embarrassed British foreign policy by its obscurity; and Salisbury returned no decisive reply to the British Minister's inquiry from Brussels as to the action Britain would take if Belgium were attacked from the French or the German side of her frontier. His silence is significant of his sense that the British people, constitutionally as well as temperamentally, wished to work unshackled by uncertain engagements and so to decide the question of peace or war on some particular issue and not through any ill-defined entanglement or understanding. This view could hardly have been more clearly presented than in his treatment, in that same year, of the Italian overture for a defensive naval alliance against France. There was no State, he wrote to the British Ambassador in Rome, with which we could work more cordially than Italy. The two countries had few differences and no grudges of long standing. But, as he wrote to the Queen, 'England never promised material assistance in view of an uncertain war of which the object and cause were unknown;'[2] nor could she promise even diplomatic co-operation against any single Power such as France. Subject to these reservations there was nothing to prevent the association of England and Italy for the maintenance of the *status quo* in the Mediterranean.

[1] The Kaiser, Frederick III, had married Queen Victoria's eldest daughter.
[2] *Life*, Vol. IV, p. 21.

M

It was Victoria's first Jubilee Year; and this affirmation of the independent basis of British foreign policy is notable. It was not the considered policy of a Conservative administration, but the conclusion of the country. It deserves to be read together with Gladstone's epitome of the principles of Clarendon in respect of foreign affairs. 'England should keep entire in her own hands the means of estimating her own obligations upon the various states of facts as they arise . . . England should not foreclose and narrow her own liberty of choice by declarations made to the Powers in their real or supposed interests of which they would claim to be joint interpreters . . . England should not assume alone an advanced, and therefore an isolated position in regard to European controversies . . . England, come what may, should promise too little rather than too much.'[1]

This was written by Gladstone to General Grey in 1869; and it serves to show how national—how English—foreign policy could be, whether conducted by a 'cynical' Conservative or a 'progressive' Liberal. The former was in truth the better constituted to get on with the facts as they were. Salisbury's correspondence bears eloquent witness to the difficulty he felt in trusting either the French or the Germans. 'For the present the enemy is France', he writes in 1887;[2] and, a year later, and more truly than he knew, he declared, 'France is, and must always remain, England's greatest danger'.[3] But Germany was suspect in his eyes largely by reason of its rulers. Though Salisbury got on none too badly with Hatzfeldt, the German Ambassador, he was profoundly distrustful of Bismarck. Nor did Wilhelm II, in spite of some amiable attentions, invite his confidence. In Salisbury's family circle someone, indeed, once suggested that he met the Emperor's advances with less benevolence than they seemed to deserve. He had, however, gauged the man with whom he had to deal correctly. Rising from his chair to leave the room, he muttered, 'False! False! False!' It was a judgment curiously in line with what Sir Valentine Chirol told me the Empress Frederick had once said to him of her son: 'The worst of Willy is that he cannot tell the truth, even to himself.'

There is a difficulty in illustrating by examples the sequence of a long period of diplomatic endeavour. A saying of Salisbury's that diplomacy cometh not by observation, has been already quoted. With two short interludes in 1886 Salisbury was at the Foreign Office from 1885 to 1892 and from 1895 to 1900, and he had an overriding control as Prime Minister until July 1902. During this long spell of power he had the means to give a very definite

---

[1] Morley, *Life of Gladstone*, Vol. II, p. 318.   [2] *Life*, Vol. IV, p. 50.

[3] *Life*, Vol. IV, p. 106. France became a great danger to us in 1940, when, after drawing our Army across the Channel, she made terms with the enemy. The utter bewilderment of British statesmen at this juncture is shown by Mr. Churchill's proposal that France and England should unite their Governments. Mercifully the French had no disposition for any such adventure.

direction to the conduct of foreign affairs and one in the main coincident with the policy of the Rosebery[1] interludes, and the Iddesleigh[2] and Lansdowne[3] locum-tenancies. Outstanding in those years was the pacific partition among the colonially-minded European nations of spheres of influence. Nobody doubted then that Europe, as the great seat of Christian civilization and the classic culture of the humanities, had, with all its faults, much to give to peoples hardly emancipated from slavery and capable of inflicting inhuman atrocities upon one another. Europe at that time had the look of being the established guardian of the idea of a peaceful society of nations. When, however, Salisbury returned to the Foreign Office at the end of 1886, the scramble for power in Africa was already well in its way. He pointed out himself in a speech delivered a few years later that pretty nearly up to that time England, by virtue of her undisputed position as mistress of the sea, had without effort dominated the African situation. Bismarck was not keen on colonial development; and France had as much as she could deal with in Algeria and its 'hinterland'. But this in Salisbury's view did not mean that England could permanently assume that the African Continent lay at her disposal without any of the sanctions of international law to govern her acquisition of territory there. He believed in a policy of 'neighbourliness'; he was not out of sympathy with German enterprise in Angra Pequena and the Cameroons, or with French and Belgian enterprise in the region of the Congo. All this while the star of Cecil Rhodes was rising. Gladstone's administration in 1886 granted a charter to the 'Royal Niger Company'; and Salisbury's own administration an East African one in 1888 and a South African one in 1889. In Egypt, under some pressure from Salisbury himself, the Gladstone Ministry had intervened in 1882 to restore order and to safeguard the Suez Canal in which Beaconsfield, as we have seen, had some years earlier, made a famous investment on behalf of England. Things were evidently moving, and negotiations, if a European War over European settlements in Africa was to be averted, became urgent. Zanzibar, where the Sultan had agreed to give up a claim to illimitable empire on the mainland for assured sovereignty over a strip of the coast-line, some six hundred miles by ten, figured rather prominently in the negotiations for territory; but it would be as impossible as it is unprofitable to follow all the wranglings in detail. Eventually, in May 1900, Salisbury resolved to tender a bait in the German Ocean and see whether he could by such means disperse the controversies that raged and rumbled around the hinterlands of Africa.

[1] Lord Rosebery (q.v. Ch. XII) was in charge of the Foreign Office during the third (February to August 1866) and fourth (1892–1894) Gladstone administration.

[2] Sir Stafford Northcote, afterwards first Earl of Iddesleigh, was Foreign Secretary for a few months in Salisbury's second administration until Salisbury himself resumed the office in 1886 combining it with the Premiership.

[3] Lord Lansdowne (the 5th Marquess) was Foreign Secretary from 1890–1902 in the last Salisbury cabinet.

M*

After an ineffectual discussion of differences with Hatzfeldt, he mentioned Heligoland. He might have said 'Open Sesame'; for the closed door to an Anglo-German deal began almost at once to turn on its hinges. Not noisily; for the Germans were not eager to betray how acceptable would be this particular exchange to an empire lately come into being and greatly concerned with the naval approaches to the newly formed Kiel Canal! Neither side, therefore, manifested enthusiasm, but in the background Wilhelm II conveyed to his Ambassador that the acquisition of Heligoland was of supreme importance and that, in comparison, concessions in Africa were negligible. Salisbury's perception of the greater advantage to Britain of gaining control of the Protectorate of Zanzibar and of the country that stretched west of Abyssinia up to Khartoum over that of retaining a barren rock in the German Ocean opposite the mouth of the Elbe, was not immediately apparent to the Queen nor to all his colleagues, though his views did not meet with opposition in the naval circles consulted. There was some little difficulty, however, in persuading the Sovereign to barter away any of her territories whatever. The Prime Minister had to stress that failure to agree with Germany would compel England to draw nearer to France and evacuate Egypt, and that Heligoland had probably passed into English hands in 1814 only because it had been a dependency of Hanover, of which George III was Elector. In face of these representations the Queen gave way. Resolutions approving the cession were passed both through Lords and Commons—a course which set a precedent against any surrender of British territory by the Crown on the mere advice of an administration that happened to be in power. The Prime Minister was, however, firmly opposed to the German Emperor's strong desire that the British Fleet should be represented at the ensuing German naval manoeuvres. That would be to court trouble and criticism in England, where opposition to his policy had on the whole been confined to a small circle of ardent Tories.

The Protectorate over Zanzibar, let it be said in passing, had one lofty attraction for Salisbury's practical mind. It could deal a deathblow to the slave-trade. His scheme was, briefly, that a railway from Uganda to Mombasa should kill the caravan traffic which carried the slaves; and he pursued it in face of the scepticism of the Treasury, of the criticism of Gladstone in Parliament and of the depredations of man-eating lions in Africa. Rosebery in due course furthered his purpose by buying out the interest of the East African Company and taking over Uganda and, though advance was slow, the railway thus reached the shores of Lake Victoria in the year before Salisbury died. The scheme, and his deep interest in carrying it through, is significant of a side to his nature which would fit more easily into the traditional portrait of Gladstone. 'Behold, this dreamer cometh!' So they had spoken of a most successful food-controller in ancient Egypt. And so, too, they spoke of an audacious Conservative, with a long imperial vision, in modern England.

Negotiations with France in respect to African possessions were hardly less tricky and contentious than those with Germany. The default of the French in Egypt, where Gambetta would have intervened in association with England, but where Freycinet, his successor, lacked both will and power to do so, left the French watching with a jealous eye the growing influence of Britain. The fuel beneath this ill-feeling was fanned into flame by the success of the deal over Heligoland and the Anglo-German understanding in respect of Africa that followed. Salisbury took the excitability of the French with his usual phlegm. The French Government was invited to approve within eight days of its publication the modification of the Treaty of 1862, which the Sultan of Zanzibar had 'freely and independently accepted'. They let their Press grumble and storm, whilst they themselves received with a sour reasonableness, in satisfaction for all that the British were acquiring in Africa, the recognition of a French protectorate over Madagascar, analogous to that of England in Egypt, and a large hinterland behind Algeria. This Anglo-French Convention, very rapidly concluded, came under the criticism of the British Press, which could only see in such 'neighbourliness' one of 'Lord Salisbury's graceful concessions'. The large accession of territory France had acquired in West Africa sprang, however, to the eye of the observer and gladdened the heart of the French journalist, until Salisbury, stung into candour to a degree unusual with him when dealing with foreign affairs, remarked in the House of Lords that this vast French acquisition was one of what agriculturists would call 'light' land. The French Ambassador caustically commented: 'You might have left us to find it out.' By that one injudicious word Salisbury had diminished immeasurably the value of a piece of diplomacy which else would seem to have allayed the hostility of centuries. It showed him, if only for a moment, a man like ourselves, human in his frailties and indiscretions.

There was worse to come, though at a later date. The problem of Egypt was the problem of the Nile and the problem, too, of the Mohammedans. When, after the Gladstone and Rosebery administrations from 1892 to 1895, Salisbury returned to the Foreign Office in the latter year, the time appeared to be ripe for clearing up the Sudanese question, which had been left over after the death of Gordon and the occupation of Khartoum by the Mahdi and by his successor, the Khalifa. An advance up the Nile and the re-capture of the Sudan was planned with care and pursued with prudence. But, before the final victory could be achieved in September 1898, events in the Far East had attracted all eyes. The murder of two missionaries in Shantung had given the German Emperor an excuse for seizing Kiao-Chau and the Russians an excuse for placing warships to winter at Port Arthur. Salisbury's comprehensive and cautious diplomacy was never better displayed than at this time. He could not play a strong hand in the Far East, for he might have a war on his hands in the Sudan. Whilst the other great Powers, therefore, secured their positions in Eastern China, Britain contented herself with the lease of Wei-hai-wei, and with some additional territory round Hong Kong as a make-weight. It was just as well; for the French, too, were moving fast towards the sources of the Nile. Marchand, with a small body of troops, reached Fashoda five days after Omdurman was fought, and forthwith set up the Tricolor to substantiate the French claim. It was a good thing that Kitchener had, as a young man, fought on the French side in the War of 1870. If he had to do a very difficult thing in dislodging diplomatically the little band of Frenchmen who had made their way with much intrepidity across Africa, he had at least such credentials as a friend to France as few Englishmen could claim. There was high tension for a few days; then the French gave way. But what had happened rankled.

'Africa', Salisbury had told a City of London audience a few years before, 'is the subject which occupies the Foreign Office more than any other.' And no wonder, when all eyes were fixed upon the Dark Continent. Portuguese eyes among others, for Portugal had set to work to create Colonies long before the idea took hold of nations that grew to be greater than herself. And her fond memory of that which once had been tempted her to suppose that her empire stretched across Africa from sea to sea, from Angola in the west to Mozambique in the east. But, between these undisputed seats of Portuguese dominion, Rhodes was now engaged in building the Rhodesian empire. Salisbury did his best to prevent the friction between England and her ancient ally rising to the status of a quarrel, yet, as he saw, Portugal 'presumed upon her weakness'; and this presumption reached a climax when a Portuguese adventurer, Major Pinto by name, took upon him to shoot down some Makololo tribesmen under British protection. Major Pinto was required to withdraw; and a naval demonstration in the waters round Mozambique drove home the British resolve to deny the antiquated claims of the Portuguese to regions where their sovereignty was represented by no more than some fortresses in decay. This gesture was, perhaps, all the Portuguese Government required to justify it, in the eyes of its own people, for giving in. It sought, however, to cover its retreat by proposing arbitration. To this Salisbury would not listen. How could the fairest-minded man arbitrate, he argued, when the question was whether an occupation that had long lapsed into desuetude was or was not to outweigh the recent activities of merchants and missionaries at the seat of trouble. A compromise was therefore sought and after much negotiation effected. But this proved no lasting settlement. For the Cortez in Portugal refused to ratify the agreement; and the British pioneers in Matabeleland, thereupon, pursued their advance.

Greatly embarrassed, the Portuguese Government put forward the plea that their Monarchy could not face a diplomatic defeat and would fall, if it occurred. This, as was thought, might result in a revolution in Spain, where the King was a child; and various influential crowned-heads became alarmed, and amongst them the Queen. Salisbury deeply resented this attempt to deflect his policy by playing upon his monarchical sentiments. The dispute passed through one or two more phases not worth narrating; and a few sentences from a letter of Salisbury's may serve as an epilogue: 'Poor Portugal! We have come to some sort of an arrangement which I trust will reasonably suit the British South African without upsetting the Braganza dynasty. But people are not reasonable, either at Lisbon or Cape Town.'[1]

The incident showed that the embers of the Revolution still smouldered beneath the surface; and another curious little affair, almost coincident with it, showed that Europe had by no means forgotten all that the Revolution had cost her and all that has been stressed at the beginning of this book as a potent feature in the fashioning and feeling of the Victorian age. Sidi Carnot, the grandson of the famous War Minister of revolutionary and Napoleonic times, had succeeded Grévy as President of the French Republic in 1887 and decided two years later to celebrate the centenary of the event in which his ancestor had figured so prominently. It appeared a memorable occasion to him, but not to all men; and, when the Powers learnt that the diplomatic corps was to be invited to assist at these, to them inacceptable, rejoicings in Paris, the sovereigns of Europe, whose predecessors had laid the revolution low, were perturbed and indignant. Salisbury, on the British Ambassador's inquiry for instructions, felt unable to dissociate himself from Germany and Austria. 'It will not do', he told Lytton, 'for you and the American to appear as supporters of the rights of man and the principles of '89.' And he recommended the time-honoured expedient of some maiden aunt suddenly discovered to be *in extremis* and necessitating the ambassador's absence from his post. But the diplomatic dovecotes were too agitated by this resuscitation of the ghost of revolution to be soothed by familiar implausibilities. The Russian Embassy fled in a compact body across the frontier. The ambassadors in general vanished. In the ungratified ardour of the French President to set all Europe dancing, as he piped revolutionary airs, there lay concealed an irony that had not yet come to sight. If the centenary that he wished to celebrate had but fallen fifty, or even thirty years later, then the French and Russian champions of the sansculottes might have marched about together, only now and again exchanging blows, as Girondin clashed with Jacobin sentiment and one type of reformer sought violently to get rid of the other.

It would be probably an over-refinement of subtlety to suggest that the

[1] *Life*, Vol. IV, p. 275.

slight inclination towards the Triple Alliance which characterized Salisbury's foreign policy owed anything to the ideology of European politics. Everywhere he respected a nation's right to choose its own form of government and all over the world his reputation grew as his continuous effort to get men to have peace one with another became better understood. In watching the way in which he turned successive corners, hardly hoping that men would show themselves perceptibly wiser than before and suffering their follies, ideological or actual, with cynical good sense, we may perhaps find some approximation to that 'grand strategy' with its long view, on the importance of which a living military critic has laid much stress. 'The study of war', says Mr. Liddell Hart, 'has taught me that almost every war was avoidable and that the outbreak was most often produced by statesmen losing their heads or their patience, and putting their opponent in a position where he could not draw back without serious loss of face.'[1]

Salisbury's policy had, as has been shown, a narrow shave at Fashoda. And there had been another shave, almost as ugly, with the United States over the boundaries of British Guiana and Venezuela in 1895, when the Americans took their stand on the Monroe doctrine. Salisbury felt sure of his case; and an unprovocative firmness on his part resulted, after a sharp exchange of views, in the reference of the dispute to an Anglo-American Boundary-Commission which, under the presidency of a Russian jurist, gave in due course an award unanimous in almost every respect which sustained the British contention. The Anglo-Saxons were slowly drawing together, very much to Salisbury's satisfaction; and his diplomacy is even credited with having prevented the formation of an anti-American coalition against the U.S.A. some few years later in 1898, when the Spanish-American War broke out over affairs in Cuba.[2] Although independence was the key-note of his policy, his hands, as his biographer once said to me, were everywhere; and very skilful hands they were.

Everywhere, that is, in the sphere of foreign affairs! But a wise foreign policy did not, and indeed could not, cover all the danger-points. The regrouping of parties at home in consequence of the state of Ireland had brought a very able but also a very ambitious man to the Colonial Office. Joseph Chamberlain was the first and also the outstandingly capable politician in his family; his sons who went into politics after him had talents, but not talents of the same order. And in the Colonies Gladstone's administration had, by granting the Boers peace and partial independence on the morrow of Majuba[3], left a most complex problem to be tackled. Joseph Chamber-

---

[1] B. H. Liddell Hart in the *Listener*, November 15th 1951, p. 830.
[2] See Low and Sanders's: *Political History of England Between 1837 and 1901*, p. 440.
[3] The disastrous engagement (1881) in which a party of Boers killed and wounded 20 British officers and 266 men without suffering a single casualty.

lain had sided with John Bright at that time, and had threatened resignation,[1] if terms were not reached. Since he had insisted on peace in 1881, the more reason that, fifteen years later, Chamberlain should have left no stone unturned to ensure it! However, in 1885 gold had been found in the Transvaal; and the accursed lust of gold had by 1895 provoked a wild rush to the goldfields. The Boers, who wished only to lead their lives in their own way, had, in face of the unwelcome immigration, raised the period required for naturalization from five to fourteen years in 1890, and in 1893 had re-elected Kruger their President for the third time. He was an obstinate old man with very little idea of the part that conciliation has to play in international affairs. Even so, the British case was far from being a strong one; and was all the weaker that Jameson had tried to carry it with violence in December 1896, by his famous raid. Chamberlain had no great illusion about the legal validity of the British demand for the concession of a vote to the Uitlanders. His official life by Garvin contains a letter to Milner in which he says 'the technical *casus belli* was a very weak one'.[2] The suzerainty which Britain had the right to claim over the South African Republic included no right to determine the suffrage. In these circumstances it is very arguable that Milner, negotiating with Kruger at Bloemfontein, should have agreed with him on a septennial qualification as the qualification for the vote, which Kruger was willing to grant, instead of standing out for a quinquennial one, which he was not. In process of time Smuts or another might have taken Kruger's place; and Smuts's subsequent career is such as to encourage a belief that a satisfactory solution could eventually have been reached with greater patience and perseverance. More drastic methods appealed, however, to both the controversialists. Without seeking to arrive at a judicial verdict on the rights and wrongs of an issue, which was differently judged at the time by Rosebery and Asquith on the one side and by John Morley and Edward Clarke on the other, the historian does wisely to play for safety by remarking that the lapse of half a century has deprived the Boer War of that clear case for hostilities which many Britons and many Boers believed they saw at the time. Salisbury's colloquies and correspondence with the Queen are alone enough to give us pause, if we study them with care. He was passing at this date, owing to the failing health of his wife, through a period of much private distress; and his great hatred of war, upon which sufficient stress has already been laid, must have been, if possible, thereby accentuated. In July 1899 the Queen enters in her Journal: 'Lord Salisbury came to see me . . . Talking of events in general he said the one cause of anxiety was the Transvaal. This country, as well as the Cabinet, excepting perhaps Mr. Chamberlain, were against a war.'[3]

[1] See Paul's *Modern England*, Vol. IV, p. 196.
[2] *Life of Joseph Chamberlain*, Vol. III, p. 457.
[3] Queen's Letters, 1886–1901, Vol. III, p. 387.

'Excepting perhaps Mr. Chamberlain!' Then in September Salisbury writes to the Queen: 'We are most earnestly anxious to avoid any rupture with the Boers, if it is possible.' But in the same letter come also the words: 'It is impossible to avoid believing that the Boers really aim at setting up a South African Republic, consisting of the Transvaal, the Orange Free State, and your Majesty's Colony. It is impossible to account in any other manner for their rejection of our most moderate proposals.'[1]

So, then, before mid-October the Boers had addressed to the British Government an ultimatum, insisting, on pain of war, upon arbitration, upon the withdrawal of British troops from the frontier, upon the removal elsewhere of all British reinforcements that had arrived in South Africa since the preceding June, and upon the non-disembarkation of any British troops now on their way on the high seas. Salisbury approved the rejection of these 'peremptory demands'; and Rosebery made public a statement to the effect that the situation had now passed beyond party polemics and that the nation should close its ranks. Yet this war, more perhaps than anything else, made a foreign policy of independence, such as both these Prime Ministers favoured, difficult to pursue, so great was the feeling aroused against Britain in Europe. It remains, however, permissible to speculate whether if either Salisbury or Rosebery had had the handling of the negotiations they might not have managed them far better than Chamberlain, who, as he wrote to the Queen when war broke out, felt things must come to a trial of force and would personally have liked 'to despatch much larger reinforcements at a much earlier period'.[2] But speculation in the region of such possibilities is an unprofitable business. Enough if we mark the decisive effect of the Boer War on British foreign policy!

Chamberlain, though the conduct of foreign affairs was neither his *forte* nor his function, had had a continental alliance in mind even before the Boer War came to strengthen his dispositions. In the spring of 1898, when for a few weeks Balfour took Salisbury's place at the Foreign Office, he had a talk with the German Ambassador at the house of Alfred de Rothschild and intimated that, if Germany would associate herself with Britain in the Far East and in Africa, there was the basis for a closer understanding. Hatzfeldt listened and reported the conversation to Bülow, the German Chancellor. Bülow was not, like Chamberlain, an amateur in diplomatic work and laid his finger at once on the weak point of the English Minister's proposal. The English administration could not bind succeeding Governments and could, therefore, give Germany no reliable support; whilst England, for her part, was already assured of German assistance in European complications by the German need of English aid in maintaining the Treaty of Frankfort.[3] Cham-

---

[1] Queen's Letters, September 23rd 1899.   [2] ibid., October 12th 1899.
[3] The main provision of the Treaty of Frankfort, 1871, was, of course, the cession of Alsace-Lorraine to Germany.

berlain, however, elaborated his lucubrations in a later interview but without making them any more acceptable to Bülow: whilst Balfour as leader in the Commons admitted to Hatzfeldt that he himself could offer no certain assurance of Parliamentary consent and adhesion. The effect of these ill-judged advances on the German Emperor's mind was to lead him to infer that Britain felt insecure; and this supposition, doubtless, was strengthened later on by the lamentable defeats which Britain sustained in the earlier phases of the Boer War.

Hatzfeldt and Chamberlain, however, met again; and the latter, though not pretending to speak for anyone but himself, renewed his advances. The Ambassador drew the conclusion that Chamberlain was trying to bring the matter to a head before Salisbury returned to resume control of foreign affairs. It came out, in the course of their exchanges, that Chamberlain, failing to effect an Anglo-German alliance, would not be indisposed to seek an Anglo-French or Anglo-Russian one. Chamberlain maintained in giving some account to Salisbury of his diplomatic ventures that the initiative had been taken by the Germans; and, if so, we need to introduce the name of Eckardstein at the opening of this informal negotiation. Salisbury in private correspondence with Chamberlain, seems to have professed himself not averse from a closer co-operation with the German Empire, if that were feasible, which he evidently doubted. In public he expressed himself rather differently: 'We know that we shall maintain against all comers that which we possess, and we know, in spite of the jargon about isolation, that we are amply competent to do so.'

Chamberlain, in reply to this, reasserted almost immediately his policy of some continental alliance for Britain. The Boer War, together with the great outburst of anti-British feeling which it evoked on the Continent, seemed to many to recommend his view.

Not, however, to Salisbury! The Prime Minister kept his head; and he was at one with Bülow in believing that, whilst friendship between Britain and Germany was in the interest of both nations, any closer relationship was impracticable. An opportunity had in fact occurred, owing to the financial embarrassment of Portugal, for a manifestation of goodwill, and it was taken, by the conclusion in August 1898 of an Anglo-German Treaty for consultation should the Portuguese Empire fall to pieces. Salisbury explained that he had no wish to see any such thing happen and treated German anxiety about the future in these localities with consideration, whilst pointing out that England was bound by treaty to respect and defend Portuguese colonial interests, and, maintaining England's right to afford Portugal financial aid.

When the year 1901 opened the South African War was moving fast to a climax and Victoria's life fast to its close. In March the Presidents of the

Transvaal and the Orange Free State solicited a peace 'on condition of the incontestable independence of both republics as sovereign international States'. This was refused; and in the September following the Government appealed to the country and received a majority not far short of what had brought them into power in 1895. Salisbury, with little inclination, retained the Premiership so as to see the war through, but handed over the Foreign Office to Lansdowne, who before long showed, like Chamberlain, a disposition to seek what he esteemed as greater security for England in a continental alliance. This is where the student has much reason to pause, for the fate and the fortunes of Britain for fifty years to come, and perhaps much more, hung now in the balance.

In May 1901 the new Foreign Secretary confronted the Prime Minister with a proposal that England should join the Triple Alliance. Salisbury, now almost in his last year of office met him with a decisive refusal; and the brief memorandum in which he did so has seemed to such critics of diplomatic history as Dr. G. P. Gooch and the late J. A. Spender, to cut the root of British foreign policy.

Salisbury remarks at the outset that the liability to defend German and Austrian frontiers against Russia was a greater one than that of defending the British Isles against France and that the bargain was consequently a bad one. He goes on to add that the policy of 'isolation' (as he terms it, despite what Lady Gwendolen rashly says of his use of it in her book[1]) had not, so far as could be judged, served us badly. Of the war against Napoleon, which offered at the date of writing the single occasion on which we were in grave peril of invasion, he observed: 'We had many allies, but they would not have saved us, if the French Emperor had been able to command the Channel.' There was a weightier objection, however, than this. 'The British cannot undertake to declare war for any purpose, unless it is a purpose of which the electors of this country approve.' A pledge given to Germany might be dishonoured, if the nation, when it came to the point, was not in the mood to fulfil it; and, even if the pact were submitted to Parliament for ratification, 'very grave objections' to it remained. Germany could not be trusted to fulfil her side of the engagement; and we ought to stake nothing important upon her doing so. For the rest he had himself for the last sixteen years countered Hatzfeldt's probings as to the course of English policy, if war broke out between Germany or Italy and France, with the observation that no English Minister could attempt to prophesy in respect of this issue and that much would probably depend upon what view the British public took of the *casus belli*.

With such an answer before him from the Prime Minister, Lansdowne was clearly in no position to pursue his design. Almost as soon, however, as

[1] *Life*, Vol. IV, p. 86.

Salisbury retired in July 1902 he resumed his purpose, only substituting France for Germany and an *entente* for an alliance. By 1904 he and Delcassé, with King Edward VII giving most effective diplomatic aid, had brought it about.

Salisbury did not live to see this entanglement displace his own policy of isolation, better named independence; still less to see it advance from its first diplomatic beginnings to its almost unnoticed military end. He died at Hatfield in August 1903; and with him disappeared, it is hardly too much to say, the epitome and consummation of the Victorian age. He had been still in office, when, in the January of 1901, the reign of the old Queen closed. It had fallen to him to serve her for more years than any of the other nine of her Prime Ministers; and it fell to him, appropriately enough, to pay tribute to the rare wisdom with which she had risen, over so long a time and to the great advantage of her own advisers, to her occasions. She had, some while before expressed what she owed to him. If Bishop Boyd-Carpenter, on whose evidence her opinion rests,[1] is correct, she placed Salisbury in the very front rank of the ten who had conducted the major business of her reign. She compared him with Peel, and said that he was a greater man than Beaconsfield. We shall not, perhaps, feel inclined to reverse, or even to revise her verdict; and still less, if we tend to share Salisbury's own modest view of the potentialities of political endeavour—that (to use some words of Lady Gwendolen's) legislation has 'a more unequivocal capacity for inflicting injury than for imparting benefit'.

As Prime Minister, Salisbury not only served longer than the rest but, possibly or probably for the last time in English history, he exercised his authority without embarrassment from the benches of the House of Lords, relieved in this manner from much of the petty dissension and discord which are the lot of party leaders at the present day. The Lords, whose constitution, as we have seen, he had long endeavoured to reform, still retained their ancient powers and showed no inclination to be reformed: and it must be very doubtful whether, had he lived, he would have encouraged them to challenge the Commons on such an issue as Lloyd George's Budget of 1909. But, however that may be, there was nothing to prevent him from doing his work in the Upper House without any disadvantage from the circumstance. He had another piece of good fortune, which can hardly be exaggerated, in the possession of a nephew[2] whose capacity to lead in the Lower House was never challenged, and also of a son in the Commons,[3] who could keep him in touch with all the gossip and by-play of party developments.

With the leadership of the party, Salisbury had never been deeply concerned. He had no high opinion of his capacity in this respect; as well another

[1] Boyd-Carpenter, *Some Pages of my Life*, p. 236.
[2] A. J. Balfour   [3] Lord Cranborne afterwards the 4th Marquess of Salisbury.

as himself. The direction of foreign affairs was what he cared about and what he felt to matter; and sagacity there meant in his eyes security elsewhere. Few would have challenged his competence for the work he chose. And many diplomatists, I fancy, would have endorsed the remark of an Italian Ambassador (Bosdari) to Lady D'Abernon that 'his considered opinion was that the late Lord Salisbury was by far the best informed and the most able Foreign Minister that England had had during the last fifty years'.[1] So much indeed becomes feasible, when foreign affairs have been set on a sure foundation, that to be wise in this department is of more importance to a Government than anything else. He, however, who would take the full measure of Salisbury's wisdom must transfer his standpoint from the year 1902 to a date about half a century later. The salient features of the landscape, owing to events abroad, will be seen at once to have greatly changed. The most part of Ireland has been lost, politically speaking, to the British Empire or, if you prefer, British Commonwealth; whereas Salisbury had made the continued unity of Great Britain and Ireland a foremost principle of his policy. 'If Ireland goes', he had said, 'India will go fifty years later.'[2] And India, too, has gone—was gone, in fact, before the fifty years were up. And both countries, in breaking off the time-honoured link with England, have themselves disintegrated, as north-east Ireland and Pakistan are there to show. Disintegration, as Salisbury warned his fellow-countrymen, was above all, the menace they had to fear at home and abroad.

If the eye is allowed to turn now from land to sea, the change will be found to be in no way less striking. Our supremacy of the Seas has passed away, though into the hands of an Anglo-Saxon Power more potent than Britain is any longer likely to be, or perhaps can ever be again. These stupendous, staggering changes, if we deal honestly by realities, can be shown to be very largely the consequence of abandoning Salisbury's foreign policy and substituting for it an unsubstantial, vagrant cosmopolitanism attended by ill-considered tributes to nationality, such as, since Byron's time, have captured the idealism of youth and persuaded it to make ventures more questionable than those of the Crusades, or even than that of the Crimean War, which, as we saw, attracted Salisbury's strictures.

The historian, however, will not find it easy to present honestly this vast alteration in a true perspective; for the judgment of his countrymen is still deeply engaged in the contemplation of these events through the fierce light with which personal grief and private loss has the power to invest them. The cause, wherein those we loved so well fought and fell, can with difficulty be considered with such detachment of mind as is now familiar in reflections upon Crécy or Agincourt, or even Waterloo. Hostilities directed against

---

[1] Lady D'Abernon, *Red Cross and Berlin Embassy, 1915–1926*, p. 127.
[2] Private information.

'the Central Powers' were, we were told by the wiseacres of the time, destined to prove 'a war to end war'; and we were simple enough to believe these false prophets. No sooner was this pack of nonsense disposed of by four years of appalling slaughter concluding in the bitter disillusionment of a dictated peace, than a fresh tribe of fortune-tellers appeared to explain that by means of 'union now' we might make 'one world' of it and reach that happy state of oecumenical fraternity which had bewitched the credulous mind of Aristide Briand in the year 1926 to the point of pronouncing it a thing well nigh accomplished. Thirteen years more babbling of politicians, six years more battling of their unfortunate dupes in the field were needed to dispel these fond, fallacious fancies. But even after that, whatever the rest of us may have thought, the political pundits pursued their will-o'-the-wisp from Geneva to Lake Success with an unfaltering faith that has had no parallel since the days of Don Quixote, whose democratic descendants in truth they were. To such Prometheus might well have addressed his boast,

τυφλὰς ἐν αὐτοῖς ἐλπίδας κατώκισα.
'I have implanted in them blind hopes.'

It is impossible to believe that Salisbury, with his deliberate, sceptical way of assessing situations, with the stress he laid on 'the cowardliness of optimism', would have lent himself to all that wealth of fancy, Utopian and idealistic, which took hold of the politicians after his death and caused his country morally and materially to suffer such immeasurable loss. His Christianity alone would have refused to assimilate it. The fall of man, a fact we must accept if any doctrine of regeneration by divine love is to make sense, and that anterior fall of angels, with all its cosmic implications, alike make havoc of a dogma of progress relying on the mere increase of knowledge for its advancement. The very coalition of Powers that dethroned Napoleon had known better than to confront him with talk of 'a fight to the finish' or of 'unconditional surrender'. The salvation of Christian civilization was to lie neither in idealism nor intransigence.

Quite apart from this, however, it is very hard to imagine Salisbury, with his highly characteristic axiom, so often stressed, that 'diplomacy cometh not by observation', encouraging the idea that peace amongst men might be permanently secured by the creation of some forum of debate where representatives of all the nations of the earth could indulge in noisy exchanges respecting their differences, exacerbating passion as they did so, and rendering collective security more questionable than ever. In every Parliament of Man, he would have pointed out, the existence of a government with cosmopolitan powers would be sure to provoke the rise of an opposition, even if he did not foresee that these oecumenical notions furnished as likely a path to the resumption of that agelong duel between East and West which, as

Mommsen had observed,[1] went back to Marathon and might well be the outcome of modern developments. The dark sayings of the German historian deserve indeed to be contrasted with Franklin Roosevelt's fond expectation at the conference at Teheran that the peace of the world could be set foursquare on the co-operation of Russia and China, America and Britain.

Any detailed speculation as to how Salisbury would have handled the crises through which the British Empire was to pass in the next fifty years lays itself open, of course, to doubt and contradiction. Salisbury was an artist in diplomacy; and his work is marked by what Newman would have termed an illative sense, which, like the strategy or tactics of an accomplished general in a campaign or on the battlefield does not readily lend itself to exact treatment. Yet some few observations can be made with something approaching certitude. Salisbury's habitual distrust of France and his abiding suspicion of Russia render it as certain as can well be that he would never have got his country into a position in 1914 where Russia, in the pursuit of her cherished purpose of possessing herself of Constantinople or at least of dominating the adjoining Straits, could, by drawing France into war as her ally, drag England also. Also it is hard to suppose that his eyes would have been blind to the fact that the real aggressor in that crisis was not, as it suited the nationalistic ideologists of the time to affirm, Austria, but Serbia, which had an unholy interest in the disruption of the Austrian Empire. His diplomacy, so far as it had a leaning, had always inclined slightly towards the Triple, and away from the Dual Alliance. Not enough, certainly, as has been shown, to encourage Lansdowne's or, for the matter of that, Joseph Chamberlain's attempt to pledge ourselves to Berlin: but enough to have averted Edward VII's subsequent diplomacy, in conformity with some rather hesitant Ministerial policy, from coming to a close understanding with France! The key to Salisbury's conduct of foreign affairs was 'neighbourliness', just as the keynote of his purposes at home and abroad was 'integration'. Beyond that, his fine perception of his duty as trustee of his country's interests would not allow him to go. He realized that there was no better guarantee for the preservation of peace in Europe than the freedom of Britain to take sides as she thought best on any particular issue at the time of its occurrence. To hold the balances evenly was a far more subtle policy than to put herself unreservedly into one of the scales; and there is no reason to think that she could not have pursued this course by building up a formidable air force, whilst maintaining her sea-supremacy at full strength and avoiding the curse of conscription. To adopt such measures would have been an easier and far

---

[1] Mommsen, *History of Rome*, Book IV, Chapter VIII 'the huge duel between the west and the east which has been transmitted from the conflicts at Marathon to the present generation and will perhaps reckon its future by thousands of years as it has reckoned its past', (translation by W. P. Dickson).

less costly method of adapting tradition to the exigencies of a changed world.

I find it difficult, too, to believe that one who, a year after the Berlin Congress, wrote to Beaconsfield that 'Austria's position in Europe was a matter in which we took deep interest and considered essential',[1] would, if he had found, or suspected that the Serbian Government of 1914 was conniving at the assassination of the heir to the Habsburg Empire—and that heir a 'trialist',[2]—have been content, like Grey, to convict the German Government of egging on its ally for its own selfish purposes without much more proof of guilt than has ever been afforded us. Again I find it quite as hard to suppose that one who had written with such admirable detachment about the remote aggressions of Poland and its neighbours upon Russian territory[3] would, if he had ever allowed a Polish corridor to be set up at the mouth of the Vistula, have placed the fortunes of his country and, for the matter of that, of France too, in the hands of the Poles and have allowed us to become involved in a second world-conflagration, in which, though Britain had acquired many Continental allies just as in 1804, she was left in 1940 to effect her own deliverance with the best part of her army on the other side of the Channel. Had the British Foreign Secretary been in a position in 1914 to anticipate Neville Chamberlain's gesture in 1938 and to meet the German Chancellor in direct discussion, there need, at least arguably, have been no war at all. The Serbs could have been compelled to deal forthwith with the Archduke's murderers; the Russians could have been restrained from that first 'general mobilization' which, more perhaps than any other single act that can be named, brought all Europe to the brink of the abyss; and the Austrians could have been given time to effect those internal changes in their Empire which the Archduke Franz Ferdinand had apparently in mind, and which were, in any case, no business of ours. All this, moreover, was in line with the discharge of those useful offices abroad that had caused Palmerston, who had no love for the Habsburg Empire, to adopt the dictum of a Czech historian and say that, had there been no Austria, we should have had to invent one.

What ought to have been effected in 1914, however, could no longer, once Hitler got into the saddle, be done in 1938. Still it was largely our British fault that Hitler ever established his mastery over the German soul. 'If you would have given me anything,' so Herbert Fisher told me Brüning had said to him, 'you need never have had Hitler.' Our Foreign Secretaries had, however, by Brüning's time long abandoned, not indeed sagacity, of which in our century it might be hard to find an example among the practitioners or pundits of external affairs, but the bare virtue of prudence.

[1] *Life*, Vol. II, p. 368.
[2] A 'Trialist' was one who was ready to put German, Magyar and Slav on an equal footing in the Austrian Empire.
[3] *Essays*, by Robert, Marquess of Salisbury. Foreign Series, pp. 13, 14.

In any study of Salisbury's statesmanship the conclusion must then be, must it not, that under his guidance, or, for the matter of that, Rosebery's, Britain would have kept free from all foreign entanglements that might deprive her of independent action on each separate international issue as it arose? This had been, almost tediously, stressed during 1886–87, when Italy and Austria approached England with a proposal for concerted action in the Mediterranean area in virtue of a specific understanding for mutual support. 'England', so Salisbury wrote to Victoria in an epitome of his remarks to Count Corti, 'never promised material assistance in view of an uncertain war of which the object and cause were unknown';[1] and he limited likewise even diplomatic co-operation, if directed against any single Power. The context is not without interest. Bismarck, as he suspected, was toying at the time with the idea of a war with France; and for this, favourable conditions would have been furnished by the preoccupation of Russia, England, and Italy in hostilities in the Near East. Salisbury was always willing for what Lady Gwendolen rightly characterizes as little more than a 'circle of acknowledged sympathies'[2]—a circle, in fact, in which England could exercise her pacific influence, but in which war, for her to involve herself, would demand a definite issue, approving itself to the mind of his countrymen. To this limitation of pledges he held on tenaciously as to part of the English constitution; and it represents, so far as exterior affairs are concerned, his lost legacy to the nation. There is something without doubt very English about it, something befitting the student of Castlereagh, something stressing both the English sense of insularity and a freedom not excluding all interest in the affairs of the Continent. For, emphatically, it does not rule out a coalition in time of war or a concert in time of peace.

On a wider view of politics, it might not be altogether absurd to say that Salisbury possessed something in common with Johnson, the Englishman *par excellence*, rough in his ruthless commonsense; attached beyond the ordinary to the Church of England, to the Monarchy, to the party which had kept these things in view, and, withal, capable of letting his wit and humour run riot among orthodoxies of belief to a degree rather puzzling to minds accustomed to move along more conventional lines. Salisbury's conservatism was in truth a way of looking at and of living life with a genuine regard for the history of the nation and a pungent respect for tradition. We have grown accustomed to hear it insinuated that all the adventures and anxieties and austerities of the past half-century carried our country on until, in 1940, it came to 'its finest hour'; and that may be, provided it is stressed that what is meant is, not the finest hour of the politicians who, if the truth be told, have shown grievous ineptitude, bringing Britain to the very edge of catastrophe by their imbecilities, but the finest hour of the fighting men.

[1] *Life*, Vol. IV, p. 21.   [2] *Life*, p. 24.

It is, indeed, no hard matter to fancy Salisbury's wit poking fun at the sanguine adventures of some of his successors, faint yet patiently pursuing the vagaries of the so-called united nations, and finding themselves, now baffled at one point, now bogged at another, now bamboozled at a third, until they had effectively demonstrated by their association to all concerned that the world had never before been so strongly divided in heart and mind, and that the one salient fact we can make sure of is that political integrity must be looked for at an entirely different level, to which, maybe, 'neighbourliness' supplies the first, firm approach and the old idea of 'Christendom' a final end.

To study Salisbury is in fact to liberate oneself from many fond and foolish illusions about the nature of man and of society; to set prudence once more among the cardinal virtues; and to define justice, after the manner of the Platonic Socrates, as a minding of one's own business. This definition, and the Dantesque verdict that 'tis love that makes the world go round' mean, according to the Duchess to Alice 'much the same thing'. Lewis Carroll is one of my earliest memories of Hatfield. I wonder whether he ever discussed with his host the Duchess's identification of these two fragments of political science. It is a matter which cuts very near the root of mortal things, and should engage the attention of every one who dares to meddle with political issues.

THERE is a passage in the life of Archbishop Lang which gives an account of a conversation at Grillions Club when he discussed with two post-Victorian Prime Ministers (Asquith and Balfour) what spectacle in late Victorian days would neither be seen again nor adequately replaced. They were agreed; and their judgment decided for 'Hyde Park on a summer afternoon in the season'.[1]

It was a good choice, perhaps as good a choice as can be made. I can recall, when still hardly more than a boy, taking a chair more than once in the strip of park that lies between Apsley House and Albert Gate so as to get a sight of it. And, as I wind up this book, the memory of those distant days returns, and I see once more the long procession of, for the most part, well-appointed carriages, rolling round the Park—rolling away into the blue mists of Kensington, upon which Matthew Arnold had long ago laid one of his magic spells. His words are, for such as can remember, still lightly winged, still able to stir the memory with thoughts of half-forgotten, far-off things, still potent to compel a sigh. Listen as they fall upon the ear with something, perhaps, of their ancient sweetness:

> Sometimes a child will cross the glade
> To take his nurse his broken toy;
> Sometimes a thrush flit overhead
> Deep in her unknown day's employ.
>
> Here at my feet what wonders pass,
> What endless, active life is here!
> What blowing daisies, fragrant grass
> An air-stirr'd forest, fresh and clear.
>
> * * * *
>
> In the huge world, which roars hard by,
> Be others happy, if they can!
> But in my helpless cradle I
> Was breathed on by the rural Pan.[2]

From that charmed cradle Victoria had sprung; and to that scene of peaceful sepulture an admirer of the Victorian Age inevitably seems to wend his way back.

[1] J. G. Lockhart, 'Cosmo Gordon Lang', p. 50.
[2] Lines written in Kensington Gardens.

A dreamer dreams on, of the horse-hoofs of that Victorian procession that held the memory of the three eminent men mentioned above, and which they regarded as the supreme illustration of the ancient charm of that large, tranquil and gracious age. With that vision in my eyes, with those sounds upon my ears, I close this book.

More seems to be borne away than a conversation. As these sounds and that vision fade, the catch of Gallic song, which my first Victorian had so often on his lips, seems to be heard again, 'Le temps que je regrette, c'est le temps qui n'est plus'.

INDEX

[The letter "n" signifies that the reference is to be found in a footnote on the page shewn.]

DATE DUE

1/20/67			
FEB 1 '67			
APR 2 8 1971			
MAY 2 1972			
OCT 2 5 1974			
AP 1 2 77			
JAN 3 1 1989			
GAYLORD			PRINTED IN U.S.A.